T0330280

LABOR AND LOVE IN GUATEMALA

Labor and Love in Guatemala

THE EVE OF INDEPENDENCE

Catherine Komisaruk

STANFORD UNIVERSITY PRESS

STANFORD, CALIFORNIA

Stanford University Press

Stanford, California

© 2013 by the Board of Trustees of the Leland Stanford Junior University. All rights reserved.

This book has been published with the assistance of the University of Iowa.

Printed in the United States of America on acid-free, archival-quality paper

Library of Congress Cataloging-in-Publication Data
Komisaruk, Catherine, author.
   Labor and love in Guatemala : the eve of independence / Catherine Komisaruk.
      pages cm
   Includes bibliographical references and index.
   ISBN 978-0-8047-5704-1 (cloth : alk. paper)
   1. Labor—Guatemala—History. 2. Slavery—Guatemala—History.
3. Ethnicity—Guatemala—History. 4. Marriage—Guatemala—History.
5. Social change—Guatemala—History. 6. Guatemala—History—To 1821.
I. Title.
   HD8145.K66 2012
   331.1097281—dc23
                                                              2012032594

Typeset by Thompson Type in 10/12.5 Sabon

For Omar

Contents

List of Illustrations

Acknowledgments

For their labor and love in support of my work on this book, I owe many people thanks. First is James Lockhart, who has been an enormously generous teacher and whose writings and teaching continue to delight and inspire me. His confidence in me has been more important than I suspect he knows. Kevin Terraciano, ever gracious and unassuming, has tirelessly supported my work in numerous ways. I also heartily thank James Wilkie, Mary Yeager, Chon Noriega, and Kathleen McHugh for their support and interest in my work during graduate school and beyond. At earlier stages I received the good guidance and aid of Catherine Clinton, who introduced me to feminist history and to the idea of graduate school, and of Silvia Castro de Arriaza, whose course—my first and only course in Central American history—I took while working as a teacher in Guatemala.

This book is based largely on research in the Archivo General de Centro América in Guatemala City, and I am profoundly indebted to the archive's staff and former staff members whose time there has overlapped with mine. In particular, I thank Anna Carla Ericastilla Samayoa, now the archive's director, and Lilian Lippmann Estrada for their help and warmth. My days at the archive were enriched also by the intellectual generosity and friendship of fellow researchers Ann Jefferson, Robinson Herrera, Oralia De León, Laura Matthew, Leo Hernández, Anne Pushkal, Franz Binder, the late Ana Margarita Gómez, Fred Opie, Jordana Dym, Justin Wolfe, Edgar Chután Alvarado, Joel Hernández Sánchez, Luqui Ramírez, Rodolfo Hernández, and Christophe Belaubre.

My work on this book has benefited from insights and suggestions offered by numerous people. John Kicza and Richmond Brown reviewed the manuscript for Stanford University Press, giving generous comments and some needed corrections. Silvia Arrom read a draft of the whole manuscript and made detailed suggestions that helped improve my arguments. Bianca Premo, Pete Sigal, Susan Deans-Smith, Ann Wightman, Camilla Townsend, Eric Van Young, Christine Hünefeldt, Matthew Restall, Julia Watson, the late Lindon Barrett, Christopher Lutz, Lowell Gudmundson, Rachel O'Toole, Colleen O'Neill, Robert Weis, Leon Fink, Karen Graubart, Nils Jacobsen, Herman Bennett, and Jennifer Morgan have given feedback on parts of the research that I presented at conferences and seminars.

I am especially grateful to Norris Pope, Emma Harper, Emily Smith, and Sarah Crane Newman for their work in the acquisition and editorial process at Stanford University Press. It has been a particular pleasure to work with the wonderful copyeditor Margaret Pinette. In Guatemala, Ana Vela Castro helped me sort through slave sale records; Erin Bates and Lisa Munro photographed key documents for me when I was unable to travel. In the United States, Matine Spence catalogued towns for the map; Wilson Juárez reformatted the bibliography; John Hammond helped me navigate Microsoft pie charts; Aldrin Magaya helped with indexing. Christopher Lutz arranged for Elisabeth Siruček to send me her translation for Plumsock Mesoamerican Studies of Inge Langenberg's book (though the pages I cite are for the published version in German). I am very lucky to have happened on Martha Bayless, Sophie Weeks, Meegan Kennedy, and Anastasia Curwood—sister writers, pacesetters, moral supporters.

During my time on the faculty at California State University, Long Beach, my colleagues there shared with me their office space, good food and friendship, and intellectual camaraderie. I am especially grateful to James Green, Dennis Kortheuer, Maythee Rojas, Liesl Haas, Rich Haesly, Susan Carlile, Bill and Linda Weber, Bonnie Gasior, the late Xiaolan Bao, Donna Binkiewicz, and Moshe Sluhovsky; and for absolutely key support and continuing friendship, I thank Linda N. España Maram.

Colleagues at the University of Iowa have nurtured my work since I first came here, and have made the campus a stimulating intellectual home for me. Leslie Schwalm, who is the embodiment of generosity, read an early version of the manuscript and made both broad and specific comments that helped improve my thinking in many ways. Jennifer Sessions and Kevin Mumford provided tremendously useful comments when I queried them at the last minute. Colin Gordon made maps and gave good advice when asked. Input and ideas from Johanna Schoen, Jennifer Glass, Ellen Lewin, Constance Berman, Barbara Burlison Mooney, Cameron Thies, Lauren Rabinovitz, Doris Witt, Rosemary Moore, Jim Giblin, Linda Kerber, Laura Gotkowitz, Jeff Cox, and Michel Gobat have enhanced my thinking and the book. Amber Brian and Brian Gollnick have welcomed me unstintingly with intellectual and personal friendship across the usual disciplinary boundaries of academe. In the History Department office, Pat Goodwin, Sheri Sojka, Mary Strottman, Jean Aikin, and Barb Robb have been key sources of assistance and good humor.

For institutional support, I am indebted to the UCLA History Department and to UCLA's Graduate Division, Latin American Studies Center, International Studies and Overseas Programs, and Center for the Study of Women, all of which provided funding when I was working on this project as a dissertation. The University of California Humanities Research Institute supplied precious aid, including the apartment where I finished writing the dissertation. At California State University, Long Beach, I benefitted from the support of the Office of University Research, the College of Liberal Arts, and the History Department. A postdoctoral fellowship from the American Association of University Women allowed me crucial time for both research and writing. At the University of Iowa, the Office of the Provost, the College of Liberal Arts and Sciences, the History Department, the Office of the Vice President for Research, and the Obermann Center for Advanced Studies have granted generous assistance. Given the extensive and expert help I have received, the book's shortcomings are certainly my own.

Then there are the purely personal debts. Friends in Guatemala have made me at home there over the years, and I thank particularly Maria Hirst; José A. Luna; Verónica Bolaños de Herrera, Andrea Herrera, and the Bolaños family; María Elena Gaitán de Herrera; Helen Herrera; the Cifuentes family (in San Cristóbal and zona 18); the Masayas in zona 7; Rosalie Zindovic; Margarita Aguilar; Ana Lilian Silva; Luis Adrián Picón; and my former co-workers and students. Laura and Raúl Cifuentes's friendship and hospitality have known no borders. In all these years in Guatemala and the United States, Elizabeth Corbett has never faltered as a friend and never acted surprised that this book was not yet done. Chris Schons has offered refreshing information, analyses, and wit. In the United States, Stephanie Rosenfeld Kurek, Jean and George Rosenfeld, Lauren Snyder, Rose Li, Julie Jones, Stephanie Bower, and Elizabeth Horvath helped keep me going. While I finished the writing, Marie Erickson, Laura Noiseux, Kara Knott, Emily Rustand, Laura Walczynski, Katie Leners, and Sarah Stuck provided child care.

My parents Ed and Karin Komisaruk have been loyal supporters despite the mysteriousness of my career and of this book project, and my sister Alex a faithful fan who has come to my aid with in-person deliveries to Guatemala, moving assistance, nighttime child care, and editorial consultation. I also thank my extended family, especially Mark and Ben DiStefano, the Valenzuelas, and the Valerios. My son Samuel has helped me understand the magnitude of my subjects' labor and love in childrearing, and though he is too young now to read these words, he has reminded me of the many joys of books. Last and most of all, I am grateful to my husband Omar. He has provided so much love, encouragement, household labor, intellectual input, and tech support that I cannot find words to thank him sufficiently. In an admittedly too-small gesture, I dedicate this book to him.

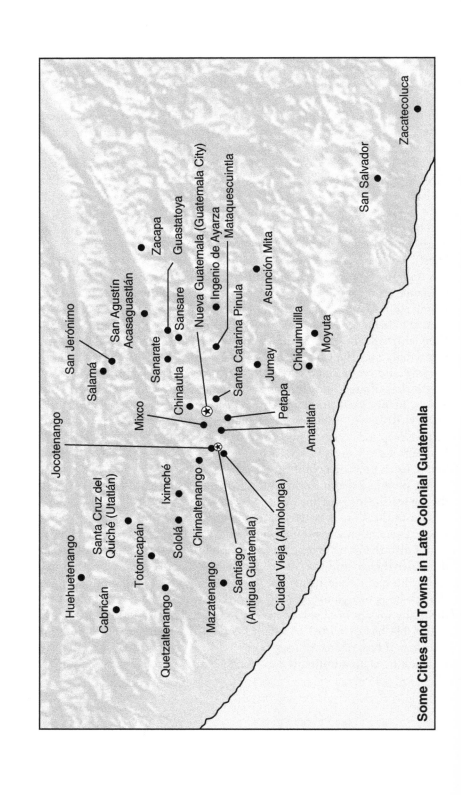

Some Cities and Towns in Late Colonial Guatemala

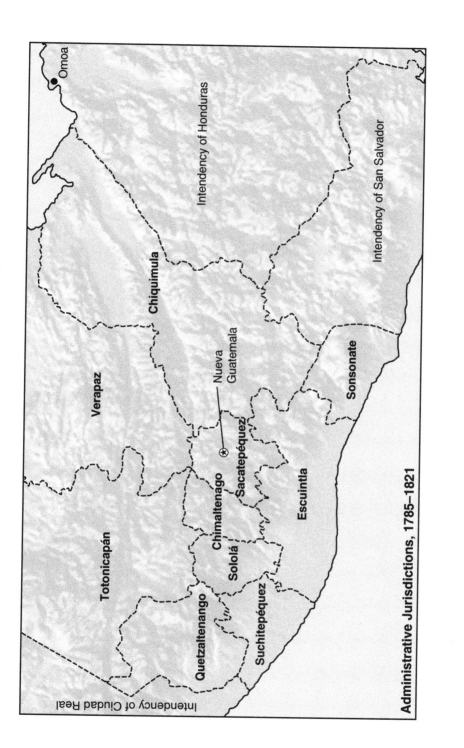

Administrative Jurisdictions, 1785–1821

Omoa

Intendency of Honduras

Intendency of San Salvador

Chiquimula

Verapaz

Nueva Guatemala

Sonsonate

Sacatepéquez

Totonicapán

Chimaltenango

Escuintla

Quetzaltenango

Sololá

Suchitepéquez

Intendency of Ciudad Real

Introduction

In a sense, we already know what happened. A similar story unfolded across Mesoamerica and the Andes over the centuries of Spanish colonial rule: populations from three continents mingled, native people and Africans became increasingly hispanized, and coerced forms of labor receded. In piecemeal fashion, hispanized wage laborers replaced Indian tribute workers and African slaves as the main providers of labor for the Spaniards. Cash tributes were gradually substituted for Indian labor drafts. Slavery was abolished in Mexico and Central America shortly after independence; abolition came somewhat later in parts of the Andes, though the emancipation process had long been underway.[1] So began the rise of the free hispanized populations whose emergence and growth have been the major developments in Spanish America's social history since the native demographic disaster.

Parts of this familiar story are still missing, though. We have yet to understand fully the mechanisms of social change. This book explores the processes of hispanization and the shift to free labor, showing that they were rooted in the gendered contours of work, migration, and families. I view hispanization as a multifaceted process. It began at the level of individuals, as native and African persons—often through labor migration—learned Spanish and adopted Hispanic cultural practices and identities. Yet it was also a reproductive process, in which increasing numbers of children were born to hispanized parents or reared as migrants in the Hispanic sphere. In its outcomes, hispanization amounted to a broad demographic shift, transforming entire populations.

The research I present focuses on ordinary individuals and families in Guatemala in the late colonial period, from the 1760s to 1821. By looking at specific lives, we can see more clearly the mechanisms that drove the broad historical changes. Systems of tribute and labor (particularly native

labor) in colonial Mexico and Central America have been studied extensively, notably in the decades immediately following World War II, when
concerns with Latin American economic development shaped much of the
scholarship on the region.[2] Here I revisit these older topics in labor history
but approach them through newer interests in gender and cultural history.[3]
The resulting view expands historical understandings by showing how gender shaped patterns of labor and migration, and how those patterns fueled
changes in cultural and ethnic identities.

In its focus on social history, the book inverts conventional perspectives on Spanish American independence. Historians traditionally have
viewed independence from the standpoint of political history, emphasizing tensions between upper-level bureaucrats from Spain and their ambi-
tious American-born ("creole") counterparts who would lead the fights for
independence under Liberalist banners. National histories tend to present
the independence movements as nationalist projects, with leaders cast as
founding heroes, while Anglophone textbooks have portrayed Latin America's wars for independence as part of an epic "age of revolutions" sparked
by the Enlightenment. Recent studies have complicated the discussion by
exploring popular political thought. One strain of this newer scholarship,
focusing on the rural armed upheavals of the late colonial era, has shown
that rank-and-file rebels articulated political ideologies grounded in local
(often Indian) concerns, which did not typically coincide with proinde-
pendence or Liberal agendas; independence thus appears as the project of
urban, Hispanic political activists, often disconnected from the concerns of
the rural majority.[4] A second, partly overlapping, strain demonstrates the
ways the Enlightenment and Liberalism reached into popular thinking (at
least among urban hispanized people), parallel not only to Liberal legislation but also to social restructuring in the late colonial and early republican years.[5]

For its part, Central America experienced no sustained movement or
war for independence from Spain. It slipped quietly out of the empire
in 1821, annexed itself at first to Mexico, and then broke away in 1823
under Liberal leadership as the United Provinces of Central America.[6] This
confederation would soon fall to internal warring, splitting by 1839 into
five separate states that would become the republics of Guatemala, El Salvador, Honduras, Nicaragua, and Costa Rica. In Guatemala, the history of
the nineteenth century, both before and after independence, has been portrayed largely in terms of an ongoing struggle between Liberal and Conservative contenders to power.[7] Participation by the poor does not appear in
these depictions until 1837, with the Conservative revolt born of a peasant
uprising in the area east of the capital.[8]

This book reframes both the foundations and outcomes of independence, suggesting that the most important legislation of the early independent-era Liberal regime was not really reformist, much less revolutionary. Rather, the laws appear essentially as the political expression of social developments that had already emerged in the colonial period. Specifically, the abolition of Indian tribute labor, the emancipation of slaves, and the compression of the colonial race hierarchy had been nearly completed by the twilight years of the colony. In this light, independence and its major "reformist" legislation appear as political changes that followed social changes, rather than leading them. The social transformations had occurred organically and gradually following the conquest, largely independent of Liberalism and the Enlightenment. In the sphere of labor in particular, changes over the course of the colonial period had ultimately made Spanish administrative structures superfluous. The process of hispanization created a free labor force that by the eve of independence had largely replaced tribute laborers and slaves. Independence in effect removed the colonial framework that had upheld the systems of tribute and slave labor, as if removing the scaffolding from a building now completed.

Guatemala may seem an unlikely country for a study about hispanization and the transformation of colonial labor forms. Among today's Latin American nations, Guatemala is one of the most "Indian." Its modern-day demographics are a legacy of the density and diversity of the region's pre-colonial population, which included dozens of ethnolinguistic groups, most of them Mayan but some Uto-Aztecan. In recent censuses 40 percent of the population has self-identified as indigenous, though foreign experts put the figure at 60 or 65 percent.[9] Those not identified as Indians are categorized as "ladinos," a term that defines people as culturally hispanized and that in Guatemala typically connotes a mixture of Indian and Spanish ancestry or entirely Indian ancestry. As in the colonial era, indigenous people in Guatemala still do much of the labor for export agriculture, the major pillar of the cash economy; also as in the colonial era, their labor is still largely migratory, with workers leaving native communities seasonally to do the harvesting at Hispanic agro-export estates. Even as recently as the 1890s, in parts of the country native agricultural laborers were being conscripted through drafts much like those of the colonial era.[10] In short, native identities and coercive forms of Indian labor have tended to endure longer in Guatemala than elsewhere in Mesoamerica and parts of the Andes.

Yet these continuities bring the complexity and limitations of the hispanization process into particularly visible relief in Guatemala, enabling us to see in the archival records not only the mechanisms of cultural change but also the persistence of native forms. For Mexico, a recent flowering of scholarship has used indigenous-language documents to analyze the survival of native forms in the colonial era. Such a corpus of mundane records in native languages does not seem to exist in Central America, but the abundance of Spanish-language records from late colonial Guatemala richly illustrates the connections among labor migration, ethnic and demographic shifts, and native communities' struggle for survival. Communiqués between colonial and indigenous states, for example, depict the processes by which native communities were losing population as the Hispanic sphere gained in numbers; native officials decried the process, appealing to the colonial state in their efforts to preserve their communities and replenish their own bases of power. Other late colonial records document specific individuals' movements from Indian communities to Hispanic cities and estates. In these records we can see that even while such journeys were culturally transformative for migrants themselves, the wages they remitted to their home communities helped sustain Indian governments and families there.

Guatemala also may seem an unlikely country for a study of African slavery. In both popular and official understandings, Guatemala is not only one of the most Indian countries in Latin America but also one of the least African.[11] The fact that Africans and their descendants were once enslaved in Guatemala is almost entirely absent from national consciousness (not to mention social studies curricula). Although a few communities and individuals in Guatemala today identify with African heritage, they trace their ancestry to groups that arrived in Central America as free people, not as slaves.[12] However, recent studies have highlighted the presence of African slaves and their descendants in colonial Central America, particularly Guatemala (these studies join a blossoming of scholarship on Africans and their descendants in Spanish American mainland areas where the slave past has been excluded from master narratives of national histories).[13] Christopher Lutz's work on Santiago, Guatemala's capital city up to 1773, has suggested that across most of the seventeenth and eighteenth centuries, blacks and *mulatos*—including slaves and free people—comprised nearly one-third of the city's adult population.[14] Robinson Herrera showed the varied roles of Africans in sixteenth-century Santiago, and studies by Beatriz Palomo de Lewin and Paul Lokken demonstrate significant numbers of slaves and ex-slaves outside the city. As Murdo MacLeod recently noted, however, we have not fully understood "what happened to these black populations."[15] I address this question using notarial and judicial records to depict the movement of people of African descent from slavery to freedom. The move into freedom, I argue, necessitated a transformation of identity that helps explain the disappearance of blacks and mulatos from the region's consciousness over the course of the colonial years.

While my analysis highlights individuals and families, it also seeks to illuminate the functions of states (both colonial and native) by linking them to their social contexts at two levels: first, by considering ways in which individuals, especially nonelites, experienced and deployed state authority; and second, by illustrating the roles played by states—and the limits of their influence—in shaping the broad social history of labor forms, ethnic constructions, and gender relations.

Colonial government in Spanish America consisted of a loosely organized set of state agencies complemented by a parallel set of ecclesiastical agencies, with each agency often acting independently of the others. While the state's primary purpose was to collect revenue, its powers were mainly appointive and judicial. Aside from the treasury's multiple instruments for amassing income, the face of the state with which most people had contact was that of the judiciary and police. These functions were fulfilled by various bodies and personnel: the *audiencias* (regional high courts with judicial and legislative power), *alcaldes mayores* (men with administrative and judicial jurisdiction over provinces), local civil and criminal courts, and local justices and alcaldes. Their records, which I call collectively "court records" or "judicial records," form an important basis for this study, largely because they contain rich depictions of social life. Yet they also open a window onto the role of the state in its most immediate responses to the cultural and economic transformations taking place largely beyond legislative control.

Local native governments in both Mesoamerica and the Andes were institutionalized within the framework of colonial rule through the Spanish construct of a *república de indios* (republic of Indians). Conceived as separate from the *república de españoles* (republic of Spaniards), the república de indios was nevertheless subject to Spanish authority. The Spaniards' initial idea had been to keep Spanish-occupied geographic spaces separate from those of the Indians, but constant spillover in both directions soon rendered the "republics" meaningful more in political and administrative than geographic terms. As native states within the colonial system, Indian *cabildos* (town councils) were both embodiments and instruments of indigenous cultural survival. The members of native cabildos held titles modeled on Spanish government, but the men were drawn from native community elders and native hereditary nobilities.[16] Native cabildos typically had one or more Indian notaries literate in the local language and/or Spanish, who enabled native governments not only to keep internal written records but also to petition the colonial state. Through such advocacy, native governments were sometimes able to gain protections for their communities, for example from egregious labor demands or territorial encroachment. Thus, Spanish colonial structures legitimated the authority of native officials within their communities and as representatives of their communities before the Spanish state, and they legitimated native communities themselves as separate body politics. In a certain sense, therefore, if a native government endured, the community endured.

Yet the authority of native governments was constituted not only by recognition from the Spanish state but also by that of their native subjects. The decimation of indigenous communities caused by repeated epidemics and out-migration diminished the constituencies of native governments and threatened their political and economic vitality. As we will see, demographic shifts in Guatemala had by the eve of independence transformed the constituencies of both native and colonial states. These transformations set foundational patterns that would persist under both Liberal and Conservative administrations in the national era.

In contrast to native communities, Africans and their descendants had no state or body politic separate from the colonial Spanish ones. Black and mulato men were employed in segregated urban militia companies, but these were part of the colonial Spanish state.[17] Africans arrived in Spanish America as an integral part of colonial society, and even though most came as slaves, they were part of the Hispanic world. Their survival and social mobility would be through inroads within Hispanic society, rather than through separate channels.[18]

The book gives particular emphasis to Guatemala's colonial capital city, its hinterland, and the linkages between the two. One reason for this is the centrality of the capital in the mechanisms of social change. Throughout Spanish America the hispanization process was closely intertwined with migration along intraregional routes—between native communities and colonial cities, between native communities and colonial haciendas, and between haciendas and cities. The Spanish capital in Guatemala was Central America's major hub of commerce, transit, in-migration, and hispanization, starting in the sixteenth century. Founded in 1541, the city of Santiago (today called Antigua Guatemala) served as seat of a colonial jurisdiction that the Spaniards called both the Captaincy General of Guatemala and the Kingdom (*Reino*) of Guatemala.[19] This jurisdiction was significantly larger in area than today's Republic of Guatemala; it encompassed all of the territory that is now Central America as well as the Mexican state of Chiapas.[20] Technically the Kingdom of Guatemala belonged to the Viceroyalty of New Spain, but Guatemala had its own audiencia, which answered directly to the Crown.[21] With some 38,000 residents in the midcolonial years, Santiago outsized all other cities in the kingdom.[22] It was at its center a Spanish city, but the center was supplied and served by surrounding Indian barrios and towns. Santiago's population across the colonial period seems to have been more heavily Spanish and ladino than that of Quetzaltenango in the northwest, but more Indian than San Salvador to the southeast.[23]

A second reason for emphasis on the capital is that its later colonial history offers a particularly revealing window onto the consequences of migration and hispanization. In 1773 a series of earthquakes damaged Santiago so severely that the colonial authorities decided to transfer their seat to a new location. They selected the site that would become today's Guatemala City, 45 kilometers east of Santiago over a mountainous road, in a cattle ranching area called the Valle de las Vacas.[24] Spanish state and church offices, colonial residences, and Indian barrios were to be transplanted according to a detailed plan that replicated the layout of the ruined city. Even the outlying Indian pueblos that had skirted Santiago were ordered to uproot and reestablish themselves at new locales chosen to preserve their position in relation to the city center.[25] Compliance with the relocation plans was only partial, especially in the outlying pueblos, but economic realities provided an incentive to move; while Santiago languished from structural damage and financial distress, construction projects at the new capital fueled a building boom into the early nineteenth century. During the 1780s and 1790s the majority of the old capital's residents migrated to the appointed site, and with their labor a new city was built.[26] This capital, Nueva Guatemala de la Asunción, was known at first as Nueva Guatemala; eventually it came to be called simply Guatemala, as it is today. (The name Ciudad de Guatemala—Guatemala City—distinguishes the city from the republic.) The old metropolis of Santiago, still inhabited albeit by smaller numbers, came to be called la Antigua Guatemala, or just Antigua.[27]

The transplantation of the capital city highlights key historical transformations in progress at the time of Santiago's destruction. Shifting labor forms appear clearly in the context of the sudden demand for workers to build the new city. Starting with the conquest generation, the Spaniards in Mesoamerica had adapted native tribute labor systems for their own profit. Indians drafted as tributaries for short-term rotary labor stints had provided the mainstay of seasonal agricultural work as well as a substantial portion of the year-round labor for colonial churches and state offices. By the time of the 1773 earthquakes, however, tribute labor (which had already disappeared in most parts of Mexico) was quickly losing ground to private recruitment in Guatemala. In the heyday of construction at Nueva Guatemala, the Audiencia issued warrants for draft laborers from a few tributary Indian communities. But the vast majority of the work was done by free laborers—Indians and others—who had made private arrangements with building contractors. I document in Chapter 1 the erosion of native tribute labor and the accompanying shifts in individuals' community affiliations and ethnic identities.

The institution of slavery was also fading. Slaves of African descent would continue to be bought and sold in Nueva Guatemala until the United Provinces declared a general emancipation in 1824, but enslaved people were relatively few in Santiago by the time of the earthquakes, and they barely figured among the workers in the building projects at the new capital.[28] Rather, many of the men were free people identified as mulatos, working for wages under private contract. As Chapter 2 shows, racial and cultural *mestizaje* (mixing) had chipped away the social bases of slavery even before it was abolished in law.

The capital's relocation also illustrates the development of the free labor force that came to replace Indian tributary workers and African slaves. Though most urban labor by the 1770s had been privatized and was no longer procured through state-administered drafts, the colonial city remained dependent on services and products supplied by Indians. The Spaniards were aware of their need for Indian labor, as we can see in the Audiencia's purposeful mandate for the relocation of native barrios and outlying pueblos to the new capital. Chapter 3 shows that the same communities, families, and even individuals often worked as free laborers providing precisely those services and products that had been demanded of them in the old tribute system. Their tribute requirements, meanwhile, had been converted as part of a broad shift toward cash tributes, underway since the sixteenth century.

The ruin of Santiago and relocation of the capital almost certainly intensified processes of social change. In Santiago the earthquakes had damaged and destroyed houses along with other structures, exacerbating the crowded conditions that typified premodern cities. In Nueva Guatemala it would take years to build enough housing for the influx of tens of thousands of people. During the two decades following the earthquakes, nearly everyone at both old and new capitals would spend time living in shared and temporary quarters. Residential mixing across families and ethnic groups had characterized the experience of migrants into Santiago also, but the massive in-migration and housing shortage at Nueva Guatemala seem to have spread the mixing across a larger segment of the population. These conditions amplified the quotidian cross-cultural interactions that had long been at the core of mestizaje and hispanization in the urban setting.

In establishing the new city, the *ayuntamiento* (Spanish municipal council) distributed lands to various Indian pueblos and elite Spanish men in 1774 and 1775.[29] This distribution was ultimately paradoxical on multiple fronts. In the first place, the Indian communities would become increasingly non-Indian as their members slipped into Hispanic identities and as the city's Hispanic neighborhoods spread outward and blended with Indian pueblos. Second, the new city would be populated mostly by women, not men. Inge Langenberg's study of census records indicates that in 1796 women in Nueva Guatemala outnumbered men by as much as 80 percent, and by independence the ratio was approaching two women to every one man.[30] Further, the female majority would be distinctly plebian, not elite. Santiago by the time of the earthquakes had also been home to a noticeable and markedly plebian female majority.[31] Both cities, like others in colonial Latin America, were drawing large numbers of migrant women to work in domestic service, while men were more likely than women to find agricultural work in rural areas.[32] As we will see, in Guatemala not only young unmarried women came to the city "to serve"; in addition, rural women whose husbands had abandoned them with children were often forced to migrate in search of wages, with domestic service their most likely occupation. These patterns of labor and migration placed women at the forefront of hispanization in the urban sphere, as both objects and agents of social change.

This female vanguard of urban hispanization calls for a rethinking of gender and hispanization. Popular understandings of both past and present in Mesoamerica portray men as the primary native (Indian) actors to engage with the Hispanic sphere. Historical scholarship on labor has implicitly echoed this understanding by focusing mainly on male workers. Women are imagined to have typically stayed (and typically to stay today) in a more rural or "Indian" setting of the home or native community, while men entered a presumably more public colonial sphere (and today enter a presumably more public Hispanic sphere) as draft workers or free wage laborers.[33] In this scenario men are cast as the main subjects of hispanization, learning Spanish and adopting European-style dress, for example; they presumably then became (and today become) the main agents of hispanization on return to their home communities and families. To be sure, men comprised the majority of migrant workers recruited to colonial agricultural enterprises. But women predominated among migrants to the city. I argue that even in the countryside women played a major role in social change, partly because of their labor in bearing and rearing children, whose care was assigned almost exclusively to women in both native and Hispanic societies.

Because reproduction—social as well as biological—is central to processes of mestizaje and cultural change, analysis of hispanization requires a consideration of (hetero)sexuality, childbearing, and childrearing. My focus on "love" in this book is essentially a focus on marriage, other heterosexual unions, and family structures—that is, on contexts of reproduction.

Throughout the book and especially in Chapter 4, I consider reproduction along with labor and migration as mechanisms of hispanization. Further, I suggest that patterns of labor and migration were themselves densely interwoven with the household and family structures that formed the bases of social and biological reproduction. Women were the largest group of rural-to-urban migrants, and, as Chapter 4 shows, they constituted the overwhelming majority of residents in the capital city—partly as a result of migration patterns but also as an outcome of patterns in love. While studies of sexuality and marriage in colonial Latin American have generally emphasized Iberian notions of honor and behavioral ideals, my research shifts the focus to love as it was actually practiced. The analysis reveals widespread informal unions and marital separations as well as non-patriarchal household and family structures. Popular opinion and the colonial state recognized and in ways legitimized these realities. In the thickly described scenarios of individual lives and circumstances, concerns about honor fade somewhat, while love—shaped by affection and desire—plays a major role in explaining behaviors and relationships.

Hispanization has not been the exclusive trend in the centuries since 1492. Throughout the colonial period and into the present, indigenous people and communities across Latin America have fought for survival, cultural vitality, and continued (or resurgent) political authority and integrity. Afro-Latin American cultures and identities also have survived and gained growing visibility, especially in recent decades. On the eve of independence in Guatemala, even as the free hispanized population in the capital city was consolidating, the tributary rolls reflected an increase the size of the kingdom's indigenous population for the first time since the conquest. The turnaround has been attributed to the distribution of smallpox vaccine starting in 1804.[34] Yet the recovery of indigenous populations was uneven across the kingdom, partly because the numbers depended not only on birth and mortality rates but also on the persistence of native ethnic identities. In the region that would become the Republic of Guatemala, the lower-lying lands east of the capital were becoming increasingly hispanized, while the highland regions to the capital's north and west, less easily accessible to Spanish commercial agriculture, remained primarily Indian. Thus the cities of Santiago and Nueva Guatemala were located on a geographic frontier between the more indigenous West and the now predominantly ladino East.[35] Like other Spanish colonial capitals, Santiago and Nueva Guatemala also served as cultural frontiers in the processes of conquest and hispanization. Both cities were sites of especially intensive mestizaje—a process I interpret broadly to include cross-cultural social interactions as well as cross-racial sexual unions and reproduction.

* * *

The research for this book is based mainly on sources from the Archivo General de Centro América (the General Archive of Central America) in Guatemala City, including notarial records (particularly wills and slave sales), censuses and other government administrative records, and judicial records. Notarial records have proved a rich source for the social history of Spanish America, particularly in the sixteenth century, but by the eighteenth century the majority of records kept by notaries in Guatemala concerned wills and transactions made by the wealthy.[36] Much of the normal activity of poor and economically middling people apparently had become routine and was not notarized. The breadth of Guatemala's late colonial society is thus better reflected in judicial records. In the Archivo General de Centro América are many hundreds of court cases—both criminal trials and civil suits—containing transcriptions of oral testimony by ordinary people who sued, pressed criminal charges, served as witnesses, or defended themselves in the judicial system. Court-appointed notaries recorded the petitions and depositions of the largely illiterate populace, often in extensive detail. Colloquial diction and hurried penmanship suggest that many of the records closely replicate the speakers' words. Similar caches of records across Spanish America have in recent decades become an important source for histories of nonelite people.[37]

In the Archivo General de Centro América, the cases heard by the Audiencia are mixed together with those heard by the capital city's municipal civil and criminal courts. This mixing is not entirely illogical, since most of the cases brought to the Audiencia originated in the capital and its nearby hinterland. The city's concentration of population helps explain this pattern, as does the ready access to the Audiencia enjoyed by people in the capital. Indeed, the records convey a sense that the Audiencia often functioned as an additional municipal court, albeit a court of appeal. Additionally, litigants in the state's courts sometimes alluded to cases brought to religious authorities. Records suggest that the various state and church judicial officers operated in awareness of one another and generally made common cause.[38] Their subjects, too, were aware of multiple available avenues of judicial redress; people might go first or in an emergency to the home of their *alcalde de barrio* (neighborhood alcalde) or to the parish priest and later to the city's judicial offices or the Audiencia, both located at the central plaza.

Because Guatemala did not have a separate Indian court like that in Mexico, the Spanish courts heard cases brought by Indians.[39] Incidents involving Spaniards as well as homicides and assaults among Indians were specifically subject to the authority of the Spanish judiciary, though native alcaldes in the urban Indian barrios and in Indian communities outside the city were empowered, like their Hispanic counterparts, to adjudicate in most internal matters.[40] Those cases from native pueblos to reach the Audiencia were mainly homicides reported by Indian officers and complaints by native town councils on behalf of their pueblos. For individual Indians beyond the city, recourse to the Spanish authorities was limited by geographic distance, linguistic differences, and perhaps the threat of retribution by local officers for challenging their authority. Nonetheless, nonofficeholding Indians who lived outside the city occasionally testified in the colonial courts, sometimes as plaintiffs and sometimes as witnesses or defendants. The office of the state's Procurator for the Poor provided counsel for Indians and others unable to pay for attorneys.

In using judicial records I am concerned not only, nor even primarily, with crimes or disputes themselves, nor primarily with the jurists' arguments. My main interest is in the litigants and witnesses—their social circumstances and attitudes as revealed in their testimonies. As Steve Stern has described for colonial Mexico, neither the people nor the situations that came before the courts were atypical; criminal violence tended to occur as an excess within normal patterns of behavior.[41] With that premise, I have read hundreds of court records in order to aggregate the social details they contain and to paint a portrait of Guatemalan society in the decades leading up to independence. I am also interested in the ways that court cases illustrate nonelite individuals' approaches to state authority and aid. The courts served as a means of redress available to the general public, including the poor. My reading shows that in Guatemala, as elsewhere in Spanish America, the magistrates sought to maintain social stability by inserting a measure of balance into economic and social relationships, and they often arbitrated with remarkable evenhandedness among parties of distinct social status. The Spanish judicial system, as Michael Scardaville has noted, "was expected to be compassionate and benevolent."[42] People went to court not only to defend themselves against civil suits and criminal charges but also to take action against those who had wronged them in any of myriad relationships, including tributary labor obligations, slavery, employment, patronage, love, and marriage.

People who testified in criminal cases were asked to state their name, place of origin or residence, and *calidad*—a Spanish concept of status that incorporated notions of race and social rank.[43] In the late colonial Guatemalan records, descriptors of calidad could express attributes of lineage, as in the terms *español* (Spanish or Spaniard) or *mestizo* (of mixed Spanish and Indian ancestry), but they could instead refer mainly to phenotype, as in *pardo* and *moreno* (both signifying someone of dark complexion). Slaves were generally identified as such when they testified but were also named with a descriptor of calidad (usually *negro* or *negra* or *mulato* or *mulata*); to be enslaved was a legal status, not a calidad. People identified as Indians gave the name of their native pueblo or barrio and, if it differed, their community of residence. Those so hispanized as not to affiliate with a particular native community were labeled simply as *indio laborío* or *naborío* (Indian attached to Hispanic society) or occasionally *indio ladino* (Spanish-speaking Indian). Although *indio* was partly a racial category, in the colonial era it was perhaps most important as a legal category, since Indians under Spanish rule were subject to specific legal structures. At the same time, Indian identities as expressed in late colonial Guatemala were about cultural and ethnic belonging; by naming their native pueblo or barrio, Indians identified themselves as members of a particular community and body politic. Those labeled as naboríos or indios ladinos were being identified as part of the Hispanic cultural and ethnic sphere.

In these racial and ethnic labels, the late colonial records convey a set of further social transitions accompanying the changes in labor systems. The complex hierarchy of sixty-four or more racial categories developed in Spanish America had broken down over successive generations of racial and cultural mixing.[44] By the late eighteenth century, no one in Guatemala was speaking in terms of the whole range of racial categories. Partly it was that phenotypes had become unreadable. Consider Hipólito Vela, a weaver-turned-petty-gangster, labeled in the 1770s alternately as mulato and mestizo. Another example is Manuel de Jesús, who was tried for theft in Nueva Guatemala in 1781. He identified himself as mulato, though various witnesses called him *negro*.[45] Across Latin America, people had been slipping across racial categories since the earliest decades after the conquest.[46] By the late colonial period, those who moved within Guatemala's hispanized world did not always know exactly what their racial background was, nor did they seem much to care. A case in point is Nicolasa de Lara, who testified as a witness in an 1808 trial. The notary wrote, "She looks to be Spanish, although she says she doesn't know her calidad."[47] Ignacio Quevedo was only slightly more certain, telling the court in 1803, "He believes he is a free pardo."[48] Rafael Vivas, an español, was arrested and questioned in 1775 about the illegal tavern he had been keeping with Rosalia Castro. Though he had been living in informal union with Castro for eleven years, he said he didn't know her calidad. (She told the court she was Spanish.)[49]

Notarial records and parish records too show fading distinctions among racial categories within the Hispanic sphere, with, as Lutz noted, "a growing failure to record race altogether."[50] For Indians, parish records were generally kept separate from those of hispanized people even in the late colonial years, reflecting the persisting perception of separation between Indian and Hispanic societies.[51] Census records follow a similar pattern.

Censuses of Indian pueblos had always been kept separate, mainly because they were used to assess tribute requirements. For the hispanized population, though, censuses in the late eighteenth and early nineteenth centuries began to consolidate multiple calidad groups into single categories; the reports for cities as well as rural areas increasingly grouped everyone besides Indians together under labels like *gente ordinaria* (literally ordinary people, meaning plebians), ladinos, or even españoles.[52] These categories were evidently sometimes chosen by individual census takers, but other times preprinted on a template from the Audiencia. The segregation of records for Indians and the consolidation of categories for other people prefigured the move after independence to official and popular understandings that retained *indio* as a separate category while collapsing all non-Indian identities into the single category of *ladino*.[53]

In the chapters ahead, I generally use the ethnic labels used in the late colonial documents. Therefore I do not use the term *casta*, which does not often appear in the Guatemalan records; nor do I use the term *criollo*, or *creole*, since people of Spanish descent in colonial Central America considered themselves to be españoles and were called españoles by other groups as well, regardless of birth in Europe or America. Indeed the word *criollo* seems rarely to have been used colloquially in Guatemala, except to describe domestic animals with spotted or mixed coloring and American-born slaves. The terms *mulata* and *mulato* in colonial Guatemala referred to people of mixed African and Indian descent, as well as those of mixed African and European ancestry.[54] Because the English *mulatto* is not quite equivalent, I use the Spanish forms. For people labeled in the archival records as Indians from specific towns, I have tried to identify the town's ethnolinguistic group, generally using the colonial-era spelling. I avoid the term *Maya*, which was not used in colonial-era Guatemala and would imply an anachronistic sense of unity among Indians.[55]

Although I have standardized the spelling of place names and most personal names, I have preserved spellings by individuals who signed their own names. After giving a person's full name once, in immediately subsequent references I use only the surname except where first names (which have gender) may make it easier for the reader to follow a narrative with its cast of characters. I preserve the honorific titles *don* and *doña* to denote the social status they conveyed in colonial-era usage; they are also ethnic markers, as they were used almost exclusively by Spaniards.

In using *don* and *doña*, I mean to reflect the fact that despite the process of hispanization and the blurring of calidad categories in the period under discussion, society was still marked by steep differences in wealth and privilege that tended to coalesce around race. The Guatemalan workforce of the late colonial years supported a small privileged oligarchy that as a group looked much whiter than the rest of the populace.

The same inequity persists today. Studies of postindependence Guatemala have necessarily grappled with continuing social inequalities and recent violence, often locating their roots in colonial-era ethnic and economic relationships. The classic example in the field of history is Severo Martínez Peláez's 1970 *La Patria del Criollo*, which together with several subsequent studies links the colonial past to the failure of the republican-era Hispanic state (and in some cases indigenous elites) to respond to the interests of indigenous communities and poor ladinos.[56] The story I tell here echoes that of colonial inequities but argues that those inequities were embedded in changing rather than static colonial-era structures. Across three centuries, the unequal racial and economic relationships fundamental to colonial rule—the race hierarchy, the labor forms—were increasingly eroded, privatized, and removed from state jurisdiction. Paradoxically, though, gendered relationships of labor and love continued to reproduce ethnic and economic inequities, even while dismantling the old colonial institutions that had once sustained them.

1 Changing Communities, Changing Identities

INDIANS AND THE COLONIAL WORLD

Early in the fifteenth century, the rulers of the Quiché kingdom founded a new capital at Utatlán and began to build an empire. They expanded their territory across the region that is now western Guatemala, extending it from the highlands southward toward the Pacific coast, until one of their subject peoples, the Cakchiquels, rose in rebellion in the 1470s.[1] The Quichés and Cakchiquels were fighting for domination of the area when the Spaniards with their native Mexican allies arrived in 1524.[2]

The invaders came by land along the Pacific coast. They turned inland and hiked up through the cacao orchards into the highlands, where they conquered the Quiché capital and then moved southeast to vanquish the Cakchiquels. The brutality of the Spanish expedition leader, Pedro de Alvarado, earned him a reputation as exceptional even among Spanish conquerors.[3] Yet he followed standard conquistador procedures, claiming Guatemala as conquered territory as he "founded" a Spanish capital (which he called Santiago) at an extant native capital, the Cakchiquel city of Iximche'.[4] The Cakchiquels then rebelled and evacuated the city, diminishing its luster for the Spaniards, who in 1527 moved their headquarters farther south and east to a site near the smaller Cakchiquel community of Almolonga. There they built a city (that is, presumably they had the Indians build it for them), which they also called Santiago (today it is called Ciudad Vieja). This Santiago was situated at the foot of the Volcán de Agua and was destroyed by a mudslide in 1541; the Spaniards again moved their base, now to a location some 5 kilometers northward in the Valley of Panchoy, still calling the city Santiago (this would become today's Antigua Guatemala). In 1773, this capital was severely damaged by earthquakes, and a final relocation followed with the construction of Nueva Guatemala (today's Guatemala City) in the Valle de las Vacas.

During the conquest in Guatemala and the area that is now Honduras and Nicaragua, the Spaniards had enslaved thousands of Indians. Many of the slaves were sold in the 1530s and 1540s for mine work in Peru and perished there or en route. Others accompanied the Spaniards to work for them in the Valley of Panchoy.[5] The enslavement of Indians did not endure, though, partly because the massive slave death toll rendered the system unsustainable. In the mid-sixteenth century, colonial legislation issued in Guatemala abolished Indian slavery.[6] The reform enforced the "reduction," or resettlement, of the former Indian slaves into several barrios within the Spanish capital and in some towns outside the city's periphery.[7]

From the perspective of the Spaniards, the main purpose of the Indian barrios and towns was to supply labor and provisions for the colony, which was centered with the huge majority of its Spanish population in the capital. In a sense this changed little across the centuries; at the time of the capital's relocation to the present site beginning in the 1770s, the city remained dependent on its Indian barrios and surrounding Indian towns for food and workers. Although the Spanish authorities announced a divine mandate for the relocation of Indian communities along with the city, earthly economic realities also necessitated the move.

Yet by the 1770s the structures of labor had changed significantly, as part of a broader process of transformation that swept across the whole of Spanish America.[8] In the first generation or two after the conquest, *encomienda* had prevailed as the major form of Indian labor for the Spaniards, accompanied in Central America by Indian slavery.[9] In the encomienda system, labor was exacted as part of Indian tributes to the Spanish. Individual Spaniards who received royal grants of encomienda, usually in payment for service to Castile in the Conquest, would enjoy the permanent privilege of a given Indian community's tribute labor. Thus an encomienda was a grant of labor (not land, as is sometimes thought). As the numbers of Spanish landholdings increased beyond the numbers of encomiendas, the encomienda form was supplanted by a system of *repartimiento*, or distribution, of tribute labor gangs among various Spanish employers.

The mechanisms of repartimiento labor recruitment in Mesoamerica are now well known to historians.[10] The drafts were administered at the corporate (institutional) level in both the Spanish and Indian spheres. In Guatemala the Spanish state was the largest single employer of repartimiento Indians, but private employers too, as well as clerical orders, applied to the colonial adminstration for repartimientos of native workers, and the administration then sent orders to native communities.[11] Indigenous community officers were charged with gathering workers and dispatching them to the job. Work crews were refreshed by rotations of laborers out of, and back into, the community—usually at weekly intervals but in some cases longer. (In Guatemala, the longer rotations were called mandamientos in the sixteenth and seventeenth centuries; by the late eighteenth century the words *mandamiento* and *repartimiento* had become interchangeable.)[12] Employers were supposed to pay an institutionally fixed wage, though shortchanging and other abuses were common.[13] The colonial state's desire to maintain steady supplies for urban populations and for export probably ensured a somewhat equitable distribution of workers.[14]

The eighteenth century would see the completion in Guatemala of a dramatic, if piecemeal, disintegration of Indian tribute labor. As elsewhere in Spanish America, this was a transition not only from draft labor to free labor but also from state-mediated labor procurement to private arrangement. That is, labor recruitment by colonial administration and by native community governments gave way to informal contracting between workers and employers themselves. This shift was closely intertwined with transitions in the population's ethnic composition. The Hispanic proportion of the labor force was growing, fed by births in the colony's hispanized world and by attrition of individuals from Indian communities. Even those Indians who maintained affiliation with their native communities, and who therefore remained subject to tribute requirements, were increasingly becoming hispanized—notably in terms of Spanish language acquisition—especially near the colonial population centers.[15] Bilingual Indians could contract their labor directly with Spanish employers or *mayordomos* (managers) without need of state mechanisms on either the Spanish or Indian side.

Thus the tribute labor system eventually became superfluous.[16] At various moments across Mesoamerica and the Andes, as native labor was privatized, the Spanish state let go of coerced Indian labor. Tributes continued, but bit by bit colonial edicts converted labor drafts to cash payments, collected locally by Indian officials and turned over to the Spanish authorities. Tributes that had once been paid in commodities also gave way to payments in coin.[17] Increasingly, Indians were recruited as free laborers who needed wages to pay their tributes. The legislation that gradually formalized this transition does not represent an activist administrative effort to enact social change; as Charles Gibson said of the collapse of repartimiento in Mexico, colonial "law provides an approximation of historical happening, or a commentary upon it."[18] In shifting to cash tributes, colonial authorities were in effect trying to maintain tributes as a source of revenue in the face of changing social and economic realities.

This chapter traces these changes in the Guatemalan context, comparing them to findings on Mexico and adding a new consideration of ethnic identities, gender, and family structures. Studies of labor and recruitment in colonial-era Mesoamerica have generally focused on male workers, and indeed the workers drafted in the tribute labor system were mostly men. Yet I show that the transition from tribute labor to individual arrangements increasingly drew entire families, as well as women and children alone, into migratory wage work. Women's work, I argue, was central in the shift to free labor and in the lengthening duration of Indian migrants' sojourns in the Hispanic world. Further, the restructuring of tributes and labor may have exacerbated certain pressures on women and children. In the new system of cash tributes, women as well as men were required to pay, and women whose husbands were absent (often having fled debts) could face dire straits.[19] My research indicates that widows and women with absent husbands were those most likely to seek wages in the cities. The restructuring of tributes may also have encouraged native parents to put their children out to work in the Hispanic cities. Wages earned by native children were normally remitted to the parents in the sending communities, who faced cash tribute collection and, often, associated debts. The migration of children from native pueblos into Spanish households provided powerful fuel for the hispanization process, since children are fastest to adopt new languages and cultures.

For native communities and ethnicities, outmigration unleashed a complex set of changes. While some migrants sent remittances that helped sustain native households and community coffers, overall the trend of departures decreased native communities' ability to meet tribute demands. Indians who worked for extended periods in the colonial sector tended to be identified increasingly with a Hispanic sphere of residence and work. This shift in identities diminished native communities' assessable populations, hence draining the consituency and authority from native states. The role of Indian polities within the Hispanic system was eroding.

Guatemalan repartimiento labor in comparative context

Historians have observed that coerced Indian labor lasted longer in Guatemala than in most areas with concentrated Spanish populations (Peru is the other noted exception).[20] Repartimiento labor had faded from central Mexico by the middle of the seventeenth century, but in Central America it persisted nearly until independence.[21] Over the years the system grew unruly in Guatemala, with local officials apparently taking authority to allocate repartimientos, until the Audiencia moved in 1761 to regain exclusive control.[22] Convention assigned work gangs from specific towns to the same *hacendados* (estate owners) year in, year out. Though each assignment was made specifically to the owner and not to the estate itself, in practice the repartimiento sometimes continued even after an estate changed hands.[23] Until about 1770, the Audiencia would quite willingly reissue an old repartimiento warrant at the request of a Spaniard who acquired an estate with a history of draft labor from a particular town.[24] Thus certain Indian towns became tied through customary labor drafts to particular estates.[25] These ties may have made the system especially entrenched in Guatemala, contributing to its persistence there.

The relatively smaller Spanish presence in Guatemala also foretells the longer duration of draft labor there, for the mechanism of change to free labor in Guatemala, like that in Mexico, hinged on hispanization. Linguistic hispanization among Indians facilitated direct arrangements between workers and employers, and the growing numbers of hispanized people living outside indigenous communities increased the availability of free laborers. Thus, repartimiento systems ended as hispanization took hold. In Mexico the hispanization process gained full speed earliest in the vicinity of Mexico City with its concentration of Spaniards and then spread outward.[26] In the Guadalajara area, the agricultural drafts ended in 1750, a century later than in the area surrounding Mexico City.[27] In the region of Antequera (Oaxaca), repartimientos continued as late as 1787 but by that point they were being used only as a stopgap measure to get workers in a pinch—particularly for wheat and cochineal production. Newer forms of recruitment had already become the norm.[28]

Likewise in Guatemala, the importance of the draft had been fading, with free labor recruitment on the rise at the time of the 1773 earthquakes, but then the construction of the new capital gave the repartimiento system a second wind in the region surrounding the city. Pueblos as far as 30 leagues away were required to send workers for the building projects. At the same time, a series of epidemics and famine further reduced the number of workers available in the countryside in the 1770s and 1780s. Hacendados in these decades were unable to get enough workers (or were unwilling to pay the higher wages needed to recruit free laborers), and their requests for repartimiento gangs surged.[29] Seeking to ensure sufficient food supplies, the Audiencia specifically exempted certain towns from labor in urban construction and drafted their workers instead to the haciendas. Thus, the colony fell back on the repartimiento system in a period of increased need and reduced supply of labor, using the draft as a way to recruit workers and to balance food production with construction.

In addition to the longer duration of coerced native labor in Guatemala, the structure of the system there placed a larger burden on Indian individuals, families, and communities. In Mexico, colonial regulations limited the weekly repartimiento drafts to at most 10 percent of a town's eligible male population during the laborious periods of weeding and harvest.[30] In Central America, by contrast, the Audiencia allowed 25 percent of a town's eligible men to be drafted in any given week. The colonial administrators in the sixteenth century had apparently meant to limit the draft to only a few men at a time from any community, but by the middle of the seventeenth century, 25 percent—the *cuarta parte* (one quarter)—had become the rule.[31] Moreover, whereas in Mexico the 10 percent allowance was substantially reduced for about half the year during the agricultural off-season, in Central America the 25 percent allowance prevailed year-round. Male adults in Central America could therefore be required to spend a quarter of the year away from their own crops and families. In many towns in the capital's hinterland and others near outlying commercial agriculture centers, where the draft continued well into the eighteenth century, indeed the full 25 percent (and sometimes numbers in excess of 25 percent) of eligible men were tapped.[32] Some employers' requests for work gangs specified a temporary or seasonal need for labor, but other repartimientos—particularly in public works—were in force during much of the year.

Despite the comparatively heavy burden of the "cuarta parte" (25 percent), indigenous responses to the repartimiento labor draft system in Central America reflected local concerns rather than disputes over differences in other realms of the empire or in other times. This pattern is consistent with the intense localism that scholars have observed in native politics, identities, and writing across colonial-era Mesoamerica. Though indigenous communities in Guatemala complained repeatedly in the eighteenth century that too many men were being requested for the drafts, they never questioned the fairness of the 25 percent proportion. Their petitions focused instead on temporary issues such as crop failures, plagues and epidemics, and church-building projects that lessened their ability to supply workers, and on the ever-decreasing numbers of people in the communities. Indigenous cabildos appealed for re-counts of eligible men and for greater numbers of exemptions for various civic and religious officeholders, but they accepted the one-quarter rule as a given.[33]

Why did regulations allow such a greater proportion of men to be drafted in Guatemala than in Mexico? It is possible that one-quarter of the eligible populations of the Indian towns around the Guatemalan capital in fact amounted to workforce sizes (in absolute numbers) similar to those near Mexico City, where numbers of eligible draftees in at least some sixteenth-century Indian communities were much higher than in Guatemala.[34] Or the difference in draft proportions also may reflect some difference in pre-Columbian labor draft systems. The matter of timing also suggests an explanation. The Guatemalan allowance of up to one-quarter of a town's eligible men became entrenched starting in the mid-1650s—precisely the time when the central Mexican draft disappeared.[35] In the decades preceding 1650, the free labor force in Mexico had been expanding and gradually supplanting the repartimiento system. During the same period in Central America, the repartimiento system was just taking shape, coexisting for several decades with encomienda and unpaid "personal service" (servicio personal).[36] By the time repartimiento became the principal method for procuring Indian workers in Central America, the Spanish population there and its demand for workers had grown, while the indigenous population had suffered multiple, infamous devastations. The Spanish government may have increased the proportion of men who could be drafted each week because of insufficient labor for colonial enterprises.

It is possible that similar proportions of indigenous community members were working on colonial enterprises in Guatemala and Mexico, but in Mexico they were being recruited as free laborers.[37] In this light, the high proportion of men drafted in Guatemala may correspond specifically to the long duration of repartimiento there. Yet, by the late colonial years, draft labor was fading in Guatemala, and on any given day some of the off-duty 75 percent of eligible draftees were working as private wage laborers. The shift to free labor was already underway.

Coerced labor fading

Though repartimiento labor lasted in one or two instances as late as 1814 in Guatemala, the system was in rapid decline by the second half of the eighteenth century, quickly being replaced by freer forms of labor.[38] Royal legislation indicates that as early as 1550 some workers in Guatemala were labeled as voluntarios (volunteers)—that is, free workers earning their pay by their own contract or arrangement. In the seventeenth century, it was commonplace for free workers to labor alongside repartimiento draftees at the same estate or enterprise, and this pattern continued in the eighteenth century.[39] (Slaves were also typically present in commercial agricultural enterprises in Guatemala. As year-round employees, people of African descent were often employed as overseers or managers, but they interacted regularly with indigenous workers, furthering the cultural and ethnic complexity of workaday life.)

By the late colonial years, estate owners in Guatemala were employing substantial portions of their workforces as free laborers. Colonial and Indian communities alike recognized the shifts that were taking place. While some Spanish employers continued to request repartimiento work crews, native communities increasingly flouted or outright rejected the Audiencia's orders, citing the widespread availability of free workers and the decreasing availability of men in the native communities.[40]

This resistance followed a centuries-old pattern of indigenous protest over the burdens of conquest, but the justifications given were specific to the current ethnic and demographic scenarios. In the early colonial years, Indian communities had written protests to the king focusing on a different set of problems—the hardships of providing tributes; the difficulty faced by men doing draft labor; the imprisonment and whippings visited on native officers who failed to deliver tribute commodities or workers; various abuses in the system, including the sale of indigenous orphans and other atrocities; and the enormous suffering of the people under these circumstances. Flight from Indian communities and shortage of men for the draft were mentioned rarely or not at all.[41] In the seventeenth century, indigenous cabildos had appealed frequently about the mistreatment— endemic in the colonial system—of draft workers.[42] Complaints arose, too, over the double burden of tributes levied in both cash and labor.[43]

In the eighteenth century, native protests came to focus primarily on the communities' shortage of people to provide conscript labor. What had been a lament about the horrific human costs of forced labor became a more direct refusal to send workers. The change is especially evident after 1760, when the Audiencia began systematic record keeping for the labor repartimiento; but there were signs earlier in the century.[44] Though epidemics, deaths, and flight had taken devastating tolls on Indian communities across the whole colonial period, the rate of out-migration from native towns appears to have increased over time. The resounding chorus of indigenous complaint in the late eighteenth century was about the departure of people from native towns. Out-migration was diminishing the communities' ability to meet tribute demands and to preserve internal structures and practices.

In 1770, for example, Indian authorities in eight towns in the jurisdictions of Chiquimula and Sonsonate (in today's southeastern Guatemala and western El Salvador, respectively) informed the Audiencia that deaths and flight had left a shortage of people to provide repartimiento labor.[45] Closer to the capital, the pueblos of Mixco, San Felipe Nerí, Santiago Sacatepéquez, San Pedro Sacatepéquez, and San Juan Sacatepéquez repeatedly made similar appeals across the eighteenth century, arguing that fewer men should be drafted in the repartimientos. They gave various reasons including the high numbers of people who had married in other towns, effectively reducing the local populations.[46] In 1774, Indian correspondents from the pueblos of Santiago Sacatepéquez, San Lucas Sacatepéquez, San Juan Sacatepéquez, San Juan Amatitlán, and San Cristóbal Amatitlán told the Audiencia that because of decreased populations and a plague of locusts, their towns were unable to send the numbers of tribute laborers requested of them.[47] In San Felipe Nerí, native officers said that they could no longer provide the numbers of repartimiento workers that they once did "because of the many Indians who have left since the last count and are away at other pueblos and haciendas." The Indian cabildo members in Mixco explained that they could not send the old number of repartimiento workers to the cornfield of the local priest, noting that "with many towns-people who leave [as free workers] for other farms, it is no longer possible to provide the people he used to have."[48]

Also in 1774, the community of San Juan Moyuta in the jurisdiction of Escuintla (in an area now in the department of Jutiapa) petitioned to be relieved of repartimiento labor at the mine of don Joseph de Córdova because of illness. It is not known if their request was granted, although Córdova responded to the petition insisting that he would give the repartimiento laborers the lightest work, since he had *gente voluntaria* (literally, voluntary people) to do the heavier chores.[49] Córdova's approach illustrates a generalized reaction of hacendados in the region: they were increasingly relying on other forms of recruitment. Even don Juan de Carrascosa, who in 1773 was issued a huge repartimiento of over 100 workers for his wheat farm in Sololá, said that he wouldn't need them in October since he already had a sufficient workforce of "voluntarios" for that month.[50]

For its part, the Audiencia continued to receive requests for repartimiento crews and attempted to assign native communities to provide the workers. The colonial authorities were following the Crown's traditional role of regulation to assure adequate supplies of food and export commodities. But the draft was increasingly inoperable because of the decreasing numbers of available men. The circumstances appear clearly in the Spanish records. Prospective employers sent their requests naming specific towns and indicating the number of workers needed. The Audiencia's personnel checked these petitions against the most recent censuses and against the numbers of townsmen needed to fulfill other obligations, including local religious and political offices as well as previous repartimiento labor warrants at other estates. Men serving on the cabildo or fulfilling religious charges, as well as those over the age of about sixty, were exempted from the draft and were to be excluded from the number of eligible draftees on which the cuarta parte was based. When there were not enough adult males for a town to meet a particular repartimiento request, sometimes the Audiencia called an alternate community.[51] In other instances, though, the Spanish authorities simply limited the draft to fewer than the requested number of workers.[52] The hacendado would then have to hire free workers to supplement the draftees' labor.

In still other cases, the Audiencia altogether rejected the hacendados' request for repartimiento labor, explicitly instructing them to get voluntarios instead—to hire workers on a private basis as free laborers. Don Thimotheo O'Connor met with such a response when he requested a repartimiento of sixteen men from Mataquescuintla and twelve from Jumay (today called Jumaytepeque) for his harvest in 1778.[53] The Indian officers of Mataesquintla rejected the request, citing mistreatment by O'Connor; and the Audiencia's representative (*fiscal*) simply denied him the repartimiento, telling him to get *jornaleros voluntarios* (free day laborers).[54] In 1776, don Manuel Ramos applied for a repartimiento of Indian workers from the towns of San Juan Sacatepéquez and Sumpango. Ramos pointed out that he had crops of maize, beans, and wheat to be harvested, but the Audiencia's fiscal flatly refused the request. "Hacendados should stop trying to cause panic about possible food shortages," the fiscal said. They should stop requesting repartimientos, "and should instead get voluntarios and ladinos"—that is, free workers and hispanized people.[55]

Both the Indian and Spanish governments were reacting to social and demographic changes that were essentially beyond their control. Although the Audiencia assumed the authority to legitimize (or reject) Indian officers' demands and decisions, ultimately the colonial state was powerless to reverse the collapse of repartimiento or the rise of free labor. Nor did the state have any underlying reason to desire a return to coerced native labor, which had never been completely satisfactory to Spanish employers.[56] In moments of particular shortage of labor, as in the 1770s, the colonists stepped up efforts to recruit coerced native laborers. But beyond these temporary crises, drafts were no longer much needed. Estates in the hinterlands that supplied the capital city had shifted to a reliance principally on free laborers, who by the second half of the eighteenth century were widely available.[57]

INDIAN AGENCY:
RENEGOTIATING THE TERMS OF LABOR

Beyond the written appeals by native community governments, a variety of informal responses to the burdens of tribute labor also contributed to the shift to free labor. One of these responses was for draft workers not to show up at the appointed enterprise or to delay their arrival.[58] The case of the Arrazola brothers' estate illustrates. In 1774, don Miguel and his brother don Andrés Arrazola requested gangs of repartimiento workers from several towns for an hacienda their mother had left them in the Sierra de Canales region just south of the capital. The Audiencia granted them a repartimiento, although it limited the crews to ten men per week, citing a decreased number of tributaries in the town of San Juan Amatitlán and a plague of locusts in San Cristóbal Amatitlán. When the native communities informed the Audiencia that ten was still too many, the Arrazola brothers appealed again, and the Audiencia repeated its order to the Indian administrators. But no repartimiento workers arrived at the estate. A few months later, the Arrazolas were still petitioning for the work crews to be sent (it is not known whether they ever arrived).[59] The same pattern unfolded in 1776 when don Juan Macía tried to get a draft labor crew from San Agustín Acasaguastlán and Magdalena for his gold mining enterprise in eastern Guatemala.[60]

Later that decade, an hacendado in Quetzaltenango noted that repartimiento workers were taking advanced wages and then "absenting themselves" from his estate. Cash advance was a standard procedure in recruiting both repartimiento and free laborers, but in this case the workers were leaving the hacienda before completing their assigned shift, and the hacendado said he had to pay them extra to get them to come back to work.[61] In effect, the workers had maneuvered for a pay increase. Though the draft order was active, the workers' ability to decamp and demand further pay before returning to the job suggests that they had restructured their work as free labor.[62]

A series of disputes over repartimiento in the jurisdiction of Suchitepéquez (in today's southwestern Guatemala) reveals the way that the Indians there collectively renegotiated the terms of their labor.[63] In April of 1792, the hacendado don Manuel Garrote Bueno petitioned the Audiencia for a repartimiento from several pueblos for his estate near the town of Mazatenango, where he had begun an indigo enterprise (a new commercial crop in the area).[64] The Audiencia granted his request. In August of the following year, though, Garrote appealed again, complaining that the workers were demanding an increased wage of 2 reales a day. The Audiencia's fiscal backed Garrote, instructing the alcalde mayor of Suchitepéquez to make the Indians work for 1½ reales, the colony's standard wage for repartimiento workers.[65]

However, the alcalde mayor, don José de Alvarado, responded that Garrote's request for a draft was inappropriate. In the twenty-two years that he had been in office, Alvarado wrote to the Audiencia, there had been no conscription of Indian workers in his district. This was a bit of an exaggeration, since there had been at least two repartimientos in the mid-1780s.[66] But Spaniards in Suchitepéquez concurred that the Indian populations were stretched thin by religious obligations in *cofradías* (Catholic confraternities), cash tribute payments, and servicio personal (the convention of providing free produce and labor) for Spanish priests in their areas.[67] Apparently, Garrote's bid for a crew of draftees was a strategy to resolve for himself what by all accounts was a local labor shortage. This shortage had given workers a measure of leverage. As the alcalde mayor explained, Indians in the area would work for 1½ reales a day, but "voluntarily and not by force, and in light work, and regular hours within the pueblo or nearby." He added that "during the periods when there is a lot of work, employers have to pay two reales per day, and even at this price they sometimes can't get workers."[68]

Thus, the Indian workers had become participants in determining their wages, and they expected this role when called for Garrote's draft. As the alcalde mayor don José de Alvarado recounted,

When don Manuel Garrote asked for the [repartimiento of] ten Indians, he wanted to pay them a wage of one and a half reales. And not wanting to go, they came to see me. One of the men spoke to me personally, on behalf of the group that was there, explaining that with the wage of one and a half reales a day, they had nothing left after paying for the food that they had to take with them for the week, and therefore they were asking to be paid two reales.[69]

The Indians were rejecting the structure of coerced labor in which the wage was set without the workers' agreement.

They maintained their refusal a few years later when a new alcalde mayor succeeded Alvarado. In 1798 the same don Manuel Garrote Bueno appears in the record, again in pursuit of workers (apparently he was the only one in the area trying to get draftees). Now he had begun a cotton-growing enterprise. He had requested a reissue of his earlier repartimiento, this time for workers to pick cotton, and once again, he was complaining to the authorities that the Indians were refusing to work.[70]

The new alcalde mayor of Suchitepéquez, don Joseph Justiniano Rossi y Rubí, wrote to the Audiencia describing the situation. His letter described how Garrote's mayordomo had come to the provincial court in Mazatenango one afternoon, asking Rossi y Rubí to apportion "thirty Indians to pick [Garrote's] cotton" and giving Rossi y Rubí money to pay the workers 1 *real* per arroba of cotton. Rossi y Rubí had then sent orders to the Indian *juez de obras* (labor recruiter) to procure a crew of thirty men—fifteen from Mazatenango and fifteen from neighboring San Gabriel—advancing them the wages fronted by Garrote in the customary fashion. Rossi y Rubí noted that the Indian juez at first resisted taking the orders and the money, but "in the end he obeyed because of my threats."

But the Indians of Mazatenango and San Gabriel balked. In the evening of that same day, Rossi y Rubí recalled,

The Indian Alcaldes, Justicias, Principales, Cabeceras, Cofradías, and others presented themselves to me collectively, giving me a written document, and telling me that they absolutely did not want to go the mandamiento of don Manuel Garrote, because they themselves had their own cacao plantations and cultivated fields to take care of, and it didn't make sense to abandon their own cornfields and cacao crops to go and work for someone else. They gave a lot of other reasons of this type, and finished by saying that they would go throw themselves at the feet of the Very Illustrious Señor President [of the Audiencia], and of the Señor Fiscal, in order to be relieved of this mandamiento that has them in ruin. And that if I wanted to punish them for this, they were ready to go to jail and they would give me the *varas* [that is, they would hand over their staffs of office], and all the people would flee into the woods rather than continue in the mandamiento of don Manuel.

   I energetically opposed this refusal by the Justicia and other Indians, and when I threatened them strongly they said that for now they would go to the man-damiento, but that they wanted a wage of one and a half reales per arroba, since that was the going rate paid by those who need workers.

Again, the Indians were collectively refusing to work without a higher wage. And they were successful in their demands, as Rossi y Rubí recounted:

Because the collection of tributes was still pending, and in order to avoid any pub-lic disturbance—which seemed very possible—I showed that I was willing to con-sent. I gave them the money they were asking for . . . and they returned home with-out incident. After this event there has been no further issue, and they have gone to do the work picking the bales that they have been assigned [that is, for which they have been paid].[71]

   Thus, the Crown's chief authority in Suchitepéquez, Alcalde Mayor don Joseph Rossi y Rubí, had ceded to the Indians' salary demands. In the most immediate sense, he did so to preempt a "public disturbance" by the Indi-ans. More broadly, Rossi y Rubí seems to have recognized that coerced labor had been supplanted in the Suchitepéquez district. As the previous alcalde mayor had argued, don Manuel Garrote's request for draft work-ers was incongruous with the manners of free labor recruitment that had become the norm in the area. The colonial economy in Suchitepéquez had become so dependent on individually arranged labor that when the colo-nial authorities in 1802 proposed a reintroduction of coerced labor, the area's hacendados resisted the idea, anticipating that they would lose the cash advances they had already made to recruit free workers.[72]

   These events show that Indian labor in Suchitepéquez had become free labor in several senses. First, labor contracts were being negotiated in what economists would call a "free" market, with wages determined by supply and demand for labor, rather than by state regulations. Second, apart from don Manuel Garrote's efforts, workers in the area were "free" laborers in the sense that they were not coerced or drafted. Even the word used by contemporaries in Guatemala to refer to these workers, *voluntarios*, was rooted in their enlistment through voluntary channels instead of the old mechanisms of coercion. Both of the men who served as alcalde mayor in Suchitepéquez in the 1790s noted that the workers themselves had explicitly indicated they would be willing to work if the wages were sufficient; and, indeed, to get laborers, Garrote ultimately had to raise the wage to a point where the Indians would choose to work. Finally, Indian labor had become more "free" in the classical Liberal sense of freedom that enfranchises individuals rather than corporate communities or governments. Repartimiento—arranged by governments on both Spanish and Indian sides—had given way to private individual arrangements. Though Indian workers might negotiate collectively (as they did in the Garrote case), their labor was not regularly being procured in Suchitepéquez through the corporate entities of the Spanish and Indian governments.

COERCED WORKERS BECOMING FREE WORKERS

The Suchitepéquez case also exemplifies another broad colonial-era pattern: free laborers (especially seasonal laborers) were often Indians, and often the very same persons who had once served under draft for the same employers. As we have seen, the Indians of Mazatenango and San Gabriel negotiated collectively to transform their labor to free labor for don Manuel Garrote. In other cases the transition was carried out individually. Men who were required as tribute laborers to trek several hours to a worksite might then opt to stay beyond the mandatory week, making private arrangements with the estate manager to earn some additional money.

An example comes from San Agustín Acasaguastlán, a Nahuatl-speaking community of about 3,000 people some 130 kilometers east of Santiago.[73] In the mid- and late eighteenth century, the town provided tribute labor for various enterprises in eastern Guatemala. Among these was doña Manuela Dardón's sugar estate, which enjoyed a repartimiento of twelve men weekly from Acasaguastlán during the height of the 1765 work season.[74] Even after the cane harvest and the draft had ended, six or eight of these men remained at her estate, working by their own arrangement.[75] These six or eight were part of a larger trend among workers from Acasaguastlán; though the Audiencia continued to receive requests for repartimientos from Acasaguastlán into the 1780s, reports indicated that Indians were increasingly leaving the town to escape the drafts.[76]

With the men who opted to stay beyond their obligatory shift at doña Manuela Dardón's estate, we can see at the level of the workers themselves the historical transition from coerced to free labor. James Lockhart has described this transformation throughout Spanish America, noting that "the villagers came to work on the estancias and later haciendas, first through encomienda obligations, then through the mechanism of the repartimiento, and finally through individual arrangements, but they were always the same people doing the same things."[77] In the case of the Acasaguastlán workers, they were quite literally the same people doing the same things.

A similar transition occurred among the men from the Mam community of San Cristóbal Cabricán in northwestern Guatemala.[78] Even while repartimiento workers from Cabricán were serving in drafts at the *labor* (farm) of the area's corregidor, other Cabricán men were going to work there and at other haciendas as free laborers. In 1812 one of the town's Indian *principales* (elders or officeholders) made a formal complaint about the repartimiento, and the Audiencia followed with an investigation in which several townsmen (both principales and commoners) testified. They all knew Spanish and had no need for an interpreter. Nicolás Pérez, an *indio principal*, said that he himself and others from his pueblo had willingly gone to work at the corregidor's *labor* "because they know that there they get nine reales a week in daily wages to maintain their families." Other men who testified echoed Pérez's statements, saying they were willing to work freely for 1½ reales a day to earn their tributes.[79]

Outside the Spanish and Indian corporate institutions that administered the labor draft, in the environment of daily contact between employers (or their mayordomos) and workers, it was a short step from obligatory labor to free labor. Workers in urban settings and public services also made the transition. For example, the Indian porters in the capital who delivered flour from the *alhóndiga* (public granary) to the city's bakeries as part of a labor draft began also to transport flour by individual arrangement with the bakery owners.[80] Both porters and bakery owners in these private deals were skirting colonial regulations. Eventually the ayuntamiento recognized its inability to control the unsanctioned activities and in 1806 legalized private flour sales. In 1810, a group of flour porters successfully appealed to the city government to stop drafting them. Yet the same men who had done the hauling under the draft continued to make the deliveries afterwards on a private basis. The inspector (*fiel*) of the alhóndiga explained that the bakeries preferred to continue service by the same people "because of the trust that the bakery owners have in their reliability."[81] Note also that some of the city's flour porters, even some of those working as draftees before 1810, were recruited as free laborers into the bakeries. Bakery workers were Spanish-speaking men of relatively low social rank, certainly among the lowest of the artisan class, some of whom identified themselves as Indians. Take for example Gaspar de los Reyes, a Spanish-speaking tributary Indian who worked in 1803 as a draftee flour porter. He was also working in don Ignacio Baines' bakery as a sifter—a low-rung job even among bakery workers.[82]

CHANGING IDENTITIES

These broad shifts in labor procurement were intertwined with transformations in ethnic identities, as reflected in the terminology people used to identify calidad and ethnic categories. Employers and Spanish state personnel in the early colonial period had referred to seasonal workers as "indios," but by the late colonial years other terms were gaining currency. Late colonial records also allude to "voluntarios," "ladinos," and "mulatos" who were working as seasonal laborers. These identities did not completely supplant the centuries-old category of "Indian," a term still used today more widely in Guatemala than in most other parts of Latin America. Yet words such as *voluntario* and *ladino* were being used in Guatemala by the late eighteenth century not only to describe a growing number of individuals within the workforce but also to label entire rural working populations in certain increasingly Hispanized areas.[83]

The term *ladino* had multiple, changing meanings across the colonial period.[84] In the early and middle colonial years, *ladino* usually meant linguistically hispanized, having the ability to speak Castilian. The term most often appeared as part of the term *indio ladino* or *india ladina*, referring to someone who was identified as an Indian but knew Spanish. By the late eighteenth century, the word *indio* was at times dropped from *indio ladino*, so that *ladino* used alone came often to describe people of Indian ancestry who spoke Spanish (if not also a native language) and were otherwise culturally hispanized. At the same time, another usage also appears in the seventeenth- and eighteenth-century records, in which the term *ladino* referred more generally to populations of hispanized workers in the countryside, without regard to their ancestry. The largest segment of these populations was hispanized Indians, but the rural workforces also included people of European, African, and, increasingly, mixed ancestry (perhaps particularly in the lowland regions south and east of the capital). The eighteenth-century censuses as well as the administrative records of the repartimiento repeatedly identified a class of "ladinos," referring specifically to people being hired instead of repartimiento workers.

The growing use of the term *ladino* by late colonial officials and hacendados was linked to several differences between ladinos and repartimiento workers, whom the records call simply "indios" or "indios de mandamiento." Spanish language knowledge distinguished the ladinos from at least some of the indios working under repartimiento drafts. The ability to speak Spanish enabled workers to contract their labor individually in the colonial economy, whereas many Indians who remained subject to the institutional labor drafts were not linguistically hispanized.[85]

Beyond language, place of residence also distinguished ladinos from people labeled as indios. Spaniards who spoke of hiring "ladinos" as free laborers in lieu of hiring "indios" through the repartimiento system were distinguishing between, on one hand, people (including those of Indian ancestry) who were living outside native communities and, on the other hand, those who continued to reside in (or return to) the native communities.[86] During the eighteenth century increasing numbers of Indians were leaving the native pueblos, finding work on haciendas and in the cities. Many left simply to earn wages to pay their tributes. Tributes were collected semiannually, and the requirements were greater than what some workers could accumulate in a single agricultural season. People who accrued overwhelming tribute debts often then left permanently or for long-term sojourns. In effect, departure from the native pueblo was sometimes a strategy to escape the burdens of tribute payment and labor drafts. Though people who absented themselves from Indian communities often maintained social and economic connections to the home town, those who remained abroad removed themselves from the reach of native government and from obligatory contributions to the community's amassment of tributes. Nor did these absentees (*ausentes*, as labeled by their contemporaries) participate in labor drafts or religious ritual and other *costumbre*—conventional social practices—within the community.

Thus, residence within the native town was tied to various aspects of community membership. In Guatemala's eighteenth-century colonial perceptions, one of the major factors that identified a person as "Indian" was residence and membership in an indigenous community. This membership, in turn, subjected people to the obligations of forced labor and tribute payment. Within the Hispanic world, identities as constituted by the ethnic labels *indio* and *ladino* were linked not only to language but also to place of residence (inside or outside native communities) and to status (subject or not) with respect to tribute and labor draft obligations.[87]

The term *voluntarios* in the late colonial records was part of this same scenario of social change. The label *voluntarios* encompassed a range of calidad and ethnic categories among which the distinctions were increasingly blurred. Because it refers to the method of labor procurement rather than calidad, the term *voluntario* was fitting for seasonal workers who were recruited through private arrangements regardless of their ethnic identity or community membership. Workers' affiliation with a corporate community became less relevant to colonial employers as labor was increasingly procured at the individual level rather than through corporate (government) mechanisms. The general meaning of the word *voluntario* (volunteer) itself illustrates contemporaries' consciousness of nondraft procurement as the factor that identified these workers.

The broadening of the term *ladino* to include hispanized working people of various ancestral backgrounds essentially maintained an earlier colonial notion that had divided society into two groups, indios and españoles. This earlier division is reflected in census records, which often took a broad view of the category "español," including in it everyone not classified as Indian. (Indeed, the word *español* itself recalled origins in Iberia, where society for centuries had been characterized by racial and ancestral diversity.) As the colonial era reached its end, the term *ladino* was supplanting the word *español* as a label for manual and agricultural workers—that is, people of middling or low social status. Yet this usage of *ladino* preserved much of the old concept of *español* with its wide inclusion of racial types (phenotypes). This configuration of ethnic categories formed the foundation for modern Guatemalan use of the term *ladino*, which describes all members of the populace not identified as Indians.

The terms *mulata* and *mulato* in colonial Guatemala connoted mixed African and Indian descent or mixed African and European descent.[88] Those who spoke of "mulato" laborers as a group in eighteenth-century Guatemala referred to people living outside native communities and performing agricultural work for wages.[89] This category included people of partially African ancestry, some of them ex-slaves, but populations labeled as "mulatos" also probably included some people of completely Indian ancestry who had married or otherwise become rooted in Hispanic society. Like Indian identities, in rural areas (especially south and east of the capital city) mulato identities were typically linked to place of residence. Late colonial ethnic labels for people in this group often included the word *mulata* or *mulato* followed by the place of residence—for example, "mulata del Valle de Sansaria," or "mulatos de la Sierra de Canales."

Thus, the terms *mulato* and *ladino* both embraced the increasing slippages among categories of social status and identity—not only slippage of individuals across these categories but also slippage among the constructions of the categories themselves. While ethnic identities are often assumed to be based on ancestry or "race," in late colonial Guatemala identities were formed by factors based more in social perceptions and understandings than in ancestry or genetic material. Key among these factors were language, place of residence, tributary status, kinship, and other social associations—particularly those of neighborhood or community. Certainly, visual markers such as dress, hairstyle, and "racial" features such as skin color also must have shaped people's perceptions of each other. Clothing is a marker easily noted by contemporaries, and in the late colonial period it likely outweighed "racial" or physical features as an ethnic identifier, as it does in Guatemala today. Visual signs of identity are not often mentioned in the colonial era's written records. (An exception is militia records, which often included physical descriptions of the troops.) Of course, style of dress—European or indigenous—is determined by environmental factors, not genetic ones; dress style is a social trait. Presumably it was normally linked to place of residence and social affiliations.

Further, labor had become a component of ethnic identities in the late colonial world. Ethnicity was partly determined by the way in which a person's labor was procured. The slippages I have described among the ethnic categories "indio," "ladino," "español," and "mulato" reflect not only the changing patterns in cultural forms like language, dress, and community affiliation but also the transformations in labor procurement. Ethnic identity was, in part, about who your parents were, where you lived, whether you paid tribute, what language you spoke, and what you wore. But it was also a matter of how you were contracted to work.

Migration, gender, and the shift to free labor

With the shift from coerced to free labor, several transitions also appear in native workers' migration patterns. First, the normal time spent working abroad lengthened beyond the one-week repartimiento stint. The journey to work was usually arduous (on foot, unpaid, sometimes longer than a day), and people contracting their own labor tended to stay for the harvest season. Some stayed more or less permanently, or at least they didn't go back to the native community. Permanent departures had been ongoing throughout the colonial years, but their rate may have increased with the growing numbers of migrants working abroad for more than a week. The longer people worked in the colonial sphere, the more likely they were to form attachments there, to become conversant in Spanish, and to continue getting work. As repartimiento faded, short-term circular migration ceased to be the default pattern.

Moreover, a transition occurred in the social composition of native migration. Under the encomienda and repartimiento systems, the conscripts sent to haciendas had been overwhelmingly male. As labor stints lengthened under individual arrangements, women and children were increasingly accompanying men to work at Hispanic estates. It was not that native women had never been forced into labor migration. In the sixteenth century, women had been drafted along with men as *tamemes* (pack carriers) and mine workers, and they had been removed from their pueblos for work in indigo processing, cloth production, food preparation, and other domestic services.[90] (For native women migrating to serve in Spanish cities, private recruitment was supplanting coercion by the 1540s, but the the imprint of the old tribute patterns—including the migration of women from specific towns to fulfill specific services—was still evident centuries later, as we will see later in the example of wetnurses from Jocotenango.)[91]

Even into the late colonial years, a number of women were also drafted along with men in the repartimientos to agricultural estates. Yet the women were far fewer. Convention required hacendados to provide three meals a day for draft labor crews, and some estate owners asked for a *molendera* or two to be drafted along with the male workers, to make tortillas—typically one female worker for six or ten male workers. Other hacendados used slave women or privately contracted women to cook for draftees. Occasionally conscripts were paid a slightly higher wage and expected to buy their meals. In any case, though, the food was infamously insufficient. Evidently, most hacendados were relying on workers' wives and mothers to pack their men a week's supply of tortillas, as mentioned occasionally in the repartimiento records. But tortillas alone were hardly enough, and Indian communities repeatedly complained that draftees returned weak with hunger as well as fatigue from the journey and week's labor.[92]

Thus, for their most basic survival, men leaving home to work on haciendas for longer than a week needed women to accompany them. Indian women who joined men in long-term migrations as free laborers on haciendas were employed primarily in food preparation, and they presumably also did the men's laundry and other female work.[93] Given the enormous amount of labor required for these services, haciendas with men staying more than a week needed female workforces.

The need appears vividly when we consider the content of women's work. The exclusively female task of preparing tortillas (not to mention beans) required women to husk and degrain the ears of corn, then to boil and soak the kernels in an alkaline solution (and women typically had to haul the water they would use for soaking). After draining this mixture, the women washed and hulled the kernels by hand to make *nixtamal*, which they then ground into dough. A woman making food for a family might spend up to six hours a day on hands and knees at the *metate* (grindstone). All this was before patting the dough into tortillas and baking them, flipping them by hand to toast each side (and for the baking, women had to gather the firewood).[94] Even in twentieth-century Guatemala, in places with no power mill women had to rise several hours before dawn to begin tortilla preparation. Linguisitic evidence too evokes the arduousness of tortilla making. The colonial-era Nahuatl term *ycxichacayulli* referred to "calluses that women get on top of the feet from grinding at the metate"; the verb *icxichacayoliui* meant "to have such calluses."[95] In today's Spanish, the idiom *quemarse las manos* means "to work hard or to the point of exhaustion," but its literal sense is "to burn one's hands." In Guatemala, it often refers literally to women's work at the comal. For readers not yet feeling exhausted, an additional thought is that preparing beans required more firewood, water for soaking, and hours of boiling.

Plus there was laundry. Laundry was (and remains in rural Guatemala) physically strenuous work. Ethnographic scholarship on indigenous societies in twentieth-century Guatemala has noted that just for their own families, women might spend two or three hours per day washing. They also had to haul the clothes, along with their small children, to and from a river or lake. Some of these children were willful toddlers. Understandably, women often worked in groups, avoiding social isolation and probably taking turns managing children.[96]

In this light, it comes as no surprise that as Indian workers began staying for several months and longer on the haciendas, more women joined in the migration. The exodus is illustrated in the communiqués sent to the Audiencia from indigenous officers lamenting that people were leaving their communities. On one level, these complaints were just routine rhetoric—part of a constant stream of petitions contesting and negotiating the nature of colonial rule. On another level, though, the native officers were not only protesting against the burdens of draft labor and tribute levies. Repeatedly their late colonial petitions came to focus on the point that whole families, not just individuals, were leaving.[97]

In 1784, for example, representatives of the común (native polity) of Chinautla, just north of the capital, appealed to the Spanish authorities, saying they could not fulfill the draft to cut wood at the estate of don Antonio Morales. They were already occupied with service in the city, they said, hauling hay, providing chickens, and supplying mules and men for the mail service. They complained of barrancos and other dangers on the trip to Morales's estate. Ultimately, they said, "The burdens have made the married people leave with their families, fleeing tribute obligations."[98] That same year, the (Spanish) priest of San Agustín Acasaguastlán reported that people were fleeing because the labor draft had become too burdensome there and in nearby Guastatoya and Tocoy. The men sent for repartimiento work were not returning, he said, and were abandoning their wives and families. "And what's more," he added, "they are even leaving with their wives and children, and so in this pueblo [San Agustín] there are more than eighty abandoned houses."[99]

In the northwestern highlands, twelve Indian officers representing the towns of Santa Lucía and San José articulated the situation in an 1809 appeal. (The record alternately identifies the towns as being in the jurisdictions of Totonicapán, Huehuetenango, and Sololá; likely they were Santa Lucía Utatlán and San José Chacayá, just north of Lake Atitlán in today's department of Sololá.) Though the officers made their petition through an interpreter, the scenario emerges in lucid terms. On the surface, they were asking to be relieved from repartimiento work at the hacienda of don Rafael de la Torre, who had previously been the alcalde mayor; but the whole of their petition conveys a more generalized outcry about the conditions of forced labor and the resulting emptying of the community. The appeal (as rendered by the colonial notary) said:

> When don Rafael de la Torre was Alcalde Mayor he mistreated them, not giving attention to the Indian townspeople nor even to the ladinos. . . . He would beat them with a stick or with his sword; and now that he owns the Hacienda de Argueta, when the natives go to work there the mayordomo mistreats them and beats them on orders of de la Torre, and doesn't pay them what has always been the customary pay.

In addition to this mistreatment on the hacienda, the petitioners said, the *hijos* (townsmen or townspeople) were unhappy because "they are compelled at knifepoint." The record is unclear as to who exactly was wielding the knife. It may have been the hacienda's mayordomo, but it may have been the Indian juez de obras (recruiter) in the pueblo. In any case, the outcomes were clear: the hijos "absent themselves from the pueblo, even leaving with [advanced] wages; they don't pay tribute; and as a consequence, they don't attend church since they aren't here; nor do they plant crops; and they leave their family abandoned." Moreover, men were leaving with their families. The San José petitioners noted that during the past year or two,

> because of the conditions described, the following families have left: Juan Xitumul with his wife and children; Bernardino Matzar with his wife and children; Diego Choror with his wife; Juan Santos Muro married with children; Francisco Matzar with his wife and children; Matías Choror with his wife and children; Pablo Coxolca married with children.[100]

From the perspective of native commoner families, women's migration along with their men out of home communities served additional purposes beyond food and laundry service. Women's work on agricultural estates increased their families' earnings, since hacendados paid women for their labor (which was mainly in food preparation). Older children also could earn wages. By migrating together, families avoided long periods of separation in which there were no means of communication.

Moreover, the colonial political economy subjected women as well as men to tribute and other pressures if they stayed in native communities. For one there was forced labor even within the pueblos. Across the colonial period, Indian women were obligated by the Spanish state to spin thread and weave cloth at their homes. (In the early years the products were demanded as commodity tributes. Later the burden was configured as a system also called "repartimiento," a reference to the distribution to native communities of cotton and wool by low-level Spanish officials. The townswomen were required to spin and weave these materials, then to turn their work over to the same officials.)[101] In addition, even with men absent, households remained subject to cash tributes. Female-headed households were by law supposed to be assessed at a fraction of the rate for dual-headed households. In practice, though, evidence from Guatemala shows that Indian officials under colonial pressure might squeeze women for full tribute payment even though their husbands had abandoned community and household. Women who stayed behind were also also subject to extortion for debts left by absentee kinsmen. These pressures, compounded with the difficulty of supporting children without a husband's labor and income, could prove unbearable in the home community, as the following examples from Jocotenango will illustrate.

Family and community structures in transition: The case of Jocotenango

Situated at the northern edge of the Spanish capital city of Guatemala, the Cakchiquel community known as Jocotenango actually consisted of two *parcialidades* or moieties, Jocotenango and Utatleca.[102] Each parcialidad had its own cabildo, but the two were united under a single Indian *gobernador* who was always from the parcialidad of Jocotenango. The community had been a key source of tribute—in labor and in kind—starting in the sixteenth century.[103] By mid-eighteenth century, Jocotenango residents were paying much of their tribute in cash. The resulting financial burden, overwhelming to many families, fueled both male and female out-migration. Meanwhile, economic pressures within the community continued, sharpened by the decreasing number of tribute-payers. The partial emptying of households and the growing financial stress began to undercut community and family structures, even as migrants sent wages back to the pueblo.

These processes emerge in the records of two investigations by the Audiencia into the employment of workers from Jocotenango. The first investigation, in 1765, focused on labor recruitment by doña Manuela Dardón—for the same sugar estate where some of the repartimiento workers from San Agustín Acasaguastlán had stayed on as free laborers. A generation later, in 1797, the Audiencia commissioned a report on wet nurses from Jocotenango serving in Nueva Guatemala. Both investigations were made in response to outcries from the pueblo—the first from the Indian government, the second from the parish priest.

WORKERS AT THE ESTATE OF DOÑA MANUELA DARDÓN

Across a large chunk of the eighteenth century, doña Manuela Dardón owned a *trapiche* (small sugar estate) located some six or eight days' walk from Jocotenango, at a place called Los Llanos in the Valley of Sansaria, in the eastern countryside.[104] Like other small sugar estate owners in the region, Dardón kept a few slaves and a salaried staff of free mulatos and mestizos, some of them employed year-round and others seasonally. She also procured repartimiento workers, as we have seen, and she recruited tributary Indians as free workers through private arrangements—not only the men from San Agustín Acasaguastlán but also men and women from Jocotenango as well as Salamá (to the northwest of her estate, over a considerable mountain range.) The Spanish state in Central America had long sought to prohibit the use of Indian laborers in sugar processing; the work was so dangerous that it had threatened in the sixteenth century to further decimate the native populations.[105] However, sugar plantations openly relied on Indians to carry out other chores in agricultural production.[106] At the trapiche of doña Manuela Dardón, Indian men were among those who cut the cane, hauled it to the mill, and raised corn; Indian women were employed grinding corn, preparing food, and running errands.

In 1765, the Indian cabildos of the two parcialidades in Jocotenango petitioned the alcalde mayor, who forwarded the complaint to the Audiencia. On its surface, the petition was about doña Manuela Dardón's recruitment tactics. The cabildos said she advanced wages to their townspeople, then sent henchmen to the pueblos to rope recalcitrant debtors into work. The roping-in was literal: "she orders them, bound in ropes, to her hacienda or trapiche." At its core, though, the petition came to focus on the community's dwindling populace. "Because the climate [at Dardón's estate] is adverse to the constitution of the townspeople," the petitioners said, "those who by chance do come back die right away. And this bad procedure of doña Manuela Dardón . . . is disadvantageous to the Real Hacienda [Crown's revenues] because of the lesser resulting amount of tributes." Ultimately, they lamented, because of the departure of people to work at Dardón's estate, "our community fund suffers great destruction and diminishment." Out-migration was draining the sources of tributes and wealth from the community.[107]

The complaint strikes a familiar chord of Indian resistance and renegotiation of the conditions of labor for the Spaniards. However, even within communities, Indians were a heterogeneous group. The Jocotenango leaders' appeal was a legitimate protest against oppressive practices by an hacendada, but it was also a tactic to gain or regain political control within the community. The petitioners faced a predicament typical throughout Mesoamerica, where Indian officeholders bore the double-edged charge of collecting tributes from their own townspeople. On one hand, native magistrates were subject to punishment if they failed to provide the Spaniards with the mandated tributes or workers. In times of epidemic, population decline, or crop failures, native officers were caught between the pressure to produce tribute payment and the shortages of commodities or labor.[108]

On the other hand, tribute collection, including tribute labor recruitment, helped delineate the distinction between Indian elites (principales) and Indian commoners (*macehuales*). Scholars have observed this pattern for various locations in Guatemala across the colonial period.[109] As Greg Grandin noted for Quetzaltenango, the intraethnic distinction between principales and macehuales was "fundamental to the political and economic power of principales, and the tribute was a tangible marker dividing the city population along caste lines." The principales of Quetzaltenango "proved particularly vigilant in collecting the tribute and, later, republican taxes."[110] For Indian officeholders, tribute collection presented an opportunity for personal enrichment as well as elevation (or consolidation) of their social and political position. The process of tribute could alternately bring fortune to Indian principales or could result in jailings or beatings if they did not meet the Spaniards' demands. But in any case it was in the officeholders' best interests to maximize what they could collect.

In this context, the petition from the cabildos of Jocotenango and Utatleca appears as a protest from a native state squeezed between Spanish demands and native population shortages. Indeed, the request that they ultimately articulated in their petition did not actually seek to reform Dardón's procurement practices. Rather, it sought the return of workers to the community and the maintenance of native officers' authority in regulating the departures. The heart of their plea was direct: "we entreat you [the Audiencia] to . . . intercept these damages, and [to stop] our townspeople from leaving for the said trapiche." Yet behind their appeal, the officers seem already to have resigned themselves to an irreversible pattern. They added a request "that we be informed of those who will go." Even if tributaries could not be kept in the pueblo, the principales were trying to restore their own political authority in the distribution of labor and payments to the Spaniards.

The colonial state shared the Indian officers' desire to preserve the pueblos, since the maintenance of tribute and social order served Spanish corporate interests. However, individual Spaniards like doña Manuela Dardón stood to gain by recruiting more Indian labor. Violations abounded against colonial regulatory measures taken to protect the Indians, and typically the state's responses to these violations had only limited impact. In the Dardón case, after all the effort of its investigation, the Audiencia fined her 200 pesos. This was a substantial sum, but the ruling was merely punitive. The fine did not change the structures that underlay the hacendados' manipulations, nor did it address the native officers' lament that the community was being emptied of its people.

The tensions between the Spanish state and private hacendados were doubtless obvious—a normal part of the business environment—for Dardón and other colonial employers. Dardón was aware also of conflicting interests within the Indian sphere. Regarding the Jocotenango cabildos' accusation that she had locked townspeople in her house, she countered that she had been sheltering them from beating and imprisonment at the hands of the Indian alcaldes. (Though she had no reason to mention it in her own defense, by lodging these people she presumably gained some household help, which according to Spanish complaints was chronically in short supply.) As for the 200-peso fine, it is not clear that Dardón ever paid in full. The final notation in her case was dated in July of 1771, nearly three years after the court's ruling. She had been paying the penalty in installments but was appealing for a forbearance on grounds of "grave illness."

The perspective of some of the macehuales (Indian commoners)—a rare perspective in the colonial archives—also registers in the Audiencia's investigation, which recorded the depositions of various Jocotenango workers and workers' relatives. Clearly the families targeted by Dardón's forcible recruitment objected to her tactics (or those of her employees who came to shanghai debtors into work). The testimony of Lorenza Saquil illustrates. Speaking Spanish without an interpreter, Saquil described how two of Dardón's men had come to her home to remove her son Mateo Lantán to the trapiche. (According to the Indian governor and one of the alcaldes, Dardón's deputies had taken yet another son from Saquil's house some four years earlier, and the young man was never heard from again.) Saquil's deposition, as recorded by the notary, reads:

About two weeks ago a mulato *criado* [employee] of doña Manuela Dardón—his name is Juan Lorenzo—entered her house around ten o'clock at night; in his company was another man she doesn't know. And as she and her son Mateo Lantán and her daughter . . . were already inside [asleep], the mulato spoke loudly telling them to light a torch, which they did, and when the mulato asked for her son

Mateo Lantán she told him that he was not in the house. And when the criado heard this he told her it was false and hastily he entered the area where her son was sleeping, and took him by one foot and dragged him out to the patio; and when she saw such unusual procedures, [as the criado was] tying him up with a lasso, as a mother and woman she began to shout to the neighborhood to impede the mulato from mistreating Mateo; and after [Mateo] managed to flee with the lasso they had used to tie him up, Juan Lorenzo [the criado] came back infuriated and he threw a stone in her face; and the other one, his companion, left to look for Mateo . . . and with this deed she went to inform her magistrates.

Lorenza Saquil's resistance that night came with a high price; the Indian governor and alcalde indicated that the stone thrown at her "for helping her son" had broken two of her teeth. Her son apparently succeeded in avoiding impressment into work at the trapiche. He was said to have sought refuge in a local mill owned by a priest and to have remained there working.[111]

Another Jocotenango Indian woman, Tomasa Larios, reported a similar episode. Agents from Dardón's trapiche had come to her house seeking to draft her son-in-law into work, to repay advanced wages. When Larios told the men that her son-in-law was not in the house, they tried to take her to the trapiche to work off his debt. They abandoned the effort, she explained, "because she resisted, telling them it was unreasonable for her to pay for what she herself had not received."[112]

Yet a majority of Dardón's workers from Jocotenango said they had gone to her estate without force. Eighteen men and women spoke for the record while actually on the road back from Dardón's estate to the pueblo; they were stopped for questioning when they crossed paths with a committee of Spanish and native Jocotenango officials sent to investigate at the trapiche. The returnees had spent five or six months at the trapiche. Now they were heading home, along with their children, for Holy Week. They said had gone to work for Dardón voluntarily, having requested and received wages in advance. As for the cabildos' charge that people who made it back to the pueblo from the trapiche "died right away," the workers en route home said that the only death among them in the past year had been that of Tomasa Supín, who succumbed to *tabardillo*—probably typhus.[113] (They may have been unaware of the death of Miguel Ordóñez, who the principales said had died in his sleep the night he returned to the pueblo some months earlier.) They concurred with the cabildos' complaint about unhealthful climate, noting that they had fallen ill in the present year with fever and chills, though they distinguished this illness, which they called "fríos y calenturas," from tabardillo. The illness with fever and chills—likely malaria or dengue—appears to have been endemic on the estate, though there is no evidence that it caused death.[114] In a deposition taken at the trapiche, Manuel Silvestre de Peña—a mulato slave around twenty years old, son of Dardón's mayordomo—said the Indians "tend to get sick for periods with fever and chills, as do the rest of the people who come to the trapiche." Peña was one of the men who had traveled to Jocotenango trying to wrangle Dardón's debtors into work, and he mentioned that he himself had "been ill with fever and chills since he came back from Guatemala [that is, Santiago and Jocotenango]."[115]

Overwork and hazardous tasks created further problems. The women from Jocotenango noted that Dardón's mayordomo required them to work even when they were ill and that medical treatment was provided only if they paid for it. (The mayordomo and some of the other permanent workers on the estate contended that the Indians got sick because of their own "desarreglos"—disorderly behaviors—such as sucking sugar cane and bathing during inappropriate hours or seasons, but the nature of the illness—with fever and chills—suggests an infectious disease. People who bathed at dusk or during certain seasons may have increased their exposure to mosquitoes, likely the vectors.) Both genders reported working long hours—from six in the morning until six in the evening from Monday through Saturday, and on Sundays an additional two hours. This schedule reflects a general pattern in Guatemala and elsewhere for sugar cane, which requires intensive labor during the harvest season, when the cane must also be processed.[116]

In a candid disclosure, Dardón's mayordomo divulged that "when there is a shortage of ladinos," the Indian men "are put to work at the furnace." He was referring to the dreaded labor in the boiling house, where through a process of evaporation and skimming, workers reduced the the cane juice and made it crystallize. The timing in this procedure demanded specialized skill; the man in charge of the boiling was, in the words of one historian, "the most valued laborer on the plantation staff"—surely a slave or another permanent worker on the Dardón estate, as elsewhere.[117] Nevertheless, the Indians (like the non-Indians) who assisted at the furnace were also subject to the extreme heat and the infamous dangers of scalding liquids. The colonial state had issued laws to protect Indians from these hazards, but numerous sugar estates in Guatemala employed Indian workers, particularly during the harvest season when boiling was in full swing, and previous scholarship has also found telltale signs of Indian labor in the forbidden tasks.[118]

Furthermore, Dardón's wages were not necessarily competitive, particularly for men, whom she paid only 1 *real* per day, whereas men on other agricultural estates were often earning 1½ reales.[119] A Jocotenango man named Josef Guerra, who had worked in the skilled trade of *albañil* (mason or builder) on Dardón's estate, complained that she paid him only

2½ reales per day, while albañales in the capital, he said, received 4 or 5 reales. He was probably exaggerating a bit; even during the construction boom in Nueva Guatemala, men in various artisan trades in the capital earned between 2 and 4 reales daily.[120] For women, the monthly salary of 2 pesos at Dardón's trapiche fell within the normal range, albeit at the lower end; among adults, female domestic servants in the capital generally earned 2 or 3 pesos a month, sometimes in addition to room and board.[121]

Nevertheless, women and men from Jocotenango continued each year to make the multiday trek to Dardón's estate and to spend five or six months working there before returning home. Dardón said in 1765 that they had been doing so for thirty years. Several reasons emerge in the workers' testimony. The Jocotenango women indicated that the estate provided tortillas and beans without charge, though they noted that "the mayordomo does not give them meat, or cheese, or other provision unless they buy it from him." In urban jobs, by contrast, only some women and few men received board from their employers. Nor did all rural estates provide their employees with food. On the San Jerónimo sugar estate in the early nineteenth century, for example, male free laborers received 1½ reales daily—half again what was paid to men on Dardón's estate—but the San Jerónimo management did not supply food.[122] Provision of staple foods represents a substantial economic increment, since agricultural workers normally spent much if not all of their daily wages on subsistence.

Moreover, Dardón was providing the Jocotenango workers with much-needed credit. Though she paid the men only 1 *real* daily, they explained that she advanced them up to 15 pesos—nearly four months' wages—before they began work, and she advanced the women up to 6 pesos—three months' wages. People in Jocotenango turned to doña Manuela Dardón as a known creditor, going to her house in the capital (a short distance from the pueblo) when they needed a loan. She also regularly covered her employees' tributes; the principales went directly to her house in the capital to collect the tributes of those townspeople working at her estate.[123] Presumably she added the tribute payments to the tabs she kept for her workers. The recruiting tactic of advancing payment for tribute fees dated back to the seventeenth century.[124]

One additional attraction of work on Dardón's estate, and other agricultural enterprises, may have been that familes remained together while they earned wages. Although women and men from Jocotenango might find jobs in the capital, domestic service did not necessarily allow workers to return home on a daily basis. Food preparation, for example, required labor from early morning until well after dusk. Some of the women from Jocotenango serving in the capital had to leave their children behind in the

TABLE I.I
**Workers from Jocotenango at the sugar estate of doña Manuela Dardón,
listed in family groups, 1765.**

Pascual Alonso; his wife Micaela Chacón; and their two *hijos grandes*—probably teenage
children—including a son named Simón Alonso and an unnamed daughter
Juan Cali
Tomasa Chacón, widow with a small child
Tomás Coc
Felipa Guerra
Matías Lantán
Pascual Lantán
Nicolás López, his wife María Santos, and two small children
Matías Lucas, his wife Micaela Coc, and their three small children
Bartolomé Ordóñez and his wife Melchora Supín
Juan Santos with two daughters
Magdalena Supín, widow with a small child

Note: For the married couples the table lists the husbands first to reflect the order in which
the Spanish notary recorded the information. It appears in the record that the investigators
(all of them male) spoke first with the men and then with the women.

Source: Archivo General de Centro América, Guatemala City, Signatura A2, Legajo 40, Expediente 830.

long-term care of relatives. Men who found work in transport might be
absent from the pueblo and their families for extended periods.

In contrast, the Jocotenango workers interviewed on the road in 1765
had gone to doña Manuela Dardón's trapiche in family groups. Table 1.1
lists the eighteen workers, with their children, whom the investigators
encountered on the road from Dardón's estate. Among the eighteen were
four married couples. Two women were widows but had children with
them, as did three of the four married couples. One man, Juan Santos, of
unidentified marital status, had two daughters in his company. It is possible that he was widowed and that one of the women in the party was
a relative and was looking after the girls.[125] One woman, Felipa Guerra,
had arrived at the estate in the company of her lover, although he had then
hightailed it out, and his whereabouts were unknown. Two workers in the
group were described as *hijos grandes* (big children—probably adolescents
or teenagers) in the company of their parents. The remaining four were
men whose relationships, if any, to the other members of the group were
not specified. Their surnames, though, suggest likely kinship relationships.
Tomás Coc may have been related to Micaela Coc; and Matías Lantán and
Pascual Lantán may have been related to each other.[126] The fact that each
of the widows—Tomasa Chacón and Magdalena Supín—shared a surname
with one of the married women in the group raises the possibility that the
widows had gone to the trapiche in the company of a sister or another
female relative and her family.

The format of the record is also suggestive. The notary made two separate lists of the workers' names. First he identified all the men and recorded their answers to the investigators' questions. Then he listed the women's names and the women's responses to the same questions. Seeing the report, one imagines that the men were gathered in one cluster and the women in another as the investigators queried them. Presumably the individuals whose names were listed sequentially were standing or sitting next to each other, perhaps sharing food or luggage. It is tempting to suspect that Matías and Pascual Lantán, named consecutively in the list, might have been brothers. Similarly, the four women who shared surnames with other women in the group were listed sequentially with their namesakes— Micaela and Tomasa Chacón appear first and second on the list of women, and Magdalena and Melchora Supín were penned in as numbers five and six, as if they were standing together.

Doña Manuela Dardón herself recognized and relied on the Jocotenango workers' marital structures in her tactics for securing labor, particularly female domestic labor, at her hacienda. When the investigators asked the women about Dardón's recruiting methods, they responded that she advanced them money and they went to the trapiche "voluntarily, and without any violence." Pressed as to whether Dardón used force if they resisted going to work, the women explained that "in case of their not wanting to go, she compels them, saying that she won't advance money to their husbands unless they [the women] go to grind corn, and for this reason they find themselves obliged to go."[127] The gendered division of labor (in both colonial and native cultures) meant that Dardón needed both male and female workers. For their part, workers got access to greater credit if they worked as families at Dardón's estate than they could get alone.

On the bottom line, it was mainly money that compelled the workers from Jocotenango to Dardón's estate. Tribute demands and other expenses pushed many adults beyond the amounts they could accumulate in the pueblo, and they were forced to seek wages elsewhere. Doña Manuela Dardón gave workers cash advances and additional credit to cover their tributes. Certainly, labor at her trapiche was undesirable work for people from Jocotenango. To get to the workplace, they had to travel a long distance unpaid. Once there they worked from sunup to sundown with no days off, and all who came to the trapiche seemed to fall ill for periods. The wages were lower than in some other places, particularly, it seems, for men. Yet other jobs in agriculture might come with the same disadvantages, and work in the city or in transportation would separate laborers from their families, whereas at Dardón's estate people from Jocotenango appear to have maintained marital and childrearing relationships in daily life while on the job.

The episodes in which Dardón (or her mayordomo) sent thugs to Jocotenango were, in effect, attempts to recover debts gone bad; her slaves were serving as collection agents. Public knowledge in Jocotenango of her henchmen's violent strategies probably deterred some people from shirking their commitment to arrive for work at the trapiche. In one case, intimidation by Dardón's agents effectively elicited a cash payment. The debtor was Miguel Lucas, a brother of one of the alcaldes and probably wealthier than most in the pueblo. The acalde described how his brother Miguel had divested himself of his property "to liberate himself from the persecution of [Dardón's] mulatos and in order not to go to the trapiche." He had "sold all his hoes and his bean fields, as well as his *solar* [lot for a house], to give his money to Dardón."[128] The same alcalde had another brother, Matías Lucas, who did accede to work at the trapiche. Matías Lucas confirmed Dardón's story that he had incurred his debt to her not in cash, but in an enterprise retailing *rapaduras* (also called *panela*, unrefined brown sugar). She had supplied him with the stuff on credit, and he had sold it in the plaza of the capital, in the company of his wife whose business was selling tortillas there. But Matías Lucas's expenses evidently exceeded his profits, as he found himself owing Dardón 7 pesos that he was unable to pay. Ultimately he went with his wife and their three children to the trapiche to work off the debt.[129]

Like most creditors, however, Dardón met with only mixed success in her measures against recalcitrant borrowers. Lorenza Saquil's son Mateo Lantán, as we have seen, dodged Dardón's agents and found work in a mill (probably a wheat mill) near the pueblo. Another of Saquil's sons, corralled by Dardón's men four years earlier and sent to the trapiche, had then disappeared. Presumably he fled from the estate rather than work off his arrears. It is easy to imagine where he or others like him went. The labor force at the trapiche included not only Indians from the distant pueblo of Jocotenango but also those from San Agustín Acasaguastlán, much closer to the trapiche; others from Salamá, to the relatively near northwest; and free mulatos and ladinos from the sourrounding Valley of Sansaria.[130] The people of Jocotenango were fluent in Spanish, and they were working in the company of people from areas near the estate. They may have left Dardón's property and taken up residence in one of the neighboring communities.[131]

Indeed, the mayordomo of Dardón's estate mentioned offhandedly, as if he accepted as normal and inevitable, "the Indians who have fled owing large quantities of money." Townspeople in Jocotenango spoke of several men who had deserted the hacienda with accounts unpaid. Lorenza Saquil told of a man named Manuel Calsón and his brothers who had "absented themselves" and had not returned. Matías Cacao, Manuel Salamanca, and

Martín Chirec were also said to have left Dardón's estate to escape their debts, and their whereabouts were unknown. These examples echo previous studies of Spanish American agricultural enterprises in suggesting that indebtedness itself did not necessarily keep laborers in the employ of an estate, since some workers simply left.[132]

In another case, Felipe Supín, whose wife had died at the trapiche, returned to Jocotenango still owing debts to Dardón. (The cause of his wife's death is unclear; she may have been Tomasa Supín, who died of tabardillo.) The widower then fled the pueblo under pressure of dunning. His mother-in-law testified that "because of the continual persecutions and hostilities that he was experiencing [at the hands] of Dardón and her criados, he absented himself and still has not reappeared and has abandoned his home." The record does not specify whether he had left children in the pueblo, though it does indicate that one of his children had been kept behind at the trapiche, presumably in the care of one or more women there from Jocotenango.[133]

The departure of people fleeing debts had the ironic effect of putting their families under increased economic stress. As in the case of the widower Felipe Supín, whose mother-in-law bemoaned that he had forsaken his home, other families also suffered when they lost the labor and income of an adult household member. In 1763, a Jocotenango man named Manuel García disappeared, escaping labor impressment at the hands of Dardón's criados. His wife was left with two small children; the notary of the cabildo of Utatleca later recalled that the wife had reported the situation to him and asked him to inform the local magistrates. It is not known what became of García or his family, but at the time of the Audiencia's investigation two years later he was still missing.[134]

The absence of tributary Indians, particularly men, from the pueblo also added to the pressure that principales faced in their efforts to amass the tributes required of them. The amounts required in Guatemala were never as standarized as they were in central Mexico.[135] Rather, they varied by town and over time, partly because Spanish policies in Central America assessed cash tributes for each town based on the commodities it had previously provided. Even for a given town, tribute levies fluctuated with commodity prices.[136] The system was full of abuses and, as Murdo MacLeod has noted, "in areas of intense economic activity, . . . tribute was notoriously exorbitant and destructive."[137] Though the colonial state made efforts to adjust assessments in accordance with the numbers of people in each community, populations sometimes dropped precipitously during the intervals between censuses. Native town governments repeatedly complained that outdated population counts were subjecting them to unbearable tribute demands.[138]

This pressure underlay much of the concern that native *principales* expressed about the departures of tributaries and the abuses by Spanish creditors and employers. The Jocotenango cabildos' petition is an example. Though on the surface they were complaining about doña Manuela Dardón's mistreatment of their townspeople, the subtext running through their petition and subsequent interviews is that of the *principales*' desperation to restore the presence of tributaries in the pueblo. "Many *solares* are currently abandoned," the Indian governor said, "and [even though] this Pueblo has some four thousand or more residents, in the present season its numbers don't reach three thousand."[139]

Paradoxically, while wage labor provided a way for tributaries to acquire the cash required of them, their work removed them from the pueblo, at least temporarily. Those who reneged on their contracts and escaped their debts through flight in effect withdrew their payments from the community's accumulation of tribute. Even those who received advanced wages and went to work them off were absent from the pueblo for months at a time. Local officials in Jocotenango were hard pressed to collect full tributes from seasonal migrants who were away from the community. One of the alcaldes and the *regidor* complained (as rendered by the notary) that "when they carry out the collection of royal tributes, they ask after some people who are not home, and the reply that the neighbors give them is that [the absentees] are at the trapiche of doña Manuela Dardón."[140] The Utatleca cabildo's notary added that in these cases, the tribute collectors had to "make repeated trips" to Dardón's house to request payments for those working at her estate and that although she might cover a portion of what was owed, she often refused or postponed giving them the entire amount.[141]

These events were part of long-term patterns in which Indian officials tried to return tributaries to their communities. Nearly a century before the Jocotenango cabildos' 1765 petition, officers from the same community's *parcialidad* of Utatleca had sought and obtained orders from the Spanish state bolstering their efforts to return absentees to the pueblo and make them pay tribute.[142] A generation after the 1765 petition, the governor of Jocotenango was struggling to collect payments from the townspeople, as we will see in the following discussion. Several of those who had gone to haciendas to earn tribute payments, he reported, had disappeared. Across Guatemala, flight was a common response by people subject to tribute collection, forced labor, or overwhelming debts.[143] Reports of women and especially men as being "ausentes" (literally, absent or absentees) abounded in the city as well as the countryside.

On one level, the example of doña Manuela Dardón's estate illustrates familiar themes in colonial Mesoamerican labor history. The timing in central Guatemala was a century or more later than in central Mexico, but the broad historical transformation in the structure of Indian labor followed much the same trajectory. Across the middle decades of the eighteenth century, Dardón's system for procuring Indian labor at her estate was shifting from repartimiento drafts, administered by the colonial and native states, to private contracts made between the estate owner and individual Indian workers. Though Dardón's trapiche was hardly one of the colony's largest agricultural enterprises, it displays the full spectrum of labor procurement forms. Her operations were sustained by a motley crew, including a cadre of slaves and free mulato year-round employees (the mayordomo among them); "ladinos" who came to cut and process cane during the harvest; repartimiento Indians from San Agustín Acasaguastlán, some of whom also stayed for short-term labor through nonobligatory arrangements; and other tributary Indians from Jocotenango and Salamá, who worked seasonally as free laborers.

On another level, the case of Dardón's estate expands the historical picture, demonstrating in particular the importance of gender and family structures among native workers. Studies of rural labor in both colonial and national-era Mexico and Central America have emphasized debt, bondage, and market forces as mechanisms of recruitment.[144] Yet the record on Dardón's estate highlights workers' agency as the flip side of labor procurement. Labor was contracted, and debts then evaded or worked off, in complex scenarios structured by a gendered division of productive and reproductive labor. Employers were recruiting workers—that is, setting and advancing wages—based on the workers' gender and family structures. Workers were making choices based partly on their families—their childrens' ages and ability to travel and earn wages, the availability of housing and employment for family members at certain job sites, the presence or absence of support from a spouse, and perhaps affection (or lack thereof) for a spouse.

Further, the 1765 Jocotenango petitions and testimonies about Dardón's estate underscore the heterogenity of interests within Indian communities. Factors such as gender and social rank within the community shaped people's concerns and often structured the conditions of their labor. Some thirty years later, the Audiencia would be prompted to make another investigation into Indian labor from Jocotenango. This time, the workers in question were women serving as wet nurses in the colonial capital. Their story will further illuminate the ways that political and financial interests diverged regardless of shared ethnicity, as conflict simmered among townspeople within a single native community.

WET NURSES AT HOME AND ABROAD

In 1797 the Audiencia received another complaint from Jocote-
nango, now at its new location just beyond the northern edge of Nueva
Guatemala. Once again, at first glance the complaint seems to focus on
Spanish practices in recruiting and managing workers from the community.
The petition came from the parish priest of Jocotenango, don Manuel de
Pineda, who was voicing alarm about Indian women being removed from
the pueblo to serve as wet nurses.[145] Apparently based on genuine concerns
about the Indians' welfare, Pineda's appeal pitted him against some of the
city's most wealthy and powerful Spaniards, who at the time of his petition
were employing wet nurses from Jocotenango in their homes. The Audiencia was typically cautious and even restrained in its judicial deliberations,
and it was perhaps especially hesitant in this case because of the stature of
the employers under scrutiny. Pineda had directed his most specific accusations at don Pedro de Aycinena, a nephew and business assistant of Central
America's most prominent aristocrat.[146] The priest identified a Jocotenango woman named María del Carmen Contán, who was serving as wet
nurse to the baby of Aycinena and his wife. Contán's own infant had been
left behind in the pueblo, Pineda said, and suffered progressive stages of
malnutrition.[147]

The Audiencia had previously ruled that Indian women with babies
should not be removed from their communities to suckle Spanish children,
but the regulation did not hold much sway. Elite Spanish parents continued
to appeal to the Audiencia for women to nurse their babies, and the Audiencia's president himself had responded by sending orders to the Indian
governor of Jocotenango for the procurement of wet nurses. The mechanisms for recruitment of lactating women within the pueblo were left up to
the Indian administration.[148]

Frustrated by Audiencia inaction on his petition, Father Pineda took
matters into his own hands. In August 1797, he sent a team of bailiffs
(probably Indian men from the pueblo) to the capital to "reclaim" two
Jocotenango wet nurses and return them to the community. These deputies
arrived at the Spanish households where the two women were employed—
the house of don Josef Antonio de Córdova, *protomédico* (chief physician)
of the Kingdom of Guatemala; and the house of don Ventura de Nájera,
an hacendado who probably owned more cattle than anyone else in Central America. Though Pineda's agents failed in their mission to remove the
women from the city, the episode caused a stir. The Audiencia immediately issued a statement to Pineda, politely but forcefully assuring him that
the wet nurses would benefit from their salaries and that their employers

would provide for the sustenance of the children who remained in the pueblo. (The statement was just that, with no mention of plans for enforcement.) The archbishop, obviously chagrined, wrote to the president of the Audiencia apologizing for the priest's disregard for state authority.[149]

But Father Pineda was relentless. He responded by bombarding the Audiencia with more than fifty pages of arguments in his own hand, contesting the assurances. He cited examples of children who had died after their mothers were recruited as wet nurses. He asserted that few of the women had been adequately paid. He railed too more generally against "the lack of justice, and even of humanity, with which those unfortunate people have been treated in the past, and even in the present." Ultimately, he urged the state to enforce a *reducción* (return) to the pueblo not only of women serving as wet nurses, but of all the women and men from Jocotenango working as servants in the capital's private homes.[150]

Pineda's outcries finally reached Spain, and the king ruled in 1799 with orders to the Audiencia. The ruling, however, was so restrained as to be almost meaningless. It prohibited the "removal" of both men and women from Jocotenango for service in wet nursing or any other occupation in the capital or on haciendas without consent of the Audiencia.[151] But the Audiencia had been providing consent all along for the removal of wet nurses, as some of them had been enlisted by order of the Audiencia's president. Presumably, the procurement of wet nurses and other Indian workers then continued, much as it had for centuries even in the face of humanitarian reform efforts.[152]

Though Pineda's campaign was thus probably largely ineffectual, it resulted in a wealth of documentation. In response to his protests, the Crown demanded a report on the Indians "of both sexes" from Jocotenango working for Spaniards in the capital and on haciendas. The resulting record offers insights into women's reproductive labor and childrearing practices as well as their engagement in both native and colonial political economies. It also depicts a system of social networks that linked survival within the native community to migration out of the community.

A notary recorded the information provided by the pueblo's Indian governor, Diego Casanga.[153] Tables 1.2 and 1.3 summarize the report, minus a few people who Casanga said had left to work on an hacienda in Sololá and had not returned. (He labeled these people as *huidos*—runaways, absent having fled. Like most of the other townspeople working at haciendas, those in Sololá had left in family groups: Manuel Ortiz with his wife and four children, Diego Sián who ran off with a widow named Angelina, and Manuel Lantán with his wife and a daughter about eleven years old.) Evidently Casanga expected other townspeople working at agricultural estates to return; he identified them as "those are who at the haciendas so as to pay me the annual tribute."[154] His wording highlights his role as collector of tributes as well as the necessity for townspeople to leave the community in order to earn the required money. Table 1.2 lists the wet nurses. Table 1.3 shows the numbers of other people named as servants (*sirvientes*) in the capital and as workers at haciendas.

A few caveats apply to Casanga's report. It has several inconsistencies, though some were probably inadvertent, normal imperfections in record-keeping. The notary's reference point apparently shifted during his cataloguing of women caring for the wet nurses' children, when he started identifying the caretakers as *su abuela* (her or their grandmother). Presumably he meant the children's grandmothers, though earlier in his list he had labeled the caretakers as *su madre* (her mother—that is, the wet nurse's grandmother). We know from María del Carmen Contán's testimony, for one, that she had left her children with her mother (their grandmother). Further, Casanga evidently did not know the details of every wet nurse's family. María Contán said her two older children were ages five and nine, but Casanga's report lists them as seven and two. Contán also had a third child—the fourteen-month-old whose ill health was at the center of the maelstrom—who is not listed in the record of Casanga's account.

More importantly, though, Casanga as governor had his own interests—he was seeking to collect tributes and debt payments—and his words should not always be taken at face value. An obvious red flag is his assertion that almost every one of the wet nurses was "content" (*contenta*). That hardly sounds credible. Consider the women whose own children had perished in the pueblo while the mothers served as wet nurses in the city. (The Audiencia's report indicates that the deaths were from tabardillo—typhus.) Father Pineda's letters allude to wet nurses who had tried to escape their employers' houses and to a teenager sent to serve as a wet nurse, whose milk dried up as a result of her fright (*susto*) on being carted (literally) out of the pueblo. Likely some of the wet nurses were grieving the deaths or stillbirths of their own infants. Odds are that some were suffering postpartum depression. Certainly they were racked by the sleep deprivation that accompanies nursing (though their total workload may have been less than at home, where they also would have had to do additional domestic labor).

Yet there is no particular reason to doubt the report's most striking pattern: few if any of the women working in the capital had spousal support. Of the twenty-one wet nurses named (Table 1.2), nine evidently had husbands who had fled, four were widowed, three were reported as "alone," and four were of unspecified marital status. One wet nurse had a husband in the pueblo, but he was described as *loco* (crazy). Only one wet nurse,

TABLE 1.2
Wet nurses from Jocotenango serving in the capital, September 1797,
as reported by the governor, Diego Casanga.

Name	Marital status	Ages of children	Person caring for children
Felipa Asig	"Her husband has fled"	None	
Rosa Cirín	"Her husband has fled"	None	
Rosa Rayo	Not specified	5; 2	Her mother
Agustina Grande	"Her husband has fled"	4; almost 1	Her sister-in-law
María del Carmen Contán	"Her husband has fled"	7; 2	Her mother
María Marta Guerra	Widow	3; 4; 5	Her (their?) grandmother
María Santos Guerra	Widow	A girl, 9; a boy, 7; a 3-month-old	Her (their?) aunt
María Josefa Canel	"Her husband is crazy"	2	Her (or the child's) aunt
Ventura Viscul	"Her husband has fled"	6; 5; 1	Her (their?) grandmother
Crespina Morales	"The husband has fled"	One child, age not specified	Her (the child's?) aunt
Aniceta Culúa	"Without a husband"	7	Her (the child's?) grandmother
Rosa Ruche	Widow	A daughter who is with her	
Felipa Sacáj	Not specified	Nearly 5; nearly 2	Her (their?) grandmother
María Timotea	"Her husband has fled"	3; 5	Her (their?) grandmother
Josefa Yscoray	*Sola* (literally, alone)	Not specified	
María del Rosario Herrera	Widow	10	Her (or the child's) grandmother
María Olaya Velásquez	Not specified	One child who is with her	
Sebastiana Juárez	*Sola*	Not specified	
Magdalena Pérez	Not specified	7	Her (or the child's) grandmother
María Matías Sacáj	"The husband has fled"	5; 5 months	Her (their?) grandmother
María Ordóñez	"Her husband has fled"	Not specified	

Source: Archivo General de Centro América, Guatemala City, Signatura A1, Legajo 154, Expediente 3063, fols. 13–14.

TABLE 1.3

People (other than wet nurses) working outside Jocotenango, September 1797, as reported by the governor, Diego Casanga.

	Servants in the capital				
	Single	*Widowed*	*Married*	*Noted as accompanied by a child*	*Noted as having no children*
Women	5	3	1*	2	3
Men	10	0	4	0	0

* "Her husband is crazy."

	Men working on haciendas (no women are named)				
Single	*Widowed*	*Married, accompanied by wife*	*Married, wife in the pueblo*	*Noted as accompanied by children*	*Children noted as in the pueblo*
2	2	7	2	3	1

Source: Archivo General de Centro América, Guatemala City, Signatura A1, Legajo 154, Expediente 3063, fols. 13-14.

María del Rosario Herrera, was reported to have a teenage child earning wages (apparently this child was in addition to her ten-year-old). Eight months later Father Pineda reported that yet another woman, Andrea Poróm, had left to serve as a wet nurse; her husband had "recently fled."[155] None of the women working as "servants" in the capital had support from husbands, either. (See Table 1.3.) Five were single and three widowed; two of the widows had a child accompanying them at work. Just one woman, Ramona Jocoyan, was married, and her husband was reported as mentally impaired (loco). Even if the report was inaccurate on a few of these women, the pattern is still clear: those without husbands present were more likely to be recruited to the city for wet nursing and other service. Given the disparity between men and women's earning power, it is not surprising that the absence of a husband could precipitate destitution, especially for women with children. Such circumstances probably induced some single and abandoned women to enlist voluntarily.

Still, "voluntary" recruitment could be complicated. The case of María Contán, the only wet nurse whose testimony was recorded at length, offers an illustration. (Recall that Contán was the wet nurse in the house of Aycinena, the focus of Father Pineda's early petition.) The Indian governor Diego Casanga portrayed Contán's recruitment in a positive light, asserting that she had taken the work voluntarily. "María Contán went of her free will to the house of don Pedro Aycinena to serve as a wet nurse," he said, "finding herself at the time not only poor and without proper clothing, but also with the husband absent because he has fled." Casanga's account clearly tried to minimize any role he had in recruiting her, though he admitted to having given her "permission" to leave.[156]

However, Contán's testimony suggests that Casanga had played a major role, perhaps even corralling her into service.[157] Speaking easily in Spanish, she insisted that she had not wanted to serve as a wet nurse in the city because she had three children. She had "been obliged" she said, by the the governor.[158] Evidently Casanga had created this obligation by dunning her for payments and seizing her house. Her testimony indicates that her husband had been in debt. The governor, she said, had tried to obligate him to work in several Spanish homes in the city. Not wanting to do so, the husband had fled the pueblo and left her with the debts. She owned a *rancho* (a small thatched house), which Casanga had then sold as if on her behalf. He took the proceeds, 6 pesos, to pay a debt that her husband owed a Spaniard. Contán alleged that her husband had already paid off part of that loan, evidently brokered through the governor (for a tribute payment, one suspects). Later in her deposition, she said she had decided to serve as a wet nurse because she had insufficient clothing and her husband had been absent for a year, though the notary's summary of this reasoning gives the sense that Contán may have simply been agreeing to the suggestion of the officer questioning her. In any case, the decision was not wholly voluntary, given her circumstances. She took the job (and left her children) in the absence of other viable options.

Whether or not the Indian governor had drafted Contán into service, his role was part of the process that had left her with no real alternatives. Under pressure of tributes, debts, and perhaps extortion by Casanga, Contán's husband had abandoned her with two children while she was pregnant with a third. The governor had then expropriated her house. Clearly Contán was bristling under the governor's authority. She noted that she was "very afraid" he would punish her if he learned of her testimony, yet even as the examining attorney and the notary ended the questioning and prepared to close the deposition, she spoke up with more; her anger (and perhaps a hope that the court would set things right) apparently overrode her fear. In her coda she explained that Aycinena's wife had given her 6 pesos to buy the rancho back. She said that she had then given this money to the governor, who promised to restore the house to her. But he reneged, she said, demanding an additional 10 pesos, which she did not have. Contán bitterly summed up the outcome: she had been "left without one or the other"—without the money and without her house. The native governor had seized her house to redeem her spouse's debts and had then taken her money as well.

Thus, one component of the story is that María Contán went to work as a wet nurse because of debts and financial need. The other part is that patterns from the systems of tribute and labor coercion had partially structured her recruitment. The procurement even of "voluntary" workers from Jocotenango was functioning based on a combination of corporate—that is, state-level—mechanisms with those of individual arrangement. Some of the elite colonial parents seeking wet nurses had turned to the Audiencia, though in hiring María Contán, don Pedro de Aycinena and his wife had apparently communicated directly to the governor of Jocotenango. (One imagines that they—or friends of theirs—may previously have appealed to the Audiencia but then learned they could speed the process by direct contact with the governor.) Aycinena testified that Diego Casanga had told him "to give [Contán] three pesos, which is the standard salary."[159] Such instruction from the governor evokes the old role of the Indian state in administering labor for the colony. For his part, Casanga in his deposition seemed to demur, saying simply that he didn't know what arrangement María Contán had made with her employers (though he said he knew the standard salary for wet nurses was 4 pesos per month plus food). Contán herself spoke of an agreement she had with Aycinena's wife, doña Javiera Barrutia, the mother of the child being nursed.[160] It is not clear whether Contán had any leverage in making the contract. She said it provided her with 3 pesos a month in addition to her food, but that Barrutia had been giving her 4 pesos "in consideration of [the fact that Contán had] children."

A portion of Contán's cash wages indeed reached Jocotenango in the form of remittances. Contán explained that she had been giving 2 pesos to each of the women whom she had entreated, in respective months, to nurse her son. The first four months, her baby was nursed by a woman named Sebastiana, widow of a man who had been notary for the native cabildo. When the baby developed a fever, Contán transferred him to the care of her mother, a woman in her mid-forties who breastfed the child along with her own youngest for the next week or so. Contán then hired another wet nurse. By the time of her deposition, she said the baby had had five different wet nurses. His health was improved. Don Pedro de Aycinena's deposition indicates that Contán's son was currently being taken to nurse at the breast of Contán's sister, to whom Contán was giving part of her salary. As for the rest of Contán's salary, she said she had kept it for herself; Aycinena said she had used some of the remaining money to buy clothing but had given most of it to her mother. He may have been referring to a gift or loan of 2 pesos that Contán indicated she had received from his wife and had then remitted to her mother.

María Contán's testimony, like the Audiencia's earlier investigation into the management practices of doña Manuela Dardón, highlights the continuing power of the Indian state and officeholders within the pueblo. The governor had pressed Contán's husband to make good on his debts, some of which may have been for tribute payments. At least one of the debts was owed to a Spaniard, though the record engenders suspicion that it was contracted through arrangements by the governor (who may have retained a portion of the money as it changed hands). After her husband's departure from the pueblo, Casanga pursued payment from Contán herself, pressing (or pressuring) her into service for wages and appropriating her property for sale. Even if Indian officeholders were no longer enfranchised as local administrators of encomienda labor or as recruiters for repartimientos, they persisted as collectors of tribute, brokers of credit and debt, and agents of labor procurement for the Spaniards. In these roles, members of the native elite continued to wield significant force in Indian social and economic life.

The response of the Spanish state to Father Pineda's petitions also echoes the earlier investigation into Dardón's sugar plantation. In its goal of protecting the Indian population, the colonial state inquired carefully about native welfare. But the Spanish magistrates were slow (or unable) to enact measures that might have achieved real reform. Although Pineda's outcry was part of a broad tradition of humanitarian clerical protest, the protesters were a minority. In general the colony's civil and ecclesiastical officers could not easily alter, nor did they necessarily wish to alter, the historical patterns that structured the recruitment of Indian workers—the Spanish demand for labor, the native officeholders' authority in the Indian pueblos, and the ongoing collection of tributes.

Additionally, the case of the wet nurses from Jocotenango helps illuminate a broader history of wet nursing. Indian women had served as wet nurses for Spanish colonial children since the sixteenth century.[161] The widespread use in colonial Guatemalan Spanish of the term *chichigua* (wet nurse, from the Nahuatl *chichiua* or *chichiva*) evokes the presence of wet nursing in pre-Hispanic times as well as colonial society's association of the role with native women.[162] In the 1570s, tribute assessments for the pueblo of Jocotenango required the town to provide wet nurses to the capital city.[163] By the late colonial years, women identified as mulatas and mestizas as well as Indians were being paid to suckle the children of elite (and occasionally middling) parents.[164] The presence of more than one wet nurse in two of the Spanish households in the 1797 report may indicate that they were also providing general child care or performing other domestic chores.[165]

Wealthy women across colonial Spanish America, like their contemporaries in Spain and Brazil, employed surrogates to suckle their children in their homes, but the majority may have done the nursing themselves.[166] Two of the employers of wet nurses from Jocotenango in the 1797 report are known to have had specific reasons to need a wet nurse. One of the infants was a foundling who had been left outside the house of a prominent Spanish family. The other baby was the child of don Pedro de Aycinena and his wife doña Javiera Barrutia. Aycinena told the Audiencia that Barrutia was "completely unable to nurse a child" because of various infirmities, some of them evidently resulting from an injury or illness that had affected one of her arms.[167] Two physicians who examined her confirmed that her "nearly continual headaches and pain in the shoulder and part of the disfigured arm, upset stomach, weakness, and nervous ailments" made her "forever unable to fulfill the delicate and important obligation of nursing."[168]

The doctors' protective stance toward the Spanish mother extended to her child as well, but not to the child of the Indian wet nurse. Early in their report, the physicians had elaborated their belief that the milk of a baby's own mother was the best for its health. Nevertheless, they then determined that María Contán's ailing baby should be nursed by another woman. Contán should continue as the exclusive wet nurse to doña Javiera Barrutia's infant, they argued, who was "very fond of and attached to the Indian Contán." Barrutia's child had begun teething, a period that the medical men contended was extremely dangerous. It would be "ruinous to try to give him a different wet nurse," they said; but "on the contrary, the son of the Indian Contán, [who is by now] accustomed to the variety of arms and milks, will surely readily accept whatever breast milk he is given."[169] The two babies may well have exhibited different temperaments, but the physicians nevertheless seem to have assigned higher priority to the health of the Spanish baby or to have allowed him more fussiness than the Indian baby.

Yet nonelite women too sometimes hired wet nurses for their children. As we have seen, María Contán hired Indian women in Jocotenango to nurse her own baby. Two of the Jocotenango women serving in 1797 as wet nurses in the capital, Aniceta Culuga and María Ordóñez, took their babies with them to the homes of the employers, where the infants were suckled by "ladina" (probably meaning non-Indian) wet nurses.[170] Women of mixed ancestry also appear among those who hired wet nurses. María de la Luz Ubeda, for example, an eighteen-year–old mestiza and single mother of a small child, employed a wet nurse in the capital city in 1775.[171]

It was common and widely recognized for women to nurse other people's infants, and contemporary Guatemalan Spanish reflected this recognition. The phrase *criar a media leche* (literally, to nurse at half milk) was used to refer to the practice in which a woman nursed two children; the phrase *criar a leche entera* (literally, to nurse at full milk) specified that a woman was suckling only one child.[172] Though wet nursing for pay often crossed lines of ethnicity and class, with Indians, mulatas, and mestizas nursing children of other groups, I have not found any evidence of Spanish women who served as wet nurses for children of Indian, African, or mixed ancestry.

The Jocotenango cases in both 1765 and 1797 also illustrate several broad historical patterns in labor migration (patterns with remarkable present-day resonance). The lists of townspeople working abroad show that departure from the pueblo to work in the Spanish economy, whether by force or voluntarily, was a regular part of life for women and men in the sending community. María Contán's testimony in particular underscores the impact of migrant workers' remittances in Jocotenango. Like Contán, most of the wet nurses in the 1797 report had left children in the care of their kinswomen, and they presumably remitted wages to the pueblo as Contán did. In fact, the Audiencia noted that Spanish families who hired wet nurses were expected to provide for a wet nurse for their employee's child as well.[173] We have seen that Contán also sent additional money to her mother in the pueblo; likely the other Jocotenango wet nurses did the same. Finally, the 1765 and 1797 cases illustrate the circular (that is, out-and-back) routes typical of Guatemalan labor migration. Among wet nurses, migration was scheduled largely by the client child's needs (or perceived needs) and the worker's bodily ability to produce milk. Twelve months after the 1797 investigation, thirteen of the twenty-one wet nurses from Jocotenango had returned home. Six were reportedly still nursing children in the capital and would probably return after the children were weaned, though some might extend their stay to work as servants, as one woman had already done. Native workers on agricultural estates and in general domestic service followed seasonal or financial timetables, but their migration also tended to assume a circular pattern.

These snapshots of Jocotenango workers are not completely surprising. Historians have previously recognized the burden that colonial rule placed on native communities and have seen the complaints brought by indigenous leaders. It is well known that flight from the communities was one outcome. Yet studies of Mexico and Central America have given relatively little attention to the ways that ordinary families and individuals, particularly women, experienced these pressures. The examples from Jocotenango demonstrate some of the challenges of preserving family structures under conquest, and suggest the efforts that both men and women exerted in the face of these challenges. These cases also underscore native women's experiences as workers in the colonial economy. Most kinds of labor were gender specific—both paid and unpaid work in agriculture, domestic service and food preparation, and reproductive or child care work. Further, wages for most women workers were lower than for men. These structural differences molded the processes of labor recruitment, migration, and wage remittances along lines of gender, distinguishing the ways that women and men experienced colonial rule and the ways they were able to respond to it. It was easier for men than for women to abandon their communities (where tributes were enforced) and to strike out alone; men commanded higher wages, they were never pregnant or nursing, and they were generally free of the work of child care. The women they left behind were especially subject to pressures and abuses of the tribute system. Women could be pressed not only for current tributes but also for debts accrued before their husbands had fled or died.[174] Subsistence too was in question for households without male labor.

Facing these burdens, widows and abandoned wives were likely to migrate alone or with their children to the Spanish city, where women's wages were generally higher than in the countryside. This pattern helps explain how the Guatemalan capital, like many colonial Latin American cities, became in demographic terms largely a city of women. The impact appears also in censuses of native communities. A record for the Cakchiquel town of San Luis de las Carretas (just north of Santiago), for example, lists the house of Marcos de la Cruz, age forty-six, "absent for many years" without paying tribute. His wife Angelina Pérez, also forty-six, was in the capital with their fourteen-year-old daughter.[175] Even more often, censuses of Indian pueblos describe houses simply as "empty." Presumably some unoccupied houses were omitted from the records altogether. Census reports do not normally show what happened to the children of parents who left native communities. We have seen in the Jocotenango cases that some of these children accompanied their parents and some stayed behind with relatives. Others, however, probably ended up among the corps of Indian child servants living in their employers' houses. Yet not all child servants were from abandoned homes. The example of Francisca Victoria García will illustrate.

A servant's life on the cusp: Francisca Victoria García

While most agricultural workers were male, women made up the majority of indigenous migrants to the colonial capital. Girls and women from numerous native communities arrived in Santiago, and subsequently in Nueva Guatemala, primarily to work in domestic service. Migrants tended to remain tied to the native community even while immersed in the process of hispanization; they often made repeated departures and return trips home, and they usually remitted a portion of their wages to their home communities. However, prolonged residence in the city, especially when it began in childhood, inevitably brought workers into the Hispanic fold. Through their experience, they acquired (or cemented) Spanish language fluency, learned how to work and survive in the Hispanic city, and developed social and economic networks there.

The example of Francisca Victoria García illustrates a life on the cusp of this transition.[176] García was born in the late eighteenth century in Ciudad Vieja (Almolonga), an Indian community of Tlaxcalan (Mexican) ancestry, 5 kilometers outside Santiago. She migrated to the new capital to work in domestic service at the age of six. One might imagine that her family was in dire economic need, although the record shows that her father would own significant real estate by the time of his death. Possibly García's parents viewed domestic service in the city as an opportunity for her to gain skills, knowledge, and associations that might later prove advantageous in seeking employment, carrying out business, or making a marriage.[177] For tributary Indian women, marriage to nontributaries (Indians or others) would bring some relief from the economic burdens experienced by all members of tributaries' households.[178]

Over the next twenty-two years, García was employed as a servant in a series of Spanish households. She married a native of the new capital, a hispanized man of Indian ancestry who was a sacristan or sacristan's assistant in the cathedral.[179] García became enmeshed, in both her personal life and her economic life, in the world of the Hispanic city.

Her case comes to light in a lawsuit that she brought at the time of her father's death in 1807. Essentially a dispute with her two brothers over an inheritance, the suit shows that a family feud had begun much earlier. In her father's will, dictated before several Indian officials in Ciudad Vieja, he left everything to his two sons and their children, excluding Francisca Victoria in no uncertain terms. He charged that she had fought with his wife (her mother) and had then been "gone [*huida*] for a long time without knowing about the death of my wife."[180]

Though a day's mountainous journey separated Francisca Victoria's home in the new capital from her relatives in Ciudad Vieja, she got wind of the will. Less than a month after it was written, even as her father lay on his deathbed, she appealed to the Spanish civil authorities in the capital. Her petition accused her two brothers—both still living in Ciudad Vieja—of seeking to appropriate her just inheritance. She complained in particular that they were acting with the help of the town's Indian governor, whom she described as "an ally of my brothers and relatives, and an opponent of me and my husband." Because the governor "is misadvised and suborned by my brothers," she said, "he is in favor of [excluding me from the inheritance], using the subterfuge that since I am not going with my husband to live in the Pueblo I do not have a right to the inheritance."[181] The Spanish judge decided in Francisca Victoria's favor, ruling that all the property in the estate should be distributed among the three siblings (following the norm in Spanish law).

Still, she disputed this judgment, petitioning the court again. She contended that certain properties in her father's estate rightfully belonged exclusively to her because they had been purchased with her wages, which she had turned over to her parents. She described how at age six, "I left the custody of my parents [and] began to serve in several houses of distinction in this capital, [and] my parents received my wages in the long period of twenty-two years that I maintained myself working." Highlighting the point that her parents had collected and invested her wages, she said, "The properties that my parents obtained . . . [were] obtained from my work from the money that they came to ask for, advanced from my salaries at the houses where I was accommodated."[182] While she alleged that her wages in all these years had totaled 760 pesos, one of her brothers countered that "she never gave my parents even a pittance." Probably both claims were exaggerated (salaries paid to other Indian girls and women around the same time would have totaled somewhat less), but the record suggests a core of credibility in Francisca Victoria's story. She was able to name very specific properties, and she was unwavering in her claims across more than a year of litigation. Her outline of the way her parents collected her salaries matches the general pattern for girls from Indian pueblos working in the capital. The Spanish court effectively legitimated her demands, ruling consistently in her favor in response to her repeated petitions.

The Indian state, however, resisted these rulings. When García brought a written order to the pueblo authorizing her to take possesssion of the properties she had claimed, the Indian commissioner (*comisionado*) stonewalled. Her description of the episode (as she reported it to the Spanish court) highlights her estrangement not only from her family but also from other members of the Indian community. She gave the Spanish court order to the Indian commissioner, she said, and

he shook his head and laughed, and after it was read to him, he began to delay, with [saying] later today, later tomorrow, and later still, by which I came to the understanding that . . . my said brothers have this commissioner very suborned and *adobado* [cooked or pickled], and as for the [Indian] magistrates of the town, well they are so banded together with my brothers and they [my brothers] so favored by the magistrates, that even with all the rightfulness and justice that accompanies me, they mock me.[183]

The colonial court then sent a request to the alcalde mayor of Sacate-péquez, the Spanish chief provincial magistrate with jurisdiction over Ciudad Vieja, asking him to intervene. Still, the Indian commissioner in Ciudad Vieja refused to cooperate.

In 1808, more than a year after García's initial petition, her husband filed a statement listing the properties at her parents' house that she was claiming as rightfully hers. The list identified some fifty items, among them seven pieces of land, four "beasts" (live largestock), a bridle, materials for making harnesses, a beehive, three hogs, a dozen chickens, hoes, axes, machetes, sickles, a mason's trowel, household furniture (tables, benches, chairs, and chests), table linens, kitchenware (grinding stones, jugs, dishes, cups for chocolate), various men's and women's garments and accessories, religious images, a cupping glass, and household tools such as a bellows, a scale, and scissors. The statement contended that her parents had taken her wages "and invested them for her in the expressed properties for her own use." The colonial court called for further testimony, but the record of the litigation then ends, with no mention of the final outcome.

At first glance, Francisca Victoria García's lawsuit is a tale of a family's undoing over filial loyalty and inheritance. Yet it also tells a story about an Indian woman's acculturation in the Hispanic society of Nueva Guatemala, and it suggests the ways in which her migration experience was transformative. Like other migrants to the colonial centers, García traversed a space that divided pueblo from city in terms of social networks, cultural practices, and identities. The rift that ultimately separated her from her parents and brothers was not only a property dispute but also a set of tensions between the native community and the Hispanic capital. Living and working in Spanish homes since age six, García undoubtedly quickly learned Spanish if she had not already known it.[184] She married an Indian who was born in the capital and was so hispanized that the word *indio* had been dropped from the label people used to describe him. Her parents, she noted, did not get along with her husband. She continued living in the city after her marriage and had no intention of moving back to Ciudad Vieja. When she learned of a threat to her inheritance, she appealed immediately to the Spanish civil authorities in the capital, and she repeatedly sought their aid. In addition to relying on Spanish institutions, she named several of her Spanish former employers as witnesses in her litigation. During more than twenty years in the capital, she had developed there a network of social connections that had become her primary alliances.

García's parents and brothers, in contrast, remained socially as well as physically rooted in the Indian community of Ciudad Vieja. Her brothers, she said, each had received from her parents an inheritance at the time of their marriages in the pueblo, whereas she had received nothing from them at the time of her marriage in the capital. The governor of Ciudad Vieja, his commissioner, and other local Indian officials colluded with her brothers by ignoring orders from the Spanish authorities and blocking her efforts to force them to comply.

On one hand, Francisca Victoria García gained relative freedom from the constraints of pueblo life.[185] Her daily activities in the capital, and possibly her mobility from one employer to the next, fell beyond the control of her mother, her father, and other Indian community elders. On the other hand, García's parents apparently retained control over her wages for at least several years. Her arguments indicate that decisions about how to dispose of her cash income fell to her parents. The properties they purchased with her salaries apparently remained in their possession for the duration of their lives.

Though she was partly estranged from her native town and her family, her ties were not completely broken. She had heard about her father's testament within the month after it was written. If she did not make frequent trips to Ciudad Vieja, she apparently maintained links in the capital to sources of news from the pueblo. The specific, extensive list of properties she named suggests she had remained familiar with her parents' home or at least that she had been informed of what they purchased with her earnings, and she had kept track of things. She knew the dimensions of the various parcels of land and even the whereabouts of a piece of ribbon (she said the stepdaughter of her brother Marcos had it). She noted that six bovine or equine beasts had been hers but that only three remained, as if she was aware that some of the animals had died or been lost or sold. She remembered a cape that she had bought for her father, two changes of clothing she had left with her sister-in-law, and some underdrawers and a *coton* (native-style shirt) belonging to her son. The list also mentions two sacks of rotten *jocotes*, conveying the sense that she had been at the house recently. (Jocotes are fruit of the tree *spondias purpurea*; when rotted they were used to make a fermented beverage.)

Perhaps most telling in her list of property is the 40-peso loan that she had given to her father "for the care of a milpa." Whether her father had tended the field himself or hired someone else to do it, Francisca had invested in an agricultural enterprise in her native community. The purchase of lands, as well as the maintenance of laborers to make the lands productive, tied the pueblo's agricultural economy to cash earned by a daughter working in the city.

Thus despite the family feud, García's story reflects the ways in which migration of servants to the capital created multiple nexuses between the native and Hispanic spheres. Some of these nexuses were economic. The money that girls and women like García remitted to the sending community might be spent on consumer products, but it could also be invested in agricultural capital and production, which in turn could serve colonial markets as well as local consumption. Migrant workers, notably women, were a crucial link between rural and urban economies.

Moreover, migrant domestics formed a central core of social connections between city and countryside as well as a vanguard of demographic change. They played the principal role in the formation of the urban hispanized population, where they numbered more than any other group of workers (figures are discussed in Chapter 3). As in the life of Francisca Victoria García, the migration experience complicated the worker's social relationships and, ultimately, her identity. García's access to property and to legal redress was contingent on her membership within specific communities, yet her identity as a community member was shifting rather than fixed. Although she identified herself to the Spanish court as an "Indian from Ciudad Vieja," the Indian officers in the pueblo and even her own family members treated her as an outsider. The trajectory of her life, including her marriage to a ladino, suggests that after 1821, in the new binary construction of ethnic categories as indio and ladino, her children would likely be classified as ladinos even within the Hispanic city.[186]

Eroding communities

It is hard to forget Francisca Victoria García's departure from home at the age of six. Other native girls too were sent to work at remarkably young ages.[187] Though their parents may have viewed domestic service in terms of opportunities or relief from the burdens of tribute, the putting out of native children to work for colonial employers portrays a grim picture at odds with present-day notions of opportunity or relief. Indian child labor appears as part of a broader, generally bleak history of indigenous family and community life under colonial rule. Native households were often unable to meet the demands of tribute. Whole families were in effect forced into labor, and many families were separated under pressure of draft or debt. The image of Indian communities that appears in the late colonial records is largely one of emptied and broken homes—men leaving under financial pressure, women and children joining them or forced to leave alone.

On one level, this scenario was a continuation of earlier colonial patterns, in which men were required to work abroad as tribute laborers for inadequate pay and women were forced into menial service positions. Though conscription had been largely eliminated by the eve of independence, the change was in certain ways superficial. People from the same communities were still doing the same jobs, and their economic situation had not improved substantially, if at all. From native workers' perspective, the structural changes in labor forms were less than revolutionary. On another level, though, there was a significant—indeed fundamental—demographic change. Flight and attrition from indigenous communities was fueling the growth of the hispanized working population and rendering the colonial administration of labor increasingly obsolete. The Hispanic state in the postindependence period would try on occasion to reinstate drafts of Indian laborers, notably after the 1850s with the rise of coffee, but these efforts had limited impact.[188] The transformation of labor recruitment had resulted from social transformations beyond the reach of legislation by either the colonial or independent government.

Cash tribute payments would be formally eliminated by the new independent government. (Though tributes had been temporarily abolished by the Cortes de Cádiz from 1812 to 1816 and again in 1820, collection persisted in some places in Guatemala, untouched by distant edicts.)[189] The abolition of tribute was accompanied by significant contentiousness between sociopolitical classes within indigenous communities, as officeholders had relied on tributes sometimes for personal enrichment and normally for the sustenance of cabildo and community coffers.[190] Though the demise of draft labor and tribute lightened the burden of native workers, it struck a blow to indigenous states and corporate communities, eliding their functions in the larger colonial (and then the national) political economy. The republican-era Hispanic goverments, particularly under Liberal rule, would be less protective of native communities than the colonial state had been.[191] For the Hispanic elites of the nineteenth century and later, intact native communities were no longer needed for labor coercion and taxation. Indian states would be mainly extraneous to the republic.[192]

2 "That They Cease to Be Truly Slaves"

AFRICAN EMANCIPATION AND THE COLLAPSE
OF SLAVERY

In 1527, the conqueror Pedro de Alvarado received a royal concession to introduce 600 African slaves into Guatemala.[1] The slave trade there
would continue for nearly three centuries in Central America until the
Constitutional Assembly declared a general emancipation in 1824.[2] Meanwhile, though, the importations of slaves slowed dramatically early in the
seventeenth century, and a remarkable demographic pattern emerged: even
though the slave labor force continued to expand until about 1690, the
free population of African and partly African descent quickly came to outnumber those enslaved. The capital city's free *negro* and *mulato* populations surpassed its slave population around the middle of the seventeenth
century. Subsequently, the growth of the free Afro-Guatemalan population
continued to outpace that of the slave population. Indeed, the number of
people enslaved decreased dramatically across the eighteenth century.[3] In
the capital city at least, the free population was increasingly African in
ancestry, and the population of African ancestry was increasingly free.[4]

The period from 1790 to the 1820s saw an increase in slave uprisings
in various American colonies. Historians have identified several contributing factors: the Bourbon and Pombaline reforms, the Napoleonic wars,
and the resulting tax increases and popular political discontent; the French
Revolution; the slave revolt in Saint Domingue (Haiti); the demise of that
colony's sugar exports and the subsequent uptick in sugar production and
slave importation elsewhere; and the political upheavals of the nineteenth
century's first two decades, which ended in independence for Brazil and
most of Spanish America in the 1820s.[5]

Guatemala, though, did not experience any large-scale slave rebellion.[6] Slave resistance there appears to have been tied only indirectly, if it
was tied at all, to external political events. This chapter argues that Afro-
Guatemalan slavery was dismantled gradually by the responses of slaves

and slaveholders to the particular structures of slavery as it existed locally. These structures were products of centuries-old Iberian understandings of slavery, and products of long-term social transformations—racial and cultural mestizaje in particular—in the colonial American context. Such transformations were beyond the control of legislation. Slavery itself was crumbling in Guatemala well before the new independent government issued the general emancipation.

Across the generations preceding independence, African slaves had come to be integrated into the colony's Hispanic culture, society, and economy.[7] Whereas slaves in the early colonial years were typically known only by a single Christian name, sometimes with an apellation referring to their race or slave identity (for example, Juan negro or Ana bozal), by the late eighteenth century most slaves were using Spanish surnames along with Christian names. Numerous slaves were paid wages and charged with providing food and other necessities for themselves and their families. Slaves exercised substantial freedom of movement, while slaveholders' efforts to recover absentee slaves were limited. As Hispanic society grew more racially mixed across the colonial era, slaves were increasingly able to pass unarrested into free society. Social networks in both rural and urban areas linked enslaved people to free relatives and acquaintances, and slaves used these networks to press the limits of their bondage. The colonial civil authorities, for their part, recognized slaves' physical mobility, and the local magistrates tended to legitimize slaves' abilities to move freely and negotiate the conditions of their servitude. In this context, the institution of slavery could not be sustained.

Backdrop for emancipation:
Historic, demographic, and legal contexts

The outlines of slavery in Guatemala reflect origins in Iberia, where slavery in the early modern period had assumed two basic forms.[8] The first form, rooted in medieval Europe, persisted in Iberia as Muslims and Christians enslaved captives during the alternating waves of conquest and reconquest that lasted until 1492. These slaves had constituted a relatively small minority of local populations. They typically served in urban, domestic labor (including artisan work), often as auxiliaries to their employers. (Such roles would be seen too in Spanish America, not only in the urban sphere but also in agriculture, where slaves often fulfilled managerial jobs.) In this older Iberian pattern, justifications for enslavement were based on cultural (especially religious) differences between enslavers and enslaved. Slaves were forced to adopt the dominant culture, and their eventual manumission in the enslavers' society was accepted and even expected.[9] This understanding of slavery would resonate in Guatemala.

A second form of Iberian slavery had developed beginning in the fifteenth century, as Portuguese incursions along the west coast of Africa brought sub-Saharan African slaves into a new European slave trade.[10] Enslaved Africans would provide the labor as European investors established commercial sugar production in Madeira and the Canary Islands. By the mid-fifteenth century large shipments of African slaves were arriving in the Atlantic islands and southern Iberia, where they worked on sugar plantations and were kept without the same expectation of integration into Iberian society. A similarly intensive form of slavery—with sizable slave communities at large estates—appeared in Guatemala, specifically in sugar agriculture.[11]

However, in Guatemala (as in Mexico and the Andes) the presence of native labor forces altered the forms seen in Iberia. On many Spanish American agricultural estates slaves filled a niche between indigenous workers and Spanish employers. Indian draft workers and free laborers of various ethnicities did much of the planting and harvesting. Slaves, on the other hand, were held as year-round employees. Fewer in number than seasonal laborers at most agricultural enterprises, slaves were often trained as artisans or placed in positions supervising seasonal workers. We have seen an example at the estate of doña Manuela Dardón in Chapter 1. Dardón's mayordomo was a free mulato; the mayordomo's son was a mulato slave charged with recruitment and management of seasonal Indian workers. Evidence indicates that the young man's mother was most probably a slave of Dardón.[12] Though free, the father was tied to the estate inasmuch as his son (and likely his wife) remained enslaved there. Even at those Guatemalan estates with large slave work forces, native laborers were also significant. An example is the Ingenio de Ayarza, a sugar estate in eastern Guatemala where owner don José Jacinto Palomo held some 100 slaves. As late as 1794, Palomo was granted a repartimiento of Indians from three towns—a total of thirty men a week—to work at the *ingenio* (sugar mill and plantation).[13]

In the late eighteenth century, most of Guatemala's slave population was concentrated in a few locations. The biggest slaveholder in Central America was the Dominican order, with several agricultural estates and a convent in the capital, all of which held slaves. The Dominicans' Hacienda San Jerónimo, a sugar estate in the Verapaz region, was home to over 600 slaves—the largest enslaved community in Guatemala.[14] Other sugar estates, mainly in the lowlands to the south and east of the capital, also figured prominently among slaveholders.[15] The Crown, however, ranked second, after the Dominicans. A few of the state's slaves labored in the arena of urban administrative offices, but the majority—around 500 people—were held at the port of Omoa (in what is today Honduras). Their labor, along with that of paid Spanish and Indian workers, sustained the port's operations.[16]

Finally, a number of slaves lived in the region's urban centers, particularly the capital, where they labored in monasteries and convents, private homes, and artisan shops. In the capital (at both locations) slaves in the late colonial years constituted only a tiny proportion of the population—on the order of 1 percent.[17] Yet they had clearly played an important role in transforming the urban population across three centuries of Spanish rule. As slaves in the capital exploited opportunities there for manumission, and as ex-slaves emancipated elsewhere migrated to the city in search of economic opportunities, the urban population of African (and partly African) descent grew. This growth spanned the colonial period and continued into the early years of independence. By the mid-1700s, the proportion of free people of African or partly African ancestry had swollen to represent perhaps the largest ethnic group in the capital city.[18] With the city's increasingly mixed racial composition, the entryway for freedpeople and fugitive slaves into the free hispanized population widened. Slaves' social networks, based heavily on kinship, were increasingly likely to include free people, who were better positioned to aid slaves in their quest for liberty. The changing face of free society in the colony made the enslavement of Africans less and less viable.

Several features of Spanish colonial law facilitated slaves' efforts to gain freedom. The judicial system allowed slaves to file civil suits and criminal charges against any subjects of the Crown, including their masters.[19] The state provided attorneys through the office of the procurator for the poor, and court records demonstrate that slaves in late colonial Guatemala were in fact availing themselves of their right to litigate. To be sure, urban slaves had easier access to the courts, but among the rural slaves who trickled into the capital, some came seeking legal recourse, usually against their masters. Their testimonies indicate that even in the countryside slaves knew of their right to appeal to authorities in the cities.[20]

The judicial system was a product of early modern Spanish legal thinking, which—following medieval patterns—essentially legitimized individual slaves' goal of manumission. This thinking is encapsulated in the Siete Partidas, the massive compendium of law codified in the thirteenth century by Alfonso X el Sabio (the Learned), king of Castile.[21] The Siete Partidas continued to influence judicial thought even in late colonial Spanish America, where judges often cited it in their rulings. In addition to Alfonso's scattered references to slaves, he included two titles (sections) in the Fourth Partida specifically on slavery. Title XXI, "Concerning Slaves," contains eight discursive laws defining slavery and its parameters. Title XXII, "Concerning Liberty," is significantly longer, with eleven laws describing ways in which slaves could be emancipated. Notably, the Siete Partidas specifically established slaves' right to litigate, albeit in a limited number of circumstances.[22] Legislation in the sixteenth century explicitly mandated that the royal courts in the Indies must hear the appeal of any black slave.[23]

In late colonial Guatemala the courts followed these principles, acknowledging the value of freedom and upholding slaves' right to litigate. At the same time, though, slaves' suits for liberty competed with the colonial state's ideal of protecting all of its subjects and their investments— including investments in slaves. The outcomes of these suits seem to have been unpredictable; the judges did not always award liberty. Still, the earlier Iberian experience with urban domestic slavery appears clearly in the records of colonial Guatemala, where Hispanic society took slave manumissions in stride.

Finally, market regulations in the late colonial years put self-manumission within the reach of a number of slaves, as slave prices were essentially fixed by state controls. In earlier times resale of slaves for profit may have been more frequent, but in the late colonial era the civil authorities recognized a slave's value as the price paid at the prior sale, or as the figure named by a government-appointed appraiser. The resulting price ceiling expanded the possibility that a slave might gather sufficient money to purchase emancipation.

Slaveholders seem often to have been willing to manumit their slaves in exchange for cash payment of the appraised value. Doña Manuela Dardón, for example, freed Juan Peña in 1775 when he paid her 250 pesos that he had saved. (Peña was in his thirties, one of the sons of the mayordomo of Dardón's sugar estate. The father had been free, but the mother remained Dardón's slave.)[24] Some slaveholders refused, but they may have been the exception more than the rule; I have found only three cases for the period after 1750.[25] In one case, the slave appealed to the Audiencia and was granted her liberty.[26] In another case, the court ruled in favor of the slaveholder (we will see the circumstances later in this chapter, at the Elegant Hoof Hacienda). The third instance is that of Juana Victoriana Medina, whose free husband had been paying in installments for her liberty—valued, he believed, at 100 pesos. When he handed over the final installment, Medina's owner arbitrarily raised the price from 100 to 150 pesos. The husband was unable to pay. Medina appealed to the Audiencia on Christmas Eve of 1819. Her petition reveals that during the years her husband was making the payments, five of their children had died in slavery. Though the Audiencia's ruling was not recorded, the tragic nature of the story suggests the kinds of hope that enslaved people and families must have pinned on freedom. One wonders, in light of the unfinished documentation, whether Medina and her husband fled before the Audiencia issued a ruling.[27]

Though slave sale prices were limited by the Crown's regulations, selling a slave allowed the slaveholder to recoup the initial investment. A slaveholder who granted freedom to a slave in exchange for the purchase price was protecting herself or himself against loss of property—a sizable risk, given that a slave who was denied the request to buy freedom might run away. The possibilities open to fugitive slaves may have expanded starting in the 1770s, when building projects in the new capital increased the demand for workers. A favorable job market may have fueled slave fugitivity, but it probably also gave slaves some additional leverage in negotiations with their masters. Another factor in slaveholders' willingness to sell their slaves may have been the scarcity of hard currency—a problem even in the late colonial years. In a cash-short economy, the specie offered for a slave's freedom could be especially valuable.

Slaves of the Crown were not excluded from the possibility of gaining freedom through purchase. In 1798, for example, a free black man ("negro libre") named Manuel Huebo bought the liberty of his entire nuclear family and his one-year-old granddaughter, all slaves at the Crown's Fort of Omoa, for 700 pesos.[28]

Resistance in the countryside:
Collective negotiation at the Hacienda San Jerónimo

A long-term dispute between the slaves and the mayordomos of the Dominican order's Hacienda San Jerónimo illustrates the flexibility of slavery in late colonial Guatemala. Early in the 1810s, some fifteen or twenty slaves traveled the mountainous route from San Jerónimo, located in what is now the department of Baja Verapaz, to the capital city. There they appealed to the royal authorities on behalf of themselves and the other slaves at the estate. The *síndico* (syndic) of the ayuntamiento, who held the ex oficio title of Protector of Slaves, wrote up their request. One of the slaves would later recall that the document had "solicited the liberty of the individuals of the [San Jerónimo] plantation, we who live under the bitter yoke of slavery, [because of] the injurious treatment with which we were being managed."[29] Their appeal demanded the reversal of several injustices: they were given insufficient food, they received greater work assignments than the hacienda's nonslave laborers, they were forced to work even on Sundays and holidays, and they were mistreated by a handful of free *negros caribes* employed as overseers or drivers on the estate.

(The negros caribes were probably members, or children, of a group of several thousand Black Caribs deported in 1797 from St. Vincent and Baliceaux in the Lesser Antilles to Roatán, in the Gulf of Honduras; descendants of these deportees today constitute the Garífuna communities of Central America.)[30]

The estate's mayordomo, himself a Dominican friar, denied the slaves' allegations. Nevertheless the order's provincial in the capital proposed some concessions, thereby avoiding, or at least postponing, further litigation. Principal among these concessions was that the slaves would be paid a daily wage of 1½ reales, the same as that received by both free and repartimiento laborers on the estate. Evidently the slaves owned some livestock; the Dominicans agreed that each slave could keep three or four animals, but beyond this the estate would charge for pasturage.[31] The remonstrant slaves returned to the hacienda, where along with the other slaves they were subsequently paid in silver rather than food.

The slaves' litigation had amounted to a conscious, collective renegotiation of the terms of their labor.[32] Clearly the slaves did not enter the litigation on an equal footing with the Dominicans in terms of social status or political power. Yet the departure of fifteen or more slaves from the hacienda and their ability to appeal to the state gave them some traction. In addition to the concession of wages, the slaves had also extracted from the Dominican administration a promise that their workload would be kept equal to that of the estate's free and tributary laborers. And the administration agreed to the slaves' demand that physical punishments would be given to the slaves only by the mayordomo (an office always filled by one of the Dominican friars) or by local civil magistrates—not by the free Black Carib overseers who, the slaves implied, had acted with excessive brutality.[33]

A series of appeals later that same decade shows that the San Jerónimo slaves repeatedly returned to the courts in ongoing efforts to loosen their bondage. In 1818 four enslaved men sued the hacienda's administration on behalf of all the slaves there. They charged that the negros caribes persisted in mistreating them, pursuing them even with firearms, and they complained that the management regularly delayed paying their Saturday wages in order to force them to report for overtime on Sundays.

In a written response to the suit the plantation's mayordomo, the Dominican friar Andrés Pintelos, sought to refute the slaves' claims. He denied that the overseers had committed any mistreatment, and he tried to justify the Sunday work assignments. The sugar would deteriorate overnight, he said, if the workers were not made to haul it just 300 paces from the boiling house to the building where it would be drained. "Because many of them are reluctant to do this small job," he explained, "one *real* is withheld from them until they do it." Pintelos was unable to mask his annoyance at the slaves' attempt to upend what he considered their proper relationship with the hacienda. "It is odd," he wrote, "that they complain of the retention of one *real* for only one night [on Saturdays], when all or most of them always have many wage advances."

Informed of the friar's response, the slaves petitioned again. They retracted their complaint about working on Sundays and demanded instead that their daily assignments be reduced on account of the Sunday jobs.[34] Pintelos ultimately acceded, grudgingly, to the workload reduction. His words convey his perception that the hierarchy of slaves and masters was collapsing; even as he submitted to the slaves' demand, his tone rose in frustration. "These slaves must understand that the master is free to give the chores by task, or by day," he wrote. His response amounts to a protest that the slaves were challenging the hacienda's power over them. In particular, he decried their repeated collective judicial appeals:

Some of these slaves are persuaded that just by going to the capital [to court] everything that they want will be conceded to them, and with this they threaten and intimidate the mayordomos when [the mayordomos] require [the slaves] to perform their work properly, and it is cause for some rebellious slaves to hoax those who are less aware into going with them and forming a group in their unjust demands and pretensions.

Pintelos had recognized the pattern: the slaves on his hacienda were using civil institutions to negotiate collectively the terms of their labor, thereby starting to restructure the social and economic relationships that constituted slavery.

The friar articulated the crux of the dispute in his closing: "These slaves," he wrote, "should not judge from the excessive benignity and compliance that their masters have had for them, that they cease to be truly slaves." Indeed, through their repeated litigation, the slaves had altered the conditions that in Pintelos's view made them "truly slaves." He brandished one of his remaining instruments of power over the slaves—the possibility of selling them away from the estate—as he admonished that "as slaves, they can be sold when and how their masters wish. And this . . . should be motive for them in the future to be more obedient, and compliant in their obligations."[35]

It was not long, though, before the slaves began seeking an injunction against their masters' power to sell them. Less than a year after Pintelos issued his warning, two of the same plaintiffs—Miguel González and José María Loaisa—appealed again to the colonial authorities in the capital.[36] They denounced the mayordomo for cruel and unjust treatment and decried an announcement that the hacienda's management was going "to sell entire families." In particular, they expressed alarm about the material and agricultural investments they would lose in such a sale: "Our possessions will become the property of the convent [that is, the Dominicans' convent]." González noted that he and his wife had a "piece of irrigated land, and a *vega* [a piece of lowland] of assorted fruit" that she had cultivated, and a field planted with beans. If they were transferred away from the hacienda, they would lose the crops they had raised to support their seven children.[37]

Litigation was not the only strategy the plaintiffs had used in attempting to alter the conditions of their slavery. Both José María Loaisa and Miguel González were engaged with the hacienda in longstanding imbroglios that had already taken shape outside the courts. At the time of their judicial appeals, both men had been reporting irregularly for work. Loaisa blamed his inconsistency on Friar Pintelos, saying the priest had "impeded" him from laboring on the estate. Because the slaves were paid in wages, Loaisa implied, his exclusion from work had cut off his source of livelihood. He said Pintelos had told him to find someone else to purchase him. Witnesses indicated that Loaisa had found paid work elsewhere. His wife was still living on the hacienda; for the record, she claimed not to know his whereabouts.

Miguel González too had come and gone rather freely from the Hacienda San Jerónimo. Friar Pintelos charged that González had fled from the estate and had been living as a fugitive for some two years, "moving about these environs [by day and] entering his house by night." The slave litigants gave a somewhat different story; they said González had been unable to work because of injuries he had suffered in a fall from a horse while herding cattle on the estate. González himself totaled his absence from work to seven months, not two years. In any case, the stories concur in depicting González's irregular attendance on the job even while he continued to live with his family on the hacienda. He ultimately returned to work in April 1819, evidently because he needed wages. But Friar Pintelos balked. When González went to collect his salary after a week's labor, Pintelos refused to pay him, and an altercation erupted. According to witnesses, González spoke insolently to the friar in front of a group of slaves. Pintelos may have beaten González (accounts vary), and the priest ordered some other slaves to tie and shackle the unfortunate man. The prisoner was dispatched to the capital, where, still in shackles, he was put to work in the kitchen of the Dominican monastery. Pintelos argued that if González had been "left without punishment it would be motivation for the rest of the slaves to do the same." Given the history of the slaves' litigation, it is not surprising that the friar feared the spread of resistance.

Miguel González was kept shackled for three or four months before he could file a complaint with the ayuntamiento. It is unclear whether he broke away from the monastery with shackles still on his body, or if they had been removed. Or perhaps he had sent for the ayuntamiento's notary to come to the monastery to take his deposition. The ayuntamiento was slow to respond to his petition. Nine months later, still slaving in the kitchen, González made another appeal. Evidently he had received news from San Jerónimo; his petition alleged that because of his involuntary absence, his wife had lost a crop of beans "that was eaten by the [estate's] cattle." Additionally, he charged, Friar Pintelos had usurped his wife's irrigated plot and the land with her fruit trees. González argued that his wife had supported him financially during his recovery from the herding accident. He noted that his health had then been further compromised by the months laboring in the heat of the kitchen. Finally, he demanded liberty. It was was the only way, he insinuated, that the Dominicans could make right on the damages they had caused. The outcome of Miguel González's case is not known (the documentation ends abruptly without a ruling).

His appeal, however, typifies a recurring pattern in which slaves contended that their financial sacrifices and suffering caused by their masters warranted the state to grant them liberty. González's narrative shows that his wife had borne the costs as well. "I had to suffer seven months," he said of his recovery from the fall, and the hacienda did not "provide me with food and medical treatment, but instead my feeble consort suffered and paid for my illness." She had also supported their children—all slaves of the hacienda—while he was unable to collect wages. Indeed, plaintiff slaves in Guatemala frequently asserted that they or their family members, rather than the slaveholder, had paid for their food, clothing, and medical care.[38] Also typical are González's charges that much of his and his wife's property (or lands they had been allowed to use) had been seized by the hacienda, and that their bean crop had been eaten by the estate's cattle. Numerous slaves similiarly demanded liberty on grounds that their masters had caused them to incur expenses or had dispossessed them of property and that their losses amounted to payment of their value as chattel.[39]

Although such suits were not often successful, they illustrate the loose nature of bondage in late colonial Guatemala. Slaves were using money, providing for themselves and their families, and managing property as their own. The San Jerónimo slave men were able to negotiate their workload and pay, refuse work when they didn't need it, leave the custody of their masters, find paid work elsewhere, and travel to the capital to litigate. Slaves' litigation itself paralleled that of free people, as they used the same courts and attorneys. Like free people, the San Jerónimo slaves owned livestock and grew their own food. The requirement to produce their food, typical for slaves in rural areas, placed an extra burden on them. Yet it also gave them a degree of independence, reducing or eliminating their reliance on the master for sustenance. Also, slaves who cultivated foods might be able to sell surpluses and accumulate cash.[40] Recall that Miguel González's wife, for example, kept an orchard and bean field. She probably intended to sell some of her produce, since she lived in a community of wage earners. The San Jerónimo slaves and others had been integrated into Hispanic society in conditions very similar to those of free workers. The economic and legal structures that distinguished slavery from freedom were crumbling.

Women seeking manumission: Cases from San Jerónimo

The records from San Jerónimo are silent on whether enslaved women performed the same chores as the men and whether the women received wages. However, it is clear that the women also sought to manipulate the terms of their labor and to gain manumission for themselves and their kin, and they used some of the same methods as did their men—appealing to the courts, purchasing the liberty of family members, gathering financial and material aid from kin. Yet like their female counterparts enslaved elsewhere in the world, the San Jerónimo women employed additional strategies specific to their gender.[41]

The life of Juana Loaisa is an example. (Her relationship, if any, to José María Loaisa is not known.) Born into slavery at San Jerónimo around the turn of the nineteenth century, Juana Loaisa was eventually freed by her mother, who paid the Dominicans the price of 100 pesos. Juana's sister continued to toil in slavery until she fell ill after the birth of one of her children. For two and a half years she was bedridden while Juana and their mother fed and cared for her and her children. Ultimately Juana's mother and sister both died, leaving the sister's two small daughters, both slaves of the hacienda, in Juana's care.

Some five years later, the estate's administrator arrived at Juana Loaisa's house and took her older niece to be sold. Loaisa followed them to the capital and appealed there to the Audiencia. She contended not only that she and her mother had provided and cared for her older niece, but also that she herself had nursed the younger niece at her own breast because the baby's mother in her illness had been unable to produce milk. She was demanding compensation from the hacienda's owners for having provided for their slaves. "I have fed for nearly seven years one slave girl of the convent," she said, "and more than fourteen months [nursed] the [smaller] girl.

I should be credited, for the eight years of supporting the two children, at least 166 pesos, supposing [a cost of] half a *real* per day." This daily rate may have been suggested by the notary; without even ending the sentence estimating a half *real* per day, he then added a protest (Loaisa's, one imagines) that this amount really "does not compensate the expense that one invests in rearing a child."[42]

However, 166 pesos would have been enough to cover the purchase price of both slave children, which would probably have totaled around 120 or 150 pesos. Indeed, Loaisa's petition hints at an underlying quest for the girls' manumission; if the convent would not agree to the payment, she proposed that she should be given "the second girl free as my own, the one that I nursed, since all wet nurses are paid and maintained for the period of lactation."[43] Her suit was probably unsuccessful. The documentation ended before any ruling was issued, but the last words recorded were those of the convent's prior, who charged that much of Loaisa's appeal was a "monstrous falsehood," particularly her claim that she had suckled her sister's baby.

Yet the story silhouettes women's efforts to free their families from bondage and to negotiate the conditions of their lives. Before Juana Loaisa's appeal, her mother had purchased Juana's liberty (and possibly also her own); Juana then petitioned the state and alleged financial and personal sacrifices for the slaveholder. Though these strategies were also employed by male slaves, much of the content of Loaisa's suit was uniquely female. Certainly lactation, through which she claimed to have sustained her niece (the slaveholder's property), was exclusively the realm of women. Loaisa referred repeatedly in the litigation to the *crianza* (rearing) of the children, a term that connoted both the labor of caring for children and the financial investment in feeding and clothing them. Whereas financial support was viewed as appropriate to either male or female roles, child care was generally considered a female task. Loaisa argued that with her mother's help she had provided all these components of crianza—both the exclusively female chores and those that might fall to either gender.

Similar arguments about women's work and slave liberation appear in the lawsuit we have seen by Miguel González. González alleged that his late mother had been unable to accumulate the cost of his manumission only because she had "sheltered and supported seven orphans of a tender age, slaves of the same ingenio who would have perished if she had not taken them in." This is not only another example of women in slave families caring for orphaned slave children; it also shows that Miguel González recognized, even expected, that a mother might purchase her offspring's freedom, as Juana Loaisa's mother had done. Further, his testimony echoes Juana Loaisa's contention that workers who reared slave children at their own expense should be compensated by the slaveholder, with money or freedom papers. "During the time of the crianza of the children," González said, "the [Dominican] convent did not give or transfer to my mother a single *real* for their food and clothing." But as soon as the children reached the age where they could work, he noted, the convent "has had the right and authority to sell them away here in the city, and to enjoy the income from their sale, having forgotten that my mother is owed for their subsistence."[44] González was arguing that the Dominicans should repay their debt to his mother by liberating him.

These cases highlight the importance of kinship networks in loosening the bonds of enslavement. We have seen too that both Miguel González and José María Loaisa lived with their wives, who doubtless helped provide food even when the men were evading work assignments and going without wages. Although the alcalde mayor of Verapaz claimed that the San Jerónimo slaves did not like to marry Indians because they were subject to tribute requirements, the noticeable presence of mulata and mulato workers on the hacienda suggests that slave–Indian free unions were not uncommon.[45] The multiethnic environment of the Hacienda San Jerónimo, with slaves laboring alongside free people and Indian tribute workers, mirrored the circumstances of most slaves in Central America in both rural and urban areas. On smaller estates where slaves comprised only minorities of worker communities, interethnic relationships were perhaps more often the norm and even more important. Slaves held in small numbers had less power to negotiate collectively, but interethnic social and kinship networks at smaller enterprises helped link them to the free world.

Social networks and emancipation on a smaller hacienda: The Elegant Hoof

The multiethnic environment at small rural estates fostered a range of social relationships—including courtship, marriage, and kinship, not to mention employment and patronage—between people of different ethnicities and between slaves and free people. The lives of María Micaela de la Cruz and José Longinos Barrientos illustrate this point.[46] Residents of the cattle-raising region of Zacapa in the lowlands east of the capital, the couple was married in the 1760s. De la Cruz was the mulata slave of a doña Lorenza Guillén; Barrientos was a free muleteer who could sign his surname in a rough hand. He is alternately described in the record as "pardo libre" (a free man of dark complexion) and "mulato."

Before she was wed to Barrientos, de la Cruz already had a small daughter known among locals to have been fathered by "a European" (whom they never named in the record). Following the marriage, the slave-holder Guillén allowed José Barrientos to move into her house to live with his new wife. But six or seven years later she sold de la Cruz and her two surviving children, the daughter of the European and a son by Barrientos. The buyer, doña Francisca Ponce de León, was an elderly single woman with no children. She lived in the Zacapa area on her estate, the Hacienda Pata Galana (literally, the Elegant Hoof Hacienda).[47] Barrientos followed his wife, son, and stepdaughter to Pata Galana and built a house there, next to the house of the new slaveowner. He eventually freed de la Cruz, paying Ponce de León for her purchase price.

However, the couple necessarily stayed at Pata Galana since their surviving children, now numbering four, remained enslaved there. Barrientos diversified his enterprises, using the hacienda as a base. Though his transport business often had him on the road or in the capital, he also kept a mule-breeding operation at Pata Galana and traded in various livestock. His efforts, presumably aided by his wife, met with some financial success. By the early 1780s the couple had accumulated sufficient cash to redeem their four children from slavery. Their story comes to light, though, because the slaveholder refused to give up her slaves, citing the difficulty of finding workers in the area. In 1782, Barrientos and de la Cruz sued doña Francisca Ponce de León before the Audiencia, demanding that she allow them to purchase their children's liberty. Unfortunately for the family, the court ultimately upheld Ponce de León's right to refuse the sale.

The decision, however, came only after lengthy and bitter litigation. The surviving record depicts the social proximity in which the slave children, their parents, the slaveholder, and various others had been living. Responding to the suit, Ponce de León alleged that Barrientos had been pasturing his animals on her estate without rent. Further, she charged, he had enjoyed free use of her patio for breeding mules and had even kept a burro tied to her house for this purpose. Barrientos countered that he, not the slaveholder, had fed and clothed the children and that he had cared for them in his house when they were struck by smallpox. Ponce de León replied that she had asked her brother, a priest, to look in on the children during the epidemic.

Barrientos complained that Ponce de León had treated the children with cruelty. Ponce de León answered that she had beaten the oldest child, Gertrudis, specifically because she disapproved of the girl's courtship with a free *negro* who worked on a neighboring estate. The suitor, a youth or man named Liandro Rivera, had reputedly offered to pay the price of Gertrudis's liberty in exchange for her hand in marriage. Gertrudis was the daughter of Micaela de la Cruz and the unidentified European; she was sixteen or seventeen years old and known locally for her beauty and

European appearance. "The slave is a pretty girl," wrote Ponce de León's attorney, "and as white . . . as an española." He argued that his client had "punished" the girl to prevent her from marrying Liandro Rivera. Ponce de León (the attorney asserted) viewed the girl with "hopes of providing her a regular marriage to a free subject of some means"—someone of higher socioeconomic status than Liandro Rivera. The claim that the beating was for the slave's own good sounds disingenuous at best, but the attorney's argument demonstrates the contemporary understanding of social realities. Social relations in the countryside were fluid enough that a mulata slave might marry someone of substantial means, and they were dense enough that a slaveholder might arrange such a marriage for her slave.

In the parade of local people called to testify, everyone knew both the muleteer Barrientos and the slaveholder Ponce de León personally. The witnesses included part-time and year-round residents of Zacapa, men from a range of social strata—two Spaniards titled "don" and a free mulato named as witnesses for Barrientos, and two Spaniards and a man of unidentified race called by Ponce de León. All of them knew the details of the case and had specific information to add. This was a community where people of various calidades and social classes interacted with each other in the normal rhythm of quotidian life. Even as slaves, Micaela de la Cruz and her teenage daughter Gertrudis had myriad associations in the area. Consider de la Cruz's previous liaison with the European father of her daughter; her marriage to a free man; the couple's cohabitation with the slaveholder doña Lorenza Guillén; de la Cruz's subsequent residence in close proximity to her next owner, doña Francisca Ponce de León; and finally the enslaved daughter's courtship with a free man of sufficient means to purchase her liberty.

Ponce de León's attorney said it during the course of the litigation: the slaveholder herself, her slaves, and the free residents of her hacienda had been living and doing their chores in "one common patio" (*un mismo patio*).[48] On a literal level, the slaves and other residents of the Hacienda Pata Galana shared living and work space inside a house and in a common patio between houses. Metaphorically as well, social and economic relations had brought the Barrientos–de la Cruz family and doña Francisca Ponce de León together into a shared patio of social and economic life.

Like Micaela de la Cruz and her children, most slaves in Guatemala were linked to social and economic networks that crossed lines of race, gender, and social status. In urban areas as well, slaves relied on social connections not only for day-to-day survival but also as avenues in the pursuit of liberty. These networks sometimes included the slaveholder and his or her family members, but the slave's own relatives and spouse were more likely allies. Paradoxically, in the face of the slave trade's practical disregard for the preservation of families, slave families repeatedly played a pivotal role in manumissions. The recurring pattern of cooperation among family members, combined with the unending stream of slaves crossing by one means or another into freedom, suggests the shape of slave emancipation as that of a collective project.

Routes to emancipation, routes to the city

In the city as in the countryside, slaves used a wide range of strategies to seek liberty or, in some cases, mitigation of their bondage. A frequent method of redemption was to pay one's own purchase price or to have a relative pay it.[49] Another path originated with the master. Some slaveholders on their deaths manumitted their slaves (or some of their slaves) in a clause in the will; others stipulated that the slaves should be sold at a reduced price, thereby paving the way to manumission. Unfortunately, people who were promised liberty or a price discount on the death of their masters sometimes then were enslaved by the masters' heirs, in violation of the wills. Litigation was one remedy, though to pursue it the slave had to know of the testament and needed access to the judicial system. A number of slaves brought such cases to the courts only years after their masters' deaths, when they were sold or taken to a new location.[50] Other slaves sued for freedom on grounds that their masters before dying had made oral promises of liberty, though such suits were not often successful.[51]

Enslaved people used whatever tactics they had at hand. In the 1770s Juan Alejos de Estrada, a slave on one of the Augustinian order's haciendas, repeatedly kidnapped four or five horses from the estate and then made demands in exchange for their return. The Augustinians' lawyer (himself a member of the order) complained that they had been unable to stop the extortion or to catch the slave.[52] In 1796 Isabel Arreze gave her master some winning lottery tickets in exchange for a freedom paper. He didn't know that the tickets were forgeries, procured by Arreze's lover specifically for this purpose. When the master realized he had been duped, he tried to revoke the manumission, but the Audiencia upheld the validity of the paper he had signed.[53]

MOVEMENT AND FLIGHT

Flight was a common route to extralegal liberation, and by the late colonial years it had sapped slavery's viability. Slave flight vexed slaveowners endlessly. On occasion they reported the runaways to the authorities, but it made little difference; fugitive slaves were rarely returned, except by their own volition. I have found only two cases documenting the return of runaways. The first case is that of Manuela Ramos, described later in this chapter (in the family history of María Apolinaria Castellanos, Ramos's mother). The other case involved fourteen slaves reported missing by sugar magnate don José Jacinto Palomo in 1775. Eleven were men; three were women, perhaps with children in tow. When the slaves—at least some of them—were finally returned, Palomo complained that the militia colonel who caught them had charged him exorbitantly for the services. Palomo could certainly afford to pay, but he may have questioned whether it was worthwhile, knowing that the returnees might again absent themselves. The most remarkable point, though, is that the runaways were captured only in April of 1779, more than four years after Palomo's initial plea. They had been circulating effectively as free people for years. Palomo knew that one of the missing men, Juan Chiapa, was working for the officer in charge of the *garita* (customhouse) in Jocotenango, just outside the capital city; another had become the employee of the *comisario* in the Valley of Chibaque, in the alcaldía mayor of Chimaltenango. Both locations were several days' journey from Palomo's estate in Jalapa.[54]

Fifteen years later, an absentee slave of don José Jacinto Palomo entered the record in a rather dazzling case of de facto liberation. The man was Manuel Antonio Hernández (possibly the same Manuel Hernández whom Palomo had reported among the runaways in 1775). In 1791 Manuel Antonio Hernández left Palomo's estate, making his way to the capital despite the crippling effects of syphilis. He was welcomed in the city by his half-sister, a free housekeeper named Apolonia Olavarrieta. Palomo sent his son to Olavarrieta's house to retrieve the slave, but to no avail. Olavarrieta refused to turn him over, and she insisted that Palomo owed her money for medicine and clothing she had bought for her brother.

After three years and no reimbursement from Palomo, Olavarrieta sued him. She alleged that she had invested over 200 pesos in her brother's medical treatment alone. Among other things, she had hired an Indian man from Jocotenango to take care of him and had paid for him to make a pilgrimage to the Black Christ of Esquipulas in the eastern reaches of Guatemala. (This image carved in the sixteenth century continues today to draw people seeking healing.) "God knows the work it cost me to make that money and see him recovered, back on his feet, as he is today," she said in her suit.[55] The eighteen witnesses she presented demonstrate her connections with a wide socioeconomic cross-section of the city's populace. Palomo countered, arguing that Olavarrieta had usurped his slave's labor. He demanded that she compensate him monetarily and return the slave. The court ultimately dismissed Palomo's suit and ruled in Olavarrieta's favor, ordering the slaveowner to pay her expenses. The judges said nothing about returning the fugitive, who was by this time was living in a rented room in the garita at one of the entrances to the city.[56]

In similar style, most runaway slaves in the colony appear essentially to have gone AWOL. Recall Manuel González, for example, who came and went for months at a time from the Hacienda San Jerónimo. The brothers Luca and José Arrivillaga, both slaves of doña Tomasa Castilla, were moving about as fugitives from her sugar estate during most of the 1790s. Castilla noted in 1799 that some of her other slaves were also on the lam.[57] Runaway slaves usually found work elsewhere, selling or bartering their labor as free people would. In the 1770s, several Spanish dons complained that the colony's provincial officers, rather than aiding in the return of missing slaves, were employing them.[58]

The preponderance of men among fugitives is no coincidence. Women's charge of child care, not to mention pregnancy, made it harder for them to strike out as migrants. But women did flee, sometimes motivated by a precipitating episode of egregious mistreatment. In 1785 a slave named Mauricia fled Nueva Guatemala shortly after her master died, when his widow doña Cecilia Gala whipped her with fifty lashes. Notably, Mauricia was only fourteen; she likely had no children. She went to Antigua, to the home of the deceased master's daughter, who was Gala's stepdaughter (and was feuding with Gala over the estate). Within a few months the stepdaughter purchased Mauricia, in effect legitimizing the slave's own arrangement.[59] The slave María Josefa Godines fled her master's home in the capital in 1789, also following a cruel punishment; her hair had been cut off and she had been locked in a dark room, brought food only twice a day. After four days she escaped through a hole she had dug in the wall. She appealed to the Audiencia, but the judge rejected her petition. It is not known whether she returned to the lawful owner.[60]

Urban slaves generally enjoyed greater access to the courts and to alternative forms of employment than did their counterparts in the countryside. For rural slaves, traveling to the city—within or outside the custody of the master—often figured as a step toward mitigation or liberation. Both Santiago and Nueva Guatemala were hubs of legal and extralegal emancipations; the concentration of wealth and Spanish homes there enabled fugitives from the countryside and other ex-slaves to find jobs.[61] Despite the predominance of adult women in the urban population, Spaniards complained of the shortage of domestic servants in the city.[62] Female slaves pursuing litigation against their masters (or simply fleeing) readily obtained room and board in Spanish homes where they offered to work.[63] As for men, the construction of the new capital starting in the 1770s increased the demand for male workers and drove their wages up.

SLAVES SEEKING EMPLOYERS: THE *PAPEL DE VENTA*

An outstanding feature of slavery and the slave market in late colonial Guatemala was the *papel de venta*—literally, "paper of sale"— a mechanism by which slaves solicited their own buyers.[64] Drawn up by the slaveholder, the papel de venta announced that the slave was for sale. It gave the slave's name and price and the name of the owner or another person for prospective buyers to contact. The paper was given to the slave, who would carry it in search of a new master. The law did not require slaveholders to sell slaves who wanted to be sold, and some slaveholders evidently punished their slaves for even asking.[65] But some slaves requested and obtained papeles de venta.

This happened frequently enough that the phrase *pedir papel* ("to ask for a paper") was understood in court documents to refer to a slave's request for a papel de venta.[66] Occasionally the papel de venta may represent a slaveholder's last-ditch effort to get some money in a sale, rather simply freeing a recalcitrant slave or risking the slave's departure. In 1817, for example, don Tomás Arroyave and his wife doña Felipa Madrid sent their slave Catalina Ordóñez to seek a new master, evidently out of exasperation. But there was no sale. The story entered the record because Catalina's son then sued for her liberation on grounds that doña Felipa had beaten her. Don Tomás responded that the injuries she was presenting as evidence had resulted from whipping by previous masters. He alleged that Catalina had been especially rebellious, absenting herself from his house for four months at one point. Other servants in the household attested that she had been doing only the lightest work. "No one wants to buy her," don Tomás complained, "not even on credit." He may have been hoping for a purchase by a mulato man named Juan Martínez, also known as Juan el Zapatero (Juan the Shoemaker). Martínez had been courting Catalina and said he planned to marry her. Indeed, he had sent her a love letter penned by a hired scribe and now sewn into the record of the suit, and one imagines he was the father of her twins. But apparently he did not have the means to purchase her liberty.[67] Ordóñez had her emancipation inscribed in the 1824 registry, saying that she had been freed by the executor of don Tomás Arroyave's will.[68]

In other cases, though, the papel de venta was in earnest, a genuine step to sell a valuable worker, as some of the following examples will illustrate. Slaves soliciting their own purchase were in a position of terrible paradoxes: they were the primary agents in the market in which their bodies and ownership of their labor were being sold.

Behind this irony, however, the papel de venta demonstrates that the distinction between slavery and free labor was crumbling. The papel de venta was predicated on slaves' freedom of movement and cultural assimilation in colonial society, particularly their knowledge of Spanish; the papel was circulated to prospective buyers by the slave's unchaperoned movement in Hispanic society. Yet slaves did not necessarily choose to exit the system by disappearing with the papel. Those who did solicit buyers were in essence applying for new jobs, seeking new shelter and sustenance or wages. These experiences mirrored those of the free laborers who lived in their employers' homes and changed jobs frequently. The use of the papel de venta—the fact that slaves chose to solicit their sale rather than to enact an escape— signals that, from the viewpoint of many slaves, slavery had become markedly similar to free labor.

BUYING FREEDOM, NEGOTIATING THE PRICE

The possibility of manumission through payment seems to have been well-known in late colonial Guatemala among slaves as well as free people. Both groups understood the words *rescate* and *rescatar(se)* as referring to self-purchase or to the purchase of a slave's freedom by kin.[69] Previous studies have shown that this phenomenon began in the sixteenth century in Guatemala (as elsewhere in Spanish America) and that it was quite common by the mid-eighteenth century.[70]

For slaves who received wages there was at least in theory a possibility of cash accumulation and, at best, self-purchase. In contrast to the slave community at the Hacienda San Jerónimo, slaves held in small numbers could hardly bargain collectively for wages. Yet some were paid with money. The brothers Mariano and Patricio Araujo, both slaves in Nueva Guatemala, maintained their wives and children with the wages they earned in their *oficios* or trades (which are are not identified in the record).[71] Francisco Ugalde, also a slave in the new capital, was earning wages and hoping to buy his liberty.[72] Bernarda Reyes was a slave at a small sugar estate evidently staffed mainly by free wage workers; she too received a salary in coin.[73] Still, wages did not necessarily enable slaves to accumulate money and purchase freedom, since the wages might be needed for necessities including food. As we have seen with Miguel González and Juana Loaisa, slaves and their free kin sometimes complained specifically that costs they incurred in supporting children and other relatives had prevented them from amassing cash to purchase freedom. Though slaveholders were legally obligated to allow slaves two hours a day to work for their own profit, it is hard to know how often this law was followed. Manuel Trinidad, for one, complained that his enslaved wife and children had never been allotted these hours (we will see his case in the following pages).

Liberty was not cheap. Young adult slaves in Nueva Guatemala typically sold for prices between 150 and 250 pesos, an amount that could buy a modest house in town. Children were appraised at lower values, often 50 to 60 pesos for a child between the ages of five and ten. Enslaved parents seem generally to have liberated themselves before their children, probably with the goal of more rapidly increasing the family's earnings. Guatemalan records do not reveal anything quite like the Cuban system of *coartación*, in which slaves formally gained partial ownership of their time or labor as they made payments toward their purchase.[74] Occasionally, though, Guatemalan slaves or their kin paid the slaveholder in installments, gradually working toward emancipation.[75]

Some slaves tried to negotiate a reduction in their prices. The archives contain appeals made to both masters and the state by slaves seeking lower reappraisals of their values. The results of these efforts varied. The enslaved man José Mariano Sínforo met with an unfortunate refusal. He was sold in childhood for 100 pesos, and when he was fourteen his price was evaluated at 200 pesos. At age twenty-five, he was sold to the Marqués de Aycinena, Guatemala's most honored Spaniard, for 250 pesos.[76] This was in 1783, when construction in the new capital was in full swing and the demand for labor at an apex. Seven years later, in 1790, as the building boom waned, Sínforo petitioned the Audiencia. His sale at the price of 250 pesos precluded the possibility, he said, "that I might ever liberate myself from this slavery, or solicit a master, if the present one should fail me." He asked that the man who last sold him be required to refund 150 pesos to the marqués, thereby reducing his price to 100 pesos. The Audiencia flatly rejected his request.[77] The *oidores* (judges) of the Audiencia may have thought that such a large cash refund would be difficult to collect, and they may have been swayed by the prestige and power of the marqués, who along with his extended family held enormous influence in the colony's elite business and political circles. Further, the ruling was not unreasonable from a legal standpoint. Since Sínforo was only about thirty-two years old, he was still valuable as property, and the Audiencia's decision served to protect the marqués's investment.

A more successful appeal was that of Manuel Trinidad, a free man who had fathered six children by his enslaved wife. Around 1809, the wife and children were sold to don Miguel López of Cahabón, Verapaz, for a total of 450 pesos—an average of about 64 pesos for each person. On his death López distributed the children among his heirs. Two of the youngsters died soon afterwards. (It is not known what happened to Trinidad's wife, who is mentioned only briefly in the record.) In 1818 Trinidad asked the heirs for papeles de venta (papers of sale) for the four surviving children. The heirs responded by raising the prices, setting the value of three of the children at 120, 90, and 80 pesos respectively. One child, probably the smallest, was offered for 50 pesos. Trinidad went to the Audiencia, accusing the heirs of mistreating his children and demanding that their prices be reduced. He argued that the masters had denied the slaves the legal allocation of hours to work for their own gain. If these hours had been allowed, he contended, the family would already have saved enough to free the children. Two of López's heirs conceded, reducing the prices of 120 and 90 pesos to 60 and 50 pesos respectively. Trinidad immediately purchased the freedom of both of these children. Though the record is incomplete, initial responses from the other two heirs suggest that they too were disposed to lower their prices.[78]

The possibility for slaves to dispute their valuations—along with the possibility to request a papel de venta—lent them some leverage in the market in which they were being sold. An example is that of Ignacio Escudero, a León (Nicaragua) house slave. Escudero was purchased around 1780 by don Pedro Soriano for 300 pesos. When the slave requested a papel de venta, Soriano raised his price to 350 pesos. Escudero turned to the alcalde in León. Soriano "has taxed me fifty pesos more," Escudero charged, "without having taught me a craft or treated me for any disease." The alcalde reprimanded Soriano for the price hike, but Soriano did not budge. Escudero later recounted how he then "went with the papel [de venta] to the house of don Manuel Taboara imploring him to do me the favor of buying me; [and] in fact he bought me for 350 pesos." Escudero's situation points to the possibility that the slave trade in regions far from the Audiencia may have been less subject to state controls. In selling Escudero, Soriano had violated the regulation that set a slave's price equal to that of the previous sale.

The violation was ultimately corrected, but only because Escudero had occasion to travel to Guatemala and appeal to the Audiencia in 1786. Apparently he had arrived there in the company of his new master don Manuel de Taboara, whose testimony in the case confirmed Esudero's story. The "price increase is very injurious [to Escudero]," Taboara said, "since he is looking to liberate himself, and I am willing to give him liberty provided that he pays me the price that I gave for him." Escudero was requesting that Soriano (the seller) be made to refund 50 pesos to Taboara, in accordance with the established price of the last buyer. The Audiencia ordered Soriano to make the rebate, in effect lowering the price of Escudero's liberty. Escudero had thus configured his sale to a new master as a step toward emancipation.[79]

Other slaves made similar plays in the market. Josefa Ordóñez of Zacapa got a papel de venta from her master, then went to the capital and petitioned the court to reduce her price from 200 to 150 pesos.[80] Isidora

Morales petitioned not for a price reduction but for more time. Her price had been set at 100 pesos, and she had already handed over 49 pesos when she was "dismissed" from her mistress's house, she said, for a "trifling quarrel." The mistress was demanding that the slave immediately pay the remaining 51 pesos. "But it is impossible for me to pay the fifty-one pesos within the brief period that I am being given," Morales said, "for one thing because my mother is supporting me, and with her small salary of four pesos she cannot help me any further." Morales added that she herself was ill, unable at the moment to find another job. She was asking for more time until she could recover her health and finish paying for her manumission. Presumably, she feared being sold and losing the 49 pesos she had already invested. The outcome of her case was not recorded, though apparently the mistress did not object.[81]

CROSSING OVER ON CREDIT

When price could not be paid or renegotiated, an another possibility remained: the purchase of freedom on credit. I can confirm that slaves used credit to buy their liberty in only two cases, but evidence hints in other cases as well that slaves or their family members had borrowed the money to pay for redemption. (Confirmation is difficult because the scattered records that mention slave manumissions by purchase do not always reveal the sources of the money.) Recall the free black man Manuel Huebo, who bought the liberty of his entire family for a cool 700 pesos—probably at least partly a loan. Slaves and slaveholders alike seem to have recognized that liberty might be purchased on credit. We have seen, for example, Francisco Ugalde, a slave who was earning wages in the new capital. Married to a free woman, Ugalde proposed to his owners in 1792 that he buy his liberty on credit and to repay the debt over the next two years at a rate of 7 pesos per month. "This is what I and my wife can earn," he said. The owners asked for a *fiador* (a guarantor to provide surety), and Ugalde named don Ventura Nájera, Guatemala's leading cattle rancher. One imagines that Ugalde had contracted to work for him. The outcome of Ugalde's proposal—whether he was manumitted—was not recorded.[82]

A confirmed example dates to 1777, when the freedman Eugenio de los Angeles gave his former master 600 pesos in cash to redeem his wife and their five children from slavery. He had borrowed the money. The case entered the courts because the slaveholder, sugar tycoon don José Jacinto Palomo, refused to liberate one of de los Angeles's daughters. Quibbling over an appraisal made the previous year, the slaveholder demanded an additional 74 pesos and 3½ reales. De los Angeles appealed to the Audiencia. His attorney, the procurator for the poor, pointed out that the plaintiff owned nothing but his labor as a *labrador* (agricultural worker), and he still needed to repay much of the 600-peso loan. (At the time of the last appraisal, Eugenio de los Angeles himself had been a slave; his value was set at zero because of his age.) Though the Audiencia upheld de los Angeles's obligation to pay the additional sum, the judges ruled that the daughter should be freed and the father allowed six more months to make the payment. Thus de los Angeles had received even further credit to pay for the liberty of his family. The record does not identify the lender of the 600 pesos, but de los Angeles's attorney mentioned that he had help from relatives. His ability to secure such a sum suggests a redoubtable network of contacts.[83]

A second case is that of Luisa Montúfar. A slave of one of the capital's most prominent Spaniards, Montúfar petitioned the Audiencia in April 1806.[84] The problem, she explained, was that her master was planning to sell her to a man from Comayagua (in what is now Honduras). It would be burdensome for her, the petition said, "to have to go to such a distant place, to leave her relatives, and above all to go to experience different peculiarities, styles, and customs," especially since she expected within six months to have the 117 pesos to purchase her freedom. She was asking the Audiencia to grant her a "moratorium for the payment of her liberty."

Her master responded that he had already sold her. The new owner, don Justo de los Campos, was impatiently preparing to leave for Comayagua. He was unwilling, he said, "to wait six months for the price of her liberty" since he didn't believe she would be able to gather the money. He also complained that on the day she filed her appeal, she left his house in the capital and had since been moving about freely. He asked that her petition be denied and that she be arrested and jailed until he was ready to depart. He did, however, leave one door open. He would consent to her remaining behind in Guatemala if she could find another buyer to pay her appraised price within six months.

Essentially de los Campos was indicating that he would accept payment from another Spaniard on credit, but he did not think Montúfar herself was creditworthy. Montúfar enlisted the aid of a fiador (guarantor), a man called Pantaleón Montúfar who owned a house in the capital and other property that he offered as collateral. Still, de los Campos refused. In early June Luisa Montúfar made a panicked appeal to the Audiencia, saying that de los Campos was preparing to leave with her the next morning for his hacienda in Comayagua. "I ask that don Justo de los Campos be ordered to accept the surety," she said, and "not to compel me to go in his company." Later that day, however, even as the Audiencia's officials were verifying the offer made by Pantaleón Montúfar, Luisa Montúfar returned to the court and alerted them to suspend the proceedings. She had found another fiador, don Víctor Zavala, evidently more acceptable to de los Campos. De los Campos had already agreed to Zavala's surety, she explained, and the case was resolved. Luisa Montúfar got her freedom on credit from don Víctor Zavala.[85]

Like Eugenio de los Angeles, to get the loan for manumission Luisa Montúfar had tapped a social network that included free people. It is tempting to think that Pantaleón Montúfar was a relative of hers, since they shared a surname and he was her creditor of first recourse. Indeed her attorney had alluded to her relatives in the area. Though Pantaleón Montúfar owned a house in the city, he appears to have been relatively humble; he lacked the honorific "don," and his credit was dubious in the opinion of don Justo de los Campos. Pantaleón Montúfar was rarely (or never) mentioned again in the city's records. Don Víctor Zavala commanded higher status; he used the title "don," his credit was honored, and his legal and financial affairs generated numerous records now preserved in the colonial archives. It is not known how Luisa Montúfar secured Zavala's backing. Perhaps she agreed to work for him, or perhaps Pantaleón Montúfar on Luisa's behalf offered something in exchange for Zavala's help.

Slaves' use of financing to buy their freedom, like other patterns of slave emancipation that we have seen, depicts their growing integration into hispanized society and social networks. It was precisely these networks that provided access to loans.

Sexual violence and manumission

Negotiations for manumission took gender-specific forms notably among female slaves and ex-slaves, whose roles included not only agricultural and household chores but also reproduction and childrearing. Recall, for example, the freedwoman Juana Loaisa of the Hacienda San Jerónimo. When the Dominican owners planned to sell Loaisa's niece away from the hacienda, Loaisa protested in court, arguing that she had reared her late sister's children and had nursed the youngest at her own breast. The slave-holders were appropriating the labor that Loaisa had provided in the form of child care and the milk that she had provided from her body. In her litigation, Loaisa was demanding compensation for some of the economic and sexual exploitations of women that that were built into American slave systems.

In addition, a number of enslaved women in Guatemala brought lawsuits over sexual violence and sexual exploitation by their masters or other Spanish men. Their suits demanded reparations or compensation, generally in the form of manumission or money that would be used to pay for manumission.[86] Some of these women charged that they had participated in a sexual relationship in exchange for a promise of freedom that had then gone unfulfilled. Manuela Ramos is an example. In 1793, she filed suit against don Pedro Ayau, a thirty-something Frenchman who six years earlier had been working in her masters' house in the capital. Ramos alleged that she had consented to his sexual solicitations with the agreement that he would give her the money to purchase her liberty—which he had then failed to do. She had become pregnant by Ayau, she said, and her baby, a girl named María de la Asunción, was born into slavery. Despite a parade of witnesses who testified on Ramos's behalf, the judges ultimately ruled that she had not proven that Ayau was the child's father. She was not awarded any money.[87] We will see more about Manuela Ramos later in the chapter. As for don Pedro Ayau, he continued to be targeted in paternity suits by various women.[88] His humble origins in Provence and his rise to fortune in Guatemala as a self-styled don are described in Chapter 3.

The colonial courts might doubt or dismiss slaves' claims of sexual exploitation even in cases involving physical force or violence. In 1814, for example, the same Manuela Ramos went to the ayuntamiento charging that her enslaved daughter María de la Asunción had been raped by their mistress's brother. The ayuntamiento dismissed the case even before hearing arguments. Ramos then appealed to the Audiencia, describing how the mistress's brother, don Francisco Argüello y Aguilar, had been staying in the house and sleeping in a private room where María de la Asunción was assigned to serve him. It was there that the alleged rape occurred. Despite María de la Asunción's "powerful resistance," the suit charged, don Francisco had "forcefully covered her mouth to keep her from shouting, as she tried to do; and as the room was without immediate communication with the rest of the house, he managed to press her down lasciviously with his superior strength."

Don Francisco's attorney sought to locate responsibility in the actions of María de la Asunción. "If this unchaste girl hadn't been so easy, nothing would have happened to her," he said.[89] She should have complained to the mistress about serving the young man, he argued, to have "remedied" the situation. The lawyer was blaming the victim rather than the rapist—a pattern that also characterized Guatemalan judicial responses to free women's accusations of sexual violence.[90] Further, he contended that María de la Asunción had willingly consented to don Francisco's advances believing that "to consent and become pregnant was the surest road to liberating herself."[91] Implicit in his statement was the idea that an enslaved woman might exchange sex for manumission or that a pregnancy by a man of means could be a route to emancipation.

María de la Asunción had indeed gotten pregnant, and she gave birth to a baby boy. But don Francisco evidently had no intentions of purchasing her liberty, much less doing anything for his infant son. Ramos's lawsuit, brought after the birth, was demanding that the mistress (don Francisco's sister) free both María de la Asunción and the baby. The proposed liberty was meant (in the words of the attorney) as "payment and indemnification for the violation of her virginity, and the criminal violence and force that she suffered." The mistress should be held responsible, Ramos implied, not only because she had placed María de la Asunción in harm's way but also because she had failed to provide anything for the baby, not even "a diaper in which to wrap him." This was another suit demanding liberty as compensation for mistreatment by a slaveholder and for debts owed for the support of a slave child.

The judge ordered a *juicio verbal*—a personal appearance by the slaves and the owner—of which no record survives, if it ever took place. It appears that the slaves had already achieved at least a tentative freedom. Shortly after the suit was filed, the mistress departed for her hacienda, leaving both Manuela Ramos and her daughter María de la Asunción behind in the city. Presumably María de la Asunción also had her baby with her, since he was still nursing. The mistress apparently had left no provisions for them, and the mistress's attorney suggested that the court declare both Manuela Ramos and María de la Asunción free to find work in the city and earn their living while the litigation was pending.[92]

From one standpoint, the attorney's suggestion that slave women might exchange sexual "consent" for liberty raises a possibility: perhaps slave women fabricated legal demands based on sham allegations of sexual coercion or on unfounded claims of promised manumission. This possibility is interesting for its implications about slave women's manipulations of the judicial system. By their nature, though, the records don't reveal whether plaintiffs' charges were true or false. However, there are cases in which women apparently participated in sexual relationships without the promise of liberty and later went to the courts seeking manumission on grounds that they had been exploited. An example is the appeal of María del Carmen Beteta on behalf of her enslaved daughter, whose baby had been fathered by their mistress's son. Beteta argued that her daughter should be manumitted or compensated by the slaveholding family, but she did not indicate that liberty had been promised. (The outcome of Beteta's suit was not documented, though it was filed late in 1821, with the general emancipation to follow in less than three years.)[93] Another suggestive case is that of Estefania Falla, who had a daughter by her master in 1766. Twenty years later, after the master's death, Falla sued his heirs for a reduction in the price of her daughter's liberty. Falla's petition did not indicate that the master had made any promises to her, nor did it state whether her union with him had been consensual. His wife was apparently aware of the relationship, though, and in her will she had dictated some small concessions to Falla's daughter. (The extant record ends with the Audiencia's instruction for officials in the Valley of Sansaria to subpoena the daughter's master.)[94]

From another standpoint, the notion that enslaved women might broker manumission through sex may have increased their vulnerability to exploitation. The coercive pressure that slaveholders and other wealthy men could exert on enslaved women was greater because the women's freedom could be put at stake. As one slave woman's attorney noted, "It is very likely that someone who wishes to have carnal knowledge of a female slave might propose to her this inducement [purchasing her freedom], which without doubt is the greatest one."[95] Not all of these men then followed through with their part of the bargain, as demonstrated by the lawsuits filed by women left without money or freedom.

Some male slaveholders did grant liberty to their female slaves who bore their children. Records of such occurrences are scarce, though; perhaps the phenomenon was rare, or perhaps the participants took pains to shield their actions from public knowledge. An example comes to light in the case of María Leandra Conde, one of eleven slaves held by don Juan Antonio Castro and his wife in the old capital. When Conde got pregnant by her master in 1799, he drew up her *carta de libertad* (freedom paper). Seeking to keep his affair secret, apparently from his wife in particular, Castro labeled the paper as *reservada* (private) and placed it with the region's alcalde mayor. Then he left town. The carta de libertad included an addendum in which Castro indicated that the document should remain confidential for the duration of his life. Perhaps he meant for Conde to be freed only on his death. It is unclear whether he was liberating her out of affection or to fulfill a promise to her, or whether he was simply dumping her to remove the evidence of his marital infidelity—her pregnancy—from the household he shared with his wife.

In any case, the pregnant Conde immediately left the house. Castro's wife then went to the authorities to report that the slave had "run away." A barrage of correspondence among judicial officials followed, revealing that not only the alcalde mayor, but also the síndico of the ayuntamiento, the notaries, and even the members of the Audiencia knew that Castro had freed Conde precisely because he had gotten her pregnant. The magistrates determined to take no action until Castro himself should return to Guatemala, and they explicitly excluded his wife from further litigation in the case. They thereby protected Castro's secret from her and perpetuated

María Leandra Conde's de facto freedom. The documentation of the matter then ended, suggesting that Conde remained in liberty.[96]

The record does not specify whether Conde had been a willing participant in the sexual relationship with her master. Yet in the context of the inherent power imbalance between slaves and slaveholders or other Spaniards, the concept of "consensual" sex is perhaps irrelevant or at best imperfect. Slave women sometimes testified that they had chosen (or "consented") to engage in sexual relations with slaveholders or other Spanish men, based either on promises offered to them or on calculations of their own, but their choices were hardly made freely. We have seen, for example, that Manuela Ramos said she had "consented" to don Pedro Ayau's solicitations in exchange for his promise to pay for her manumission. She made that decision seeking liberation from enslavement—a situation that nobody would choose or consent to voluntarily. The violence that characterized and facilitated slavery throughout the Americas persisted in late colonial Guatemala. Even as the viability of the institution there was crumbling, evidence of severe beating of slaves entered the court records.[97] Violence against slaves created an environment of terror, lending slaveholders a degree of control that enabled them to subject slaves to work and to unwanted sexual relations. A single violent episode could help sustain this environment, reminding slaves of what might befall them if they didn't obey their masters.[98] Episodic violence could therefore govern the "choices" that slaves made, in effect eliminating any real alternatives, even without the use of constant or immediate force.

Recall Manuela Ramos's daughter María de la Asunción. We have seen that she was raped by her mistress's brother, who "forcefully covered her mouth to keep her from shouting, as she tried to do; and . . . managed to press her down lasciviously with his superior strength." As an enslaved servant, María de la Asunción was required to go into this houseguest's bedroom on a daily basis. The fact that she became pregnant suggests that she likely suffered more than a single episode of sexual assault during the year he was staying in the house. It is possible that he used physical force repeatedly, each time he had sex with her. Or it may be that after one or a few of these incidents, she calculated the futility or the danger of trying to resist, and that he was then able to continue abusing her sexually without also stifling her and pinning her down each time. Although this latter scenario would not have been equivalent to repeated use of physical force, we should still recognize it as repeated sexual assault. If the assaults were indeed ongoing, then this was a case of chronic rape.[99] The pregnancies that resulted from so many slave–Spaniard unions are evidence that such sexual relationships were often ongoing, rather than single episodes.

Consider the story of Ana María Villalonga y Sabater, who survived chronic sexual violence at the hands of her master. Several archival snapshots of Villalonga show her riding various currents of slavery's demise—including bondspeople's physical mobility, slaveowners' inability to recover runaways, slaves' agency within the slave market, and their use of the court system. But Villalonga's life also illustrates that even within a context where slaves might maneuver for their liberty, they were still subject to multiple forms of dehumanization and assault.[100]

Born in western Africa, Villalonga survived the Middle Passage and was sold in San Juan, Puerto Rico. In 1776 she was taken forcibly to Guatemala. She got a papel de venta in 1781, and shortly thereafter she sued for manumission, but the suit was unsuccessful. Ultimately she was sold to don Juan Jacinto Herrera, who took her to his home in Tegucigalpa where he chronically beat her and raped her even as she kept house for him. She explained later that she had been unable to escape in Tegucigalpa because she didn't know people there, whereas Herrera was so well known there and so "greatly supported" that she knew it be useless to seek help from the Spanish authorities. (Indeed, Herrera held the highest civil office in Tegucigalpa—alcalde provincial y regidor perpetuo.) Villalonga made her move when he brought her on a business trip back to Guatemala, where she immediately appealed to the state.

She argued that she should be manumitted because Herrera had sexually exploited her and mistreated her with cruel beatings. "When I entered the power of this Herrera," she said,

I was a virgin maiden (*niña doncella*); beginning with the journey [to Tegucigalpa] he began to solicit me, and when I did not want to submit he gave me mistreatment with punishments [that is, beatings]; and one day he pretended to be sick and asked me for some water and in the bed he grabbed me unexpectedly; not wanting to go through mistreatment and in order to get my freedom as he promised me, I had to consent; with this, he continued using my person whenever he wanted, from which I became pregnant; this was a motive for him to hate me, punishing me, and from the blows that he gave me I miscarried the baby.[101]

As Villalonga said, she "had to consent" (*hube de conscender*) to Herrera's demands, hoping to get her freedom. Yet her history of enslavement (including her removal from home and kin in Africa, and her foiled efforts to escape the custody of various owners in America), as well as the immediate circumstances of mistreatment, left her no viable option but to submit. Force and "consent" were indistinguishable. Villalonga noted bitterly that she had asked her master for the liberty that he had promised but that he had failed to deliver. Though she had come to realize that his promises were lies, she still had no real choices about "consenting" to the sexual abuse as she was under the duress of his beatings.

The outcome of Villalonga's case hinged on social contacts that she had developed in the capital city, perhaps during her long residence there before the sale to Herrera. After filing the suit, she found refuge with the parish priest of Jocotenango. Presumably she was working for him as a servant; she told the court she expected he would purchase her if she did not obtain her liberty in the suit against Herrera. With the legal action still pending, Herrera returned to Tegucigalpa without her. After two years of long-distance written litigation in which he repeatedly demanded that the authorities aid him in recovering his slave, the court finally legitimized what had become a de facto liberation. Villalonga had been in Central America for eighteen years. Her age was not recorded.[102]

The transition from slavery to freedom: Three families

The following three family portraits provide case studies of the transition from slavery to liberty. While they demonstrate the difficulty that slaves faced in achieving manumission, they also illustrate the possibility that ex-slaves might gain some mobility in Hispanic society. The first two histories are of families with the surname Castellanos, both held at one time as slaves of don Ignacio Guerra Marchán and perhaps related to each other. The third family, that of María Gertrudis Salgado, is presumably unrelated.

MARÍA APOLINARIA CASTELLANOS AND HER FAMILY:

FOUR GENERATIONS

María Apolinaria Castellanos was the mother of Manuela Ramos, whose legal actions we have seen against don Pedro Ayau and don Francisco Argüello y Aguilar.[103] A slave described as *negra*, Castellanos was sold in 1775 along with two of her children for a sum of 400 pesos. The sale transferred them from sugar baron don José Jacinto Palomo and his Ingenio Ayarza to don Francisco Barcena and his house in the capital city. Seven or eight years later, Castellanos purchased her own liberty from Barcena for 80 pesos. This relatively low price (especially in light of the earlier total valuation) may indicate that Castellanos had grown elderly or infirm, but it may be that Barcena was disposed to liberate her because of his difficulty subjugating her. He later testified that during the years she was his slave, she had repeatedly fled from his custody, "trading and doing commerce for herself, as if she were free and in charge of her own will, without giving me one cent."[104]

Castellanos's goal of liberating her son and daughter, however, proved more elusive. In a series of petitions to the Audiencia in 1783 and 1784, she complained of Barcena's mistreatment of her children, especially her daughter Manuela Ramos who was being held in jail at Barcena's request (he said it was because she had escaped from his house).[105] The *rectora* of the women's jail confirmed Castellanos's allegation that Barcena had neglected to pay the required 2 reales for Ramos' daily sustenance, which Castellanos (the slave's mother) was therefore forced to provide. Further, Ramos had fallen ill in prison, and her mother paid for her medical treatment as well. Castellanos was asking the Audiencia to make Barcena reimburse her for 10 pesos she had borrowed to pay for medicines. She was also demanding a papel de venta so that both her daughter and son could look for another master. Evidently they got the papel, but Castellanos then filed an appeal charging that Barcena had drastically inflated their established prices; he was asking 300 pesos for each of them. Barcena retorted that Castellanos had surreptitiously entered his house after her emancipation and "robbed" her daughter (his slave) from him on two occasions. The second time, he said, he had paid another Spaniard 42 pesos to retrieve the slave from a location outside the city where the mother had her "hidden" for seven or eight months. He also alleged that Castellanos and her children had stolen money and other valuables from his family members. "I will pay her what is just," he said, when "everything of which I am accusing her is paid for."[106]

Thus, Castellanos had pursued her children's liberty along several avenues even before she appealed to the Audiencia: she had sought to appropriate valuables from Barcena, presumably with the goal of purchasing her children's emancipation; she had removed her daughter from the slaveholder's house and had attempted to hide her; and she had requested papeles de venta for both her son and her daughter. Litigation was yet another tactic, but it faltered when Barcena left the city for his hacienda and apparently failed to respond to a subpoena. Documentation of the suit ended abruptly.

However, later records show that Castellanos continued her campaign for her daughter's freedom. (Her son is not mentioned again in the records; his fate is unknown.) First she suceeded in getting Ramos's price lowered. Even while Ramos was still being held in the jail, a woman called doña Josefa Corona purchased her from Barcena for 200 pesos—100 pesos less than what Barcena had hoped to charge.[107] Corona noted that she had bought the slave partly "motivated by the pleas of her mother [Castellanos]." The 200 pesos she paid was half the total sum that Barcena had paid for the mother, son, and daughter, and thus represented an increase over the price for Manuela Ramos at the previous sale. But an escalation was to be expected given that Ramos was a child at the time of sale to

Barcena and a teenager by the time of sale to Corona.[108] In Corona's custody Ramos gained not only relief from her imprisonment but also some
opportunities to accumulate cash. Assigned the daily chore of going to
the plaza to buy things for Corona's household, Ramos evidently took to
siphoning the shopping money. Corona partly blamed Castellanos, complaining that Ramos was "influenced by her mother . . . in the swindling."[109]

It was while she was a slave of doña Josefa Corona and her husband
don Agustín Zavala that Manuela Ramos gave birth to her daughter María
de la Asunción. The question of who the father was caused substantial
dispute. Various people testified that when Corona learned of the pregnancy, she tied Ramos up and made her "confess" the identity of the baby's
father. Ramos named José Estanislao Lara, a free mulato around nineteen
years old who worked at a tannery next to Corona's property. One witness recounted how Lara "would jump over the walls of [Corona's] pas-
ture to meet with la negra [Ramos], and that she took out the pans [of
leftovers] each day, at the time that her masters were asleep in their siesta,
to sustain the boy."[110] Lara had in fact begun the ecclesiastical paperwork
for marriage to Ramos, but the process was stalled because he lacked the
few pesos to complete it. The marriage would never take place. When the
baby girl was born, rumor spread that she was "the thrust of the horns of
a white bull" (*cornada de toro blanco*)—the child of a European. Indeed, a
week after the birth don Pedro Ayau, who several months earlier had been
living in the same house, reportedly came to give Ramos a small amount
of money. To the neighbors, this proved that Ayau was the child's father.[111]

Some six years later, Manuela Ramos sued don Pedro Ayau in the
Audiencia, in the case we have seen earlier in this chapter. She attested
that he, not José Estanislao Lara, had in fact fathered her child. Ayau had
solicited her affections and she had consented, she said, because he had
offered to purchase her freedom. As for her earlier statement to her owner
that José Estanislao Lara had fathered her child, Ramos explained, don
Pedro Ayau—at the time still a fledgling upstart in Spanish society—had
instructed her not to accuse him of being the father. "I blamed someone else
to save don Pedro because he had told me not to show him in a bad light
before the masters."[112] Understandably, Ramos would not have wanted
to cross the man who she was expecting would liberate her from slavery.
Even the spurned suitor José Estanislao Lara recognized Ramos's reasoning. Called to testify in her suit, Lara corroborated Ramos's statements. He
maintained that he never had sex with her but that she had named him as
the father of her baby "to free . . . don Pedro so that he would not lose the
convenience of being accommodated in the house of . . . Ramos's masters."
Lara said that Ramos herself had told him she was pregnant by Ayau and
that other people in her masters' household had confirmed her story.[113]

In her suit Ramos was demanding that don Pedro Ayau fulfill his promise of redeeming her from slavery ("me cumpla lo prometido"). Her anger at him is obvious in the record. She noted that he had not even deigned to speak with her since the birth, and she railed against his failure to liberate her from slavery even while he enjoyed a sizable personal fortune. "Seeing that it has cost me my life [that is, freedom] and that the baby will be left suffering travail as a slave," she said, "I have availed myself [of the courts] . . . so that [Ayau] does not remain as he has up to this point [scot-free] . . . in possession of more than a thousand pesos and with his own house."[114]

Even after Ramos presented her witnesses, Ayau continued to protest, insisting that José Estanislao Lara was the child's father. In the absence of DNA testing, the Audiencia sent one of its notaries to examine visually both the lass and José Estanislao Lara, and to record a description of their "features, color, and physiognomy." The findings failed to implicate a match. The child, the notary wrote, was

of white color, though not perfectly so, aquiline face, regular mouth, eyes that border on black, and Roman nose, and in everything very distinct from the features of José Estanislao Lara, since he is of swarthy color, somewhat flat-nosed, and in the mouth, eyes, and form of the face, very different from the physiognomy of the daughter of . . . Manuela Ramos.[115]

No description was recorded of either Ayau or Ramos. Ayau evidently had not even seen the child but was quick to dismiss the notary's implications and to point the finger at Lara. Invoking racialized notions of physical appearance, he argued that the description showed the child to be the daughter of mulatos, not of a European.[116] (Incidentally, Manuela Ramos was elsewhere described as negra, not mulata.) Ayau was avoiding the point that the child of a mulata (or negra) and a European might in fact have looked like the child of mulatos, and might in fact have looked just like Ramos's daughter. Racial labeling in the colony—and indeed people's perceptions of race—had become quite fluid and often contradictory; perhaps Ayau was seeking his escape in this conceptual mayhem.

As we saw earlier in this chapter, the Audiencia ruled in Ayau's favor, absolving him of Ramos's demands. The judges recorded no explanation for their decision, but likely they considered the evidence of Ayau's paternity inconclusive since it was limited to Ramos's claims, hearsay, and descriptions of physiognomies. Further, Ayau had been jailed pending resolution of the case, and he had begun complaining to the Audiencia that his imprisonment and the seizure of his property were making it difficult for him to recruit help in his defense. He was sentenced to pay only for his share of the court costs—some 29 pesos.[117]

Meanwhile, Manuela Ramos remained a slave. After the birth of her daughter the records of her life show one further sale—from doña Josefa Corona to don Ignacio Guerra Marchán. Guerra Marchán was one of the notaries for the Audiencia and apparently a neighbor, if not also a relative, of Corona.[118] Ramos' daughter María de la Asunción, a toddler at the time, was also sold to Guerra Marchán.[119]

Guerra Marchán's testament left Ramos and her daughter to his wife, doña Petronila de la Cerda, and they continued to serve in de la Cerda's household. In 1814, when María de la Asunción was about twenty-seven years old, Manuela Ramos filed the lawsuit charging that her daughter had been raped by de la Cerda's brother, who was visiting from the province of León (Nicaragua).[120] Though the record is inconclusive, the court granted license to Ramos and her daughter to work freely at least until the litigation was resolved. Given the contemporary context, it is hard to imagine that anyone was able then to reenslave them. Neither María de la Asunción nor her son—the child born of the rape—appears in the 1824 registries of the general slave emancipation in Guatemala City. Their absence there seems to bolster the hunch that they remained free after the 1814 lawsuit.

While in the custody of don Ignacio Guerra Marchán, Manuela Ramos was married to another slave, Mariano Claro Aguilar.[121] The two had at least one child, a son named Julián Aguilar, born around 1803. Guerra Marchán sold Julián as a small boy to another Spaniard, in whose custody the child remained until fleeing as a teenager. Residing in the capital as a young man, Julián Aguilar became a tailor and registered his liberty in the records of the 1824 general emancipation. He noted that his parents Manuela Ramos and Mariano Aguilar were living in Mataquescuintla, a town in the cattle-raising region east of Guatemala City with a predominantly mulato population.[122] Mataquescuintla lies on the route to the Ingenio Ayarza, don José Jacinto Palomo's sugar estate, where Ramos and her mother María Apolinaria Castellanos had lived before their 1775 transfer to the capital. It is tempting to think that Ramos was reunited in Mataquescuintla with relatives from the ingenio, which was only about fifteen miles away.

JUAN EVANGELISTA CASTELLANOS AND HIS FAMILY

Another enslaved family held by don Ignacio Guerra Marchán also used the surname Castellanos.[123] Juan Evangelista Castellanos and his wife Ignacia Antonia Velasco had been slaves of the priest don Francisco Feijóo. Feijóo freed the couple on his death in 1795, but their two small children passed as slaves into the custody of Guerra Marchán, the estate's executor. At the time, María Apolinaria Castellanos and her daughter Manuela

Ramos were also slaves in Guerra Marchán's household. Juan Evangelista Castellanos may have already been their kin. María Apolinaria Castellanos and Manuela Ramos had tried a decade earlier to get Ramos sold into Father Feijóo's household; Ramos's then-owner doña Josefa Corona described how Ramos had gone with her mother and "a *negro* of the priest don Francisco Feijóo" to ask Feijóo to buy her. (Feijóo agreed to the purchase, but Corona was unwilling to make the sale.)[124] The "*negro*" was probably Juan Evangelista Castellanos, who was the slave of don Francisco Feijóo at the time.[125] One imagines that that Juan Evangelista Castellanos may have been the brother or another relative of María Apolinaria Castellanos, given these efforts as well as their shared surname. (Slaves sometimes used their parents' surnames but other times took the slaveholder's name.)

Like María Apolinaria Castellanos, Juan Evangelista Castellanos struggled for much of his lifetime to free his children. He had been Feijóo's slave for twenty or twenty-five years before being liberated in the priest's testament, and then he and his wife continued working for Feijóo's executor so that they could remain with their enslaved children.[126] Six years after the priest's death, the executor don Ignacio Guerra Marchán began to seek a sale of the two slaves. Juan Evangelista Castellanos then petitioned the Audiencia. He argued that he had been feeding and clothing the children himself, and it was therefore unjust for Guerra Marchán to sell them. He pleaded that the sale be halted and his children declared free. As Guerra Marchán resisted, his attorney's arguments revealed various ways in which Castellanos and his wife had already tried to redeem their children. They had voluntarily been separated from their son and daughter, the attorney alleged, leaving the household "with the pretext that they were going to try to [raise the money] to liberate the two children." When a long time passed in which the parents did not present Guerra Marchán with payment, he decided to sell the youngsters. Their father then requested more time, and asked Guerra Marchán for 40 pesos to invest in "commerce." Guerra Marchán gave him the 40 pesos, the attorney said, and Castellanos began "making trips to the provinces of this kingdom and those of Mexico." However, seeing that Castellanos was still not paying him for the children, Guerra Marchán became suspicious that the family might flee. He proceeded with arrangements for the sale of Castellanos's son, Mariano.[127]

A procurator was assigned to represent Castellanos. For reasons not clear in the record, the procurator altered the demand, dropping the plea for the children's outright liberty and instead asking for Guerra Marchán to pay for the food and clothing that Castellanos had provided them. Presumably this payment would have helped enable Castellanos to purchase their freedom himself, but documentation ends abruptly with no outcome recorded.[128]

In the 1824 records of the general slave emancipation in Guatemala City the daughter of Juan Evangelista Castellanos and Ignacia Antonia Velasco, Eduarda Gertrudis, appears registering her liberty. She reported her surname as Feijóo and age as twenty-seven, and said she was married to a free man named Domingo Gómez. Though she identified both her parents, the registry did not record their whereabouts. Her occupation was listed as "sirviente" (servant). The notary indicated that she had been passed by inheritance from citizen Francisco Feijóo to citizen Ignacio Guerra Marchán but had not "been in the custody of the owner."[129] Perhaps she had fled the household of Guerra Marchán with her parents, just as Guerra Marchán had feared would happen. As for her brother Mariano, a free man named Mariano Castellanos appears in the criminal records of 1803, convicted of stealing a cloak and a hoe and carrying a concealed weapon, but I cannot confirm that this was indeed the same Mariano Castellanos.[130]

MARÍA GERTRUDIS SALGADO AND HER CHILDREN

María Gertrudis Salgado, of calidad "parda," was born into slavery around 1722.[131] She was married to a man named Manuel Alvarez, by whom she had six children who survived into adulthood. (It is not known whether Alvarez was a slave or free, or what his occupation was.) In 1762, Salgado's owner sold her and five of her children into the capital city home of doña Antonia Rodríguez Bayona. Rodríguez had purchased Salgado's three daughters; a tenant or guest in the house, the licentiate don Juan Manuel de Zelaya, bought Salgado and her two sons. Salgado's sixth child, a son, was born subsequently into slavery. Zelaya eventually was appointed as the *asesor* (advising lawyer) for the Audiencia of Guatemala—an officer whose opinion nearly always determined the ruling of the Audiencia's judges.

Sixteen years after the sale, still in Zelaya's custody, María Gertrudis Salgado appealed to the Audiencia where her master was asesor. She argued that based on the total purchase price paid for her and her children, her freedom should be set at no more than 100 pesos. Further, she contended that Zelaya owed her several debts. For years she had been required to provide food and clothing for herself and her youngest son, who was born as Zelaya's slave. (Zelaya may have neglected this child in particular because he was a dwarf.) The previous year she had fallen ill for two months and evidently hovered near death, as she was given the last rites. During these two months, she complained, Zelaya had not provided her with sufficient wages to pay for her medical treatment or to support her youngest son; her other children, by this time free, had assumed these responsibilities. Her son Francisco, she said, had spent more than 50 pesos because of her sickness. She alleged that the illness had left her "very scarce of vision and of memory, unable to work" and that Zelaya had therefore orally conceded her liberty but had then reneged when she decided to leave the service of his household.

Zelaya disputed the charges, and the Audiencia ruled in his favor (hardly surprising given his position as asesor). Yet the information in his testimony helps depict the transition Salgado's family made between slavery and freedom. One of her daughters died in childhood; the other two were manumitted after the death of their owner doña Antonia Rodríguez, in accordance with her will. Salgado's eldest son, eighteen or twenty years old when the family was sold to Rodríguez and Zelaya, soon fled to Veracruz and found employment at the port. He was then imprisoned there at Zelaya's written request, but he escaped by setting fire to the jail. Zelaya did not hear further of him. Another of Salgado's sons, Gregorio, was about four or five at the time of the sale. Zelaya had Gregorio jailed several times before age twelve because of "various sizable robberies" (Zelaya's words), then sold him to someone who planned to take him to Havana; for reasons that are not known, though, the lad remained in Guatemala. Salgado's third son, Francisco, was liberated (the records do not specify how) and went to the northwestern Guatemalan city of Quetzaltenango, where he obtained work as an apprentice silversmith in the shop of a wealthy Spaniard.[132]

As for Salgado's husband Manuel Alvarez, Zelaya claimed that the man had "not contributed anything" to support his wife and children, and that the couple had "maintained continual war." When Zelaya moved from Santiago to the new capital, he intended for Salgado to stay behind to care for his property, but she asked him "to take her because she could not suffer her husband." Thus she had moved along with her two daughters and youngest son to the new capital.

Subsequent records are suggestive of the ways that Salgado's two elder sons were integrated into free Hispanic society following their manumission. Francisco Alvarez's employment as an apprentice silversmith in Quetzaltenango and his ability to pay 50 pesos toward his mother's medical treatment demonstrate significant advancement in the Spanish world, and his mobility continued further. In 1785, residing in the capital again, he applied to the silversmiths' guild to be examined as a master of the craft. He had financial backing from an unspecified source to fulfill the royal *quintos* of gold and silver and to open his own shop. He received the license in 1786, gaining entry into Spanish America's most elite artisan trade.[133]

Francisco's brother Gregorio Alvarez, who in childhood had been repeatedly jailed for thefts from his owner, became a tailor. He was married to a woman named María Timotea Aguilar, whose trade of weaving *huipiles* connotes Indian ancestry. Gregorio Alvarez surfaces in the city's criminal records for 1790, arrested for drunkenness. Apparently he had fallen into domestic discord; it was his wife and mother who had reported him. He had been inebriated, they said, for two days, "raising scandal in [their] neighborhoods, wanting to burn down the thatched house where he lives." Interrograted in jail, he denied having been drunk. Rather, he claimed that he had grown impatient because his wife was not home at 5 p.m. to heat his chocolate. He had burned two of the sticks from her loom, he said, in an attempt to make a fire and cook the beverage for himself. He was released from jail and sentenced to pay court costs, but he disappeared and could not be located by the authorities or by his wife or mother. Notable in the judicial record is the beautiful hand in which he signed his depositions.[134]

It is not known whether his mother María Gertrudis Salgado had attained freedom by this time. She would have been about sixty-eight. However, Gregorio Alvarez's testimony indicates that her two surviving daughters continued to live with her.[135]

These three family histories underscore several prominent features of Guatemalan slavery and emancipation. All three stories depict slaves' struggle for liberty as a project closely intertwined with the trajectories of their families. Though the strategies used varied widely, certain patterns emerge. Slaves aiming to purchase liberty consistently worked to adjust prices in their favor. Those who deployed the courts typically demanded compensation for their masters' failure to provide support or other wrongdoings. For their part, slaveholders willingly engaged in litigation against their slaves, seeking to preserve the slaves as their property. Testimonies from such cases reveal that personal relationships and familiarity between slaves and masters were normal. So were marriages and informal consensual unions between slaves or ex-slaves and free people (plebian people, not slaveholders).

The three families also highlight the gendered structures in slavery and manumission. These structures were created partly by the law's approach to slaves and childbearing: children's status as enslaved or free at birth was determined by the status of the mother, not the father. Slave women who bore children by free men might pursue their children's freedom through cooperation or negotiation with the fathers or, as did Manuela Ramos and her daughter Asunción, through litigation. Gender also undergirded patterns of physical and social mobility. In general, men were more able than women to escape slavery through flight, since women were constrained by the responsibilities of pregnancy, nursing, and child care. As exemplifed by ex-slaves Julián Aguilar the tailor and Francisco Alvarez the silversmith, men could gain social mobility in various trades that yielded greater income than did most female trades. Additionally, previous studies have shown the importance of military service in social mobility of men of African ancestry.[136] Yet the links that migrant slaves and ex-slaves forged between countryside and city transcended gender, enveloping both men and women in long-distance social networks that often served as bases for the transition to freedom. Slaves' quests for freedom did not usually yield immediate success. Their struggles often stretched beyond a single lifetime—across families, across generations.

Emancipation and the transformation of identities

By the late eighteenth century slavery in Guatemala was increasingly unsustainable. Slaves themselves were availing themselves of legal institutions and social structures to unravel their enslavement, and as the numbers of people of African and partly African descent grew in free society, so did the possibilities of slave liberations. Kinship and social networks, as well as passing unstopped into free society, continued as primary mechanisms for emancipation, while the state and reigning social ideologies persisted in legitimizing manumissions.

When the general emancipation was declared in Central America in 1824, the civil authorities recorded the names of all the slaves who came to the offices in the capital to claim their liberty. Only fifty adults and eighteen children were registered—barely a blip on the demographic screen in a city where thousands of residents were identified as *negro* or *mulato*.[137] The emancipation law of 1824 appears to have been largely a commentary—a ratification of a long-term social transformation that was already almost complete.

The enslavement of African-descended people ended because of a specific kind of social *mestizaje*: slaves had used physical mobility, self-employment, access to wages and credit, and the judicial system to mix into free Hispanic society. On one hand, the ongoing emancipations of slaves contributed to the growing numbers of blacks and mulatos in the free population. On the other hand, this crossing over into free Hispanic society helped occlude consciousness in the nineteenth century of African heritage and the history of slavery in Guatemala. Ex-slaves were absorbed into a free populace whose members increasingly viewed their ethnically mixed society not as Africanized, but as hispanized or "ladino," a term that came to be defined in contrast to the non-Hispanic cultures of the region's Indians.[138]

The colonial nomenclature of ethnic and racial labels, which had recognized African ancestry in terms such as *negra, negro, mulata, mulato,* and the occasional *Guinea,* was ushered out of official use at the time of independence from Spain. In the independent era, both state and ecclesiastical institutions adopted the single label *ladina* or *ladino* to describe all members of society not identified as Indians, and the term *ladino* continues today as the predominant popular and official descriptor for non-Indians in Guatemala. This sense of *ladino* had already appeared in the parlance of the late colonial era, when the word was widely used to identify culturally Hispanized people, particularly in juxtaposition to Indians living in native communities.

Thus, the structure of slavery underlay several historical transformations in Guatemalan society—including slave emancipation, the incorporation of an African-descended population into ladino society, and the collapsing of Afro-Guatemalan identities (along with several others) into a single ladino identity. The same processes by which slaves gained emancipation also contributed to the assimilation of free blacks and mulatos within Hispanic society and, paradoxically, to the erasure of the slave past in Guatemalan historical consciousness.

3 A Quiet Revolution

FREE LABORERS AND ENTREPRENEURS IN THE HISPANIZING CITY

By the time of the 1773 earthquakes in Santiago de Guatemala, most of the city's adult inhabitants were free laborers, not tribute workers or slaves.[1] The same would be true at Nueva Guatemala. The rise of this free labor force was the outcome of transformations we have seen in native labor and African slavery. At both locations, the capital was a major destination for migrants—including Indians and Africans escaping coerced labor systems and people seeking wages or markets to sell their wares. Social change in the capital was also rooted internally, as people from tributary Indian barrios within the city became hispanized through out-marriage or flight, changing their identities and removing themselves from subjection to tribute.[2] For people of African descent enslaved within the capital, the city's concentration of judicial institutions, along with its large population and labor market, created opportunities to cross, legally or extralegally, into free Hispanic society.

Thus, the city was a hub of hispanization and the related transformation in labor forms. Guatemalans in the late colonial years still recognized racial and ethnic distinctions, which persisted in their construct of "calidad," but for most workers in the city and a growing number of those in the countryside, the form of labor procurement was no longer institutionally linked to ethnicity. Although construction of the new capital in the 1780s motivated the Audiencia to instate some new repartimiento drafts, these were short-term measures taken to augment the workforce for particular building projects. The city already had a resident labor force of thousands of free workers.

This chapter focuses on the capital city's free labor force, which embodied broad regional transformations in ethnic identities and labor forms. In the early decades at the Spanish capital of Santiago, state-administered Indian tributes in goods—especially foodstuffs—had helped sustain a relatively small colonial (Spanish) population. By the end of the colonial era, Indian tributes had been largely converted from commodities and services to coin. Indigenous people were now being recruited as free wage workers. The city's population was buying its food and other supplies mostly from private enterprises. Small businesses, some licensed but many informal, had largely replaced tributes in providing commodities for local consumption. Similarly, the role of coerced African labor in serving the city had faded. Though Santiago's slave labor force had grown along with the rest of the urban population into the 1680s, the numbers of slaves then decreased dramatically across the eighteenth century.[3] Workers in the late colonial years were procured principally without state support or controls. The provision of goods and services for the city had been privatized.

Though tribute labor and slavery were also eroding in the countryside, the shift from coerced to free labor assumed unique forms in the urban economy, particularly that of the colonial capital. In Santiago and its successor Nueva Guatemala, the concentrations of Spaniards, government offices, and large-scale mercantile activity created demand for services from various kinds of workers, especially women. Indeed, the performance of services for money underlay a central experience of city dwellers: they lived in a cash economy. Money defined daily existence in ways specific to urban life. In particular, the content of urban labor—the nature of work itself—differed from that in the countryside, where households functioned largely on a subsistence basis and even commercial enterprises were largely agricultural and pastoral. In contrast, the capital city's economy was dominated by services and manufacturing—particularly textile and clothing production—and, for the first generation at Nueva Guatemala, construction. A number of men were registered in the urban censuses as labradores (farmers or farm hands), and a few city dwellers may have been raising pigs for a living, but these people totaled less than 5 percent of the workforce.[4] Though most capital residents worked with their hands, their work was often indoors and not with the earth.

The urban focus of this chapter helps complete a picture of the gendered processes of migration and hispanization. We saw in Chapter 1 that outmigration from native communities to agricultural estates was constituted not only by whole families but also by men leaving alone; in the aggregate it was a primarily male migration. In contrast, this chapter shows that migration to the city was primarily female, as women and girls came to work as domestics. Thus, whereas men comprised the majority of rural workers in the expanding free labor system, by the mid-eighteenth century women had come to comprise the overwhelming share of adults in the capital. Servants were hired to fulfill mundane domestic services in individual homes, yet their migration into the city would have far-reaching outcomes. Domestics would form the core of a largely female underclass that peopled the city's overarching social trends—its hispanization and racial diversification. The mainly female stream of arrivals would also shape the economy, as women's domestic labor underwrote the diversification of urban industries.

Just as urban workers were enlisted for the physical construction of the new capital, the twilight decades of the colonial era also witnessed the emergence of a new urban society. Begun in the early colonial years, a fundamental restructuring of ethnic identities, gender demographics, and economic life had transformed the regional capital of Spanish conquest and colonization into a racially mixed, culturally hispanized, mostly female city that ran on a cash economy. These transformations amounted to a quiet revolution that on the eve of independence was already long underway.

The hispanizing city: Changing ethnic demographics

Clear signs of the colonial-era transformation appear in the capital city's demographic picture. The Spanish city officials who planned the layout of Santiago in 1541 had intended the city's center for Spaniards. Outside the center, Indian barrios (neighborhoods) would be established in association with each of three religious orders (the Franciscans, the Dominicans, and the Mercederians); beyond these urban barrios lay communities of Indians who had survived enslavement and early epidemics. A series of decrees between 1541 and 1563 formally liberated the Indians from slavery but kept them in subordination as tributaries like the indigenous people elsewhere in the region. The Spaniards' idea was for these Indians to serve them, providing the city with a labor force. Thus, the city center—the Sagrario parish, anchored by the cathedral—was ringed by tributary neighborhoods and, beyond those, tributary towns. In subsequent generations, the Sagrario would remain the most ethnically Spanish and the wealthiest of the neighborhoods. But the entire city, especially the Indian barrios, would be increasingly diversified by ethnic mixing.[5]

Though census records for the capital at Santiago are very limited, Christopher Lutz's work helps fill the gap with analysis of baptismal and marriage records from the city proper and tribute records from four surrounding Indian towns. In general terms, Lutz estimated that the population of this area grew to 38,000 people by the 1680s, then remained fairly stable until the 1773 earthquakes.[6]

Beneath the apparent stability, however, Lutz demonstrated a dramatic increase in the numbers of *gente ordinaria* (literally, common people), whose records were kept in separate parish registers from Spaniards and

tributary Indians. The gente ordinaria group was linguistically hispanized but racially diverse. It included blacks and mulatos (both enslaved
and free), mestizos, and naboría Indians—hispanized Indians not tied to a
native tributary community and not subject to repartimiento duties.[7] The
numbers of gente ordinaria nearly doubled between the 1590s and the
1750s. Even before the 1650s, these people had come to outnumber the
city's Spaniards and Indians put together. By the 1750s, the gente ordinaria
included an estimated 25,041 people—about 65 percent of the city.[8] The
rise of this new population, Lutz has shown, resulted mainly from growth
in the free mulato and mestizo populations. Since both mulato and mestizo
identities were defined in terms of race mixture, the uptick was presumably
fueled by interracial unions. Indeed, parish records confirm high rates of
interracial marriages in Santiago.[9] Free unions were also often interracial
and were widespread.

Yet not only the mulato and mestizo populations were growing. The
numbers of naboría (nontributary) Indians in Santiago also expanded,
notably between about 1660 and 1720.[10] Tellingly, the growth of the
naboría population coincided with a sharp decline in tributary Indian
populations in the urban barrios.[11] Part of the tributary population loss
was due to epidemics, but there is also evidence that individuals from the
tributary group were crossing over into the nontributary group. Though
legal codes defined tributary status as inherited from the mother, some
people born to tributary Indian mothers were dropped from tribute rolls,
evidently overlooked or forgotten after they migrated or married outside
their place of birth. Others acquired official nontributary status through
appeal to the courts or by joining a militia.[12]

Tributary status was less ductile in the Indian towns beyond the city
limits. Even while the urban tributary population was shrinking, tributary
communities outside Santiago itself made strides toward population recovery after the late sixteenth and early seventeenth centuries.[13] Compared to
urban barrios, Indian towns outside the city were more ethnically homo-
geneous. Outsiders were generally known to be outsiders; the rest of the
people were locally born, of known ethnicity, and (save for a few settlements of Mexican auxiliaries to the conquest) subject to tribute. Within
these communities, there was no nontributary world into which a person
could disappear.

In contrast, the heterogeneous setting of the city facilitated attrition
from the tribute rolls, as Santiago's residential patterns and economic life
fostered interethnic social and sexual relationships. The offspring of an
interethnic couple would be legally exempt from tribute if the mother was
not a tributary; if the father was not a tributary, the child might be at
least positioned through association to avoid tribute. The city's multiethnic

neighborhoods enabled some individuals to slip undetected into the mix of gente ordinaria, evading pursuit and tribute collection by native officers. Increasingly, urban Indians were nontributary.

African slaves, too, were enveloped in Santiago's hispanization process. Lutz's analysis indicates that the number of black slaves in the city plummeted after reaching an apex in the 1650s. The overall slave population remained constant for a few decades, fed by the rising number of mulato slaves, but then shrank—from an estimated 1,580 persons in the 1680s to only 400 persons in the 1750s.[14] The mechanisms of manumission and integration that we have seen in Chapter 2 had been at work in Santiago, part of the broad process of mestizaje.

Thus, the so-called gente ordinaria—a hispanized group of varied ancestries—had come to predominate in Santiago long before the city's destruction in 1773. The colonial state eventually recognized this shift, as we can see in the administration's changing approach to urban censuses. The state had taken pains since the early colonial years to count Indians for tribute assessment, and it had occasionally counted or estimated the numbers of *vecinos* (Spanish household heads).[15] But there had been no census in Santiago before 1740 of mulato, mestizo, or naboría (nontributary) Indian populations. (Lutz's work with parish records was key in demonstrating the rise of these groups precisely because of their absence from the censuses.) A census taken in 1740 was the first to include mestizos and mulatos as well as Spaniards.[16] Similarly, a survey following the 1773 earthquakes sought to count every member of every household.[17] This shift to inclusion of all ethnic groups reflects changing perceptions.[18] At least among the Spanish officials who made the censuses, a new understanding had emerged in which mestizos, mulatos, and independent Indians were part of Hispanic society.

Censuses taken at Nueva Guatemala suggest that the state's *mentalidades* about ethnicity had gone even farther than in the 1740 count at Santiago. Not only were all ethnic groups included, but generally calidad was not recorded. Calidad categories were noted in the 1796 census of the barrio la Habana, but not in the other two extant barrio reports for that year and rarely in the smattering of surviving barrio censuses from 1805, 1813, 1819, and 1820.[19] A census form preprinted by the Audiencia for 1819 included two categories—español and ladino (Indians evidently were meant to be enumerated separately or simply to be counted as ladinos if they were living in the city). The form essentially mirrors the parish registries' tripartite construction, substituting the label *ladinos* for *gente ordinaria*.[20] In 1824, the new independent government took a thorough census of Nueva Guatemala, and reports survive for all twelve of the barrios delineated in 1791 (in the intendancy reform).[21] The records give block-by-block registries of every house, with names and ages of everyone, not just the household heads. None of the 1824 records makes mention of calidad. Presumably, every household head was sufficiently ladinized to speak to the census takers; no interpreters are mentioned in the reports.[22]

It was not that race and ethnicity had become unimportant. Rather, the distinctions among hispanized Indians, mestizos, and mulatos were increasingly murky. Even the lines separating these groups from Spaniards had blurred somewhat. Indeed, New Spain's eighteenth-century racial nomenclature reflected the notion that someone with a bit of Indian ancestry might still be a Spaniard: the offspring of a mestizo and Spaniard was labeled as *castizo*, and the offspring of a castizo and Spaniard as "Spaniard."[23] Phenotypes must have varied even among Iberian-born Spaniards, given that the Peninsula had long been home to descendants of people from North African and the Middle East as well as Europe and, starting in the fifteenth century, to sub-Saharan Africans. In Guatemala, by the late colonial era many mestizos, and mulatos had evidently passed into the ranks of poor Spaniards.[24]

Increasingly, the term *ladino* came to describe people of mixed or unclear race, generally replacing the term *gente ordinaria*. Though it had once been used mainly to emphasize linguistic hispanization in non-Spaniards, the word *ladino* came to be used as an ethnic label that sidestepped issues of race and phenotypical appearance. It was especially useful for identifying members of a population in which racial distinctions had become muddied.

The changing meaning of the word *ladino* suggests the two senses in which the Guatemalan capital, at both Santiago and Nueva Guatemala, was hispanizing. The city's social environment, where Spanish was the lingua franca and hispanized people increasingly abounded, fostered the hispanization of migrants coming from elsewhere. That is, the city's cultural milieu shaped the people arriving there. Yet the city was also being shaped by its residents. For individuals, hispanization was often necessary for escape from labor drafts, tribute collection, or slavery; it was also often necessary for contracting for wages. As people sought free status and urban employment, they molded their identities and their behaviors (such as language use and dress), thereby augmenting the Hispanic population of the city. Thus, the city itself, with all its Indian and African heritage, was becoming ladino.

City of women: The demographics of gender

At both Santiago and Nueva Guatemala, hispanization in the late colonial era was led by women, who made up the majority of migrants coming from the countryside. Early censuses of Santiago's vecinos had essentially counted Spanish household heads, most of whom were male. However, starting with the 1740 census—the first to count people of all ethnicities, and the first to count people other than household heads—the reports reveal a remarkable gender disparity. Women were a noticeable majority at both Santiago and Nueva Guatemala. This was true also of other cities in late colonial Latin America, though the disproportion appears exceptionally large in Guatemala.[25] The surviving record of the 1740 census is brief, disaggregated by ethnicity but not gender. But the census taker made a point of noting that among the "common poor, . . . the feminine sex abounds in total profusion."[26] Population estimates for Santiago in 1770 by Archbishop don Pedro Cortés y Larraz also reflect a great predominance of women. The archbishop registered gender for two parishes—the Sagrario, where he recorded 5,478 women compared to 3,159 men, and the Candelaria, where he reported 821 women and 630 men among "ladinos" (Indians there were counted separately, without a record of gender).[27]

The censuses at Nueva Guatemala were more detailed. Inge Langenberg's analysis of the records demonstrates the order of the gender disparity, indexing about 50 percent more female residents than males in the surviving reports from 1796 and 1824.[28] Notably, for both years, the sexes appear in nearly equal numbers among children under fourteen who comprised about one-third of the city's populace. The imbalance was concentrated entirely in a phenomenally lopsided teenage and adult population—that is, the workforce. For 1796, records survive for three of twelve barrios. They list a total of 2,492 women age fourteen and over and only 1,367 men age fourteen and over—a ratio of about 1.8 to 1. The records of the 1824 census, extant for all twelve barrios, list 8,408 women age fourteen and over and only 4,288 men—a ratio of 1.96 to 1.[29]

Granted, men were more likely to go unreported in the censuses. Presumably some Indian men purposely eluded the census-takers in efforts to dodge tribute and labor drafts.[30] Women were more easily counted because their jobs as domestic servants placed them within households, which were the basis of census surveys.[31] Still, the imbalance reported in the censuses is too large to be explained only by evasion and other inaccuracies. Both late-colonial Santiago and Nueva Guatemala were, by large majorities, cities of women. The urban female majority can be explained mainly by the migration of girls and women into the city to work in domestic service. This in-migration continued—and may have increased—across the late colonial years, almost certainly expanding the city's population. I suspect that Lutz's population estimates mask this growth because they are based on marriage records. In a population with nearly twice as many women as men, the proportion of women who got married had to be especially low. Further, many of the migrants in the city returned regularly to their home towns, and many were living only temporarily in the city; hence, some would return to their home towns to be married if not also to live. In effect, urban population growth was comprised largely by people who would not have been well represented in the city's marriage records.

It is impossible to calculate exact numbers of women in service; not all the barrio censuses list female occupations, and those that do so are haphazard. The reports sometimes list numerous teenage and adult women in a single household—presumably including servants and wage-earning tenants—without giving occupational information. Comparison with other kinds of records confirms that some of these women were in fact working for wages. For example, Apolonia "Túnchez" Fuentes was listed in the 1796 census without an occupation, but court records show that she was practicing various trades, as described later in this chapter.[32] Only one woman was listed in the 1796 census as a *panadera* (bakery owner), and not a single woman was identified as a panadera in the 1824 census.[33] Yet bakery inspection reports show at least sixteen or eighteen women operating bakeries in 1777 and in 1829.[34] María Magdalena Mijangos, named in the 1796 census without an occupation, appears in court records as a full-time private teacher for girls (more on her business later).[35] Some of the 1824 barrio census reports identify women's occupations simply as *oficios mujeriles*—literally, womanly jobs. Yet most women who testified in the city's court records stated a more specific occupation. One suspects that the census-takers who repeatedly recorded "oficios mujeriles" (or just ditto marks) did so for all women they judged to be earning wages, without inquiring for details. It is also possible that some women demurred when asked about their occupations. They may have been informally piecing together various sources of income, or operating a business without license (Apolonia "Túnchez" Fuentes, for one, was doing so).[36] Women who aspired to a certain social status may have preferred not to mention a manual trade.

Despite their omissions, however, the censuses demonstrate that enormous numbers of women were working in domestic service. Langenberg's analysis shows that "servant" was the most commonly reported female occupation in both the 1796 and 1824 censuses, and in fact female servants outnumbered girls and women in all other occupations combined. That is, more than half the women with identified occupations were servants—299 women, or 55.7 percent, in the 1796 census and 1,117 women, or 54.9 percent, in 1824. Additional women were identified specifically as washerwomen and cooks.[37] Judicial records also point to domestic service as the predominant employment for women, especially migrants into the capital.

It was commonly understood that rural girls and women came to the city from the surrounding pueblos for the express purpose of "serving"—that is, working as domestics.[38]

By contrast, the censuses identified only seventy men as servants in 1796 and only 212 men in 1824—5 percent or less of the male workforce in each year.[39] Even if we add sacristans, coachmen, cooks, *peones*, day laborers, and slaves to the male "servant" category, the whole group comprised only 11.8 percent of the male work force in 1796 and 9.3 percent in 1824. No single occupation dominated urban male employment in nearly the proportions that domestic service dominated female work. The largest male occupational sectors were textile and clothing production, which together accounted for about 16 percent of the city's men, followed by the building trades, agriculture and animal husbandry, metalworking, and baking.[40]

Though some men came to the city seeking economic opportunities, their numbers were fewer than women. Men from rural areas were more likely to find paid work in agriculture than to go to the capital. (Even some of the men living in the outer reaches of Nueva Guatemala were listed in the censuses as agricultural laborers.[41] Their womenfolk likely worked in services in the city.) Other rural men found jobs outside the city in transport, commerce, and military service. These sectors also employed men from the capital, thereby removing them from the city. Male convicts were generally exiled to distant presidios or sent to public works projects outside the capital. With remarkable frequency, when census takers and other administrative officers queried women as to the whereabouts of their husbands, the response was recorded simply as "ausente" (absent).

Thus the late colonial capital city was a mostly female world in which households often departed from the model of patriarchal family structure. Although some domestic servants lived in their employers' homes, the city's female majority was not wholly absorbed into male-headed households. (We will see a specific quantitative analysis in Chapter 4.) Below the socioeconomic rung of elite Spaniards, households typically consisted of various adults and children who were not necessarily related to each other as nuclear families or as masters and dependents. Urban jobs and housing were often short-term arrangements, as workers—men and women alike— were wont to frequent changes of employers and lodging (not to mention return to home communities). The displacements caused by the 1773 ruin and relocation of capital must have been partly responsible for the ephemeral quality of households over the next couple of decades, but there were other reasons as well. The old "push" and "pull" factors that had fueled migration to Santiago (including the arrivals of women, who "abounded" in the 1740 census report) persisted even during and after the construction of the new city. In effect, the huge female majority in the 1824 census demonstrates the continuation of old migration patterns fifty years postearthquake. While men were exiting native communities primarily to work at haciendas, women were leading the migration into the city.

Seismic shifts in women's work; slippage in the guilds

Women's migration into Santiago and Nueva Guatemala unfurled a complex set of transformations in their labor and ultimately in the economic life of the city. In material terms, women who came to the capital from small towns or rural areas experienced changes in the actual content of their work. In economic terms, the urban structures of labor recruitment, compensation, and distribution also differed from those in the countryside. The city's particular economic characteristics—its cash economy, large female labor force, and array of industries—underwrote a greater diversity of work for urban women than their rural counterparts. Across the colonial era, the range of urban women's trades expanded as female migration into the city facilitated specialization of labor. Women domestic workers, many of them from the countryside, prepared the food and cleaned the homes and clothing of urban people—both men and women—working in other industries.

For women arriving from the countryside, a most important change was embedded in the city's daily bread. In the urban diet, wheaten bread had partly replaced hand-ground maize as the carbohydrate staple. The wheat was ground at several privately owned mechanized mills in or around Santiago (they were built starting in the early colonial years).[42] Tributary Indian men hauled the flour to a host of bakeries in the city, where salaried workers made it into bread. The bread was then sold to households, ready to eat. In 1777, twenty-five bakeries had already been established at the new capital; by 1793, that number had doubled.[43]

In the countryside, in contrast, the diet relied almost exclusively on corn tortillas as the starchy staple. Maize grinding was not mechanized until long after the colonial era (the spread of mechanization is still ongoing, though power mills had reached most areas of Guatemala by the late twentieth century). Before mechanization, once the corn was harvested, women processed the grain and prepared the tortillas in their homes in an extremely labor-intensive process. Women cooking for their families might spend upwards of six hours a day at the grindstone alone, in addition to the work of husking and degraining the ears, boiling and soaking the kernels in lime, and washing and hulling them to make nixtamal before grinding. After grinding the nixtamal, women patted the resulting dough into tortillas—a task requiring enormous skill (as anyone knows who has ever tried to form a tortilla by hand)—and cooked them on the *comal*. Tortilla preparation alone had for millennia defined one-third of women's waking lives.[44] In the colonial capital, consumption of wheaten bread meant that less labor was required for average per-capita tortilla consumption than in the countryside. The presence of bread and bakeries thus released urban women, as a group, from untold hours of blistering, knee-bruising labor at the metate and finger scorching at the comal.

It did not completely release them, however. Maize was generally cheaper than wheat, and tortillas remained popular even in the capital city, as they do today.[45] The 1824 census of Nueva Guatemala identified eighty-two *tortilleras* (tortilla sellers). Some of these women may have made the tortillas themselves, but presumably many of them also involved their daughters or other women in the processing. Further, some of the city's legion of female servants were at times grinding corn and making tortillas in the households where they were employed. In contrast to rural women who were producing tortillas mainly for their families, however, tortilleras and servants were working for income. Tortilla preparation for the city was thus partly subsumed in the cash economy, and although the work of making tortillas weighed heavily on the vast majority of rural women, it was shifted in the city's cash economy onto a proportionally smaller group. Like the presence of wheat mills, the presence of domestic servants and tortilleras also freed up untold hours for other women in the capital. These hours gave some urban women greater time than their rural counterparts had for sleep, leisure, and other kinds of labor.[46]

After food preparation, cleaning—especially, doing laundry—consumed the biggest share of women's labor. Washing differed in the city from that in the countryside, both materially and economically. Rural women hauled their families' laundry (along with their small children) to lakes or rivers where they would soak the clothes, then scrub them on flat rocks before rinsing. Some urban women took laundry to the rivers at the edges of town, but many washed right in the city. At both pre- and postquake locations, the capital enjoyed an aqueduct system that piped water into wealthy homes, fountains, and several outdoor public washing facilities.[47] All of the arrangements inside the city presented the challenge of maintaining a clean tub of rinse water without an infinite supply. The launderers could scrub clothes in shallow sinks or on nearby rocks, but they had to tease out the soap by pouring water from a small tub or pitcher. Rural girls and women coming to serve in the city had to learn these techniques. They also had to learn how to wash and iron a variety of foreign fabrics.

Laundry was especially burdensome during the rainy season. Guatemala is renowned for its torrential downpours.[48] They turn the earth to mud, and the mud gets on everything. For months on end, rain and humidity make it difficult to dry wet clothes and linens before they mildew and need repeat washing. Compounding these problems for launderers in the late colonial capital, the city lacked adequate drainage. In Nueva Guatemala, only the streets closest to the plaza mayor were cobbled before independence; the rest were unpaved dirt—and in the rainy season, mud. Rainwater and sewage ran together and filled even the cobbled streets with an infamous muck that soaked shoes, socks, and hemlines.[49] A passing horse or cart could splash and soil an entire outfit.

Like urban food preparation, urban laundering was often performed as part of the cash economy. Women who could afford to hire laundry out gained significant time, since those doing laundry for their families might spend two or three hours at it per day.[50] Hints of the city's laundry task appear in the late colonial census records. The three extant barrio censuses for 1796 registered thirty-one laundrywomen (*lavanderas*), and the 1824 records identified fifty-five of them (all these were in addition to those listed as sirvienta or *criada*).[51] The actual numbers of both washerwomen and general servants must have been higher, given that the census takers often omitted women's occupations.

Thus, several factors—the capital city's bread industry, its aqueduct system, its cash economy, and its abundance of female workers—facilitated specialization of labor among women as well as men. The cash economy and the rise of the new free labor force brought migrant girls and women into economic structures and activities not seen in the countryside. Further, those women who were relieved (or partly relieved) of cooking and cleaning chores were able to do other kinds of work. Though domestic service clearly dominated female employment, urban women in the late colonial era earned wages in a range of other occupations. The spectrum of trades in which women operated seems to have expanded across the colonial period. In sixteenth-century Santiago, women had dominated in bread and chicha sales, but few if any other enterprises.[52] By the mid-seventeenth century, a group of mulata peddlers were retailing beef in the plaza and distant neighborhoods, and by the 1770s women had entered the ranks of cigarette makers, gunpowder and fireworks makers, tanners, weavers, storekeepers, and hatmakers.[53] Before the end of the colonial period, they were working also as *salitreras* (saltpeter refiners), potters, and teachers and in various trades in the textile and clothing industries.[54]

In 1784, the Crown ruled that women be allowed to practice their trades in Spain despite guild restrictions against them, and in 1799 the restrictions were lifted in New Spain as well.[55] In the Guatemalan capital at least, these laws clearly lagged behind practice. Several women had already received formal guild recognition, some but not all of them widows carrying on their late husbands' enterprises. Further, even before the legislation in 1784 and 1799, women in were operating outside the guilds in numerous trades.[56]

Male craftsmen too had increasingly been working at the margins of the guilds in Guatemala and elsewhere.[57] Héctor Humberto Samayoa Guevara has noted that the Guatemalan guilds were in "disorganization and decline" even before the 1773 earthquake.[58] To be sure, their exclusivity had waned. Once the preserve of Spanish men, the guilds had gradually opened to Indian men and then to mulatos and blacks.[59] Within the guilds, too, social hierarchies had loosened somewhat. Men who testified in Guatemala's late colonial courts typically identified a craft but often without mention of their status as apprentice, journeyman, or master. Few artisans in late colonial Guatemala used the honorific title *don*, and it did not correlate with master status, not even in the traditionally high-ranking crafts such as silverwork.[60] Consider, for example, the master silversmith Antonio Avila, always named without the honorific *don*, and the three men he employed in 1785 in his shop—the español don Juan José Cabrera, age twenty (his guild status is not specified in the record); a mulato named Francisco Froilán Calderón, in his early thirties (again, no guild status specified); and an apprentice (no calidad mentioned) named Pascasio Monzón, in his teens or early twenties.[61]

Even among those artisans who attained master status, socioeconomic backgrounds varied widely. Compare for example the silversmith Luis de Avila with his contemporary Francisco Alvarez. Avila was the son of a silversmith (and possibly the brother of the master silversmith Antonio Avila previously mentioned). He was examined and licensed as a master in the same trade in March of 1777.[62] Within a few months he was established with at least one other silversmith, likely a journeyman, working for him in his shop.[63] He later expanded successfully into the baking business. In 1785 his bakery was supplying bread for the city's main hospital (San Juan de Dios) and grossing between 100 and 150 pesos per month.[64] In contrast, Francisco Alvarez was born a slave, the son of María Gertrudis Salgado and Manuel Alvarez (their family was profiled in Chapter 2).[65] It is not known how Francisco Alvarez attained his freedom, but he appears in the archives again in 1785—he would have been in his late twenties or thirties—petitioning to be licensed as a master silversmith. Journeymen applying for master status in a trade had first to demonstrate their material readiness to open a *tienda pública* (public shop).[66] Alvarez was relying on credit. "I am soon to give the surety," his petition said, "to cover the *quintos* [royal taxes] of gold and silver that I will work." The surety (*fianza*) was money that Alvarez had borrowed; it would serve as collateral to guarantee his payment of the taxes on precious metals. His petition and exam were successful.[67]

The "disorganization and decline" that Samayoa Guevara has described in the guilds did not go unnoticed by late colonial elites, who repeatedly sought to expand and codify regulations for the guilds. An example is the Sociedad Económica de Amigos del País (Economic Society of Friends of the Country), founded in 1794 by a group of elite men interested in Liberalism's economic promises but cautious about social change.[68] In 1798 the Sociedad Económica presented to the capital's ayuntamiento a detailed plan enumerating no less than 254 rules and regulations for the guilds, followed not long afterward by an addendum amending some of the articles and outlining three new ones. The plans were concerned not only with shaping (and controlling) artisans' behavior in the interest of social order for the city as a whole but also with maintaining the hierarchy of social order within the guilds—that is, among artisans themselves.[69] The ayuntamiento evidently did not adopt the plan, but in 1811 the president of the Audiencia revived the matter, citing concerns about workers' "habits" (*costumbres*).[70] This time the ayuntamiento passed a regulatory code consisting of 224 clauses divided among nine articles. Still, elite anxieties persisted about slippage in the guilds (and presumably the slippage itself also persisted). In 1812 the capital's Consulado de Comercio—the merchant guild, a decidedly aristocratic group—appealed to Guatemala's representative in the Cortes of Cádiz for further reforms and control over artisans. "Their trades are necessary in the Republic," the Consulado admitted, but "are exercised by habit, capriciously and arbitrarily . . . without the formality and honor of accredited masters."[71]

Paradoxically, even as the ayuntamiento and the Consulado were elaborating their regulatory goals, across the Atlantic the Cortes of Cádiz was issuing decrees in 1811 and again in 1813 meant to abolish the guilds altogether—a move by Liberals toward freeing trade and industry. The administration in New Spain echoed with its own equivalent decree in 1814. The guilds were legally reinstated in the empire in 1815 (after restoration of the Bourbon king to the Spanish Crown), then abolished again in various edicts issued in 1820.[72]

Despite the relaxation of the guild structures, women remained largely ghettoized. There were far more non-Spanish men than women of any calidad in the guilds. Martha Few has observed in her study of seventeenth- and early eighteenth-century Guatemala that "even in the context of economic expansion, . . . women tended to work on the margins on the colonial economy."[73] The tendency continued into the nineteenth century as part of a broader pattern that reached beyond Guatemala.[74] Not all that far removed from the condition of domestic servants, most tradeswomen in the late colonial years were working in relatively low-prestige and low-paying industries, concentrated in the conventionally female tasks of food and beverage preparation. Thus, the guilds had lost some of their traction, and there had been remarkable openings along racial and ethnic lines as labor coercion eroded. There had also been some openings along lines of gender. Yet women were still subject to occupational inequities that often superseded ethnicity.

The lives of domestic servants: Linking countryside and city

Domestic service was the city's largest single occupational sector and by far the largest source of urban employment for women. Household service acted as a dual mechanism of social change. As girls and women migrated to the city to work as domestics, they became hispanized—they learned Spanish, acquired skills for survival and work in Spanish households, and developed social networks within the Hispanic city. Migrant servants who stayed in the city often formed kinship ties there, through marriage or concubinage and motherhood. Their presence thereby shaped the urban ladino population, making it largely Indian and African in ancestry. Thus, household service was at the center of hispanization and mestizaje. Women in domestic service played a key role in the transformation of urban ethnic demographics across the colonial period.

It is not possible to determine the numbers of households that maintained live-in servants in the colonial capital, since most of the censuses do not state the roles of the various members of each household.[75] However, the frequency with which female domestic workers left jobs and found new employment demonstrates that women's labor was in significant demand in the city. Many paid servants worked for only a few weeks before leaving to stay with relatives or friends or going to work in another household.[76]

Court records show that numerous Spanish households included someone identified as an *indizuela*, an Indian girl or young woman employed to do chores and errands; indigenous boys are also mentioned occasionally as workers.[77] Girls working as domestics were sometimes called *hijas de la casa*—daughters of the home—suggesting a pretense of protection and affection by the employers. But treatment of Indian servant girls was at best paternalistic. Like adult female servants, girls typically worked for a cash wage plus bed, board, and often clothing; but they received lower wages than adults. Their earnings were generally turned over to their parents.[78] Robinson Herrera's study of sixteenth-century Santiago has identified notarized records in which indigenous parents contracted their children's labor to Spanish employers.[79] By the late eighteenth century such agreements had evidently become normal enough to be left unwritten.

A lawsuit filed in 1799 by Domingo López illustrates.[80] López and his wife (whose name was not recorded) were tributary Indians in the Pocomam town of Santa Catarina Pinula, 6 kilometers outside Nueva Guatemala. For two years their daughter had been in the city working as an *hija de la casa* for a Spanish couple, who had advanced her a salary of 9 reales a month for two and a half years.[81] The daughter's name and age never appear in the suit, though the salary suggests she was a preteenager. Domingo López described how his daughter had unexpectedly returned one night to her parents' house in Pinula, because her mistress had begun "to hit her and mistreat her" on finding "a little slab of chocolate broken." The employers, López explained, were saying that his daughter had broken some dishes and allowed a bird to escape, and they wanted the parents to pay for these things plus the advanced wages not yet worked off. But López argued that "it is not reasonable that we be charged for kitchenware that was broken while in use in that very house." He contended that "the only thing our daughter does owe is . . . five pesos and five reales"— the remainder of the salary advance. The court backed López, ruling that he owed only the wages and allowing him six months to pay. The record notes that the judge did not issue any decision about some petticoats or skirts (*enaguas*). López said the employers had given them to his daughter as a gift, whereas the employers wanted payment or the garments returned. The clothes apparently stayed in the daughter's possession.

Like other parents of Indian children, Domingo López and his wife seem to have retained control over their daughter's income. Presumably they had invested her wages or used them to pay tributes or debts. The parents also provided a measure of security for their child, taking her back into their home and appealing to the court to help clear her debts. A similar pattern unfolded with Micaela de los Santos, a young Indian woman from Ciudad Vieja who served in a Spanish house in the capital. When she was sexually assaulted in the house, she sent for her father, who came to take her home. He also filed a suit on her behalf.[82]

In contrast, orphaned servant children could not count on these protections. Orphans generally appear not to have been given cash wages, receiving instead only their food, shelter, and clothing. Masters may have treated servant children somewhat like their own, especially in nonelite families where children were expected to help their parents with chores.[83] However, at the hour of dictating their wills, people made a distinction, leaving more valuable inheritances to biological or adopted children than to servants.[84] Poor orphan children surface very rarely as plaintiffs in litigation, but census and notarial records (especially testaments) indicate that a substantial number of children without parents survived by working in other people's homes. The virtual absence of recorded judicial appeals by these children suggests that they had little recourse to protection from the state. These conditions would make orphans especially subject to the authority of their employers and to abuses of that authority.

Even children who did have parents were vulnerable. Francisca Victoria García from Ciudad Vieja, whose life was described in Chapter 1, was sent at age six to work as a domestic in the new capital. Other children, too, were placed in service at remarkably young ages.[85] Child servants were subject to the authority and whims of their employers, often for years at a time during the most formative periods of their lives. Their wages came at the price of not only their labor but also great potential for mistreatment. Moreover, daily life with their own families was sacrificed. For small children in particular, being put out to work and to live with strangers must have been enormously traumatic.

Why did parents in indigenous communities send their children to work in the city? They may have viewed domestic service for Spaniards as an opportunity for their daughters to enjoy a plentiful diet and material comfort and to gain some mobility in colonial society. The clothing typically provided to servant girls was not only something in which they might take pleasure; it was also a visible marker of status and dignity. As such a marker, clothing itself—elegant clothes or extra changes of clothes—could constitute a component of social mobility. Clothing of European style or fabric could be a step for Indian servants toward a more hispanized identity.[86] Further, native girls serving in Spanish homes would acquire knowledge and associations that might later be valuable. Servant girls learned to do laundry in the urban facilities and to cook for Spanish households, catering to Spanish tastes and using European-style stoves, cookware, and ingredients. They gained fluency in Spanish. By living in the city, child servants developed contacts with a range of hispanized people who might later become their creditors, employers, clients, or spouses. Children from tributary families sent to work in the city would be positioned to marry nontributaries or to blend into the nontributary population. Such a marriage or assimilation would relieve them (and their children) of the burdens experienced by dual-tributary couples.[87]

Parents of girls working as domestic servants could use their wages to make investments for their future. As we saw in Chapter 1, Francisca García's parents used her salary to purchase land and livestock for her in the hometown while she worked in the city. Likely her parents and brothers benefitted from these properties in her absence, but her lawsuit suggests that the investments were meant to be for her. Her income had also been used to buy furniture and housewares that her parents were keeping for her. Her parents may have imagined—perhaps hoped—that she would return to the pueblo to get married or to live there with her husband and children. Some girls sent to serve in the city did return to live in their hometowns as adults.[88] Although Francisca García decided to get married and make her life in the capital, the properties her parents had bought for her in the pueblo could provide rents and other income for her. She had given her father 40 pesos "for the care of a milpa" back home, and she expected to get the money back; evidently they were treating the milpa as a source of income. The use of migrant servants' wages to buy properties in the sending communities may have been part of a larger strategy by families to develop vertical integration in business. Investments in the native community could provide supply lines—such as maize for a chicha or tortilla business, or livestock for sausage making or lunch sales. Grown daughters with lives established in the city could operate the downstream end of these businesses, processing the raw materials and selling the products to urban consumers.[89]

Indeed, women who had served as domestics in their youth were likely as adults to develop their own small enterprise in the city or to make a business circulating between hometown and city to sell products like tortillas or thread. Marriage typically heralded the end of live-in servitude, since the woman would go to live with her husband rather than her employer. Granted, urban residences were not necessarily patrilocal. Especially at Nueva Guatemala, housing was crowded and often shared by people unrelated to each other, who slept in rented rooms. But if a domestic servant got married and moved to her husband's lodgings, she would no longer need a bed in her employer's home. In effect, domestic service was often a stage of life that preceded marriage. Of the 1,117 women age fourteen and older registered as servants in the 1824 census, 1,043 were single; only thirty-four were married, and forty were widowed. They also tended to be young; 435 were between fourteen and twenty-three years old, and 315 were between ages twenty-four and thirty-three. In contrast, for all other female occupations—in which women were most often self-employed, not living with their employers—the census reports the greatest concentration of workers in the age group between twenty-four and thirty-three.[90]

Women's small enterprises engaged them in some of the same kinds of labor that domestic servants performed, notably laundry and food preparation. Petty businesswomen prepared tortillas, tamales, and entire meals in their homes for sale there or nearby. Their enterprises ranged from single-handed operations to larger outfits with several employees. Even women with very small enterprises enjoyed greater autonomy from their clients than did live-in servants.

This autonomy had its limits, though, notably for lavanderas (laundry-women). Lavanderas occupied an especially low rung, partly because of the low input costs and the strenuous work. Hauling and scrubbing clothes are backbreaking chores, and the task of wringing can cause repetitive strain injuries in the hands and wrists. Moreover, the nature of washing meant that lavanderas with well-heeled clients—whose houses enjoyed running water—would work within the client's home (a pattern that continues today).[91] Though these women might live out and even rotate among the homes of various clients across the week, they were subject to oversight and discipline while on the job. On the plus side, their work may have been steadier than that of women working on their own account, and their income greater than that of lavanderas serving a more plebeian clientele. Ildefonsa Cañas, a married woman around forty, noted in 1818 that she had been a lavandera for about seven years in the home of don Tomás Arroyave and doña Felipa Madrid in Antigua (Santiago). The Arroyave-Madrid family may have been Cañas's only client; with the clothing and linens of an elite family and their guests (not to mention their numerous servants), the household must have generated plenty of laundry. Given that the Arroyave-Madrid residence would have had piped water, at least Cañas didn't have to haul the clothes beyond the patio.[92]

Manuela Gálvez, a single mother of five, worked independently as a lavandera, but the income wasn't enough to support her family. Gálvez was a mulata, originally from Villa Nueva de Petapa but living in the new capital. She was thirty-six when she was arrested in 1803, on reports that she was running a late-night gambling den in the house where she was renting a room. She didn't deny the charges, though she tried to foist responsibility onto her landlady. In any case, she admitted to having in the past sold *aguardiente* (liquor) to supplement her washing business.[93]

Like lavanderas, tortilleras performed physically exhausting work—blistering, backbreaking hours over the grindstone, and finger scorching at the comal. However, women identified as tortilleras had a bit of independence since they were generally selling tortillas made at home, rather than working in the home of an employer. (Those hired to grind corn and make tortillas in other people's homes were called molenderas.) Though the 1824 census registered only eighty-two tortilleras living in the city, women also came from the peripheral Indian towns to sell tortillas, as they had done at Santiago.[94] Dorotea Flores, an Indian from Ciudad Vieja (at its postearthquake location), was among those selling tortillas in the capital in 1805. She did not know her age but was said to look about forty; she was married with a daughter and small grandchild. Flores said she maintained ties to her home in Ciudad Vieja even though she often resided in the capital, where her daughter evidently lived. Likely her daughter was helping make the tortillas.[95]

Other food-preparation enterprises similarly facilitated women's self-management in jobs that amounted to domestic labor.[96] In Nueva Guatemala in 1781, twenty-four-year-old Manuela Bustamante was known among her neighbors as "la Tamalera" (the tamal-maker). She made the tamales alone in her rancho (small house). Married several years earlier to a mestizo baker, she had separated from him because he was given to drink and had beaten her repeatedly. It is unclear where the husband was lodging, though he was still in the capital.[97] A woman named Nicolasa de Lara, around forty in 1808, was known as "Chuchito." One imagines she was in the business of making *chuchitos* (a Guatemalan variation on tamales, with a piece of pork or chicken at the center). She entered the record when a tenant in her house was allegedly assaulted there by an acquaintance. Lara/Chuchito testified that she hadn't witnessed the attack; she had been outside, she said, meeting with two swineherds who had stopped by to sell her some pigs. Presumably she would be making her chuchitos with pork.[98] Though Lara/Chuchito was married, her husband was away, stationed at the presidio in Trujillo, in what is now Honduras. The record does not clarify whether he was there receiving a military salary or serving a penal sentence.

Though these small businesses released women from the pressures of live-in servitude, the profits were generally meager. Women providing cooking and cleaning services as independent entrepreneurs often drew income from an array of trades to make ends meet. We have seen that the lavandera Manuela Gálvez resorted to bootlegging and (if we are to believe her neighbors) illicit gaming to support her children. Other women, too, notably single mothers, faced similarly tight circumstances. Inés García earned some income doing laundry and making cigarettes, but she was known to support herself and her three children mainly with illegal aguardiente production.[99] Felipa Velis, age twenty-nine, had been a live-in cook for a financially middling couple. When the wife died, Velis moved to other lodgings with her teenage daughter, but she continued doing occasional work for the widower. As she explained it, she would stop by his house and he would give her a *real* or two, and she would then work it off by doing some sewing or laundry for him.[100] In the context of these women's lives, the term *oficios mujeriles* (womanly chores or work) assumes a particular significance (even beyond its apparent use by the census takers as the default female occupation). Women without a thriving business or support from a spouse could face precarious circumstances, especially if they had children. They often used multiple skills, doing a variety of womanly chores, to cobble together an income.

Contact zones: Servants and employers

Girls and women who migrated to the city as servants escaped some of the patriarchal constraints of village life, but they exchanged the vigilance of their families and townspeople for that of their employers.[101] By definition, servants were subject to their employers' authority. They often referred to their female employers as their "señora" (lady or mistress), and to employers of either gender as their "amo" or "ama" (master), connoting the authority implicit in the employer's position. Servant–employer relationships embodied, at the level of individuals and households, "contact zones"—a term that Mary Louise Pratt has used to describe "social spaces where disparate cultures meet, clash, and grapple with each other often in highly asymmetrical relations of domination and subordination."[102] In Guatemala, domestic service was the principal vehicle bringing Indian and African women into personal contact with the colonial employer class. Household service turned the most private space of Spanish society—the interior of the home—into the venue of some of the most fundamental interactions in the formation and structure of colonial society.

To be sure, not all employers clearly differed culturally or ethnically from their domestic servants. In 1770, an Indian woman named Antonia Ajau, from the pueblo of San Cristóbal el Bajo just outside Santiago, was living and working as a *mesera* (monthly wage laborer) in the home of another Indian woman in the neighboring community of Santa Isabel. (Both communities are Cakchiquel.) Ajau also worked for an Indian woman in the house next door, who employed her to bring "the daily ash for her soap[making]" operation. And Ajau served at times in a third house, grinding maize for tortillas. Her husband, an Indian from nearby San Cristóbal el Alto (also Cakchiquel), worked as a haymaker or transporter of hay (*sacatero*).[103] Examples also abound within the city limits. In the new capital, Rita Oaxaca employed a woman named Petrona as a servant in her house.[104] Oaxaca's surname indicates that she herself was probably of Indian or partly Indian identity.[105] Leoncia Barrientos Pinto, in her mid-forties and married to a carpenter, was identified as *parda libre* (a free woman of dark complexion); she employed a girl named Francisca to work in their home.[106] We saw in Chapter 2 that Apolonia Olavarrieta, a free mulata domestic servant, hired a young Indian man to care for her ailing brother, himself a fugitive slave.[107] Bonifacio Rogel, who with his wife had employed Felipa Velis as cook, was identified as pardo. He was a tailor with three horses and a small thatched house but without his own shop; his wife, while she was alive, was selling *chicha* (a fermented maize drink)—by no means a prestige occupation.[108] Thus, domestic servants came from a wide range of social groups, and they were hired by employers from a very broad spectrum. Young women who worked in other people's houses might later head their own households, and they might quit domestic service to work in their own enterprises.

However, in the capital city, ethnic demographics clearly distinguished domestic servants, as a group, from their employers. Most women who served in households in the late colonial capital were of Indian, African, or mixed ancestry, whereas their employers were concentrated among the Spanish population. Domestic service in the city was partly a stage in life, but it was also linked to station in life.[109] The majority of the capital's female servants were employed by people who outranked them in hierarchies of both ethnicity and wealth. Girls working in the homes of middling artisans or small entrepreneurs may have aspired to attain the status of their employers, and such aspirations may have nourished the servants' discontent if their fortunes did not release them from servitude. But for plebian girls and women working for elite Spaniards, it was obvious that the servants would never come close to the masters' level of wealth and privilege.

The inequities between servants and masters came into sharp relief in the substance of their daily lives. Domestic workers slept in their employers' houses, prepared and served their employers' food, washed their dishes, laundered their clothes and linens, emptied and cleaned their toilets, made their beds, overheard their arguments and their affections, and breastfed their children. These were highly intimate relationships. Household servants are often viewed by historians as "dependents," and indeed they were dependent on employers for housing, food, and often clothing as well as wages. But employers were also dependent on their servants for the most basic daily upkeep. In the context of such intimacy and mutual dependence, the inequalities could be especially glaring to servants. At the same time, employers' dependence on their servants may have opened some space for servants to resist the inequalities.

Servants' thoughts were rarely documented, but there are various signs in the archival records that tensions did erupt. Studying Inquisition records, Martha Few has identified cases in which servants denounced employers before the Holy Office in Guatemala.[110] Perhaps the subtlest evidence is simply the frequency with which domestic servants left jobs. Some worked only a few days or weeks before quitting. On servants being fired, the records are nearly silent.[111] This may be partly because wages were often advanced; employers may have then been reticent to forfeit their investment by letting a servant go. Moreover, though, there was little reason for a servant's dismissal to generate a written record. Firing must have normally gone undocumented. Servants who quit or were dismissed might go to stay with relatives or find work in another household. If they had saved some cash, they might rent a room or space in a shared room. Employers' power was limited somewhat by the city's demand for female labor, which enabled disgruntled domestics to vote with their feet. Nevertheless, wages were generally paltry, and servants had few sources of leverage besides the need for their work.

In this light it is not surprising that domestic workers might resort to illicit means to squeeze some gains from their position. Servants leaving jobs sometimes took with them wage advances or other valuables, typically without the employers' consent.[112] In effect, the workers were playing the labor market—trading their jobs for advanced wages or stolen goods, then finding other jobs. Their strategy mirrors that of their contemporary agricultural workers in Guatemala and elsewhere in Spanish America, who sometimes decamped from haciendas where they owed advanced wages.[113] However, compared to rural workers, urban domestic servants who abandoned wage debts or stole from their employers were more easily arrested because they tended to stay in the city.

María Estéfana García, an Indian born in Nueva Guatemala, is an example.[114] Her case illustrates a complex set of power dynamics between employer and servants in a household contact zone. When she entered the record in 1814, she was in her twenties, single. She had been working in the home of Mercedes Mendizábal, a widow (likely mulata) with two children.[115] Mendizábal had a lunch-service enterprise with two employees—García working in sales and preparation, and another woman as a molendera. While Mendizábal went daily to sell lunches in the plaza, her employees stayed at her house to prepare and sell lunches there. In July 1814, Mendizábal reported to the civil authorities that María Estéfana García had stolen from her the sizable sum of 85 pesos and 4 reales (on the order of two or more years' wages). Mendizábal explained that she had kept a jar of money buried in the dirt floor under a bench in her bedroom. One day after taking some money out, she had been hiding the jar again when García entered the room and presumably caught sight of the stash. Some days later Mendizábal went to withdraw more money and found it almost all gone. Meanwhile, García had left her service under pretext of illness.

García was arrested and held pending bail. The court heard evidence from various witnesses, including Mendizábal's molendera—a woman named Francisca Aquino from Cubulco, an Achí-speaking town some 200 kilometers north of the capital.[116] Testifying through an interpreter, Aquino said she had seen María Estéfana García in Mendizábal's bedroom, standing next to the bench stuffing money into her petticoat and into a tobacco pouch "the size of a large orange." García had allegedly given her 1 or 2 reales and instructed her not to say anything. Aquino claimed in her deposition that she had been reluctant to take the hush money and that she had told García she was going to report the theft to Mendizábal. But she didn't report anything. Queried by the court about her silence, Aquino said that "since her señora does not understand her, she does not speak with her." Presumably she was referring to the language barrier. (As for the language of communication between Aquino and García, the record is unclear, identifying García only as "Indian.")

García was not easily cornered despite the statements against her. She contended that Aquino had been "advised" by her employer before testifying and that the deposition was "all false." The jurists essentially dismissed Aquino's story, perhaps believing it was concocted under coaching or perhaps discrediting her because she was not hispanized. Other witnesses included two men who had frequented the house to visit García and to eat lunch. One of them, a thirty-seven-year-old tailor with a practiced signature, admitted to a love affair with García but denied any knowledge of the missing money. Ultimately, the court determined that there was insufficient evidence, and García was freed from jail.

Like Mercedes Mendizábal, most employers who charged their former servants with theft were unsuccessful in recouping their losses, although the ex-servants were often jailed while the courts investigated. As we have seen, Domingo López's daughter left her employers still owing them five months of work. Her father was ordered to repay the cash advance, but the employers were unable to recover the additional money and goods they sought. María Estéfana García apparently left Mercedes Mendizábal's employ with a small fortune in coins stuffed into her skirt and tobacco pouch. To be sure, she then spent nearly four months in prison before the case was dismissed. At Santiago in 1769, a domestic named María Candelaria Ansueto evidently filched 200 pesos worth of clothing, silver, china, and crystal from her employer before quitting his service to work for someone else. The aggrieved employer was don Gabriel Rodríguez. He went to the law when he spotted a pair of his missing trousers being worn by the brother of Candelaria's new employer. A tailor called as a witness described having made exactly those breeches for don Gabriel Rodríguez; they were of fine dark brown wool, with gold galloon straps and gold buttons. But before a final ruling by the judge, Rodríguez dropped the charges. He realized he had little to gain. María Candelaria's "crime has in a sense been cleared by three months that she has been in the women's jail," he said, "and I recognize that she is insolvent and cannot pay me."[117] In 1796, a servant named Juana Velásquez evidently stole some silver dishes from her elite Spanish employer. The employer managed to recover some property but not exactly his dishware; by the time the silver surfaced, it had been melted down. Velásquez spent some two months in jail before being released when the silver was returned.[118]

Despite the leverage that servants sometimes managed to exert, their power was generally less than that of their employers. Servants were subject to seemingly infinite kinds of abuses.[119] Because judicial records were generated specifically in cases where disputes had erupted openly, the archives convey a picture of contestation by servants, but such contestation may belie the quotidian norm. Even when servants found ways to resist, oppressive treatment and mistreatment must have been enormously taxing psychologically, especially for workers who lived in their employers' houses. Lodging was often without even a private bedroom.

The case of Sebastiana Vásquez is suggestive. In 1794, Vásquez contracted to serve in the home of doña Ignacia Ugalde for 3 pesos a month. After a month, Ugalde increased the workload, putting Vasquéz in charge of the kitchen. The employer promised a 1-peso raise, but Vásquez later explained that eventually "because of the mistreatment that the señora gave me, I quit her service." Ugalde responded vindicitvely. She refused to pay Vásquez for her last month, and she seized a chest containing her clothes. Vásquez continued working for another nineteen days, trying to recover her clothing and collect her salary. She complained to the alcalde, who sent a commissioner ordering Ugalde to pay the wages and return the clothes. But Ugalde did not comply. Vásquez then filed a formal suit, in a petition that conveys her outrage. "In front of the commissioner himself," she said, doña Ignacia Ugalde "threw herself at me like a wild beast, wanting to get rid of me by slapping me. And it is unjust that in addition to my lacking the salary that with such fatigue I earned from doña Ignacia, she should have mistreated me." The court's notary managed to retrieve Vásquez's clothing, but efforts to recover her wages proved fruitless.[120]

Five years later, the same doña Ignacia Ugalde literally trapped another domestic servant in her employ. For reasons not given in the record, she locked the unfortunate worker, Juana Pérez, inside the house. Pérez escaped through a window, only to be arrested when Ugalde complained to the alcalde. The court held Pérez in prison for seventeen days before hearing her side of it. She said she had left because "being free [of slavery or other bondage], she did not want to continue in the service of the house." The alcalde ordered her released from jail pending presentation by doña Ignacia Ugalde of any evidence. Ugalde's husband came forth on his wife's behalf, but he was evidently unsuccessful in returning Juana Pérez to the house. The record does not specify whether Ugalde had advanced any wages to Pérez. The husband did not mention an advance in his appeal.[121]

On one hand, doña Ignacia Ugalde's repeated judicial run-ins with servants may indicate that she was an exceptionally abusive employer. On the other hand, her cases are consistent with broader patterns in legal disputes between employers and domestics. Notice that Ugalde appeared in the first instance as a defendant charged by a servant, and in the second case as a plaintiff bringing charges against another servant. Servants and masters alike could make appeal to the courts; the colonial state sought to protect workers from abusive employers and to protect employers from theft or breach of contract by workers. Yet servants and masters were not equals before the law. The state's interventions were shaped by its broader effort to uphold the colonial class hierarchy, which reflected early modern ideologies about the natural order of society. Egregious behaviors could be questioned and even punished, but the inherent inequalities between masters and servants were generally accepted by the state, employers, and servants themselves. Free labor did not mean that laborers were considered to be the equals of employers, not even in the late colonial years when Liberalism was becoming fashionable among some of the colony's elites. Though some workers successfully challenged abuses by their employers (or abandoned those employers), female domestic workers were unable to alter the larger social order that kept them poor and working in menial tasks. Perhaps the most telling pattern in litigation between employers and servants is the courts' discrimination in jailing. Whereas domestic servants were normally held in prison while under investigation for crimes, I have found no cases in which employers charged with abuse of servants were jailed.[122]

It was not only judicial ideologies that kept servants from equal footing in the courts; it was also the practical matters of legal personnel and administration. The Spanish colonial state (like its successor independence-era state) was embedded in the employer class—the same elite individuals who, along with their friends, were major employers of domestic servants. In the abstract, colonial ideologies charged the state with protecting all its subjects. But in practice, the personal interests and sympathies of the governing officers themselves could overshadow the interests of workers.

An example is the 1814 case of Efigenia Ascencio, a mulata servant in her mid-thirties.[123] When she suffered a beating at the hands of her well-heeled employers, their political connections nearly kept them above the law. The employers were don Ignacio Taborga and his wife doña Josefa Rodríguez, prominent Spaniards with houses in both Nueva Guatemala and Amatitlán, a cattle-raising center some 30 kilometers away.[124] Efigenia had been working at their Amatitlán residence when a conflict between the mistress and the maid erupted in blows. In the melee that ensued, both doña Josefa and her husband don Ignacio struck Efigenia with pieces of firewood, causing her serious injuries. She escaped when an unexpected visitor happened upon the scene. Don Ignacio and doña Josefa then immediately spoke with Amatitlán's top colonial officer, the alcalde mayor, who evidently tried to help cover their crime. Efigenia came to him soon afterwards, but he dismissed her charges, telling her, "You've got it wrong" (*estás mal informada*). He did arrange her transportation to the hospital in the capital, indicating that don Ignacio would pay the costs. The court then opted not to pursue her case; officials said it was not a serious one, and they were burdened with pending business. Eventually, though, gossip chipped away at the legal barricade. Three weeks after the incident, the court decided to investigate, noting that the matter was "being whispered about too much among the public." Efigenia was still in the hospital with a head injury, her recovery uncertain.

Her deposition, recorded at the bedside, depicts a background of ongoing tensions with her employers, particularly doña Josefa. On Efigenia's first day on the job, she found that the bedroom she was given was damp (this was the rainy season), and she had to ask another servant to share her room. Within the week, doña Josefa reprimanded her because a half *real* worth of bread was missing. When Efigenia responded that she had never stolen anything, doña Josefa threatened to hit her, brandishing a kitchen knife. Efigenia backed down at first. But the sparring resumed the next Saturday night when, according to Efigenia's testimony, doña Josefa and don Ignacio arrived home "somewhat drunk." Doña Josefa rebuked Efigenia for not sleeping where she was assigned. Efigenia answered that the room was wet. Doña Josefa insisted, adding (as rendered by the notary taking Efigenia's deposition) "that she [doña Josefa] could hit her and she had authority over her." Efigenia retorted with: "Who had given [doña Josefa] the authority to hit her?"[125] It was then that doña Josefa allegedly "took a stick of firewood and with it gave her a blow in the head that threw her to the floor." Doña Josefa "tore [Efigenia's] shirt and grabbed her by the braids, keeping her [down] while she called her husband." When don Ignacio came into the room, Efigenia testified, he began batting her body and head with a piece of firewood even while she pleaded for mercy.

Efigenia's deposition conveys her perception of appropriate standards for her dignity and personal authority even as a subordinate. Her mistress had repeatedly violated these standards—with the damp bedroom, the accusation of petty theft, the explicit verbal assertions of authority (*dominio*) over her, the threats of physical punishment, and finally the assault itself. In her deposition, Efigenia freely admitted various ways in which she had resisted these affronts, finally fighting back when struck to the ground: "She scratched her señora on the face, managing to get on top of her, although she was unable to get [doña Josefa] to let go of her braids." And she had ultimately appealed to the legal authorities for help.

Neither doña Josefa nor don Ignacio testified for the written record, though a certification from the hospital verifies Efigenia's injuries—a major contusion on her head as well as other bruises, puncture wounds, and inflammation accompanied by a fever. Fortunately, she recovered and was released from the hospital after about two months. A juicio verbal (personal court appearance) followed, at which Efigenia agreed to give up rights to further litigation in exchange for a payment of 40 pesos from don Ignacio. Thus she was ultimately compensated to a degree. Measured by our modern sensibilities, though, the settlement seems meager compared to the employers' wealth and the violence of the injuries.

The case is suggestive about the limits of state protections—protections that were more in the hands of masters than of servants. Doña Josefa and don Ignacio had used their social position to avoid prosecution, recruiting the alcalde mayor to give them legal protection. Their elite status nearly gave them impunity—in effect, license to mistreat their servant. The court finally decided to hear Efigenia Asencio's case only because of the pressures of public opinion ("it was being whispered about too much"). Her story suggests that other cases like hers were perhaps never tried and never recorded. The employer class had more control over what appears in our archives than did their servants.

Notwithstanding, the judicial archives are peppered with appeals by servants and other workers, particularly people who lived in and near the capital city, which offered access to various offices of the state's judicial apparatus. Workers as well as employers viewed the colonial authorities as potentially protective. Though the state was not uniformly supportive of the poor, it was often benevolent. As it did for slaves, the judiciary provided attorneys for poor free people, enabling household workers to litigate. They sued for such things as back wages, personal damages, and—as we will see below—child support. More often than not, domestic workers who initiated litigation against their employers were awarded some settlement, though the amounts granted tended to be relatively small compared to the wealth of the employers.

Maids and lovers: Coercion and inequality
in master–servant sexual relations

Social inequalities shaped the relationships between domestic servants and their employers even when these relationships were sexual. Scholars have recognized sexual violence against indigenous and African women as a tool of conquest and enslavement.[126] Three centuries after the initial Spanish conquest in Guatemala, in the "contact zones" of households, sexual coercion and violence persisted as expressions (if not also instruments) of ongoing subjugation based on ethnicity and class as well as gender.[127] The nature of domestic service empowered employers with enormous authority over workers' whereabouts and tasks, giving the masters opportunities—or enabling them to create opportunities—to use sexual coercion or force against their servants.[128] In the seclusion of their private households, employers could easily make abusive demands, coerce their servants with threats or actual punishments, and force them physically.

Legal culture and popular ideologies bolstered masters' power to coerce and rape their servants. Many sexual acts that modern expectations would categorize as rape were not clearly defined as criminal, either in Spanish law or in popular understandings in late colonial Guatemala. There was no word with meaning equivalent to today's concept of "rape" (or *violación*). The term *estupro*—defloration—applied only if the woman was assumed to have been virginal before the act in question. Further, "estupro" did not involve any consideration of whether the woman had consented to have sex; the concept was not concerned with women's right to refuse.[129] In practice, the Guatemalan courts limited criminal investigation for estupro to cases of victims under age thirteen. For men accused of sexual "force" against teenage and adult women, early modern Spanish laws distinguished the crimes, prescribing differing punishments, according to the woman's socioeconomic status. The punishments were lesser for sexual assaults on women of low social status. Thus, servants' right to refuse sex was diminished at best.[130] Like their contemporary servants elsewhere and like their local counterparts today, domestic workers in colonial Guatemala were highly vulnerable to sexual assault and coercion.[131]

In light of the courts' approach, however, it is not surprising that few cases of sexual violence were brought to trial. In my random sampling of over 300 criminal court records for the period from 1765 to 1824, only five cases involve scenarios that appear as sexual assaults on nonenslaved women.[132] Three of the five were assaults on preteenage girls, none of them servants; all three were tried as estupro.[133] Only two cases involved adult victims. One of these was a domestic servant, a twenty-three-year-old Indian widow serving as wet nurse in an elite Spanish household. She described having been forcibly assaulted by her mistress's brother, who was living in the house. The court heard the case but ultimately dismissed the charges, explicitly displacing responsibility onto the victim. The defendant was never arrested or jailed.[134] The other adult plaintiff's case—against a man of middling socioeconomic status—had the same outcome.[135] The judges' disposition in these instances highlights the possibility that other women may also have reported sexual attacks, only to be dismissed by local alcaldes before a written record was generated. Further, some victims may have chosen not to report sexual assaults for fear of punishment by their employers, family members, or rapists. The wet nurse we have just seen, for example, noted that she was afraid her ill-tempered master would beat her if she told him that his brother-in-law had raped her. She abandoned the job and returned to her home community before reporting the crime.

For free women, the personal costs of reporting a sexual assault generally outweighed any potential gains. Aside from fears of retribution, plaintiffs had to endure a discussion among witnesses and judicial personnel about their sexual histories and behavior. If the charge was estupro, the girl would additionally be subjected to gynecological examination by a midwife and/or surgeon, who would pronounce judgment about the victim's state of "virginity." In the two trials identified for sexual attacks on free adult women, the courts ultimately blamed the plaintiffs for the assaults against them, in effect publicly denying their violation.

A comparison with charges brought by slave women is suggestive. In Chapter 2 we saw a pattern of lawsuits filed by slave women on grounds of sexual coercion or abuse by the master or another man, typically the master's relative or houseguest. These were essentially civil suits, not criminal trials; the plaintiffs were seeking liberty or money to purchase their liberty. The plaintiffs described scenarios of sexual coercion and force in which the aggressors had promised them manumission in exchange for their "consent." Compared to free women, slave women had greater reason to testify about their subjection to such pressures, since the possibility of their emancipation was at stake. As shown in Chapter 2, there was widespread awareness among slaves that the judicial system would facilitate their manumission if they could prove it had been promised to them.

In contrast, free domestic servants had little reason to explain that they had been forced or manipulated to consent, since they were not seeking manumission. In their litigation against men with whom they had had sexual relationships, free servants were usually seeking child support. To win a settlement, they needed to prove paternity, not force or coercion. Free women who could provide convincing evidence of paternity were almost assured of winning some settlement, but their willingness or lack of willingness to participate in the past sexual relationship was irrelevant to building their cases. This is not to suggest that free domestic servants were not subject to rape and sexual coercion; it only indicates that they had less potential gain than did enslaved women in recounting the details to the men who ran the courts. It also follows that free women may have been somewhat less likely to be compelled into sex; since they were free of bondage, not even their employers could coerce them with an offer of liberty.

What about consensual sexual relations between servants and employers? As Sharon Block has demonstrated for early Anglo America, there is a continuum between coercion and consent. It can be difficult for historians to locate a given instance of master–servant sex precisely on this continuum, since "the power of mastery could blur the degree of coercion."[136] In the context of colonial Guatemala, the power of mastery over servants was often augmented by the power and privileges of Spanish ethnicity. Still, it is reasonable to think that not all sex between employers and servants was coerced or forced. Consider the case of twenty-two-year-old Petrona Alvarez. In 1799 and 1800, she had an affair with don Pedro José Esnao, a year her senior, who had hired her to wash and mend his clothes. Though both were identified as *españoles*, Esnao held higher socioeconomic status. He had come alone to the new capital from León (Nicaragua) to study Latin, with no need to earn wages. He used the honorific *don*. Alvarez, not a *doña*, lived with her widowed father, a tinsmith, in a little shop attached to one of the city's inns. She was working for a living. But she was clearly a willing party in the relationship, as she revealed under interrogation by the alcalde de barrio (this was after a neighbor complained about a pattern of trysts in Esnao's rented room). Alvarez admitted that sometimes after her father was asleep, she "would take out the key and go meet the student [Esnao]" at his lodgings. Witnesses confirmed that she sometimes spent the whole night with him.[137]

In another set of examples, lawsuits brought by free women seeking child support from their former employers hint at mutual affection in the relationships, despite the fact that those couples whose cases came to court had ended in dispute. These relationships generally appear to have been unequal but consensual, and even—up to a point—loving. The case of María de los Angeles Aragón illustrates. Identified in the records as an Indian servant of the parish priest of Mixco (just west of the new capital), Arargón did domestic work for several people and seems to have moved easily among their households. One of her employers was don Blas Bahamonde, a fledgling merchant who traveled frequently between his home in San Miguel (in what is now El Salvador) and Guatemala. While in Guatemala he stayed in Mixco and hired Aragón to do his cooking and laundry. Before long it was common knowledge in the town that Aragón and Bahamonde were carrying on an affair. People who lived in the various houses where María de los Angeles worked observed that don Blas often spent the night with her. They also noticed him visiting her at the hour of the siesta, furtively entering her employers' houses through side doors.

In 1778, Aragón (who was not married) got pregnant. Bahamonde, then in his early thirties, soon left for San Miguel, and he did not return to Guatemala for fourteen years. During those years he wrote several letters to María de los Angeles inquiring about their daughter and expressing concern for her, but he was rather unwilling to provide financial support. He ultimately amassed a great fortune in San Miguel. It was only with a lawsuit that Aragón managed to extract from him a child-support settlement—a one-time payment of 50 pesos. Years later, when their daughter was about thirty, she sued her father for additional support. By this time she was married and keeping a tavern with her husband. The court awarded her the hefty sum of 600 pesos, plus the extensive costs she had incurred in litigation. The record shows that she successfully collected.

On one level, this story depicts a domestic servant whose more privileged lover abandoned her and their child, refusing to help support them. As one witness in their daughter's litigation pointed out, both Aragón and Bahamonde were unmarried at the time of Aragón's pregnancy; he was free to marry her if he wished. Thus the case can be read as one in which social inequalities ruled, and an Indian domestic servant struggled to support her child while the careless Spanish father lived a life of luxury in San Miguel. On another level, though, the story depicts two relatively poor women, Aragón and her daughter, who deployed public institutions to demand payments from a man who had abandoned them.[138]

A similar scenario developed three decades later in the lives of Paz Palala and the priest don Francisco Carrascal. As a child or teenager, Palala had lived in the home of Carrascal's mother, doña María Josefa Aparicio, who employed her as an hija de la casa. Palala was probably an orphan or the child of an impoverished family; she worked without a salary, receiving only her food, lodging, and clothing. The surname Palala suggests Mexican Indian ancestry.[139] When Aparicio died in 1814, Palala continued in the service of the son, the young don Francisco Carrascal.[140] Carrascal was ordained in 1815 and began service as the parish priest of Asunción Mita in southeastern Guatemala; a year later, he was assigned also the parish of San Miguel Petapa, just south of the capital. In 1821, service in the parish of Chinautla, a few kilometers north of the city, was added to his duties.[141] Though he was frequently traveling among his parishes, Carrascal played a prominent political role in Guatemala City and in the early independent Central American federation, signing the declaration of independence and then serving as a *diputado* (representative) for the state of Guatemala.[142] He retired from parish service in 1829 and continued to live on the income from his *labor* (farm), whose profits he split with its manager, and from two *capellanías* (chantries) of 1,000 pesos each.[143]

Paz Palala remained in Carrascal's service for twenty-three years until his death in 1835. She traveled with him to the pueblos where he worked, washing his clothes, preparing his food, and managing his domestic life generally. He gave her money each week, which she used to make purchases for their daily living, including food and his cigarettes.[144] In July of 1821, Palala gave birth to a daughter. It was no secret that Padre Carrascal was the child's father. During her pregnancy and for the first year or two of the baby's life, Palala stayed in the capital while Carrascal traveled to his parishes. Friends saw that she sent him his daily cigarettes, and he was known to send her baskets of chickens, ducks, and other gifts. After the birth, Carrascal himself told several people that the girl was his daughter. Neighbors knew that he provided for her clothing and other needs. She was said to look like him.[145]

In the later years of his life, Carrascal named an executrix for his will.[146] In a memo he noted that the executrix had been instructed to use his property "as I have communicated to her, confidentially, to cover the only responsibility I have." Presumably he was referring to his daughter.[147] (It was common practice for priests to conceal inheritances left to their offspring, even when their paternity was common knowledge among neighbors.)[148] But after Carrascal's death, the executrix distributed little if anything to Palala and the daughter.

Palala then sued Carrascal's estate. She demanded not only child support and alimony (*alimentos*) but also wages that she argued she had earned. She presented eleven witnesses, including the priest's sister, his nephew, and the servant of another priest who for a time had shared a house in the capital with Carrascal.[149] (His sister, apparently his only sibling, had been excluded from his will after an earlier falling-out.)[150] Though the record is incomplete, it is clear that someone tried to block Palala from tapping into the estate. Perhaps it was the executrix or the manager of Carrascal's *labor*. The attorney for the estate argued doggedly against Palala's impressive evidence. He protested that Carrascal might not have been the father of Palala's child, and he sought to counter Palala's demand for back wages, suggesting that the weekly allowance Carrascal had given her was more than sufficient. "Padre Carrascal dressed only in black," the attorney wrote, "and the washing of his shirt and underwear could not have consumed four pesos monthly, which was the salary that she received for her service in the kitchen and laundry of a single man."[151] But Palala and her witnesses indicated that she had spent the money Carrascal gave her on his household expenses. The estate's attorney countered that she had been "remunerated with the clothing and furniture she needed and with use of the kitchen, hens, ducks, etc."[152]

Though the outcome of Palala's suit is not known, her case clearly repeats a pattern seen with María de los Angeles Aragón: a female domestic servant of relatively low social status appealed to the state demanding payment from a Spanish employer who had fathered her child. Both Palala and Aragón perceived that they (and their daughters) deserved greater provisions from their employer-paramours. This was despite the women's much lower socioeconomic status than that of the men. Neither Aragón nor Palala had completely internalized the colonial ethnic and class hierarchies.

Some elite men did make provisions for domestic servants with whom they had affairs, or at least for the children of these affairs. We saw that Padre Carrascal probably meant to leave an inheritance for the daughter he had with Paz Palala, though his plan may have been foiled after his death. In the late 1780s, don Francisco Maz gave a rancho (small house) to the daughters he had by his maid Paula Antillón.[153] The priest don Miguel de Aragón made Josefa de Guzmán his universal heir; she had been his domestic servant for many years and appears in the record as the probable mother of his daughters.[154]

Yet the provisions were not always congruent with the men's economic means, and bequests were often contested or unfulfilled. The cases we have seen were recorded precisely because the women had appealed to the courts in a struggle to obtain or retain support. Because none of these women was married to the father of her children, none enjoyed the legal benefit of inheritance as a spouse, nor would the children inherit automatically. Elite men who engaged in sex with their maids usually did not intend to marry them, regardless of emotional ties. Don Pedro Esnao, the Latin student from Nicaragua, had no plans to marry Petrona Alvarez, though both were eligible. When the alcalde put the two under questioning, Esnao said he "wanted to pursue his literary career without her." Don Blas Bahamonde is another example. His letters to María de los Angeles Aragón demonstrate his affection; and as a witness attested, he had been free to marry her at the time their child was born. But he absconded to San Miguel. We can only presume that he chose not to marry her, following the normal pattern among Europeans in Spanish America, because of her low socioeconomic status. He later married a Spanish woman of some means.[155] The 50 pesos that the court awarded María de los Angeles Aragón was a paltry sum compared to the wealth Bahamonde was amassing in San Miguel. Even the 600 pesos later awarded to their daughter represented only a small fraction of the father's net worth. Though the judicial system was available as a potentially protective recourse, the overarching economic inequities between domestic servants and their elite employers persisted—through amours, *desamores*, and shared parenthood.

Men in domestic service

Though fewer in number than their female counterparts, male domestic servants spanned a broader range of career trajectories. Boys and men in domestic service in late colonial Guatemala were usually called *criados* or *sirvientes*, terms used interchangeably. Though the lexicon made little distinction, the tasks that male servants performed varied widely, and the workers themselves comprised a wide socioeconomic spectrum.

At the lower end of the spectrum, the recruitment and demographic profile of male domestic servants looks similar to what we have seen for female servants. Native and African men were procured for domestic labor through mechanisms that gradually shifted, like the mechanisms of female recruitment, from tribute labor and slavery to free wage labor. In the early and mid-colonial eras, Indian men had fulfilled various domestic roles as tribute workers, drafted under the catchall category of "servicio personal"—personal service for high-ranking colonial officials in both church and state. In the late colonial years the drafts of men for servicio personal continued in some cases, notably to serve rural parish priests, but in the capital city men recruited as free domestic servants were replacing draftees. Men from Chinautla, for example, had been drafted for servicio personal in the capital as late as 1742, for numerous jobs including cooking. By 1784, the Chinautla draft was diminished to include men only for the mail service.[156]

Even after the shift to free labor, some Indian men continued to provide the same kinds of domestic service as their predecessors from the same communities had provided as draftees. In the 1570s, for example, a crew of men from Jocotenango had been drafted three days a week to clean the palace of the Audiencia.[157] Two centuries later, a 1797 report from Jocotenango listed fourteen Indian men working as free laborers in the capital. Two of them, Alfonso Clemente and Isidro González, were serving in the palace of the Audiencia. Presumably they were providing janitorial service, as their forebears had done under the old tribute system. Another three of the men in 1797 were also staffing government and ecclesiastic offices (cleaning, one imagines). The remaining nine were employed by specific individuals, evidently in their homes.[158]

At the upper end of the spectrum was a class of sirvientes or criados comprised of young men, some of them from Europe, working as assistants to Spanish merchants. This class appears as the equivalent of Mexico City's *cajeros* (a term not used widely in Guatemala).[159] They generally aspired to become independent businessmen in their own right, and those who succeeded attained much higher levels of wealth and status than did any women called sirvientas or criadas. Yet even well-born servant men were not exempt from manual labor. Don Blas Bahamonde, the father of María de los Angeles Aragón's child, is an example. During his early residences in Guatemala, Bahamonde had lived as a criado in the home of don Pedro Martínez, with duties including gardening at one of Martínez's properties.[160] As we have seen, Bahamonde eventually made thousands as a merchant in his own right.

When they traveled, Iberian merchants in America usually brought at least one slave or free servant, often a young male. These workers might assist with the business, but they also functioned more generally as personal assistants, helping their employers procure the daily necessities. An incident at the old capital in 1775 offers some examples. Several Spanish-born merchants were staying at an inn. Among them were don Jacinto Martínez Mesa, an indigo trader, and his younger brother, who apparently assisted in the business. In the Martínez Mesa brothers' company was their criado, a free mulato in his twenties or early thirties named Juan Francisco Osorio, originally from the Valley of Cuscateca (now in Honduras). Also living at the inn was a man known as Lázaro el Maltés (Lázaro the Maltese). Though his agnomen connotes Mediterranean birth, Lázaro's lack of the honorific "don" suggests lower social status than that of many European men in the city. He was known to the Martínez Mesa brothers and their servant Juan Francisco Osorio before coming to the inn; all of them had attended an indigo dye fair five months earlier in the town of Apastepeque (in what is now El Salvador). In Apastepeque, Lázaro el Maltés had been working for a Genoese man, most certainly a merchant, with whom he had then traveled to Guatemala. The Genoese had subsequently left the capital, and Lázaro remained, working as a servant for the priest who owned the inn.

Lázaro's tenure with the priest, however, was short-lived. One March day around noon, the criado Juan Francisco Osorio went to the inn's kitchen to get a plate of food for his employer. In the kitchen, Osorio and several others witnessed a scuffle between a large dog belonging to Lázaro el Maltés and a smaller dog. Seeing that the smaller animal was leading in the fight, Osorio made a crack about the cowardice of Lázaro's dog. Lázaro took offense, challenging Osorio to fight ("ponte tú conmigo"—roughly: let's go at it, you and me). Osorio replied that "there was no reason to fight," but Lázaro threw a punch and drew his knife. Osorio was unable to escape quickly enough from the narrow kitchen; Lázaro stabbed him in the abdomen before fleeing to the street. Fortunately, Osorio showed signs of a quick recovery. After being treated by a doctor, he returned to the inn.

Later that day the alcalde arrived and questioned witnesses, including the inn's two cooks. One was a woman over age fifty whom the other residents called "the nun," apparently referring to her spinsterhood. She identified herself as Indian and spoke Spanish without an interpreter. The other cook was a twenty-three-year-old mestiza. Her husband had also been present, evidently engrossed in the dogfight. (He was a free mulato tailor, age twenty-seven, who signed his deposition in a smooth hand.) The witnesses all confirmed Osorio's account. But no one could find Lázaro el Maltés. In his absence, the authorities seized the property he had left behind—9 pesos, a new pair of stirrups, a mule bridle, a linen shirt, and two old pairs of underdrawers. (The record makes no further mention of Lázaro's dog.) Eight weeks later, with Lázaro still missing, Juan Francisco Osorio requested and was granted the impounded clothing to use on a trip he was making to San Salvador in the capacity of a servant. The rest of Lázaro's property was given to the priest who owned the inn, in compensation for the costs he had paid for the investigation.[161]

This episode typifies several patterns in male domestic service. Boys and men of various ethnicities worked as criados. They appear in rather tight pecuniary circumstances, relying on their employers for lodging, food, and even clothing. Yet like their female counterparts, men in domestic service floated in and out of jobs. They might stay with a given employer for only a few weeks. Compared to women, though, male servants enjoyed prospects for much greater fortunes. This was not only because men's salaries tended to be higher but also because some of the men working as servants, especially those of European descent, were positioned to develop their own business in long-distance commerce, notably in regional and transatlantic exports like indigo. Lázaro el Maltés, for one, aspired to a certain degree of material wealth, as suggested by the stirrups and bridle (if not a mule or horse) among his belongings.

Textile and clothing workers

After domestic service, textile and clothing production was Nueva Guatemala's largest employment sector. The textile industry continued to thrive in Santiago as well, even after the 1773 earthquakes; Santiago alone was said to have around a thousand looms in 1795, producing 20,000 *arrobas* of cloth annually.[162] Commercial textile production would suffer after about 1798, with a collapse in the region's indigo market and competition from textile factories in England.[163] Still, the industry commanded a large sector of the economy. At Nueva Guatemala, the 1824 census registered 461 men, or 10.1 percent of the city's adult males, as weavers—more men than in any other trade. Tailors ranked second, with 285 men, or 6.2 percent of male workforce.[164] (Men do not appear as spinners in Guatemala, in contrast to Mexico.)[165]

Women also worked in significant numbers in the textile industry, mainly as spinners and seamstresses. Though the 1824 census identifies only sixty spinners and 128 seamstresses (3.0 and 6.3 percent of the female workforce), these figures are probably deceptively low.[166] Women who spun thread tended to combine it with other sources of income, described by census takers as "oficios mujeriles." Spinning was rather low-status work. Prisoners in the women's jail were put to work spinning cotton as well as preparing their food (proceeds from the thread were used to generate a salary for the *madre rectora*—the woman who served as warden).[167] Sewing and fancywork were the most genteel of women's crafts, and those earning income as seamstresses may have passed in the censuses as housewives without an identified occupation. Both women and men worked as dyers, hatmakers, and buttonmakers; men also worked as upholsterers and *galoneros* (making fabric braid or trim) and women as lacemakers.

The records on textile workers illustrate the transformation of the workforce with the rise of free labor. Textiles had been produced for the early colonial Spanish economy mainly by coerced workers, both male and female. As part of a colonial imposition called *repartimiento de algodón* (distribution of cotton), Spanish corregidores turned raw cotton over to native alcaldes, who distributed it to their townswomen. The women were forced to work unremunerated at their homes spinning the fiber into thread, which was then returned for the profit of the corregidores. Women not completing the task are known to have been whipped. Additionally, indigenous women wove the cloth demanded of their communities in tribute and at times by corregidores.[168] Men's labor also was coerced for clothing production. Tribute lists for some native communities include finished garments as well as cloth, and men probably did some of the tailoring.[169] In early Santiago, men of various ethnicities had been put to work in weaving sweatshops (*obrajes*) as a form of punishment or correction. Note that the locations where weaving was performed, the equipment, and the techniques were gendered; while women weaving at home used the pre-Hispanic–style backstrap loom, men in the obrajes used treadle looms (foot-pedal looms), built on the Spanish model if not imported.

By the late colonial era, coerced labor had largely given way to free labor in textile and clothing production. The one exception was the persisting forced labor of Indian women spinning cotton, although it was documented only in the northwestern highlands (the corregimientos of Totonicapán and Huehuetenango, and Quetzaltenango), not in the region surrounding the capital.[170] Thread spun in those northwestern provinces may have been partially supplying the capital's looms; though free spinners abounded in the city, more workers were required for spinning than weaving.[171] In any case, much of the spinning for the late colonial capital was done by women on their own account. In addition to spinners of various ethnicities in the city, Indian women in surrounding towns worked freely spinning thread for sale in the city.[172] Similarly, native women's work in weaving (beyond that for their families) had also been transformed into free labor, subsumed in the cash economy as tributes in commodities were replaced by coin. The coercion of male weavers had ended; by the late seventeenth century, Santiago's penal obrajes had disappeared as Indian men in the city and beyond adopted the treadle loom to weave for cash.[173] In the late colonial years, men identified as Spaniards, mestizos, mulatos, and pardos were working as weavers in both Santiago and Nueva Guatemala.[174] The master weaver Julián Cota, over age fifty when he testified in 1812, said he had been born in Africa; presumably he was an ex-slave.[175] Few if any of the city's weavers in the late eighteenth century were identified as Indians.[176]

A number of urban women also were operating as weavers, though they were fewer than the men. Nine women are listed as weavers in the three extant barrio censuses for 1796, and fifteen female weavers are identified in the 1824 census.[177] Some of these women were likely working at backstrap looms.[178] The 1824 census did not register treadle looms among the property of any of the women weavers.[179] (Backstrap looms, which are homemade, would not have been given attention as potentially taxable property in the census.) But the census didn't catch everything. As early as 1745, the weavers' guild recognized a woman named Francisca Gelista as a *maestra* (master), in a document contracting a youth named José Tiburcio to learn the trade in her shop. Presumably Gelista and her apprentice worked on a treadle loom.[180] Notarial records also show that a number of women were operating weaving workshops in their homes. In the 1770s, Josefa de Cárdenas of Santiago owned four treadle looms. The looms were hers alone, not an inheritance from her husband; he was still alive, with a mercantile trade in thread and cloth. Cárdenas noted that her husband had brought no property to the marriage. Probably he was supplying her thread and selling cloth from her shop.[181] The widow Tomasa de Cartagena had six treadle looms and related equipment in her home.[182]

Despite the large weaving industry in both Santiago and Nueva Guatemala, workshops were small, with only a few workers, not on the scale of the Mexican obrajes with dozens of employees.[183] Some looms in Guatemala were operated without guild recognition, by men trained in other crafts who had turned to weaving to supplement their income.[184] Even those operators with recognized, dedicated weaving shops were hardly captains of industry. Take Cristóbal Iguana of Santiago. Implicated in the stabbing of another man in 1775, Iguana fled the crime scene and disappeared. In the standard procedure, the authorities went to his house and impounded his movable property. He had a workshop with four looms, but precious little else. There is no mention of spinning wheels or dyeing vats; Iguana had not achieved vertical integration. In addition to his looms, the officers found forty-five spools of white and blue thread, totaling sixteen and a half pounds; three warp beams, two with half-done pieces of cloth and the third with a warp started; twelve iron treadles; an iron chain (part of the treadle mechanism); six shuttles (part of the weaving mechanism); two benches; one small bottle; a flask of "ordinary glass pieces"; and some chickens. Everything was sold, with 6 pesos of the proceeds used to cover court costs and another 8 pesos awarded to the stabbing victim. The remaining 26 pesos and 2½ reales were turned over to Iguana's wife, who was evidently left in precarious financial straits and had been "clamoring" to the court.[185]

Among weavers, as in most other crafts, status in the guild seems not to have mattered much. Having a loom or looms is what determined whether a weaver worked for someone else or for himself. The records occasionally label a weaver as master (*maestro*), journeymen (*oficial*), or apprentice (*aprendiz*), but more often the notaries simply indicated that a man was a weaver in his own shop or someone else's.

At both Santiago and Nueva Guatemala, weaving shops were concentrated in the barrio of San Sebastián.[186] Apprentice and journeymen weavers—that is, weavers who did not have their own shop—tended to live in rooms near their workplace, if not in the master's house. Thus, though the shops themselves were small, San Sebastián was home to a large community of textile workers who lived and toiled cheek by jowl. Research in the parish's marriage records has suggested that the quotidian proximity contributed to a high rate of intermarriage and ethnic mixing among weavers' families.[187]

The appearance in the late colonial capital of dyers (*tintoreros*) represents another shift to free labor, since dyeing had previously been done without pay, part of the production of cloth given in tribute.[188] People in indigenous communities surely continued dyeing the thread and cloth they produced for their own families, but commercial dyeing in the capital came to be done by women and men specializing in the trade, identified as dyers (tintoreros) and occasionally as fabric printers (*estampadores de ropa*). Some dyes were made from cochineal and indigo, both raised in colonial Central America for export and processed near the fields by Indian workers. Merchants brought these dyes into the capital.[189] In addition, even as late as the twentieth century, indigenous artisans also used various native flora and fauna to make dyes in numerous colors; some of the colonial-era tintoreros must have been using the same methods.[190] Indian men and women from Santiago's neighborhood of San Antón, which had originally been a tributary barrio, worked often as tintoreros in the late colonial years.[191] One suspects that the barrio's tributes in earlier centuries had included dyed yarn, or provision of people to dye, and that later generations were continuing the craft as free workers.

While some dyers worked at their homes, others were employed in weaving shops. At the new capital in the 1780s, Manuela Trinidad Cantero, a married woman in her forties known by neighbors as "la Tintorera," dyed thread in a tub in her house.[192] An 1814 case hints that a tintorero named Cecilio Ramírez Hernández was put to work in a weaving shop. Ramírez was identified as mulato, age twenty. Originally from Antigua's barrio San Sebastián, the center of the city's textile industry, he was living in a rooming house in the new capital when he was arrested in the death of a Jocotenango Indian man. The fatal injury had occurred while the victim was out drinking with friends in the new capital's barrio San Sebastián. Testimony from various witnesses in the neighborhood reveals a loose-knit community of men who worked in textile production and fraternized in their free hours, gathering to drink, strolling in groups of mixed company, and (as on the night of the murder) engaging in altercations. Eventually, suspicion was shifted from Ramírez to another man, and the authorities somewhat cautiously released Ramírez from jail into the custody of a master weaver. Presumably Ramírez had been (or would be) working at his craft of dyeing in the weaver's shop.[193]

Like weavers, tailors (*sastres*) in the late colonial years were mostly men of ethnically mixed ancestry, though a few were identified as Indians or Spaniards.[194] At least two were former slaves.[195] Evidence suggests that in native communities, cutting and sewing clothes—that is, tailoring—was largely men's work, while women and possibly men did the weaving.[196] In the early colonial era, tributes demanded from various communities in Guatemala included finished clothing articles as well as raw cloth.[197] Some men therefore had presumably been doing unpaid tailoring as part of the tribute system. At the same time, European tailors were present in the colony starting in the 1520s, and in Santiago they began training Indian apprentices by the 1550s if not sooner.[198] Thus some native men had crossed into the early colonial Hispanic world as tailors.

With the growing population of Spanish and hispanized women in colonial society, seamstresses (*costureras*) paralleled tailors, sewing clothing for women. They also did lacemaking, embroidery, and other fancywork. Seamstresses named in judicial records were often identified as Spanish, a few with the honorific "doña," though some were of mixed ancestry.[199] At least a few slave women were skilled as seamstresses.[200] Needle crafts required substantial training and practice and were viewed as appropriate activities for girls and women of high social rank. A few other lines of business—shopkeeping, urban real estate investment, and rural estate management—were also acceptable, but needlework was the only type of manual labor that would not tarnish the gentility of a woman's public image. Sewing and fancywork required little investment and property compared to estate management and other aristocratic enterprises. (The craft of making cigars or cigarettes was arguably genteel, but not as prestigious

as needlework.[201] Cigarette making required less training than needlework
and was widely practiced by non-Spanish women. Though Spanish women
too may have rolled cigarettes for profit, they rarely reported it for the
written record. Only eight cigarette makers were registered in the capital's extant 1796 censuses, and thirty-six in the 1824 records. Seamstresses,
on the other hand, reported their work in larger numbers—seventy-four
women in 1796; 128 in 1824.[202]) Privileged women who had acquired
needlework skills and subsequently fell on hard times could support themselves, albeit austerely, with their own labor.

Contemporary understandings clearly distinguished the trade of seamstress from that of tailor. Tailors had an organized guild, even though some
men were practicing outside it.[203] There is no evidence that any women
were called "tailors" (sastres) or recognized by the tailors' guild. Granted,
trade guilds were mainly a male phenomenon, but some of them formally
legitimated female practitioners, as we saw with the master weaver Francisca Gelista. The guild of *coheteros* (gunpowder and fireworks makers)
also recognized women, some of them widows carrying on their late husbands' trades. So did the guilds of saltpeter refiners, bakers, potters, and
tanners.[204] There was no seamstresses' guild—no formal guild officers or
exams. However, residents of the late colonial capital did recognize certain women as "maestras" in needlework and other genteel crafts. These
women were known not as commercial seamstresses, but as private teachers for girls.

"An adequate royalty": Maestras

Women operating as private "maestras" (female masters or teachers) served Nueva Guatemala's privileged circles, paralleling a class of
girls' teachers called *amigas* in colonial Mexico City and Lima.[205] The term
maestra echoed the vocabulary of the guilds, and similarly the Guatemalan
maestras referred to their students as *niñas aprendices* (literally, apprentice girls). The pupils were españolas, children and teenagers whose parents
paid the maestras a monthly sum, though the system of compensation was
somewhat unstructured. In exchange, maestras instructed their charges
(often several at a time) in needlework, religious doctrine, and reading and
writing. Some teachers or their servants may also have taught the girls to
cook and do laundry. A pupil would spend much of each day at the maestra's home, if she did not live there. Some of these girls were orphans or
children of widowers, and maestras served them in lieu of a mother, providing child care and attending to general upbringing. One maestra spoke

of "care for the girl, as much in teaching her as in serving her, doing her hair, making her food, and all that is necessary."[206]

Private female teachers coexisted with a *colegio* for girls from Spanish families as well as three *beaterios* (institutional communities of pious laywomen) that offered formal education for girls of various ethnicities. (Convents evidently were not running formal girls' schools until after independence.)[207] The teachers staffing the girls' institutions were also mainly women.[208] From the parents' perspective, the appeal of private teachers over institutions may have been simply the availability of enrollment space or proximity to home.[209] Lower costs were also likely a factor.

Women with private teaching enterprises played counterpart to the city's male teachers (*maestros de escuela*, literally schoolmasters) who ran boys' schools in their homes. Records show four such male teachers working in the late colonial years, in addition to boys' educational institutions run by religious orders as well as a state-run secondary school.[210] Male private teachers were by law subject to the *media anata*, an annual tax assessed to guild officers and master craftspeople, but the legislation that established the media anata in the 1630s did not mention female teachers.[211] By the late eighteenth century, however, maestras had established a recognized profession in Nueva Guatemala.

A picture of their enterprises emerges in a dispute between the maestra María Magdalena Mijangos and the father of one of her pupils.[212] Mijangos was identified in the 1796 census as mulata, age forty-eight, single, and living in a house headed by her brother Mariano Mijangos, a mulato tailor in his late thirties. Several other adults with the same surname, all labeled as mulatos, were also living in the house.[213] It is not known how María Magdalena Mijangos learned to sign her name; perhaps she had been educated in one of the city's beaterios. In any case, like other maestras both in private operations and in the beaterios and colegio, she was forced to earn her living.

In 1798 Mijangos, now about fifty, filed suit against don Juan Antonio Aróstegui, whose daughter had been her pupil from 1790 through 1794. The teacher alleged that Aróstegui had failed to pay her, and she demanded a back payment of 6 pesos per month. "That is the least amount," she said, "at which I evaluate my work." She described how Aróstegui had placed his daughter in her care,

with the agreement that I would teach her, and educate her, and he would give me a *real* and a half every day for her food, promising me that at the end of the instruction he would recompense me, so that I would have a way to subsist in the future.

This girl came to my house, it was necessary that I give her a bed, and linen for it, she stayed five years in my custody, I taught her (with the exception of laundry and cooking) everything that in this city it is the style for a woman of honor to know, helping at the same time with her spiritual education.[214]

Aróstegui had promised, she reiterated, "that at the end he would give me a gratuity with which I would be able to finish my days"—that is, on which she could retire.

Informed of the suit, don Juan Antonio Aróstegui balked. He insisted that there had been "no specific contract, much less any obligation" on his part. Mijangos had taken his daughter "voluntarily," he contended, out of "the great love that she had for the girl." He said the teacher had been "reluctant" even to take money for the child's food.

Testimony from various witnesses reveals that maestras' agreements with their pupils' parents were generally unspoken, but the teachers expected a gratuity or gift in addition to the costs of the girls' food. One aristocratic witness explained that "it has never been customary to pay teachers materially, nor much less have there been contracts," but she confirmed that "the parents of the pupils recompense [the teachers]" and that it was "appropriate that Mijangos be recompensed for her work."[215] The maestra Bernarda Amaya agreed that Aróstegui should pay Mijangos "her gratuity." A man identified as a music teacher described similar understandings between male teachers and their students' parents. A man whose two daughters had been pupils of Mijangos testified "that he did not pay anything for her teaching; but his wife gave her each year an adequate royalty." Because his daughters came home to his house to eat and sleep, he explained, their maestras had never charged him. But he did give the teachers "their *obsequios* [gifts]." Even Aróstegui's daughter doña Josefa, sixteen at the time of the lawsuit, knew the etiquette. Questioned in the proceedings, she said she had studied with other maestras before Mijangos and that "it is necessary that teachers be compensated for their work, with some gratuities or obsequios; but paying them has not been the custom."

Thus, in the usual arrangement, parents and teachers tacitly assumed that money was part of the contract. María Magdalena Mijangos's protests that she "was reluctant" to receive don Juan Antonio Aróstegui's money for his daughter's food were a polite façade covering the fact that Mijangos depended on payments from her students' parents. Though she spoke of teaching the child out of love, she expected to be understood in the context of a patron–client relationship informed by local customs. And why did Aróstegui take Mijangos so literally? Again the depositions offer an explanation. Mijangos noted that "don Juan Antonio is a person who is not only economical but excessively so" (*don Juan Antonio es un sujeto no solo económico, sino que peca de tal*). The music teacher said although he had never done business with Aróstegui, he had heard of the man's thriftiness. Even a witness identified as a compadre of Aróstegui, queried on the issue of frugality, had to concede "that it is true." Don Juan Antonio Aróstegui was a well-known tightwad.

Evidently angered by the litigation, Aróstegui went so far as to suggest that Mijangos should reimburse *him*. She had educated his daughter inadequately, he charged, failing to teach her to wash clothes and cook. Mijangos replied that Aróstegui had told her not to teach the child those chores because he was going to buy her two slaves to do them. Aróstegui said the maestra had taught doña Josefa "nothing more than embroidery" and then shamelessly sold the child's needlework for her own profit. Mijangos answered that she had to sell a few pieces because she had bought the fabric with her own money. Both father and teacher then accused one another of feeding doña Josefa insufficiently. Mijangos said that when the girl had gone home every two weeks, the father sent her to prayers without giving her chocolate or anything to eat. The father retorted that on the contrary, his daughter had been fed on visits to his house but had complained of shortage at the teacher's.

In the continuing sparring, the record reveals a complex relationship between parents and teachers. Aróstegui described how during the years his daughter was under her tutelage, Mijangos had come with various members of her family to visit at his house on festival days. He said he had always "made them a grand reception with great expense" for liquor and food and had once given her leftovers to take home. He even presented an itemized list of expenditures he had made—totaling 72 pesos and 6 reales—"in obsequio [generosity] to the maestra Magdalena Mijangos and her siblings." Mijangos acknowledged the visits, but she disputed the quality and quantity of food. "Whatever he himself was eating," she said, "they gave her." The holiday visits served multiple purposes. In Aróstegui's estimation, inviting Mijangos and her relatives into his home to offer them food and drink showed his magnanimity. He also may have erroneously hoped that Mijangos would accept his hospitality as compensation for her work. But Mijangos explained her visits as an extension of the job. She said she had called at Aróstegui's house "to serve him, out of charity, [because] of the situation in which he found himself, and still finds himself today," presumably referring to his widowhood. She may have enjoyed food at his table, but she did not view it as payment for her labor.

The state backed her. "It is apparent," the asesor wrote, "that don Juan Antonio made [the expenditures] more to fulfill as an honorable man the political obligation of hosting her visits, than to pay for the services." The court determined that Aróstegui owed Mijangos some additional amount, but the asesor rejected Mijangos's demand of 6 pesos per month. Rather, he called for an assessment by two *mujeres peritas*—qualified women experts in the field.

The notion of "mujeres peritas" conveys the court's view of maestras as practitioners of a legitimate, skilled trade. Indeed, various maestras were well known; as each party to the suit raised objections about various prospective expert witnesses, the jurists had to float five names before even one was finally accepted by both sides. The woman called was doña María Ignacia Castro, identified as a "maestra de niñas" (a girls' teacher), age fifty-seven. She signed her name in a fairly practiced hand. Having seen the embroidery of don Juan Antonio's daughter, Castro said she was sure the girl could "support herself honorably and honestly with the work of her hands." She believed Mijangos had satisfactorily "served this girl in the three roles of mother, teacher, and criada." Given that the father had paid for the child's food, Castro said, Mijangos should be given 5 pesos and 4 reales for each month of her service. For the full five years, this would amount to 330 pesos.

The next *perita* to testify was the reverend mother of the Beaterio de Belén, where Aróstegui's daughter had been a resident for the past year at his expense. (The reverend mother was not a nun, but lived the pious life of a *beata*—a woman who has not taken vows.) Though the reverend mother's client–patron relationship with don Juan Antonio Aróstegui was mediated by the beaterio, she presumably recognized and supported the institution's interests, since her salary depended on its survival. The beaterio, in turn, depended on financial support from wealthy families who placed their daughters there.[216] Hence it is not surprising that the reverend mother's recommendation supported Aróstegui most enthusiastically. She said his daughter had been "taught very little of that which should have been taught" before she entered the beaterio. In "the teaching of a young woman so that she may be called a complete woman," the reverend mother opined, "good instruction consists of Christian doctrine, which is the first [in importance]." As for practical skills, she continued, there is a "variety of sewing, embroidery, artificial flowers . . . cooking, laundry, very essential to the female sex, even in the most noble . . . [and] reading in which certainly as in the rest, this girl is very limited." The reverend mother concluded that "sewing and fine embroidery," were all that Mijangos had taught young doña Josefa. "In the rest the child was ignorant," with the exception of reading, which she only "half knew." Only since entering the beaterio, the reverend mother added, had the lass made significant progress. The maestra Mijangos should not be given anything, she said; but she allowed that if don Juan Antonio wanted to give her something out of generosity, or "better to heal his conscience," she suggested "about thirty pesos."

With such disparity in the experts' recommendations, the court called a third perita, the maestra doña Gertrudis Flores, whose shaky signature suggests an advanced age. She offered a decisive assessment: "For the teaching, education, and service of the child doña Josefa Aróstegui, her teacher Magdalena Mijangos should be given five pesos per month." But the asesor was dissatisfied with Flores's appraisal. The peritas, he said, were supposed to determine a "gratuity for the whole period of learning, not a fixed monthly salary." He ordered the estimates discarded, and yet another perita to consult.

By now over a year had passed since Mijangos initially filed suit. It had been four years since the child had left her tutelage and since she had begun asking the father for payment. Exasperation must have contributed to her candor in telling the jurists, "It is not relevant to the case whether it is called gratuity, or salary." She was bringing into the open what everyone already knew—she was teaching to earn a living. The court assented. It ruled that Aróstegui would pay Mijangos 5 pesos a month for the time his daughter had been in her charge. He was also sentenced to pay a substantial portion of the court costs, since Mijangos's witnesses had attested to her poverty. Despite several attempts by Aróstegui to withhold or reduce the amount owed, within six months Mijangos did extract from him a cash payment of the full award—280 pesos and 5½ reales. He then grudgingly came forth with the courts costs of 93 pesos and 1½ reales.

The Mijangos–Aróstegui story demonstrates that a cadre of women in the late colonial capital was making a living as private teachers for girls. They were practicing unofficially, with no guild or licensing, essentially self-employed through private contracts. But everyone in elite circles, at least, seemed to know who they were and what their occupation was, and the state implicitly recognized the trade, calling various maestras as expert witnesses in Mijangos's suit. Maestras working in institutions as well as those in private enterprise knew how to sign their names—something few of their female contemporaries in Central America could do. The skills in which they trained their pupils had been acquired during relatively privileged childhoods or youths, but maestras were typically women who, like Mijangos, found themselves in stretched circumstances, in need of wages.

Doña Gertrudis Flores, the last perita consulted in the lawsuit of María Magdalena Mijangos, is another example. Flores had been widowed more than two decades earlier and like many of the city's residents she had suffered what she described as a "lack of money . . . much expenditure, and financial loss" since moving her family to the new capital.[217] The maestras in the girls' colegio and beaterios fit a similar mold. The sisters doña Perfecta and doña Ana Dominga Gordón, both unmarried españolas, worked as teachers in the Beaterio de Indias. They were known to be without any valuable property, living off the charitable support of people who would "provide them some alms" for their work in the beaterio. In 1792, an uncle of theirs died intestate in León. Though they tried to avail themselves of some of his property, they evidently met with no success.[218] Later in the 1790s, doña Perfecta was appointed as the rector of the prestigious Colegio de Niñas, a position from which she was eventually ousted under accusations of fiscal mismanagement.[219] Her sister doña Ana Dominga apparently continued teaching in the Beaterio de Indias.

In addition to reflecting a variety of economic activities practiced by privileged women, the records of the female teaching trade also illustrate elite ideologies about girls' education and women's intellectual life. The goal of formal education was not to offer social mobility but rather to prepare children for the roles society expected them to fulfill. Well-heeled Spanish women in the late colonial era were expected to do fancywork, to write with at least rudimentary skill, and to read. Indeed, elite women in Guatemala were reading for pleasure. We get a glimpse with the example of doña Dominga Durán. She took several novels along when she and her husband traveled from the capital to spend a few weeks at their farm in 1820. Her reading list—including *Tom Jones, Carolina, Memorias de Rosaura*, and *Las heroidas*—comes to light because the books were impounded by the Inquisition at the customhouse on her return to the city, and her husband then petitioned for their return. He mentioned that the books had been lent by a friend, doña Encarnación Gutiérrez; she too was obviously reading for pleasure.[220]

Scholarship on Spanish America has shown that new ideologies in the Bourbon period and the nineteenth century emphasized education for girls particularly to prepare them for motherhood, which Liberal thinkers linked to the welfare of families and the state.[221] Like its counterparts in Mexico, Guatemala City's Colegio de Niñas had expanded its enrollment and curriculum by mid-nineteenth century.[222] However, neither formal female education nor the colegio itself was new to the independent era. Elite Spanish girls in Guatemala's colonial capital had received formal schooling from a class of professional teachers just slightly less privileged than themselves.

The building trades

The relocation of the city beginning in the late 1770s fueled a construction boom that lasted into the early 1800s, and the building trades grew accordingly. Although the state attempted to direct the forced labor of Indians and convicts toward the construction projects, the coercive efforts proved generally unsuccessful and insufficient.[223] As people sought housing in the new location and the crown ordered the construction of public buildings and other large-scale projects, scores of jobs for free male laborers opened in the building trades.[224] Langenberg has shown that in 1796, the building trades ranked second among male occupational sectors, surpassed only by textile production. Private construction leveled off after about 1810, however, and the industry contracted again after the cathedral was completed in 1815 (it had been started in 1782). The 1824 census confirms that the number of men employed in construction had shrunk substantially.[225]

Meanwhile, the construction boom and the accompanying demand for building materials catapulted a few men from relatively humble origins into considerable financial success. An example is Bernardo Ramírez, a mulato who became the chief architect for the new city. He successfully petitioned the crown to grant his descendants the right to hold jobs and honors normally reserved for Spaniards. His story has received attention from a number of historians.[226]

Less known in the annals of history is Francisco Mesi, an illiterate shoemaker from the French region of Provence. He claimed to have deserted a group of colonists bound for the Americas when their ship docked briefly on the Yucatan Peninsula (though one wonders, considering his later behavior, whether he was ejected from the ship involuntarily). Adopting the alias "Pedro Ayau," he initially found employment as a sailor along the route from Campeche to Honduras, but he soon made his way to Nueva Guatemala, arriving there in 1786.[227] He secured lodging and work as a stonecutter at the quarry of don Domingo González. By 1792, though he still spoke only limited Spanish and was completely unable to read or write, Ayau had assumed the title "don" and was contracting independently to provide stones and sand for building projects in the new city.[228] Two years later, don Pedro Ayau owned one of the city's quarries, with a staff of men somewhat younger than him working there.[229] By 1795 he had fathered some four children by three different women in Guatemala, but he could not be coaxed to the altar. (The reader may recall from Chapter 2 that Ayau also refused to pay for the freedom of a slave woman he had allegedly impregnated under promise of manumission. Nor would he liberate the child.) In 1796, easily able to pay the child support settlements and court costs awarded to two free women who had sued him, don Pedro Ayau finally was wed to a Spanish woman, doña Atanasia Mesa. He was thirty-nine years old.[230] His trajectory of immigration to Guatemala as a young man, concubinage, rise to fortune, and later marriage into a high-status family fits a familiar pattern among European-born men in Spanish America.[231]

Manuel Luciano Alcayaga, a locally born mestizo, also rose to pros-
perity in the building-supply trade, but his success was more limited and
ultimately ill fated.[232] Alcayaga had worked as a brick maker in the old
capital. In 1778, at age twenty-seven, he contracted with the overseer of
construction for the Convento de la Concepción at the new capital. The
contract allowed Alcayaga to use a *ladrillera* (brick-making facility) and
kiln that had already been built next to the site assigned for the institution. In exchange, he would supply bricks and tile for the construction
of the convent's new building. He promised 12 pesos' worth of materials
per month, with tiles (*teja*) valued at 11 pesos per thousand, and bricks at
14 pesos per thousand. Ensuring his profits, Alcayaga contracted also with
the university and the Convento de Santa Teresa to supply bricks and tiles
for their new buildings.[233] Among the workers he employed at the plant
was his nephew, a man of mixed ancestry who earned between 2½ and
3 reales a day.[234]

In 1782, Alcayaga requested and was granted a repartimiento of Indian
workers to help operate the ladrillera. He was one of very few non-
Spaniards, if not the only one, to receive a repartimiento grant in the region
of the capital in the late colonial years.[235] When his enterprise exhausted
the usable clay on the rented property, Alcayaga petitioned the Audiencia for "license" to remove clay from the adjacent field of a Spaniard. His
request emphasized "the benefit that certainly results also for the public."
Probably he had already been entering and taking clay from the lands of
the Indians of Jocotenango, which also adjoined the ladrillera; though he
denied having done so, at the same time he complained to the Spanish
authorities that the Indians "have threatened to take me out of there by
blows." The Audiencia granted Alcayaga permission to take clay from the
adjoining Spanish-owned field and issued an order to the Indian authorities of Jocotenango "that on no pretext should they impede" Alcayaga in
his operations during the city construction projects.[236]

Alcayaga fell from fortune at the end of the building boom, when the
projects that he had been supplying were completed. In 1809, unable
to pay one of his creditors, he described his finances in an appeal to the
court. He had suffered a series of losses, he said, and had been left with his
house as his only valuable property. Badly in arrears, he was then forced
to sell the house, worth 200 pesos. The buyer gave him 120 pesos as a
down payment, but Alcayaga spent the majority of this money paying off
a batch of bricks that had been ruined in the baking process. "I now find
myself in the street and without any means," he said, "experiencing two
thousand needs, my wife without decent clothing [*en cueros*—literally,
stark naked]."[237] Indeed, Alcayaga's wife, a mulata about twenty years his
junior, appeared to be headed for her own ruin. Beginning at the time

of the slowdown in urban construction, she had taken to drinking, fighting with her husband, and even robbery. In 1810 she stole a set of silverware from a well-to-do Spanish household; after confessing to the crime, she was released into the custody of her husband. She was jailed again in 1811 for a repeat offense. The court transferred her to the hospital when she was injured in a jailhouse fight, and she was apparently then released, but she was arrested yet again for another theft in 1813. Alcayaga had come to her defense in earlier trials, but in this final case there is no statement from him. It is unclear whether he was still alive at that time; if so, he would have been sixty-two years old. His wife was sentenced to a full year in the women's prison.[238]

The rise of upstarts like don Pedro Ayau and Manuel Alcayaga was possible partly because the building industry was staffed with little regard to guilds. Construction workers included albañiles (masons or general builders), carpenters, stonecutters, brick makers, cabinetmakers, *aparejadores* (master builders or draftsmen), painters, and sculptors. During the construction boom, some of these workers were recruited from the ranks of craftsmen in other trades.[239] Bárbaro Arriola, for example, a thirty-five-year-old mulato who had been trained as a weaver, was working in 1801 as a *peón* (a daily wage laborer) for a master albañil.[240] An Indian man named Cristóbal Santiago who was known as a candle maker was working on the construction of a house abutting the Convent of San Francisco in 1803.[241] The relocation of the city may have increased fluidity in jobs and crafts, but even before the earthquake instability of employment and movement across urban trades had been typical.[242] The same was true elsewhere in Spanish America also.[243] Men and women were getting work where they could, when they could.

"From time immemorial": Tavern keepers

For centuries, women in Guatemala had been making alcoholic beverages for popular consumption. A 1679 petition from an Indian cofradía in Ciudad Vieja requested license for the sale of pulque, noting that Indian women had been selling the drink "from time immemorial."[244] The licensing request was necessitated by the colonial state's regulatory measures, which in part sought to limit alcohol consumption. In this goal, the authorities were battling against the ritual and social importance of alcohol. But regulation was meant also to garner revenues through licensing fees and *estancos* (state monopolies on beverage ingredients and sales). The state teetered in an awkward balance between its desire to stop the masses from getting drunk and its desire to make money as they did so.[245]

In Nueva Guatemala, consumers could choose from an array of alcoholic beverages. Pulque (made from the maguey plant) was available but not widespread.[246] In the central plaza, a group of women sold *batido*—a spiced *atol* (porridge-like beverage) fortified with a bit of alcohol content. For buyers with deeper pockets, shops near the central plaza stocked wine and liquor from Spain and Peru. The most popular drinks, however, were aguardiente (made from sugarcane juice) and chicha (made from maize fermented in sugar water or fruit juice, with relatively low alcohol content).[247] A state monopoly for aguardiente, established in 1753, sought to capture tax revenues from the sale of sugarcane itself as well as tavern licensing fees. But extralegal sales of both the ingredients and the liquor persisted. Chicha was even harder to control, as maize was ubiquitous.[248]

Chicha was the consummate plebian drink. It was produced by poor women in humble houses, sold there by the producers and consumed on the spot by people walking through the neighborhood, often on their way home from work (or on finding themselves without work). Chicha producers covered the full spectrum of calidad categories. The industry had long been regarded by the Spanish state as illicit, operating off the regulatory grid. By 1799, though, the ayuntamiento instituted a licensing system for chicha sales, in effect legitimizing the trade in the capital while also trying to collect on it.[249] While applicants for license to produce and sell aguardiente were primarily men, their counterparts in chicha were mostly women. City records on *chicherías* (chicha taverns), available mostly for the 1820s, show that the monthly licensing fee hovered around 10 pesos, with the number of licenses ranging between thirty-four and forty-four. If too many or too few bidders came forward, the ayuntamiento adjusted the fee and restarted the bidding. Though the monthly tax of 10 pesos suggests that the enterprises had a sizable profit margin, the records show that *chicheras* (chicha makers) sometimes relied on creditors to cover their fees.[250]

The potential savings of operating without the rather pricey license must have been obvious. An unlicensed chichera had relatively little to lose, provided that she avoided a law-enforcement sting. The product had a fairly long shelf life, the enterprise required little space, and the labor could be carried out by family members during their spare hours.[251] Producers fermented the maize in vats in their kitchen or patio, sometimes in the same room where customers were served. In unlicensed taverns, the fermenting liquids and equipment were typically buried underground or hidden in a back corner of the house, in an attempt to conceal them from the authorities. But it was hard to hide drunken revelers. The archives are laden with the records of countless law-enforcement raids on unlicensed chicherías.

A bust in March 1795 at a clandestine saloon illustrates the typical pattern. The alcalde of the barrio Ojo de Agua, making his nightly rounds

with his deputies, heard a noise coming from inside one of the neighborhood's thatched houses. They noted that "it sounded like people drinking."
The squad went in and found eight men, who by their "countenance and
eyes" were judged to be "somewhat drunk, and in a disposition to continue drinking." All eight customers denied it, but on further inspection the
officers found a "tub stinking of chicha" and a buried vat filled with the
fermenting juice. In the standard procedure, they smashed the containers
and dumped the liquid in the patio. The head of the household, a mulata
in her early twenties named Juana Luna, admitted to being the chichera.
She gave the usual excuses: she was poor; she had children; and although
she was married, the money that her husband made as a tailor was insufficient. Luna and the customers were taken to jail. (Her husband was inexplicably absent; the authorities left her house and children in the charge of
her aunt.) After three days, the customers were sentenced to pay the court
costs and were freed from jail. Luna, unable to pay the fine for bootlegging,
was sentenced to twelve lashes and eleven more days of imprisonment. The
lashes were to be administered inside the women's jail, a punishment considered lighter than public whipping.[252]

Petrona Téllez, a tributary Indian making clandestine chicha in 1809,
appears to have been somewhat better off financially. She too was arrested
at her home in a raid by the alcalde de barrio (in the barrio del Perú). Téllez
was known to have "another line of business, which is dyeing thread," and
was therefore considered relatively guiltier for bootlegging. She gave the
usual excuses: "being a poor woman, and her earning power never being
enough to sustain her family, which is large." Reprimanded with the facts
that her yarn dyeing provided an alternative means of support and that she
also had a husband, she said

that because what her occupation yields is not much, and her husband's earning
power not being enough, although there are days that she has something left over
when there is yarn [to be dyed—that is, when she has work]; nevertheless, that
when there isn't [yarn,] there is nothing left for them, and in order to be able to
support herself she has resorted to chicha.

Téllez was sentenced to a month in prison. Her Indian identity exempted
her from corporal punishments such as whipping. But she and her husband
came forth to present a fine, saying that they would rather pay "so as not
to suffer the month of reclusion." The judicial authorities agreed to release
her.[253] Thirteen years later, a woman named Petrona Téllez, likely the same,
was licensed to operate a chichería in the capital, and again another seven
years after that.[254]

Téllez's reliance on more than one source of income was typical. Even
those chicheras who depended at any one time exclusively on their taverns

were likely to engage in multiple enterprises across the course of their lives. Consider Apolonia Fuentes, an española born in Santiago. She left her mother's home as a youth because she did not get along with her stepfather. Known in Nueva Guatemala as Apolonia "Túnchez" or "Tunche," she landed in prison on more than one occasion after various women accused her of liaisons with their husbands. One wife was especially galled, complaining in 1782 that Túnchez had been coming to her house trying to collect money from the husband. Túnchez explained in later testimony that the man owed her for the burial of a baby he had fathered. A month later, one of the alcaldes conducted an investigation "in response to repeated complaints made against Apolonia Túnchez for being an illegal huckster of meat, a brawler, a scandalous woman, a perturber of marriage . . . , and other disorderly excesses, which constitute a totally criminal conduct, damaging to the commonwealth and deserving of the most severe punishment."[255] Several witnesses testified, and Túnchez was jailed, but as no formal sentencing was documented it is unlikely that she was held for long. The following decade, the tables had turned, as Apolonia Túnchez found herself repeatedly appealing to the law about her own husband. She accused him of carrying on affairs with other women, being lazy, failing to provide financial support, misspending her money, physically mistreating her, and threatening to kill her. In the 1796 census, she was listed as the head of a household in which her husband did not appear, and indeed she subsequently noted that he had long been living in other places with his consorts.

Apolonia Túnchez continued for decades in enterprises on the margins of the law. At the time of an 1809 raid on an unlicensed tavern at her home, the alcalde de barrio reported that hers was "one of the biggest chicherías in the city." He noted that she also was in the "business of [illegally] slaughtering cattle, making soap, and other lines of trade." Although Túnchez was "a repeat offender in the manufacture of chicha," the alcalde lamented, it was difficult to punish her. "She always puts up an Indian woman to take the blame so that she herself can avoid paying the fines." Sure enough, Túnchez denied all responsibility in the 1809 raid. She said the house belonged to her niece, and the chicha to a woman named Ana María Jobel. Jobel, a fifty-year-old mulata, admitted to being the chichera, giving the excuse of financial necessity. Nevertheless, she came forth with two silver buckles to cover the fine rather than spending time in jail. Ultimately, the tavern persisted. Túnchez appears again in the record two years after the 1809 raid, by this time well over sixty years of age, running a tavern with several other women (her niece among them) in her employ. Evidently, though, she was now licensed.[256]

The expansion of state regulation and licensing of alcohol producers in the late colonial era is suggestive of more general transformations in business life. It was not that native women were new to making pulque and chicha; they had been doing so even before the conquest. Rather, it was that these drinks had now entered the sphere of Hispanic commerce. As the capital city's working people—its beverage producers and primary consumers—had become increasingly hispanized, they brought pulque and chicha with them into the Hispanic fold. At the same time, aguardiente had been added to the popular drink menu as sugar cane estates popped up in various parts of Guatemala. A widening array of beverages and producers had thus entered the colonial capital's Hispanic social mainstream. Colonial regulatory legislation followed.

In a discussion of taverns, we might wonder about prostitution.[257] Indeed, a late-afternoon stroll through the oldest neighborhoods of Guatemala City today gives the distinct impression that the saloons in certain blocks are housing a sex trade. Yet the colonial-era evidence suggests a separation between taverns and prostitution. Whereas the judicial records tell of seemingly infinite raids on bootlegging operations, venues of prostitution are mentioned rarely and only obliquely. A woman named María Josefa Paz was arrested in 1798 in a "suspicious house" known as "las Enganchadas" (literally, the Women in Love). The alcalde charged that Paz was "one of those women who do not stay in one place and do not want to live *sujeta* [subject to authority or propriety]." No release or sentencing was recorded.[258] In 1802, journeyman baker José María Parejo was arrested on charges of "insulting" a woman named Casilda Martínez, having scaled the walls of her house and entered her bedroom. Witnesses referred to the building as a "house of Sodom and Gomorrah." Perhaps it was a brothel (or perhaps Parejo had been under that impression when he was scaling the wall).[259] Neither the house of "las Enganchadas" nor the so-called house of Sodom and Gomorrah was labeled by witnesses as a tavern.

No doubt informal prostitution occurred in various settings.[260] Yet sexual "consent" and money appear to have been more frequently exchanged within relationships described by contemporaries in such terms as "concubinage," "illicit friendship," or "illicit communication." These relationships were more ambiguous and complex than simple prostitution. Like marriage, unsanctioned sexual relationships often involved not only the transfer of credit or cash but also shared childrearing responsibilities, common business ventures, and the division of domestic chores. Transfers of cash, credit, and property often flowed from women to men as well as from men to women in relationships that contained a sexual component. Popular ideologies about gender roles may have prescribed that men provide financial support to their wives and concubines. But in practice, financial responsibilities were typically shared between sexual partners. The histories of the bakery owner doña Tomasa de Lara and the cattle and beef tradeswomen in the following sections illustrate the complex and varied interplay among sexual, economic, and social relationships.

The bread also rises: Bakers

By the late colonial years, European-style bread wasn't just for Spaniards. The quintessential Spanish-introduced food in America, wheaten bread had risen in popularity with the rise of Santiago's free hispanized labor force. In Nueva Guatemala, bread appeared in the diets of urban working people, prisoners, and even slaves. Furthermore, the city had a sweet tooth. A 1786 report by the síndico of the Ayuntamiento indicates that the bakeries' biggest seller was *pan de manteca* (literally, shortbread)—a pastry made of flour, eggs, sugar, and shortening. Of 100 *fanegas* of flour consumed daily in the city, seventy-eight were for pan de manteca. (A fanega is about 1.5 bushels.) "The use of pan de manteca in this capital is very old," the síndico (himself a bakery owner) reflected in his report.

It came into use (without a doubt) as a special particular treat; and without noticing it, comfortably fixed people gradually became fond of it because of the way it delights the palate, and they began to designate it to have with [hot] chocolate. From here it passed to other people of lesser means, and little by little it has become universal, to the point where there is not a poor day laborer who doesn't use it, principally with that wretched-quality chocolate that they are accustomed to drinking.[261]

While laborers were enjoying this sweet stuff perhaps once a day, gentility sometimes called for chocolate in the morning and the afternoon—a schedule that facilitated two daily servings of pan de manteca.[262] Still, maize was cheaper than wheat and less subject to price fluctuation.[263] Given that much more flour was being used for pan de manteca than for plain bread, one imagines that many people were eating pan de manteca with their chocolate, and tortillas with their larger meals (much as urban Guatemalans today eat pan de manteca with their coffee, and tortillas with meals).

It wasn't only bread consumers whose profiles had changed across the colonial era. The demographics of bakery ownership and labor had also shifted, reflecting broader trends in the city's ethnic composition and labor market. In early colonial Guatemala, as elsewhere in Spanish America, women seem to have started the first commercial baking. By 1589, though, several well-heeled men in Santiago had also entered the business, using the labor of their servants and slaves.[264] As bread consumption spread from Spaniards to other ethnic groups, so did bakery ownership. Women continued to figure prominently among owners, but gender roles had changed at the level of laborers.[265] In the sixteenth century, female baking entrepreneurs had actually been making the bread they sold, and in the seventeenth century women were probably still doing some of the baking. But by the late eighteenth century, the labor of commercial bread production had shifted almost entirely into the hands of men—specifically, free wage laborers.[266]

These men typify the rise of the urban hispanized free labor force. As we saw in Chapter 1, the work of tributary Indian men delivering flour brought them into contact with bakery owners, thereby facilitating the hiring of the same Indian men to work for wages inside the bakeries. An Indian man named Gaspar de los Reyes (we saw him in Chapter 1) was working two jobs in the capital in 1803—hauling flour to various bakeries, and sifting it in the bakery of don Ignacio Baines. Reyes lived in the house of a mestiza clothing trader; she gave him lodging in the kitchen or corridor out of charity, she said.[267] Other bakery workers slept in the bakeries themselves.[268] In 1799 the ayuntamiento decreed a prohibition against nighttime work in the bakeries, citing concerns about bakery workers being drunk by day.[269] Such concerns were hardly unusual, given the Spanish elites' frequent complaints of laziness and drinking among their colony's workers. (The prohibition against nighttime baking apparently didn't last.)[270]

An 1808 homicide case gives us a peek inside a bakery in the barrio de la Habana, at the home of owners Victorino Paniagua and his wife, Flora Arbestren. Their baking enterprise entered the record one January night when an intruder barged into the dough-making room and fatally stabbed one of the employees. The victim, José Luciano Hernández, had been out drinking earlier with the assailant, and insults were exchanged before the two parted company. That night the assailant came to the bakery to rebuke Hernández, who by this time was asleep there, as were two other employees. Wakened by the intruder's challenging words, Hernández punched him, and the intruder responded with the fatal stab. The alcalde arrived with a notary, and Hernández's deposition was recorded as he lay dying. Though he had worked in the bakery freely for wages, he identified himself as a tributary Indian from Santa Isabel (on the city's outskirts), in his mid-thirties. As for his housing, he noted that it was usual for the workers to sleep in the bakery "until work time." Separate documentation reveals that he was married with children and sometimes slept at home. (His wife was also identified as an Indian from Santa Isabel.)[271]

The other workers' testimonies depict a division of labor that seems to have been the norm in bakeries. The *hornero* was in charge of the baking itself; the *cernidor* or *ahechador* did the sifting, and one or more others

kneaded the dough. Horneros occupied the top rung in a fairly loose hierarchy among bakery workers. In the Paniagua-Arbestren operation the
hornero, an illiterate Spaniard, smugly pointed out that "it is customary
that while the other assistants knead, the hornero sleeps." The operation's cernidor, incidentally, was labeled in the record as mulato. Other
bakeries too were multiethnic workplaces, though occupational hierarchy
did not always correspond to calidad hierarchy.[272] Bakery owner Victorino Paniagua himself, employer of the workers interviewed, was identified as mulato and in his mid-forties. His wife's calidad and age were not
recorded. Evidently husband and wife shared in the roles of management.
When they were awakened by the commotion that fateful night, it was
Flora Arbestren who got out of bed and went to confront the intruder.
She grabbed the candle he was holding (the only light in the room at the
moment), and told the workers to keep him there until the police came.
The husband got up only later, he explained, because he was "impeded in
both legs." The workers alternately identified both the husband and the
wife as their employers; Hernández described the enterprise as "the bakery of Victorino Paniagua," while the cernidor referred to the wife as "his
Señora Maestra Flora Arbestren," connoting that she was his boss. Neither
the owners nor the workers knew how to sign their names.[273]

Despite the ethnic diversification of the bakery-owning class, the business commanded a degree of social prestige. Even at the end of the colonial
era, many bakery owners were apparently Spanish, some with the honorific
"don" or "doña." Bakery owners (and their family members) might attend
customers at the storefront, but they kept their hands out of the dough.
For women in particular, this exemption from messy and sweaty labor
made bakery ownership and management compatible with high social status. Also, baking enterprises required sizable start-up capital. In addition to
the space (typically in the owner's house), the owner needed an oven and
utensils, raw materials, and workers. The workers' salaries might amount
to only a few reales a day, but in years of poor wheat harvests ingredients could cost upwards of 10 pesos for one day's bread. Even with these
investments, the Guatemalan baking operations were small compared to
those in Mexico City.[274] They were numerous, though, scattered generously
throughout both Santiago and Nueva Guatemala. Customers came from a
small radius and expected to get their bread home still warm.[275]

While the manual labor of baking had become men's work, ownership
of a significant proportion of bakeries remained in female hands. In a 1777
list of the twenty-five baking enterprises in the new capital city, nineteen
were headed by women, with some of the operations apparently run by a
partnership of sisters. (See Table 3.1.) By 1786, the number of bakeries in
the new capital had nearly doubled to forty-six. A list of bakery owners

TABLE 3.1
Gender and bakery owners in Guatemala City, 1777, 1786, and 1829.

	1777	1786	1829
Total bakeries identified by women's names	19	19	19
Women with "doña"	11	17	18
Women without "doña"	6	2	*
Partnerships of women sharing the same surname	2	0	1
Total bakeries identified by men's names	6	28	19
Men with "don"	2	13	*
Men without "don"	4	15	19
Bakeries named by location or surname only	0	0	4
Total number of bakeries	25	47	42

*The honorific "don" and "doña" were dropped from official use in 1821.
Source: Archivo General de Centro América, Guatemala City, Signatura A3, Legajo 2537, Expediente 37179; Signatura A1, Legajo 41, Expediente 1014; and Signatura B84.1, Legajo 1127, Expediente 25848.

for that year included nineteen women, but the roster apparently named the husbands of other women who were actually running the bakeries. For example, José Santizo was among the men named, and other recrods show that he was the husband of doña Tomasa de Lara, who had started her bakery enterprise more than a decade before their marriage. Just three months before the list was made, she had received license from the ayuntamiento to continue operating the bakery. Her husband was often out of town. (We will see them again later.) Because bakeries were located in the owners' houses, people associated the operations with certain households. In naming a head of household (such as José Santizo), the list was probably understood by locals to indicate a certain bakery with which they were familiar.[276]

An 1829 inventory identified forty-two bakeries in the city, giving the names of the owners or in some cases only a surname associated with the house where the bakery was located. About half the individuals identified were women. Like two of the bakeries in the 1777 roster, one of the 1829 operations may have been run by a partnership of sisters; the bakery was identified as "las Alvarez." The appearance in each roster of certain surnames at more than one bakery suggests the clustering of particular families in the trade. In 1777, two of the largest operations were owned by women surnamed Domínguez, and two people named García appeared on the roster. In 1786, the same two Domínguez women were listed, as were two each of owners called Alvarez, Guzmán, Molina, and Guerra. In 1829, two people named Artiga, three named Ruano, and three named Marín were running bakeries.

At first glance, the bakery rosters give an impression of substantial changes in ownership between 1777 and 1786; only four of the twenty-five owners named in 1777 surface again for 1786. Yet some of these changes in lists may be merely an alteration in the way the notaries identified each operation, rather than actual changes in ownership or management. Presumably some real turnover occurred with migration from Santiago to Nueva Guatemala during the intervening years. Still, several owner surnames from 1777 reappear in 1786, and several from 1786 reappear in 1829, suggesting that some families continued in the business from one generation to the next.

An example is the family of doña Tomasa de Lara, who owned a bakery in the old capital beginning in the 1740s. She moved to Nueva Guatemala in the decade following the 1773 earthquakes and reestablished her baking business. When the city faced a flour shortage in 1785, the ayuntamiento renewed its efforts to limit the number of baking operations. Lara was excluded from a list of twenty-five bakeries named to be allotted flour and to continue their operations. She petitioned the ayuntamiento, saying, "I have been excluded without due consideration of the fact that I have maintained myself in this exercise, serving the public for more than forty years, and his Majesty for some six years, making the *bizcochos* [hard biscuits] needed for provision of the *castillos* [forts and presidios] in the kingdom." By emphasizing her service to the community and Crown, Lara's petition evoked her social status and respectability, implying that she deserved the right to continue in her trade. At the same time, her appeal expressed dire need. It was a combination of merit and humility that typified petitions throughout the empire. Lara described 5,000 pesos' worth of losses that her enterprise had suffered in the ruin of the old capital. The losses had reduced her, she said, "to this state of poverty, in which I have maintained myself, continuing nevertheless in the exercise of bread making." She added that she was over the age of sixty, crippled in one leg, and without any means other than the bakery to maintain herself and the ten persons in her family.[277] Within a few days of her request, the ayuntamiento added her to the roster.

Lara's baking business had apparently been her main means of support for most of her life. Widowed in her first marriage, she was married again in 1764, this time to José Joaquín Santizo, a mestizo merchant who traded in flour, sugar, and textiles. At age twenty-six, he was some fifteen years her junior. It was not a happy marriage. During more than twenty years of wedlock, Santizo frittered away Lara's money and mistreated her verbally and physically. Repeatedly she appealed to the civil and ecclesiastic authorities, accusing him of chronic drunkenness, concubinage, failure to provide money for their household, maltreatment with indecent words, and cruel beatings. Her witnesses attested to his wrongdoings. One noted that when Santizo "joined his wife's household he had various debts that she has since paid off little by little." On at least one occasion he took sugar from her stores to sell for his own profit. (Among his infidelities was a long-term affair with a niece of his stepfather. She owned a bakery in Quetzaltenango, where Santizo frequently traveled with his commerce. No doubt she obtained some of her baking ingredients from him.) Although Lara succeeded in getting Santizo locked up for short periods, she never obtained the divorce she sought. Ultimately she outlived him, continuing her baking business after his death.[278]

Doña Tomasa de Lara had ties to the trade in baking ingredients through her son-in-law as well. Her adopted daughter Teresa de Jesús, a foundling who had been left at the door of her house, was married to a man who ran a flour mill. Teresa and her husband lived in doña Tomasa's house during the first few years of their marriage in the 1770s. It appears that Teresa also went into the baking business; a Teresa de Lara was listed in 1786 among the capital's bakery owners.[279]

In concert with the broad pattern of labor privatization, the late colonial years saw a softening of state controls over bakeries and wheat flour distribution. Starting in the sixteenth century the colonial state had used several regulatory mechanisms in its effort to ensure the bread supply for the capital.[280] The capital's ayuntamiento administered bakery licensing and dictated prices per pound, though illegal profits were probably common, as intimated by complaints that bakeries were selling poor quality and underweight bread.[281] In an effort to curb such practices, in 1693 the ayuntamiento ordered bakers to stamp their bread with an identifying mark.[282] In the seventeenth and early eighteenth centuries, both the Audiencia and the ayuntamiento enacted legislation intending to channel wheat into the capital and thereby prevent price speculation and shortages.[283] The ayuntamiento also regulated the cart service that distributed flour within the city.[284] But at least in good crop years, there were extralegal channels. People applying to the ayuntamiento for bakery licenses in Nueva Guatemala openly noted that they already had the oven, utensils, and flour to begin their operations.[285] In 1789, following an abundant harvest, a group of Indians from various pueblos officially supplying wheat to the capital appealed to the ayuntamiento to allow them to sell their wheat outside the city. They noted that they had already been selling it privately to various bakeries in the city.[286] (While some Indian wheat growers hired muleteers and accompanied them with the harvest into the capital to sell the crop, others sold their produce to wholesale merchants who would take it to the city.)[287] For their part, these wholesalers were Hispanic and their businesses highly privatized. Many of them also dealt in sugar and panela (raw brown sugar). The scale of their enterprises enabled them to supply ingredients on credit to bakery owners.[288]

In the early nineteenth century, the ayuntamiento began to relax its regulatory stance. In 1806 it discontinued its efforts to control flour deliveries to the bakeries. Then in 1810 it ended a draft of Indian porters to make the deliveries.[289] Thus, wheat and flour sales and distribution were placed legitimately in the hands of private merchants and privately contracted wage laborers.

Meat suppliers

Though beans were (and are) the cheapest and most popular source of protein in Central America, meat has long been the favorite. A troika of European-introduced animals—the chicken, the pig, and the cow—became dietary mainstays in the Spanish colonial capital. In the late colonial years, even prisoners were given their daily meat.[290] The workers and enterprises that supplied the city with meat help illustrate the broad social transformations of the colonial era. Trends for all three of the staple meats reflect deregulation and privatization of labor as well as changes in the workforce profile, as free hispanized laborers—notably people of ethnically mixed ancestry—increasingly assumed the work of meat production and trade. The mechanisms of distribution and retail sales were also increasingly privatized, and markets expanded as meat consumption spread among a growing cash-earning population.

POULTRY AND PORK

In the early colonial years, the Spaniards had demanded chickens and turkeys from the Indians in tribute, though Indians from areas around Santiago were soon coming to the city to sell chickens and eggs for cash.[291] Once commodity tributes had been converted to cash, poultry raising was essentially unregulated and hardly documented. Still, scattered references confirm that by the late colonial years hispanized people as well as Indians were keeping chickens for consumption and sale. (As it is not unusual for people in today's Guatemala City and Antigua to keep chickens in their patios, we can easily imagine that many of their colonial-era predecessors did the same.)

Swine husbandry was concentrated among a more specialized personnel. The colonial state's administration of labor in the pork industry was more long-lasting than in poultry, but the trend was also toward free labor and privatization. In the early colony, tribute laborers had been forced to tend the hogs of the *encomenderos*.[292] As late as the 1730s, tributary Indians from the pueblo of Jocotenango and the city's barrio de la Candelaria were obligated to carry out pig slaughtering and lard making in their homes.[293] Tributary Indians living in the new capital's barrio de la Candelaria continued to work as pork butchers even beyond 1800.[294] By the late eighteenth century, though, women and men of mixed ancestry had also entered the trade in porcine products, and they and their Indian counterparts were processing and selling pork without state intervention. Both men and women appear in the records as swineherds and pork butchers, but retail sales of raw pork, sausages, and tamales seem to have been exclusively female work.

The late colonial pork and poultry trades were staffed mainly by people running their own small enterprises. An 1809 case gives a profile of some of the women working in retail sales in the central plaza. Like city plazas throughout Spanish America, Guatemala's central square was home to a range of businesses, from the upscale shops under the arched *portales* along the square's edge, to the humble enterprises of ambulant vendors (many of them Indians who came from surrounding pueblos to sell foodstuffs). Near the bottom of this hierarchy were women who sold their wares in the plaza itself under rented *sombras* (umbrella-like shade covers). Our 1809 case entered the record because of a dispute over payment for these sombras. To collect the rents, the alcalde had commissioned one of the plaza vendors, a mulata widow whose work was selling lime (*cal*, used to make tortillas). One Sunday morning she sent her teenage daughter, Rosalia Arroyo, to collect from Lucrecia Valdés, a mestiza in her mid-thirties who was sitting in the plaza with her basket, as she would later tell the court, "selling her pork meat, which is her career." Arroyo approached and told Valdés she was supposed to have paid the previous Monday. But Valdés said that her sister, who worked with her, had already paid. Clearly Valdés took umbrage with the girl; witnesses later recalled that she scolded her, saying, "Hex on the soul who gave birth to you! You all are trying to suckle from two teats" (*malaaya el alma qe. te pario qe quieren mamar a dos tetas*).[295] The young Arroyo responded in kind, and further insults and racial epithets were issued in both directions. Valdés then reportedly threatened Arroyo with a stick. Arroyo responded by taking some sausages that Valdés had for sale and throwing them in her face. Valdés's sister and Arroyo's mother and sister all came to intervene. More insults and vulgarities were exchanged. Ultimately, Rosalia Arroyo's sister Bernardina hit Lucrecia Valdés in the head with a piece of firewood. Bleeding, Valdés was hospitalized and given the last rites. Fortunately she ultimately recovered. Bernardina Arroyo was jailed briefly before being released because she had a small child.[296]

In the judicial proceedings that followed, several additional women testified as witnesses to the scuffle—another mestiza seller of pork (not related to the Valdés sisters), an Indian soap dealer, a salt vendor, and three poultry sellers (two mestizas and one of unidentified calidad).[297] Like the Valdés sisters, who rented their sombra for seven days a week, these women were regulars at the plaza; they all knew each other by first name and trade, if not also surname. Non-Spanish working-class women entrepreneurs had come to occupy the very center of the colonial capital. Though the city center had originally been intended for the Spanish population, by the late colonial era free non-Spaniards with petty businesses there were recognized and in effect institutionalized by the colonial state, as the city rented sombras to them for their operations.

The outcome of the 1809 case is also suggestive. The court sentenced Bernardina Arroyo to compensate Lucrecia Valdés for her medical expenses and for the income she lost while unable to work for several weeks, and to pay the court costs. Valdés's husband testified that she made about 4 reales per day; the total income loss was calculated at 27 pesos 6 reales, and the court costs at 28 pesos. Bernardina Arroyo, who worked with her mother selling lime, was unable to cover this amount. Three years after the court ruling, with no payment yet logged, Bernardina's mother went on record promising to make the payment herself within four months. The mother, age forty-seven, was a widow with eleven children. The four months elapsed and still she had paid nothing. In the fifth month, she came forward with 8 pesos, and documentation of the case ended.

Like the rents charged for the sombras, the court's willingness to hear the case (and to record detailed depositions of nine women who worked as vendors in the plaza) connotes the state's implicit legitimization of enterprises run by low-status women in the city center. The court personnel themselves, or their wives or servants, may have purchased meat and other groceries in the plaza; consumers depended on the vendors there. Poultry and tortillas were no longer provided by Indians in tribute, and hogs were no longer raised by draft laborers. A new hispanized urban underclass was supplying the products for sale in the city.

Further, the record in the trial of Bernardina Arroyo suggests the court's recognition of the importance of women's labor and income. Arroyo was released from prison quickly (by the standards of the day) partly because she had a small child. Her husband was present, but in a society that defined the care of small children exclusively as women's work, her labor in the home was crucial. Note also the court's decision that Lucrecia Valdés should be paid for income lost when she was unable to work. The judges subpoenaed Valdés's husband so they could ask him about her daily earnings; his answer served as the basis for calculation of the damages owed. The state was thus acknowledging and endorsing women's free wage labor and their roles as breadwinners for their families.

Though their operations were small, the plaza vendors' business strategies mirrored those used by even the largest entrepreneurs. Family businesses typified elite economic activities across Spanish America; relatives might work together or they might work apart from each other but as partners (or employer and employee). Likewise, Rosalia and Bernardina Arroyo and their mother were working together selling lime in the plaza. One of the witnesses, a forty-year-old Indian woman named Simona Juárez, was working with her mother selling soap. Sisters Lucrecia and Presentación Valdés shared the rent for their pork-selling operation. In another business strategy, owners of large enterprises often sought to achieve vertical integration or at least to achieve it as families if not as individuals. Recall bakery owner doña Tomasa de Lara, for example, whose second husband was a flour and sugar wholesaler. The trade in hogs and porcine products was a more humble realm than bakery ownership, but examples of vertical integration do appear. In 1812, Florencia Castillo Roldán was operating at several levels of the industry in the Nueva Guatemala; she herself raised pigs, slaughtered them, and sold tamales—presumably containing pork—in the central plaza.[298] Lucrecia and Presentación Valdés must have concentrated on sales (if not also processing—that is, making sausage), given that they paid to rent their sombra for seven days a week. However, their family as a whole had achieved vertical integration in the business; the sisters surely got at least some of the pork they expended from their brothers Victoriano and Mariano Valdés, who in a separate record both identified themselves as pork butchers (*matadores de cerdos*).[299]

BEEF AND ITS MARKET FORCES

Compared to poultry and pork, almost everything about beef was bigger: bigger animals, bigger spaces needed to raise them, bigger investments, bigger profits, bigger retail sales, and bigger government regulation.[300] State regulatory measures, however, tended to be overruled on the ground by the powers of the market. Legislation proved unable to control either the growing population of free laborers seeking gains in the beef trade or the appetites of cash-earning consumers eager to enjoy beef. As free labor activities and the consumer market expanded, the state gradually revised and began to retract its efforts to regulate the beef industry. The story of beef thus illustrates the erosion of colonial governing structures in response to changing social realities.

Beef processing and sales for the capital city were regulated by the ayuntamiento through the administrative structure of the *abasto* (public supply system), with the primary goal of maintaining a steady supply of meat. A corollary goal was to maintain stable prices and quality. Moreover, the *abasto de carne* (public beef supply system) generated significant income for the ayuntamiento, as ranchers paid an *alcabala* (tax) on each head of cattle sent through the city slaughterhouse. In the early decades at the new capital, the abasto de carne was the principal source of income for the city government.[301] Beef was big business for both private enterprises and the state.

Starting in the sixteenth century, the ayuntamiento had contracted annually with various *hacendados* (ranchers), who each agreed to supply a given number of cattle on assigned days.[302] The hacendados hired men to drive their herds to the city slaughterhouse. In the slaughterhouse, tributary Indian men from the pueblo of Santa Isabel, working as draft laborers, butchered the animals.[303] The meat was then sold in a central retail outlet, or *carnicería*. As demand grew over the next century, the ayuntamiento expanded the abasto, adding carnicerías in several neighborhoods and awarding to a private bidder a concession for the carting of beef to these various shops. The men and women who contracted for the transport monopoly were themselves cattle ranchers or members of ranching families. They hired Indian men, recruited privately as free laborers, to do the work.[304] By the late colonial era the official carnicerías too were partly privatized, with stalls rented from the ayuntamiento by *carniceras*—women working as independent retail vendors. Rents were charged in the form of a licensing fee. The carniceras dealt directly with herd owners, obtaining meat on credit, sometimes after it was butchered, occasionally on the hoof.[305]

This expansion of the abasto expanded the opportunities for illegal sales of beef and hides, and illicit trade was entrenched in Santiago by the 1680s. Ranchers, cattle thieves, and even slaughterhouse officials joined in the smuggling. Contraband beef reached consumers by way of an informal sales force of women called *regatonas* (hucksters), who were mostly mulatas and mestizas, unauthorized by the ayuntamiento. Some of the meat they peddled had been butchered legally in the city slaughterhouse, purchased with cash or on credit from the ranchers; but because they had not paid for rights to sell, the regatonas were working illegally and subject to arrest. Their prices may actually have been higher than in the licensed carnicerías (some regatonas were simply reselling meat they had bought from legal retail sources), and they were reputed to use trick weights.[306] But they offered consumers various advantages. They sold smaller portions than one could buy in the carnicerías, where the half-*real* minimum purchase was beyond reach of most people's wallets (and no one had ice to keep extra meat).[307] If the regatonas didn't come right to their clients' homes, they sold in locations more numerous than the carnicerías, and some took meat to communities outside the city.[308] Popular opinion held that the regatonas sold better meat than the carnicerías; because of the ayuntamiento's price ceilings, ranchers usually sent their thinnest and sickest animals to the city slaughterhouse and reserved the better specimens for the black market. Finally, regatonas could save customers frustration at the carnicerías. The shops were often crowded, and contrabandists had cornered the market to the point where the official retailers tended to run out of meat.[309]

The ayuntamiento attempted repeatedly to curtail the black market, but to little avail.[310] By the late colonial years, ranchers were so resistant to selling their cattle through official channels that they had to be forced by a state-administered system of obligatory turns to send herds to the city slaughterhouse. The system was given teeth by the threat of a 500-peso fine for sending too few beasts on one's assigned day (though ranchers who offered an excuse were often exonerated or assigned to make up the shortfall another day).[311]

The whole beef trade, both licit and illicit, was carried over from Santiago to Nueva Guatemala. Ranchers who bought cattle at the government-sanctioned livestock fairs remained subject to the same obligatory system of provision. A new slaughterhouse was built, and Indian men from the pueblo of Santa Isabel (at its new location) continued being drafted to do the butchering.[312] Soon after the city's founding, a central retail carnicería was established; more were added in 1779, and in 1792 the ayuntamiento planned for yet another four.[313] Still, the government was unable to harness the entire beef market within the law. Licensing fees for stalls in the carnicerías remained high, and illicit sales by regatonas persisted as people relocated to the new capital. The regatonas in Nueva Guatemala were the very same people (and their daughters) who had been in the business in Santiago.[314] Rustling also persisted, and fraud surfaced in the public slaughterhouse. The manager was repeatedly accused of falsifying the numbers of cattle butchered; evidently he was sequestering carcasses for illegal sale.[315] Word was that regatonas were slaughtering cattle in their houses.[316] The ayuntamiento discussed the problems, with some members arguing that the uncontrolled trade actually helped keep supplies plentiful.[317] (Notably, some of the major cattlemen were themselves members of the ayuntamiento.)[318]

In 1800 the ayuntamiento lifted the ban on private retail sales of beef, thereby transforming the regatonas into carniceras plying an authorized trade. The measure further allowed retailers to buy the animals on the hoof. Such pre-sales to regatonas had already been happening, but illicitly.[319] The new rules enabled ranchers legally to contract with anyone to sell meat from their herds.[320] Though most carniceras apparently continued to purchase their merchandise after it had been butchered, a few of them regularly procured live animals. These few paid the fees at the slaughterhouse and were inscribed in the abasto's registry before selling the meat to consumers.[321] Thus, starting in 1800, the abasto's record of daily suppliers lists the names of some of the carniceras along with elite hacendados and smaller ranchers, showing each carnicera supplying up to two or three animals a day. The regatonas had begun illicitly, upstarts outside the law, but they had ultimately loosened the colonial structures enough to gain formal admittance into the beef trade.

Still, the state had not lifted its ban on unofficial slaughtering of cattle, and the amount (and quality) of legally butchered beef remained insufficient to meet demand.[322] Clandestine slaughtering persisted unabated. The reticence of the ranchers to fulfill their abasto obligations signals the profitability even for them of the black market. Although the taxes collected for official butchering at the slaughterhouse diverted only a small portion of the price of each animal, the setback was substantial in absolute terms for ranchers who sent large herds for the abasto.[323] The abasto in Santiago on the eve of the earthquakes was butchering seventy head of cattle a day, and the number in Nueva Guatemala in the 1780s was similar; by the 1780s, the abasto in Nueva Guatemala was butchering sixty-five or seventy-five head of cattle each day, often provided entirely—or almost entirely—by a single hacendado.[324] Further, carcasses sold outside the official channels could fetch higher prices than those sold legally under state price controls. For cattle rustlers, of course, illegal slaughtering and sales were the whole point; profit margins were high when no money was invested to purchase the livestock. Distribution from illegal points of slaughter evidently operated among social networks like those that structured more legitimate businesses. Late colonial court records indicate that bands of cattle thieves were active on the city's outskirts and in the nearby countryside. With almost uncanny consistency, the records reveal that these men had female kin or housemates identified as regatonas de carne (beef hucksters), *almuerzeras* (lunch sellers), or *tamaleras* (tamal makers). Cattle thieves were apparently turning meat over to their wives, sisters, and other associates to sell it raw or in prepared foods.[325]

The booming black market in beef reflects the broad shift toward free, privatized labor. Although private slaughtering was illegal, it was widespread; without it, beef supplies would have been inadequate to meet demand. The state's abasto had become ineffectual in maintaining sufficient and steady supplies, and private enterprise was filling the gap. Illicit butchering had thus assumed a role mirroring developments that we have seen across various industries: it was supplementing the state-administered labor of tributary Indians (in this case, those who staffed the slaughterhouse). As we might expect, most people named as clandestine butchers and vendors in the late colonial years were identified as mulatos or mestizos.[326] They were part of the new free hispanized labor force that was replacing tribute labor generally. Thus, the relaxation in 1800 of state efforts to control retail beef sales followed developments that had already been consolidated; scofflaw butchers and regatonas had wedged their way into the market, outside the colonial structure of the licensing system. In effect, the 1800 legalization of private sales served merely to legitimize the regatonas' work and to relieve them from danger of arrest.

Signs of the new hispanized population appear in the beef trade's higher echelons as well. Even at the conventionally elite level of cattle ranchers, by 1800 a parvenu class including people of mixed race had entered the records as suppliers to the abasto. A closer look at some of the personnel in beef will illustrate these points.

BEEF TRADERS:

HACENDADOS, POQUITEROS, AND CARNICERAS

Spaniards had introduced cattle, and Spaniards persisted as owners of the largest herds across the colonial centuries. A group of aristocratic men and women, many of them related to one another, dominated the business of supplying cattle to the capital city's abasto de carne. Known among their contemporaries in Guatemala as "hacendados" (owners of haciendas), they fit the mold that has been described for hacendados in various parts of Spanish America.[327] Guatemala's elite ranchers actively bought and sold land and other property, but most of them acquired their initial base of wealth, including land, through inheritance. They used marriage and other kinship ties to maintain and consolidate their holdings. Men predominated among this group, but some women also sent large herds to the city's abasto de carne.[328]

The Nájera clan provides an example. In the 1770s, 1780s, and 1790s, the name Nájera appeared more than any other among registered beef suppliers to the capital. There were the siblings doña Josefa, doña Lugarda, and don Ventura Nájera, along with don Manuel, doña Manuela, and doña María Josefa Nájera—probably siblings or cousins of the former three.[329] (Indeed, doña María Josefa and doña Josefa were two different people.

Although in 1796 doña Josefa Nájera owned an hacienda managed by a mayordomo, in that same year doña María Josefa did not own any ranch. Doña María Josefa was a major supplier of cattle to the city, however. She grazed her animals on other people's haciendas, presumably paying rent.)[330] The Nájeras of the late eighteenth century married into other large ranching families and perpetuated the business in the next generation.[331] Doña Manuela, for example, was wed to a member of the Rivas family (also cattle ranchers) and bore two daughters, doña Teresa and doña Serapia Rivas. Doña Teresa and doña Serapia shared ownership of an hacienda in the region of Escuintla (south of the capital toward the Pacific coast). Along with other members of the Nájera family, they continued to supply cattle to the city's abasto well into the nineteenth century.[332]

At the same time, a class of smaller ranchers had entered the abasto's registries as suppliers of cattle to the city. These people were named without the honorific "don" or "doña." Their herds were relatively small; they were assigned fewer days to send cattle to the abasto, sometimes sharing responsibility for a given day with another rancher. In cattle-dealing circles, these small ranchers were called *poquiteros*—meaning people with small businesses.[333] Especially in the areas of Petapa and Sansare (to the south and east of the capital), where large numbers of slaves had been employed in sugar production, people identified as mulatos had entered the ranching business.[334] Marcos Marroquín, for example, identified as mulato, owned a small cattle ranch (*sitio*) in the Valley of Sansare. He did not know how to sign his name.[335] A Sansare woman named Francisca Carrillo, identified as a free mulata, also owned livestock. She entered the record in 1802 when she reported a stolen mule. (The local alcalde later spotted the missing equine in a mule train headed to the Atlantic coast, and he eventually recovered the animal.) Probably this was the same Francisca Carrillo who appeared as a frequent supplier of cattle to the abasto in Antigua Guatemala (Santiago) in 1803–1805 and again in 1809.[336] This Antigua supplier sent enough animals that she could hardly have been called a "poquitera," yet despite the size of her livestock holdings she was not labeled as "doña." Notably, in the records for San Salvador, León (Nicaragua), and some other cities in the areas now comprising Guatemala and El Salvador, such nonelite names appear as the major cattle suppliers, albeit for smaller markets than the capital city.[337] Spanish ethnicity and high birth were no longer requisites for landownership and cattle ranching.

The poquiteros and other nonelite ranchers acquired and managed their wealth using strategies similar to those of the largest landowners. Like the aristocrats, the nonelites too acquired property through inheritance and other transactions among kin; an example is the sisters Josefa Antonia and Paula de Jesús Rodríguez, who inherited eighty head of cattle in the area of

Amatitlán.[338] Yet small-time ranchers also actively bought and sold properties across their lifetimes, frequently assuming substantial debts in order to acquire and consolidate holdings. And like their wealthier counterparts throughout Spanish America, Guatemala's minor ranchers tended to diversify their investments across multiple industries, not limiting themselves to livestock alone.

A capital city woman named Rafaela Izquierdo typifies these smaller cattle dealers. She was named through much of 1774 as a regular supplier to the abasto de carne, but her participation was short-lived; after that year she does not appear again.[339] Her investments were quite fluid. In the 1770s Izquierdo shifted her assets several times among various endeavors—ranching, agriculture (wheat fields and a flour mill), urban real estate, and consumer retail supply.[340] Her wealthier counterparts in ranching also frequently liquidated and reinvested their holdings, but their fortunes were sufficient for them to maintain a wider range of ventures at any one moment, and as individuals they tended to appear in the beef abasto registries more frequently. Smaller investors like Izquierdo owned a narrower range of properties at any one time. With a shift in the focus of their investments they might disappear from the abasto registries altogether, as Izquierdo did after 1774.

The records do not identify Rafaela Izquierdo's calidad. If she was Spanish, she was clearly of lower status than some Spanish women, as she lacked both the honorific "doña" and the ability to sign her name.[341] One imagines that her father, Salvador Izquierdo, may have been of ethnically mixed ancestry. With the military title of Sergeant (*Sargento*) and not a "don," Salvador Izquierdo fits the profile of mulato and mestizo men at lower ranks of the colonial militias.[342] He was able to write his name in a rough hand, and he had a number of business endeavors, including a small extralegal slave trade.[343] Rafaela Izquierdo's mother, Manuela Antonia Ramírez, was the legitimate daughter of a family with some property, but she too lacked the honorific "doña," as did her own mother and siblings.[344] Rafaela was married to a man named José García, who bore the military title of Captain but not the honorific "don." The illegitimate son of a woman who was not a doña, García invested primarily in pastoral and agricultural ventures while his wife managed her agricultural properties and urban real estate.[345] He was able to sign his name, albeit in a most unsophisticated hand. Rafaela Izquierdo's brother José, her only sibling to survive infancy, assumed the military titles Ensign (*Alférez*) and Captain and appears to have earned his living as an intercity merchant.[346] Like Rafaela, José was married into a family of middling social rank. His wife was of illegitimate birth, neither she nor her mother a doña. José and his wife had two children who survived to adulthood, both male. One went to serve in the household of a prominent Spaniard in Havana and then in Mexico, while the other remained in the Guatemalan capital.[347]

Rafaela Izquierdo relied on kin throughout her adult life not only for inheritance but also for business partnerships and credit. Most likely her husband was cooperating with her in her ranching enterprise; at the time of her participation in the abasto de carne in 1774, he was renting and managing an hacienda that pastured 300 head of cattle annually.[348] Izquierdo also used her family network in her urban real estate activities. In 1749—one of her earliest investments—she bought a house in Santiago's barrio de Chipilapa. She had money enough for only half the 200-peso down payment, but her father covered the other half.[349] Over the next thirty years she inherited several houses from her maternal grandmother and uncle, gradually paid off the mortgages, and sold the properties at considerable increases over their previous prices.[350] Using her profits on these sales as well as further help from her father and a number of mortgages, she then bought more houses, including the one where she would live.[351]

To her good fortune, Izquierdo sold three of the houses in 1770, presumably clearing at least some of proceeds before the 1773 earthquakes, when many debts went bad. Her remaining properties probably sustained some damage, and the evidence suggests that her fortunes suffered: in 1779 she was long overdue on 220 pesos owed to the Convent of Santo Domingo, which had given her a loan for some houses she bought in 1770.[352] But all was not lost. By 1786, she owned outright two houses in the new capital and another lot on which she was planning to build (though she would ultimately sell it still empty).[353] At the time of her death in 1794, she had sold off some of her properties but still owned a rancho (small house) and a tienda de pulperías (general store), as well as the house where she resided, which was then appraised at the impressive value of 714 pesos.[354]

Like larger ranch owners, Izquierdo provided loans, employment, and ultimately inheritances to a network of her relatives and fictive kin. In 1764, when she charged one of her nephews with collecting some debts, the power of attorney she gave him listed seventeen people who owed her money, among them several dons and doñas.[355] Izquierdo did not have any direct heirs; her only child died before reaching adulthood.[356] In her will she made bequests to her two nephews as well as her criadas, her sister-in-law, and the daughter of a man named Francisco Córdova. Francisco Córdova had become important among Izquierdo's contacts by 1770, when he contracted to buy a wheat field and mill from her for 2,550 pesos (to be paid over several years). She named him coexecutor of her will in 1786 and bequeathed some kitchenware to his daughter "as a sign of affection."[357]

In the years before Izquierdo's death, four girls or women lived with her as criadas. Though her two nephews would inherit the very valuable house in which she resided, her other real estate holdings were to be distributed among the servants. One of them, whom Izquierdo said she had raised, bore her surname and was chosen to receive the best of the small houses, a *rancho de teja* (small house of brick or with a tiled roof). Another criada was to receive a *rancho de paja* (small thatched house). For the third criada, Izquierdo initially planned to leave an empty lot and some building materials for a house, but the plan was dropped when the maid fled Izquierdo's service. The fourth criada was disabled, and Izquierdo sought to assure that someone would employ and support her. She designated 50 pesos and some clothing for "whoever might take charge of the mute Sebastiana, a poor disabled person whom I have maintained with me." (Sebastiana herself would not receive any real property.)[358] In her later years Izquierdo sold the ranchos intended for the first two servants and bought another one that they would share after her death.[359]

Though Rafaela Izquierdo's background and fortunes were a far cry from those of the Nájeras and other aristocratic Spanish hacendados, her ranching business positioned her comfortably on a higher level of the beef industry's socioeconomic ladder than the carniceras (retail beef dealers) on the next rung down. Carniceras often worked in family enterprises, but none seems to have been vertically integrated, save for some operations in cattle rustling and meat laundering. That is, carniceras and their families do not appear to have owned ranches or herds, nor were they integrated downstream in meat curing or processing. However, their networks of borrowing and lending extended both upwards and downwards. They procured animals and meat from ranchers on credit, and they often sold their overstock on credit to *cecineras* (makers of cured beef). An 1807 lawsuit against the carnicera Jacoba Avedaño, for example, names several cecineras who had debts to her.[360]

At all levels of the trade, beef dealers' financial networks tended to merge with social networks, engaging them in a range of relationships that stretched across socioeconomic and ethnic lines. The case of the Monroy sisters illustrates. Their family members had long been in the business of selling beef tallow and probably meat in the old capital, where they were known by the aliases Flaco and Flaca.[361] (Flaco—literally, thin or lean—is often used as a moniker describing a physical attribute. In the Monroys' case it may have been an ironic reference to the family business.) In late 1794 the four sisters, identified in the record as mulatas, decided to move to the new capital. They were fleeing a 300-peso debt for some cattle they had taken on credit; they claimed they were unable to pay following a robbery of silver and other valuables from their house, though their creditors disputed this contention.[362] Arriving in Nueva Guatemala, the Monroy sisters lodged in the home of a woman named Dominga Rodríguez. They

sold her a silver reliquary or locket for 2 pesos and used the money to pay
her for their food. Rodríguez's husband then joined the sisters as partner in
a business. He gave them 500 pesos to procure a market stall in the central
plaza and merchandise to sell, with the agreement that he would keep 50
percent of the profits in the first six months. The Monroys opened shop
selling both dry goods and beef. In a matter of weeks they had become
some of the principal beef retailers in the city. Credit continued to play an
essential role in their operation, as they financed livestock from both elite
and smaller ranchers.[363]

In 1800 one of the Monroy sisters, Máxima, was targeted in a lawsuit
by don Máximo Coronado, a large cattle rancher and one of the major
suppliers of beef for the capital. He was demanding 90 pesos for meat
he had given her on credit and some other debts. Máxima Monroy was
twenty-seven years old and unmarried. During the litigation it became clear
that her relationship with the rancher had involved more than just beef.
She argued that there could be no cause for her to owe him any money,
since there had been no keeping of accounts. She explained (as recorded by
the notary):

> He [don Máximo] supplied the meat and she [supplied] her work in selling it, and
> she spent on food for the two of them, on the washing and sewing of clothes which
> she paid for because she could not do it herself since she was selling the meat, on
> bread and chocolate and everything that was necessary to attend to him, and he
> took cash [from her purse] when he wanted without making the least note of it.[364]

At first Máxima Monroy said she was omitting certain factors in her
defense because she did not want to "damage the honor of don Máximo,"
but eventually she divulged that she had been in concubinage with him.
Witnesses confirmed her statements and told of a lovers' quarrel that had
ensued in Máxima's house before don Máximo filed the suit.

Ninety pesos would seem to be a lofty sum for a carnicera, but Máxima
was not without recourse. The court record shows that she had nurtured
an extensive network of creditors and debtors, with beef advanced from
numerous ranchers. Among Máxima's nine witnesses were three dons and
two carniceras not related to her (both living in her house). Her contacts
also included the women she had hired to make cigarettes and chocolate
for don Máximo, and those who did their laundry and sewing. At the conclusion of the lawsuit, when the court ruled that Máxima should pay don
Máximo 51 of the 90 pesos he was demanding, she proved to have substantial liquidity, paying off the settlement within a few days.[365] Her client–
patron relationships with cattle ranchers gave her access to credit on a
level not available to all petty vendors. (Recall the lime seller Bernardina
Arroyo, whose family was able to cover only 8 pesos of a much larger

fine.) Though Máxima Monroy depended for a time on a lover from the ranks of the hacendados, he was hardly her only financial connection. In a sense, she was an independent businesswoman.

The Monroy sisters and other meat suppliers we have seen illustrate several aspects of the division of labor in the late colonial years along lines of gender. Below the level of ownership and property management in most industries, women and men often performed different kinds of work, and their earning power was unequal. Men were generally paid more than women, even for the same jobs. However, entrepreneurial behaviors were similar. Both genders used kinship and other social networks to get loans and build their businesses, mirroring patterns that have been observed for large-scale enterprises throughout Spanish America.[366] Rafaela Izquierdo inherited property through her maternal line and relied on her father for cash loans to expand and consolidate her holdings. The carnicera Máxima Monroy went into business sharing a market stall with her sisters, using money invested by their landlord; she subsequently relied on her paramour and other connections to advance her the credit she needed to carry on her enterprise. Lucrecia Valdés plied the trade in pork and sausages with her sister, sharing the expenses of their shade cover in the plaza and probably sharing the work of making the sausages. Presumably they got the main material input from their brothers, whose business was raising hogs. Similarly, the Valdés sisters' contemporaries who sold soap and lime in the plaza were working there in family groups. These vendors help complete a picture in which women of various ethnicities and social classes operated their own businesses, albeit sometimes barely making ends meet.

Economic activities, gender, and society

As the coerced labor systems of tribute and slavery faded, free labor and small enterprises grew, creating an extensive cash-based economy in the colony's hispanized sphere. In effect, the capital city's labor scene was an outcome of the disintegration of forced labor—a hub of migrants exiting the coercive procurement systems, seeking employment through private contract. Yet certain aspects of the free labor market bore remarkable resemblance to tribute labor and slavery, as individuals from the same towns and even the same families often continued doing of the same kinds of work their forebears had done as coerced workers.

Domestic and public lives in late colonial Guatemala (as elsewhere in the early modern world) tended to overlap. Businesses often operated in the owner's home, and employees often lived in their workplaces. In the most public places, including the central plaza, families ran small enterprises.

Economic and personal relationships merged as kinship and shared residences tended to translate into business partnerships, employment, or credit. Although women were barred from most political offices and from the priesthood, they were not excluded from the public spheres of economic and social interactions. Their integration there—combined with the continuing migration into the city by people of African, Indian, European, and mixed ancestry—undergirded the rise of a hispanized society in which domestic and public worlds were enmeshed so closely together as to be at times indistinguishable. Interethnic relationships, both personal and economic in nature, perpetuated the city's role as a site of cultural and ethnic mestizaje well beyond the colonial period.

Notably, women and children were the vanguard troops in this process. Women fleeing gendered burdens in the countryside were likely to migrate alone or with their children to the city, where they could earn higher wages than in rural areas. An enormous predominance of adult women in the city's demographic structure resulted partly from the demand for their labor in traditionally female roles of food preparation and laundry. At the same time, women entered various lines of work shared by men, including several kinds of artisan work, rural and urban property management, and mercantile trades. As we will see in Chapter 4, the skewed gender ratio assumed its own role in structuring households and daily life. Women's ability to find work and develop enterprises in the city meant that they did not always depend on male kinfolk for their survival, and certainly they did not depend exclusively on men. Husbands in late colonial Guatemala were often absent. Further, many women did not marry, and others were widowed. Households, therefore, were often female headed—sometimes permanently and sometimes seasonally or temporally in accordance with men's work schedules outside the city.

4 Broken Rules in Love and Marriage

HOUSEHOLDS, GENDER, AND SEXUALITY

At a basic level, the dissolution of the old ethnicity-based coerced labor systems was an outcome of racial mixing and cultural hispanization; Indian tribute labor and African slavery were made superfluous as a population of free hispanized laborers emerged to do the work. These transformations played out through several mechanisms. As we have seen in the previous chapters, a principal mechanism was individual crossing-over from coerced labor into free labor, and often from one ethnic group into another. The crossings were facilitated by increasingly widespread venues of social mixing—notably colonial haciendas and cities, where Indian draft workers, African slaves, and free laborers of various calidades worked and lived in close contact. The other main mechanism of demographic change was the birth of growing numbers of children into the free hispanized population. These births were fruit of relations between men and women who moved at least partly in hispanized circles. Thus the same social environments that fueled attrition from the coerced labor pools also fostered sexual unions, both sanctioned and unsanctioned, of which the children would be reared in the hispanized world.

This chapter links the historical trajectory of hispanization with an analysis of gender relations and sexuality. A view of gender relations and sexuality is crucial for explaining shifts in racial and ethnic categories because, as historians have noted, race is embedded in gender; persistence of racial categories depends on patterns of reproduction, which are shaped by gender relations.[1] The chapter focuses largely on the capital city, the colony's hub of hispanization. We saw in Chapter 3 that hispanization was a gendered process led in the city by women, who dominated migration from rural areas. In addition, women's roles in reproductive labor—childbearing and child care (and hence socialization of children)—made them key agents of hispanization. We will see in the following pages that the numbers of women heading households in the late colonial capital contrasted sharply with Spanish patriarchal ideals.

Indeed, this chapter shows that various aspects of gender relations in late colonial Guatemala assumed forms not anticipated in Spanish literature and laws. These findings offer several additions to the history of gender and sexuality in Latin America. I demonstrate that marriages in the urban setting were less important and less durable than mandated in church law. An informal style of divorce, not codified in canon or secular law, was widespread, as were illicit unions. Regardless of codified civil laws to the contrary, the courts supported property rights for informally divorced women. This was before the rise of Liberal republican states and secular divorce in Guatemala and elsewhere in Latin America. We must therefore adjust our view of social changes supposed to have been introduced by postindependence legislation.[2] Additionally, studies of Guatemala and other parts of Spanish America have used baptismal records to identify high rates of illegitimate births.[3] This chapter's study of judicial testimonies helps explain these births by depicting permissiveness in courtship as well as fluidity in marriage and a marked (if incomplete) social acceptance of illicit unions. Finally, while historical scholarship on Spanish America has analyzed courtship and sexual relationships in terms of a patriarchal "culture of honor" rooted in medieval Mediterranean societies, my analysis refocuses the lens, foregrounding additional factors to help explain behaviors and thought.[4] In the resulting image, honor is recast as part of a broader scenario that features universal sentiments such as anger, desire, and affection.

The dissonances identified in this chapter between prescription and actual behavior are not completely surprising following the flowering of studies on gender and sexuality in the early Americas. Steve Stern's 1995 study of late colonial Mexico, for example, posited "multiple and contested gender codes in the [Latin American] social body" and called for exploration of these codes and contestations with the goal of better understanding the "dynamics[,] contradictions, and wider significance of patriarchal traditions in Latin America."[5] This chapter represents such an exploration as well as an effort to connect the history of gender to that of labor. Specifically, it links "multiple and contested gender codes in the social body" to the shifts in ethnic and labor forms seen in the previous chapters. Those transformations in ethnicities and labor took shape along the gendered contours of migration patterns, household and family composition, and sexual relationships. Thus, the story of gender relations and sexuality helps complete the picture of a society in which racial and ethnic mixing had dismantled the old labor forms.

Gender and households

Ideal households in Spanish colonial law were patriarchal. Following Roman legal concepts, Spanish law empowered fathers and male heads of household with authority over their children, wives, and slaves. Husbands by law controlled their wives' property and most of their legal transactions. In certain transactions, as Silvia Arrom has described, a wife did not legally need her husband's permission: "to accept an unencumbered inheritance . . . , to testify in court . . . , or to make her own will." The law also allowed a wife to file suit against her husband in certain situations. "Still," Arrom notes, "there were few areas in which married women could exercise their will."[6] Civil law was less restrictive of single adult women, but it did not give them equality to men. Perhaps most notably, women were barred from holding public offices and from working as lawyers or clerics.[7] The law also gave fathers signficantly greater power than mothers over their children. The Spanish notion of patriarchal authority was intertwined with male economic power, and the laws explicitly linked paternal authority to fathers' financial responsibility for their legitimate children and to their usufruct of children's property and labor.[8] Beyond law itself, men's power as family patriarchs was underwritten economically by the fact that they were paid higher wages than women. Ecclesiastical prescriptions also supported the subordination of women and children to the patriarchs who headed their families.[9]

Nevertheless, female-headed households were frequent in cities across late colonial Latin America.[10] As we saw in Chapter 3, both Santiago and Nueva Guatemala were home to large female majorities. Furthermore, both the 1796 and 1824 censuses show remarkable numbers of female-headed households. Because the census reports were made by the various neighborhoods' regidores (councilmen), their formats vary, and some register individuals without showing any divisions among households. But in all three extant barrio reports from 1796 and in eight of the twelve reports from 1824, the regidor or his assistant drew a horizontal line between households, or numbered each household. An accounting of gender of household heads listed in these reports—the first person listed for each household—is presented in Table 4.1 and Figure 4.1. (The table and figure do not include military installations, monasteries, convents, the hospital, prisons, beaterios, or the girls' colegio.)[11]

At first glance it seems that in the 1796 records, male-headed households formed a majority (460 of 837, about 55 percent), whereas in 1824 female-headed households predominated (784 of 1454, about 54 percent). However, 113 of the women named as the head of households in 1824

TABLE 4.1
Gender and marital status of household heads in Guatemala City censuses, 1796 and 1824.

Year	Female heads of household					Male heads of household				
	Married; husband appears to be present	Married; husband not present	Single	Widowed	Total female heads	Married; wife appears to be present	Married; wife not present	Single	Widowed	Total male heads
1796	19	16	129	213	377	383	4	43	30	460
1824	113	33	313	325	784	538	16	67	49	670
Total for 1796 and 1824	132	49	442	538	1161	921	20	110	79	1130

Sources: Archivo General de Centro América, Guatemala City, Signatura A, Legajo 2752, Expediente 23682 (El Tanque 1796); Signatura A, Legajo 5263, Expediente 4422I (La Habana 1796); Signatura A, Legajo 5344, Expediente 45056, (Capuchinas 1796); Signatura B, Legajo 1130, Expedientes 25977 (San Sebastián 1824), 25980 (Ojo de Agua and Santa Rosa 1824), 25981 (El Tanque and El Marrullero 1824), 25984 (San Juan de Dios 1824), 25989 (Sagrario and San José 1824).

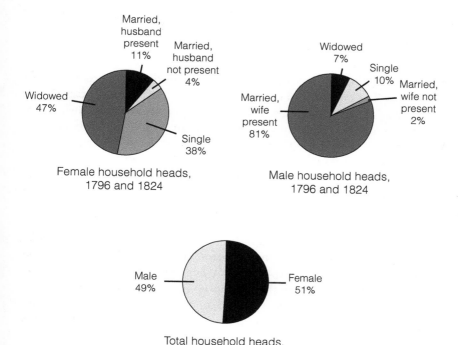

FIGURE 4.1 Gender and marital status of household heads in Guatemala City censuses, 1796 and 1824.

Sources: Archivo General de Centro América, Guatemala City, Signatura A, Legajo 2752, Expediente 23682 (El Tanque 1796); Signatura A, Legajo 5263, Expediente 44221 (La Habana 1796); Signatura A, Legajo 5344, Expediente 45056, Capuchinas 1796); Signatura B, Legajo 1130, Expedientes 25977 (San Sebastián 1824), 25980 (Ojo de Agua and Santa Rosa 1824), 25981 (El Tanque and El Marrullero 1824), 25984 (San Juan de Dios 1824), 25989 (Sagrario and San José 1824).

were wives whose husbands were also listed. This apparent inversion of patriarchal authority raises questions as to whether these wives were indeed the household heads, and, more basically, what colonial people understood household headship to mean. As a whole the census reports convey the impression that the first person listed in each household was construed as its head; all those named first were adults except in three or four cases, such as a twelve-year-old boy living with only his disabled father.[12] In most of those households headed by a married person with spouse present, the husband is listed first, followed by the wife—a pattern suggesting that patriarchal authority was indeed associated with household headship. Yet in 1824 the census takers varied on this. While some of them always or almost always listed husbands before wives, others were inconsistent. For the Cuartel de la Candelaria (which encompassed the barrios del Sagrario and San José), the recorder penned seventy-seven wives' names above those of their husbands and only thirty-four husbands above their wives. The report from the barrio of San Sebastián names twenty-one wives ahead of their husbands, versus 178 husbands ahead of their wives. In San Juan de Dios thirteen wives are listed ahead of their husbands, versus eighty-six husbands ahead of their wives. Perhaps the census takers in these neighborhoods were simply listing people in the order they came to the door to answer questions. But it is also possible that the officials conceived of some wives as household heads. That conception would not have been incongruous with the more general pattern in which women frequently headed households.

Even if we discard as uncertain the 113 households apparently headed in 1824 by wives with husbands present, we are left with 671 female-headed households and only 670 male-headed households. In some of these female-headed houses there is no adult male named, and in other cases the male residents appear (based on ages, relationships, or occupations) to have been tenants, relatives, or employees rather than husbands. Likewise, in some households headed by men, women were registered who do not seem to have been married to the household head. These women were presumably servants, tenants, or relatives.

Perhaps a most significant point is that the majority of households in both 1796 and 1824 did not have a cohabiting married couple at the head. In 1796, 402 households were headed by a husband or wife with spouse present, while 435 were not; in 1824 651 were headed by a husband or wife with spouse present, whereas 803 were not. Thus the majority of households were evidently not constituted by patriarchal families.

The census records do not allow us to calculate the rate of marriage, since they report people's marital status only in some barrios. Even then it is unclear for some of the married individuals whether they were cohabiting or separated from their spouses. In the crowded conditions of urban housing, married couples often lived together as tenants in someone else's household; but the censuses are often mum on these situations, since in Spanish naming patterns women keep their maiden surnames regardless of marriage (and in the colonial records the census takers did not add the husband's surname). Nevertheless, it is clear in the censuses that marriage and the nuclear family did not generally define household structure in Nueva Guatemala. Research on Guatemala's ladino eastern countryside has made a similar suggestion.[13]

Women in the capital did not normally move into the homes of their husbands' parents at the time of marriage. Patrilocal residence patterns, with daughters-in-law laboring in the households of their parents-in-law, have been described for other areas of Mesoamerica and may have been frequent in the Guatemalan countryside.[14] However, censuses of Indian communities in Guatemala in the late colonial years show households composed of nuclear families, and most towns tended to register a native son or two as well as a few native daughters "married in other pueblos." Granted, Indian populations were counted mainly for tribute assessment, which was based on marriages; hence the Spanish state-appointed notaries who recorded the censuses of Indian pueblos may have aimed to shape their reports to the mold of nuclear families. Scholarship by Robert Hill suggests an additional explanation. In colonial-era Cakchiquel communities (in central Guatemala), Hill notes, "Women generally went to live with their husbands in or *near* [my emphasis] the house of the [husband's] father."[15] Nuclear-family households may have been clustered in patrilocal hamlets within native communities.

In the countryside, both a woman and a man were needed to form a household because subsistence agriculture and food processing formed the basis of survival. Labor in the rural economy was divided along lines of gender, with children taught how to perform those tasks appropriate to their gender. Each household therefore required the work of both husband and wife; men knew how to tend the milpa, and women knew how to make the tortillas. Rural people got married largely because they needed a partner for the gendered labor of the subsistence household.[16]

In the city as well, households functioned as economic units, serving not only as dwellings but also as sites of production. But urban household enterprises were not necessarily based on a combination of male and female labor. In the urban cash and credit economy, household businesses specialized in particular commodities or services, and workers often purchased their daily food and drink. Men working on the construction of the cathedral, for example, bought prepared food from women in the central square. Men of greater means living in the capital without their families paid for their meals in private homes—sometimes the same houses where they rented sleeping quarters and paid for laundry service. Salaried workers and apprentices often slept in the employer's home or shop, and those who did not eat in the employer's residence might eat for a monthly fee in another house or might purchase their meals from vendors. A number of men lived in rooms at the garitas around the city, in the military barracks, or in structures standing on agricultural lands or pastures at the edges of town. Presumably vendors came to sell food at these locations. Some men working just outside town may have boarded in private homes, purchased meals in public areas or in *tabernas* (which sometimes sold food along with drink), or prepared their food themselves.[17]

Thus, to survive in the city a person did not necessarily need a spouse to provide complementary subsistence labor. Some married couples in the capital worked together in cottage industries, notably liquor production, but these cooperative ventures generally supplemented income from work in other industries.[18] While a conjugal relationship could function as an important node within a person's economic network, marriage was only one of several types of associations that enabled city dwellers to conduct their business and earn a living.[19] More than their rural counterparts, urban workers could stay afloat without being married, or without the presence of their spouses.

Marriage and de facto divorce

In early modern Iberian law the authority to execute marriages was the exclusive reserve of the church. Canon law defined the marital bond as a lifelong union, unbreakable until death parted the couple. A type of separation was authorized by the church (hence the term *ecclesiastic divorce*) but only in a limited number of circumstances: cruelty, physical mistreatment, or threat of murder of one spouse by the other; an incurable contagious disease in one spouse; attempts by one spouse to compel the other to commit criminal acts; heresy or paganism in one spouse; adultery by one spouse; or abandonment by a husband and failure to provide for the wife.[20] Studies of Spanish American ecclesiastic divorce suits suggest that relatively few unhappy spouses ever brought such suits, and even then the majority of plaintiffs were not ultimately granted divorces.[21] Moreover, ecclesiastical divorces did not pretend to dissolve the marital bond. Rather, they were meant to be temporary, with the stated goal that the couple would eventually reconcile. Only in cases of adultery would legitimate separation be permanent, and in any case remarriage was precluded until one spouse died.[22] In effect, ecclesiastical divorce amounted to permission from the church for a couple to separate, rather than permanent dissolution of the marriage.

Nevertheless, in late colonial Guatemala spouses were often described as being *ausente* (absent) from one another—a term that could refer to various degrees of estrangement. Sometimes it meant only that one member of the marriage, usually the husband, was away temporarily on business and was expected to return. In other cases, though, "ausente" connoted a more long-term or generalized absence from which a return was uncertain or unlikely. An example is Gregorio Alvarez (son of Gertrudis Salgado, whose family was described in Chapter 2). Alvarez abandoned Nueva Guatemala after being jailed briefly in 1790 at the behest of his wife and mother, who had complained of domestic discord and of his drunkenness. When officials went to his house nearly six years later to try to collect the court costs, his wife said he was "ausente" and she did not know his whereabouts. She had been left with their children, she said, without financial support.[23] In another example, a twenty-seven-year-old slave named María de la Luz was sold in 1776, with the record indicating that her husband Casimiro José was "ausente."[24] The fact that no surname was given for Casimiro José suggests that he too was a slave. He may have absented himself to escape bondage. In 1810 a woman named Bonifacia Martínez reported her marital status as widow, while at the same time her adult son said that her husband was "ausente."[25]

In written records the word *ausente* sometimes follows a name as an epithet, as if the person's absence had become well-known and perhaps permanent. María Agustina Magarín, head of a household where at least one other middle-aged woman lived, testified as witness to a mugging outside Santiago in 1775. In recording Magarín's marital status, the notary indicated that her husband was "Vicente Pensamiento ausente."[26] That same year, when Rafaela Bonifacia Vásquez was questioned about a suspected homicide in her neighborhood, the notary reported her as married to "Antonio Cabrera ausente."[27]

While the authority to marry people belonged to the church, civil law also defined individual rights—notably property rights—within marriage. Spanish legal codes allowed adult women to own property but stipulated that property acquired after marriage was jointly owned and would be controlled by the husband.[28] Wives' dowries, too, and *arras*—property given by the husband at the time of marriage—were to be administered by their husbands.[29] Further, the law stated that a married woman must obtain her husband's permission to enter into a contract or to litigate, except to sue her husband for mistreatment, misuse of her property, or failure to provide for the family.[30]

In practice, though, these legal restrictions on married women were not always upheld. Studies of colonial Ecuador and Yucatán have indicated that regardless of the law, married women carried on business and legal activities on their own behalf.[31] In late colonial Guatemala, married women who bought and sold property or filed lawsuits occasionally noted that they did so with the consent of their husbands, but more often their petitions made no mention of such permission. Some said that their husbands were away in one province or another; this explanation was sufficient in practice to allow wives to litigate and carry out financial transactions for themselves or on behalf of their husbands. When their husbands' absences were ongoing, women still apparently faced little difficulty doing business and even taking control of property that the men had left unattended. Doña Manuela Gómez, for example, mortgaged a house while her husband was away in San Salvador.[32] Micaela Galana sold a house while her husband was in Mexico.[33]

Bárbara de Cárdenas's real estate sale of 1786 is especially telling. The previous decade, title to a sitio (lot) in the barrio of San Sebastián had been granted in the name of her husband, Pedro José Castellanos, as part of the distribution of lands in the new capital. Two *ranchos pajizos* (thatched houses) had subsequently been constructed on the property. When Cárdenas sold the lot with its two ranchos in 1786, she acted without her husband. The notary recording the sale indicated that although the title of the sitio was in the husband's name, Cárdenas had built the ranchos "at her expense from her means and without the least cooperation of Pedro José Castellanos her husband, who always as today is absent and separated from her." The record further explained (presumably based on what Bárbara Cárdenas told the notary) that the commissioner for the distribution of sitios had erred in recording the husband's name. The husband had "neither been present to solicit the land nor contributed in any way to the construction," the notary wrote, "because not only had he always behaved very badly when he was together with her for some short time; but also according to common knowledge he had [left] her abandoned and was always away, as he has been at present for more than three years."[34]

Bárbara Cárdenas was not legally divorced, nor does the record give any indication that she ever thought of pursuing a legal (that is, ecclesiastic) divorce. But she had obtained much of what an ecclesiastic divorce would have done. Though law stated that married women needed the permission of their husbands to enter into contracts (such as for the construction of Cárdenas's ranchos) and to sell property they had acquired while married, Cárdenas proceeded unhindered. She called on four witnesses who confirmed before the notary that her husband had been absent and that she alone had paid for the ranchos, and the sale went forward.[35] In essence, the community recognized her situation and enabled her to conduct business without consent or control by her husband, and the civil authorities implicitly legitimized the couple's separation, overriding the codified laws. To be sure, many of the laws on management of women's property were meant to protect their interests, albeit in a paternalistic way.[36] Thus it might be said that magistrates who allowed women to conduct business without their husbands' consent were following the spirit of the law, at least in cases where husbands were not acting in their wives' interests.[37]

Besides marital ruptures in which a spouse was described as "ausente," another style of separations appears where both husband and wife may have remained in the same city or area. These couples, contemporaries said, "are not conducting married life" (*no hacen vida maridable*); or more briefly, "they aren't making life" (*no hacen vida*). Simply put, they were not living together. Frequent references and use of abbreviated terminology (no hacen vida) indicate that people recognized the phenomenon as a familiar one.

Examples abound in the court records. In Chapter 3 we saw briefly Manuela Estéfana Bustamante ("Manuela la Tamalera"). In 1781 she stated that she had not "made life" with her husband in some three years, and witnesses confirmed that she and her husband "were continually separated."[38] Her husband was still in town, though, as we will see later. A woman named Antonia Mena, labeled as parda (of dark complexion), around thirty years old, testified in her husband's 1770 trial for various misdeeds. She said he had not "made married life with her at all," and she accused him of multiple adulterous affairs. "When she has seen his face," her deposition continued (as rendered by the notary), "and he has maintained himself for some days in her house it has been because he found himself out of favor with [the other women]."[39] In 1792 Santiago Miranda, who signed his name in an elegant hand, complained that his mother-in-law and stepfather-in-law had sought to separate him from his wife, María de San Carlos Gaitán. "They have influenced my wife," he wrote, "so that . . . she will not make life with me." San Carlos Gaitán, a twenty-five-year-old cigarette maker who said she did not know her calidad, contended that her refusal to "make married life" resulted from shortcomings in her husband's behavior.[40]

Some individuals who were said not to be making married life had also absented themselves from their spouses at long distances. In 1770 Juan Francisco Valle, a forty-nine-year-old mulato silversmith, noted that he was married in Nicaragua to Catarina Mayorgas "with whom he has not made life for twenty years now." Valle had been living in Santiago and had become established there socially; he was serving as a *ministro de vara* (constable) and had taken up with another woman.[41] It is not clear whether Catarina Mayorgas knew her husband's whereabouts, but it is easy to imagine that she would have described him as "ausente."

Most informally separated women experienced financial hardship with the loss of access to their husbands' wages—not only because women's earning power was less than men's, but also because women generally retained informal custody of children. (In a formal ecclesiastic divorce, a husband was required to provide support for his family only if he had been found to be the guilty party, though we don't know how often this requirement was enforced.)[42] In one instance in the capital, an informally separated woman—Gertrudis Carrillo, a free mulata around thirty— claimed that the civil authorities had told her estranged husband (a weaver, mestizo) to give her 2 reales a day to support her and her daughter. The alcaldes, however, said they didn't remember any such order.[43] Lawsuits brought by other women suggest that such a ruling would have been unusal; more frequent were orders for couples to reunite and fulfill spousal duties, including financial support by husbands. (Indeed, such an order was the ultimate outcome of Gertrudis Carillo's case.) It is difficult to gauge the impact of these rulings, since the courts did little follow-up beyond attempting to collect fees for litigation.[44]

Although the majority of marriages probably did not end in separation, the rate of breakups was significant. Studies of late colonial Spanish America have emphasized the importance of marriage, especially for women, in establishing social and economic standing.[45] Yet it is clear in Guatemala's records that people there could hardly count on marriage as permanent. Historians have also recognized the phenomenon of unauthorized separations elsewhere in Spanish America; as Stern noted for Mexico City, "conjugal rupture, whether temporary or prolonged, seemed embedded in the fabric of social practice and expectation."[46] The frequency of marital separations in Guatemala, along with their widespread popular recognition and the courts' allowances for separated women, amounted to an institutionalized sort of de facto divorce. As we have seen, women who were separated informally from their husbands were able to conduct business and legal affairs rather independently, notwithstanding the restrictive aspects of civil code law. Thus de facto divorce as it was practiced in Guatemala was not only more accessible, but in a sense more permissive, than ecclesiastical divorce. De facto divorces allowed women to manage their property and enter into contracts, and in effect often allowed both men and women to participate in subsequent informal conjugal relationships, as we will see later in this chapter.

Spousal roles, spousal conflicts:
Ideology, behavior, and the courts

Though the authority to unite couples in wedlock and to grant legal (if limited) divorces belonged to the church, numerous marriages came before the state authorities as individuals sought help dealing with wayward spouses and marital strife.[47] Their cases reveal much about contemporary understandings of appropriate spousal roles, which were reflected in the ways plaintiffs and their attorneys constructed their complaints and in the judges' rulings. Women's litigation, as well as the courts' responses, invoked notions that a husband should provide financially for his wife and children, apply himself to his work, and be kind and faithful to his wife; he should not abandon the home nor drink or gamble in excess and should not dishonor his wife with obscenities or insults. Testimonies from men, as well as admonishments issued by judges, demonstrate that a wife was expected to obey her husband, subordinating herself to his authority and to his and their children's needs. The wife's expected role required sexual fidelity and modesty outside the home, and service to her husband in domestic chores, particularly preparing food and washing clothes.[48] To the extent that these idealized roles might structure a marriage, a husband would have the right to give orders to his wife and to punish her (including corporal punishment) if she disobeyed him or otherwise violated understandings of appropriate behavior.[49]

Research on various regions in colonial Spanish America has suggested that people internalized dominant ideologies of appropriate spousal roles and behaved accordingly. Stern noted for Mexico that "the notions that men and women were fundamentally different; that such differences implied natural (and socially beneficial) distinctions of right, restriction, and social standing; and that such distinctions granted men superior freedom while consigning women to greater restriction resonated deeply with the wider political and religious culture."[50]

At the same time, however, scholars have also emphasized wives' resistance to husbands' authority and particularly to corporal punishment.[51] Several studies have suggested that while wives accepted (at least publicly) the premise that husbands had a right to use corporal punishment, they disputed the degree of acceptable violence.[52] In her study of Lima, Christine Hünefeldt argues that the presence of domestic violence itself indicates an underlying struggle. "In some cases," Hünefeldt found, "women subjected to violence had overcome—in the eyes of their husbands, overstepped—gendered economic and social boundaries."[53]

My analysis of Guatemalan court cases suggests that litigation was inherently structured by prevailing colonial attitudes about marriage; these ideologies formed the bases for secular and canon law, and both plaintiffs and defendants (as well as their attorneys) made their cases accordingly. It is not surprising, then, that the argumentation presented in judicial cases tends to depict strong social prescriptions about appropriate conduct of husband and wife. However, a close reading of testimonies shows that people did not consistently act out the idealized marital roles; everyday concerns and behavior often hinged on factors beyond the supposed rights and obligations of each gender. While husbands tended to complain of their wives' infidelity or drunkenness, women's charges typically included these problems but also ran to misuse of money and violence. Most appeals were filed by women, and they portray disheartening patterns of violence. Wives complained repeatedly that their husbands had mistreated them with *golpes* (blows) and *castigos* (literally "punishments" but connoting beatings). Though women who filed charges against their husbands professed a belief in notions of mutual obligation, they objected to the realities of their husbands' behavior.[54]

An example is the litigation of Apolonia "Túnchez" Fuentes (her chicha enterprise in the new capital was detailed in Chapter 3). In 1798, she went to the alcalde de barrio charging that her husband had "pulled his knife on her several times, injuring her, tearing her clothes, and telling her he ought to keep going until he kills her." It was not only that she objected to the physical abuse and threats. She said that the cause of her husband's violence toward her was her effort (in the alcalde's words) to "correct him for his laziness" and to "get him to end his extramarital affairs." Thus, Túnchez had openly objected to her husband's behavior and struggled to get him to change before she turned to the court.[55]

Litigation provided women with a way of publicly exposing and punishing malfeasant husbands—a means to a degree of retribution as well as a period of relief. Wives in Santiago and Nueva Guatemala who came to the civil authorities with complaints about their husbands consistently obtained a speedy intervention.[56] Normally the plaintiff's husband was jailed until an investigation could be carried out and a ruling issued. (This contrasts with the state's response to domestic servants' complaints about abusive employers; as we saw in Chapter 3, the employers were not jailed.) Surely many wives endured mistreatment without reporting it, but the archives' abundance of petitions demonstrates that women in the city were widely aware of their access to judicial recourse against husbands, and some chose to use it.[57]

In response to the complaint by Apolonia Túnchez about her husband Miguel García, that same evening the alcalde and his deputies picked García up on their rounds. Specifically, they caught him at the house of a woman named Cayetana Ramírez in a rather compromising position. "He was sleeping with her in the same bed," the alcalde reported, "and both of them were drunk." Presumably Túnchez had told the alcalde where to find him. The officers took both the husband and the paramour to jail.[58] (Consorts caught in such cases were normally taken into custody, then questioned and admonished before release.) Although the final outcome was not documented, the arrests illustrate the state's quick response to complaints about violent or unfaithful husbands.

Even if the offending husband was not apprehended in such incriminating circumstances, a wife's complaint was sufficient for arrest. Apolonia

Túnchez again illustrates. In May 1802, nearly four years after she got her husband arrested in the liaison with Cayetana Ramírez, Túnchez appealed again, now saying that her husband (still Miguel García) was in an affair with a woman named Juana Luna. The authorities jailed both García and Luna. In the trial that followed, Túnchez accused García of not only infidelity but also drinking, gambling, failing to provide financial support, and physically maltreating her. The litigation continued for five months as witnesses called Miguel García a philanderer, wife beater, drunkard, gambler, fighter, and even a murderer. Meanwhile, García escaped from jail and disappeared. He does not appear in the court records again. His consort Juana Luna was declared innocent and freed.[59]

Wives who appealed to the judicial authorities were using a strategy that Stern has called "pluralization of patriarchs."[60] That is, in seeking protection from their husbands (household patriarchs), these women were turning to patriarchal authorities beyond their households—alcaldes, lawyers, and judges. Notably, wives' petitions in Guatemala were largely an urban phenomenon; few spousal suits by rural women (or men, for that matter) surface in the archives.[61] Small-town alcaldes and Indian officers may have been inclined merely to admonish abusive husbands or to dismiss complaints rather than forwarding them to distant tribunals. Further, household patriarchs as a group may have had greater power over women in the countryside than in the city, since rural people depended for their subsistence on the labor of the dual-gendered household.[62] Urban women as a group enjoyed easier access to judicial recourse than their rural counterparts had. The capital city in particular, with its extensive law-enforcement apparatus, offered women more avenues to the deployment of state (and clerical) authority.

A somewhat different view of marital conflicts and violence emerges in criminal charges brought by people other than aggrieved wives. Typically such cases were reported by neighbors or discovered by the alcaldes through happenstance on their rounds. The whole of these records is probably disproportionately weighted toward incidents involving major injuries or neighborhood disturbances (hence the reporting by other people); but the episodes did not necessarily differ from other spousal altercations in origins or dynamics, given that the degree of injury or noise was often unintended or unexpected. In trials instigated by neighbors or night patrols, women tend not to appear as defenseless as in suits that they themselves initiated. Wives as well as husbands appear among the perpetrators of injuries inflicted on their spouses.

Consider the criminal proceedings against Manuela Tujulla. At their home one afternoon in 1770, Manuela assaulted her husband Manuel Medina with a bone, causing a chest wound some two or three inches deep. Manuel survived, and Manuela was brought to trial after neighbors reported the incident. Though Manuela's testimony was not recorded, Manuel and other witnesses alleged that she had been drunk when he arrived home that afternoon. One of the neighbors said the dispute began because Manuela had found some strings of candy missing. Yet admittedly Manuel had played a key role in escalating the conflict. He himself described how before the stabbing he "had closed the door and bolted it, leaving her outside, to prevent her from trying anything crazy because of her inebriation." He then went to lie down while she was locked out. She managed to push the door open, he said, and she stabbed him as he was getting up. Though the outcome of the trial was not recorded, the case suggests sovereign assertiveness in both members of the marriage. Manuela Tujulla did not adhere to the ideal of a wife's subordination to her husband.[63] (Her drunkenness, by the way, is typical; like their male counterparts, women who committed violent acts were often inebriated. Recall Cayetana Rogel, for example, wife of brickmaker Manuel Luciano Alcayaga, described in Chapter 3. Rogel was given to drink and was known to have beaten her husband repeatedly.)[64]

Still, husbands were more often the aggressors, and wives who assaulted husbands were sometimes acting in self-defense, perhaps even more often than the records would indicate. A 1781 criminal case illustrates. The couple was Josefa Casimira Calderón, an Indian, and her husband Manuel Toribio Granados, mestizo, a baker in his mid-thirties. They were living in the new capital in the house of an Indian woman who said she was lodging them out of generosity. An altercation erupted one day when Josefa came home from a shopping errand shortly after noon. Manuel had arrived drunk a while earlier and was evidently irked not to find Josefa in the house. The landlady testified that Manuel began bombarding his wife with insults, including "saying that she was a whore." The tensions escalated into a physical struggle, and Manuel got the upper hand, stabbing Josefa in the chest with a piece of firewood or a kitchen knife (accounts vary). Testifying in the hospital, Josefa contended that her husband was a habitual drinker, wont to fight with her when intoxicated. She confessed that she had also injured him in the fray, though obviously she had been trying to protect herself. Less than two weeks later she died in the hospital. The magistrates regarded Manuel somewhat mercifully since the wound was not immediately mortal; the barber-surgeon who examined Josefa at the crime scene had judged the gash to be only skin-deep, and Manuel's attorney (the procurator for the poor) contended that Josefa had died because of bad medical treatment. Manuel was sentenced to 200 lashes and four years in the capital's presidio laboring on public works.[65]

Manuela Estéfana Bustamante ("Manuela la Tamalera") also injured her husband in response to violence and threat. He was a mestizo bakery worker named José Santiago Albizures. They had separated when she was in her twenties, and their story was documented some three years later, in 1781. One May afternoon while Bustamante was making her tamales, Albizures unexpectedly entered her house while drunk. He approached and put his arms around her as if in an embrace, then stabbed her in the chest and abdomen with a knife. She bit him and managed to twist the knife from his hand. As they struggled, he reached for her braids; she made a superficial cut first on his head and finally thrust the knife into his chest. Her teenage brother happened upon the scene while stopping by on his way from work, and he broke up the fight by threatening Albizures with a piece of firewood. But it was too late. By the time the neighbors arrived, Albizures was dead.

Bustamante was hospitalized with chest wounds while her trial got underway. She and her neighbors surmised that the motive for Albizures's attack was jealousy over her interactions with another man—jealousy that she argued was unfounded. Her testimony and that of witnesses portrayed Albizures as a habitual drunk who beat her repeatedly during the time they lived together. Following their separation, he had allegedly accosted her in the street and threatened to kill her. Though Bustamante readily admitted to having stabbed him, she maintained that she had not meant to kill him. She was "carried away by anger upon finding herself wounded," she said, insisting that her intention had been self-defense. Her attorney too stressed the defensive nature of her crime; he noted that she was still in danger even after she wrested the knife from her husband, who might have killed her had she not struck back. The judges also viewed the incident in this light. There was some dissension among them as to the length of time for her jail term, but they agreed that she should be sentenced to "the softest penalty" and ultimately condemned her to serve only one year.[66]

Though in actions they sometimes departed from ideals of submission, women as a group clearly bore the brunt of domestic violence. In his analysis of eighty-five spousal assault cases in the Guatemalan capital between 1740 and 1824, Leonardo Hernández found that 75 (88 percent) involved female victims.[67] Even though presumably much of the domestic violence went unreported (or unrecorded), its frequency nevertheless is clear in the court records, conveying a picture easily likened to other times and places. In today's Guatemala spousal violence (mainly against women) is so widespread as to be, in the words of one recent study, "an assumed occurrence."[68] Only in 1996 did legislation recognize intrafamily violence and prescribe steps to address it (though the law falls short of defining such violence as criminal).[69] A saying still used in Guatemala attests fatalistically, *Quien quiere, aporrea* (One who loves, beats). For various other regions in colonial Spanish America and early modern Europe as well, scholarship has confirmed widespread domestic violence, especially against wives.[70] The preponderance of husbands over wives as perpetrators of marital violence is part of a wider pattern—the norm in most societies past and present—in which men are more often the culprits in violent crimes.[71]

Despite the colonial state's rapid response to wives' complaints, few men charged with adultery and wife beating in Guatemala were sentenced to much time beyond the duration of their trial. While wives were able to punish their husbands with jail time and the public exposure of imprisonment and a trial, this strategy did not necessarily end the problem, since the men might return to their violent or philandering ways on their release.

Indeed, reform was unlikely in many abusive husbands. Some of them appear repeatedly in the court records, relapsing after release from prison. Lucía de los Dolores Sunsín brought charges against her husband Ramón Ortiz in 1775, alleging mistreatment across sixteen years of marriage. Ortiz was held in jail for about three months, freed only after being fined for the court costs and being made to swear that he would improve his behavior. But less than six months later Sunsín was again petitioning the court. She complained that she herself had been penalized financially—not only with the fine her husband had to pay but also with the cost of a cape he had hocked while gambling in prison. Furthermore, her petition read, he

[has] proceeded with more force and vigor in his wretched life, daily drunkenness, maltreatment, and dishonor of me, already having gambled away the new cape that I made him; finally coming home every day drunk, having lost at gambling, to cruelly maltreat me, and dishonor me by shouting in the doorway, giving various fathers to his children he has had with me [that is, accusing her of infidelity and promiscuity].

She was requesting an affidavit that she would use in pursuing an ecclesiastical divorce.[72]

The divorce did not go through. By 1782 the couple had moved to the new capital, where Ortiz evidently was unable to hold down a job in his trade of button making, and he continued beating his wife. Again she appealed to the civil authorities. The judge sentenced Ortiz to work in the shop of another button maker, but to little avail. Within the month, Sunsín filed another petition. She complained that Ortiz was not working and was "continually drunk." She had been giving him money knowing that he would spend it on aguardiente, she said, because she wanted "to avoid quarrels, maltreatment, and that he should hit me or take something valuable." When she didn't give him money to drink, she explained, he would furtively take articles of her clothing and sell them, and would even sell items that his clients had left him to work on. Sunsín noted that Ortiz had been imprisoned on "eight or ten previous occasions" at her request, "but it hasn't been enough because each day he gets more and more insolent." She was asking the judges to send him to one of the presidios outside the city. If he is held "in the Presidio of San Carlos in this city," she said, "I will have to live in the imminent risk that he will at some point escape and violently take my life." Ortiz was eventually transferred from the jail to the presidio—apparently the one in the capital. Still, Sunsín had gained at least a period of relief, since he had been jailed for a year. There is no record of how long Ortiz was kept in the presidio, but it is not hard to imagine that if he did ultimately return to his wife's house, his bad behavior resumed.[73]

A number of trials for marital infidelity and violence ended when the wife rescinded her charges. In recanting, women did not usually deny that their husbands had committed the transgressions, though some wives said that the men had promised to mend their ways.[74] The reason for recanting appears at times to have been the woman's fear that if she pursued litigation and further jail time, she would face greater reprisals when her husband was released. María Concepción García filed charges in 1811 against her husband, a tailor in his mid-thirties described as pardo libre. She accused him of infidelity, drunkenness, failure to provide financially or help her in the house, preventing her from attending church, and beating her severely over their fourteen years of marriage. She had not gone to the court sooner, she said, "because of the fear that if I did, I would have to pay for it later." At first she insisted that she was "entirely resolved not to be reunited with my husband." A month later, though, while her husband waited in jail for his trial, García came forward to recant. She said she had forgiven her husband and wanted to be reunited with him "to live in peace." Given the brutal mistreatment she had described, a peaceful reunion hardly seems to have been likely. She may have recognized the inevitability of her husband's release and had second thoughts about pursuing the litigation against him, fearing retribution.[75]

A woman named Petrona Juárez appealed to the law in 1796. She was a twenty-something mulata, a dealer in stolen cattle; her husband was a baker, mestizo, also in his twenties. Juárez said he had beaten her one night during an argument and threatened to decapitate her if she alerted the neighbors. The magistrates jailed him, but after two days the wife recanted her charges.[76] In light of his threat, it would not be surprising that she was afraid he would retaliate.

Some women dropped charges because of financial need, being unable to support themselves and their children without their husbands' income. The case of Antonia Cartagena and Pedro Nolasco de Avalos is telling.

Identified in the record as mulata, Antonia was twenty or twenty-one when they were wed around March of 1777; Pedro was a journeyman silver-smith, mestizo, nine years her senior. They already had a child together. In the early months of their marriage, Antonia complained to the civil author-ities several times about Pedro's infidelity, his violence, and his threats to kill her, but she did not request his arrest. The police finally jailed him that September on charges brought by an old flame (he had gone to her house one night trying to reignite the affair; when she refused he grabbed her neck and knocked her to the ground in an effort—ultimately unsuc-cessful—to make her submit). But Antonia petitioned for his release. With-out him, she explained, she had no source of income for herself and their baby. (Pedro was sentenced to pay court courts and freed. As was typical of contemporary sexual assault cases, the jurists argued that the woman who brought the charges—the old flame—was partly to blame. The court ordered her to return to her husband and make married life with him.)[77]

A woman's ability to get by without her husband's financial support depended not only on her social class but also on her access to income and social networks. Apolonia "Túnchez" Fuentes, who petitioned repeatedly for her husband's arrest, evidently did not need his wages to support herself and her teenage daughter. Though identified as española, she was of relatively low status; she did not use the honorific "doña" (nor was her husband a don), and she practiced trades—in meat and chicha—dominated by women of Indian and mixed ancestry and often operating outside the law. Yet these enterprises brought her an income independent of her husband. She also rented out rooms in her house.[78] Her husband reported no occupation. The second time she charged him with adultery, she testified that he was "of no use, because far from [her] having received from her husband even a single cent, he had in the past misspent good quantities of her pesos."[79]

Women could be caught between the desire on one hand to punish their husbands or protect themselves by having their husbands jailed, and the need on the other hand for financial support. Consider Isidora Cárde-nas. In 1800 she brought criminal charges against her husband Severino Vásquez, a silversmith, accusing him of an affair with another woman. As a result of the liaison, Isidora said, "Severino has abandoned me and our legitimate children, making the help that is necessary for our food scarce and at times lacking; continually absenting himself from my house, he has gotten to the point of separation, living alone in the shop where he works, and finally mistreating me in deeds and words." Isidora presented several witnesses, but after they testified she told the judges that she had recon-ciled with her husband, and she asked them to drop the case. Nine months later she reversed her position, renewing the litigation. Her husband was again arrested, and more witnesses testified. But the following month, the charges still pending, Isidora again came forward, inexplicably asking for her husband to be released from jail. She made several appeals this time before the authorities freed him somewhat hesitantly, sentencing him to pay court costs and warning him about his future conduct.[80]

Six years later, Isidora brought new charges against him, this time for his affair with yet another woman. Severino was incarcerated during the trial and then sentenced to two months' service on public works. A few days after the judgment, Isidora petitioned the court. She asked that her husband's sentence be doubled to four months and that instead of service on public works he be required to stay inside the jail, working at his trade as a silversmith and remitting his wages to her. Otherwise, she argued, she would be unable to support her family. Her request was granted.[81] One suspects that her previous vacillations about his incarceration were motivated by financial duress. The second time around, savvy to possible contingencies, she used the legal system (as well as a network of witnesses who testified on her behalf) to punish her husband and to gain several months of safety from him while retaining access to his wages.

In sum, women who recanted their charges against husbands seem to have acted based on economic needs or fear of retribution. Research on villages in late colonial Mexico has suggested that women who rescinded accusations against men may have done so under social pressure from male community elders.[82] In the record of the late colonial Guatemalan capital, though, wives evidently appealed to the courts independently; there is no evidence that they necessarily sought the guidance of men in doing so. In one sense, women's litigation deployed—perhaps even reinforced—patriarchal and colonial hegemony embodied by the legal system. The judges in Guatemala usually favored the preservation of marriage, seeking to reunite separated spouses couples and admonishing them about the prescribed roles of husband and wife. At the same time, though, the magistrates nearly always jailed men whose wives brought charges, and they always sentenced those husbands whose trials were carried (at least in the record) to completion. Ultimately, separated couples sometimes disobeyed court orders to reestablish *vida maridable* (married life), continuing to live apart, and some women explicitly refused to be reunited with abusive husbands.[83] While the colonial courts exalted marriage as the basis of household structure, this ideal did not always translate into daily life.

City dwellers, at least, appear to have been widely aware of Spanish precepts of spousal roles. Yet actions often varied from expressed ideology. Further, frequent spousal separations belied the permanence of the matrimonial sacrament. Abandonment of marriage and its concomitant economic duties provided an escape hatch from prescriptions that may have been impractical or irrelevant in city life. In the urban context, the mandated gender roles for husbands and wives were rendered somewhat illogical, since labor and domestic arrangements did not necessarily depend on a household headed by a heterosexual couple. Marriage was unseated as the basic structural unit of urban households.

Informal unions

Given the fluidity in the duration of marriage, it should not be surprising that a remarkable proportion of the urban populace engaged in unsanctioned sexual unions. Informal unions were not systematically documented, but their numbers are suggested by the rates of out-of-wedlock births recorded in baptismal registries. Lutz's work with the registries from Santiago shows the pattern from the 1630s to 1772, a period when records were kept segregated for three ethnic groups: tributary Indians; gente ordinaria (blacks, mulatos, mestizos, and nontributary Indians); and Spaniards. The records for the city's tributary Indians have been lost, but 69,195 records remain for the other groups. Among gente ordinaria, illegitimate births ranged from 42 to 49 percent of all births during each decade from 1700 to 1769. In the last three years before the earthquakes (1770–1772), 57 percent of the 1,626 gente ordinaria baptisms were for babies born out of wedlock. The rates of illegitimacy were somewhat lower among infants identified as Spaniards—between 26 and 37 percent of baptisms each decade between 1700 and 1769 and 24 percent in 1770–1772.[84]

These findings are harmonious with other colonial Spanish American cities, where studies have similarly shown that the numbers of illegitimate births approached, and occasionally surpassed, numbers of legitimate births.[85] Also typical is Lutz's finding of lower illegitimacy rates among Spaniards than other groups. Historians have explained this difference in terms of elite concerns about maintaining social status and honor, which would depend partly on legitimate births and female chastity outside marriage.[86] Additionally, elites had greater economic reason to be concerned with keeping family fortunes among legitimate heirs.[87] Proportions of out-of-wedlock births may have been lower in the small towns and hamlets of the countryside, where people were more often living with their families and hence might have been less desirous of seeking affection in an illicit union, or simply more subject to parental or spousal oversight.[88] The migration patterns seen in the previous chapters, with great numbers of single and abandoned women arriving in the city, also contributed to the urban demographics of illicit unions and illegitimate births.

The high rate of out-of-wedlock births is echoed by the frequent mention in the court records of informal unions. The plethora of words used in Guatemala's late colonial parlance to denote such relationships in itself suggests their significance. *Concubinato* (concubinage), with its related forms *concubina* and *concubino*, was perhaps the most general of these terms; *amancebamiento* (also meaning concubinage), and the related *amasia* and *amasio* were used somewhat less frequently. Couples in consensual unions were sometimes said to be in *mal vivir* (literally, bad living).[89] Slightly more euphemistic was *ilícita amistad* (also *amistad ilícita*, literally, illicit friendship), a term that surfaces in numerous court records. A more faithful transcription of speech may be *mala amistad* (literally, bad friendship), which also often appears. *Ilícita amistad* and *mala amistad* were sometimes shortened to a simple *amistad*, which invariably in court records referred to a sexual relationship, or at least a romance. *Trato ilícito* or simply *trato* referred specifically to sex itself but might also allude to an ongoing relationship of concubinage. *Acceso*, on the other hand, was more limited in its connotation, tending to pinpoint carnal knowledge without evoking other components of a relationship. All of these terms applied to relationships outside the bonds of marriage, regardless of whether either person was married to someone else. As far as the wording used to name these relationships, contemporaries did not distinguish between affairs that were adulterous and those that were illicit simply because the couple was not married.

In late colonial Guatemala, none of the terms referring to illicit liaisons necessarily implied that the couple were living together.[90] It might appear that that couples in unsanctioned unions rarely headed households together; even though some of the barrio censuses do indicate relationships among residents of each household, concubina/o and amasia/o are not mentioned. This may indicate only that respondents did not reveal their illicit relationships to the census taker. Perhaps the census takers listed couples who lived together as married, as Arrom noted was done in the Mexico City census of 1811.[91] Yet the enumerators of the Guatemalan censuses were perhaps less prone to such euphemistic simplifications; whereas the Mexico City census listed "women living with children but without husbands as widows," the Nueva Guatemala census of 1824 tended not to designate single mothers as widows. Presumably some men helped support extramarital households in which they lived sporadically with mistresses, but likely these men were not entered in the census records of those households.

One cohabitation case that does come to light is that of Rosalia Castro (alias "Bonita") and her partner Rafael Vivas, who lived in Santiago's barrio of San Francisco.[92] Bonita was unmarried and claimed to be an española (Rafael said he did not know her calidad). Rafael himself, also unmarried, said he was español, although a neighbor believed him to be the illegitimate son of a mestiza mother and a Spanish father. Bonita and

Rafael had been living together as a couple for eleven or twelve years when they were arrested in 1775, following an anonymous tip on unlicensed aguardiente production and their illicit relationship. Bonita said she was thirty-five at the time; Rafael was around thirty-four. They admitted to the illegal liquor trade in their house and to their unsanctioned union, explaining that they had sought to get married some two years earlier. Their plans were thwarted, though, by an ecclesiastical impediment that surfaced in the nuptial proceedings: Rafael had previously had a sexual relationship with one of Bonita's relatives. Bonita knew of the affair. Both she and Rafael contended that they had pursued a dispensation (to allow their marriage to take place), but the process had been interrupted by the 1773 earthquakes. They had then resumed living together in the same house, which Bonita had bought in 1771. Their 1775 arrest resulted in a one-year sentence for each of them for the aguardiente, but they were released before twelve months had elapsed—Rafael because he developed kidney stones and was transferred to the hospital, and Bonita because of "continuous outcries that she direct[ed] to the court." Though their subsequent story is not documented, one imagines that once again, as they had done after the priest separated them in 1773 as part of their ill-fated marriage proceedings, they returned to their life in Bonita's house.

However, Rafael was neither legally nor financially the patriarchal head of household. Nor would it be quite right to say that he and Bonita were joint householders. Bonita apparently commanded sizable means. She alone had acquired title to the house for the rather stately price of 390 pesos, to be paid over time. Presumably the aguardiente business helped her pay off at least some of the mortgage. Under interrogation, she testified that in the week of her arrest they had sold two arrobas of aguardiente at 28 reales per arroba—a gross income of 56 reales (7 pesos) for the week. As for who had purchased the drink, she pleaded ignorance, saying that Rafael had sold it. The record depicts Rafael in somewhat tighter pecuniary circumstances. His property was impounded after his arrest, and the inventory included seven chairs and some other pieces of furniture, some empty trunks and boxes, mirrors, candleholders, several paintings and saints' images, and twelve chickens. This was more than most manual laborers owned, but it doesn't measure up to Bonita's house and movable property (which would have included kitchenware, if not also furniture and other things). When the magistrates asked Rafael why he had succumbed to involvement in the illegal sales, he said he had no other way to pay an 8-peso legal settlement that he owed—a relatively paltry sum compared to the fortunes of his consort. He was trained as a silversmith but said he had not practiced the craft since his late teens. Instead had been earning his living as a clerk or assistant (*cajero*) in several taverns.

Even Bonita may have kept or hired Rafael as no more than a clerk in an operation where she acted as the controlling partner. She owned the house where the enterprise was run, and in her testimony she pointed out that Rafael was living there only because she let him; when the magistrates reprimanded her for the long-enduring concubinage, she asserted that she had sought not only at one point to marry Rafael but also at another time to "throw [him] out of her house"—unsuccessfully, she said, because he insistently came around looking for her. Ultimately she had continued in the amistad, she conceded, because of her own weakness.

Thus, although Rafael was Bonita's partner in the aguardiente businesses and in their sexual relationship and although he lived with her, he did not share equally in heading the household. The title of the rather costly house where they lived was in Bonita's name alone, even though she purchased the property at a time when she had already been living with Rafael for some seven or eight years. Rafael had no legal right to inheritance of the house, or to any other property belonging to Bonita, for that matter. Though the couple's fortunes were clearly intertwined, they were nevertheless more separate than those of a married couple.

Property rights constituted a key distinction between marriage and informal unions, since inheritance was largely subsumed within the legal structure of marriage. When a married person died, the surviving spouse was generally entitled by law to inherit two-fifths of the shared property. Another two-fifths would be divided equally among the couple's legitimate children, and the testator could leave one-fifth to other parties. (Wives' dowries and the property each spouse brought to the marriage did not become part of the shared property.) Married couples might easily own a household together; the house itself, unless brought by one spouse to the marriage, and the rents paid by tenants were common property (*bienes gananciales*).[93] For unmarried couples living together, there was no such legal structure. The Guatemalan state granted recognition with property and inheritance rights for couples in consensual unions only in 1964.[94]

The disarticulation of property rights from informal unions can help explain the relatively lower rates of illegitimate births among elites. Throughout Spanish America, the privileged colonial classes recognized that marriage was intertwined with property holding, and they strategized accordingly. An ideal marriage would present the opportunity to expand the family's wealth or to consolidate it (as in cousin marriage).[95] Keeping childbearing within marriage secured the legal process for inheritance of family fortune.

City dwellers in consensual unions seem to have kept their accounts more separate than did married couples. Unlike Bonita Castro and Rafael Vivas, most of the unsanctioned couples who entered the archival record appear not to have formed households together, or to have done so only for short periods. Overall, the records convey an impression that the ephemeral nature of household formation underwrote illicit unions. Migrants and other workers in the old capital had generally lived in rented and temporary lodgings, and domestic arrangements were even more haphazard in Nueva Guatemala during the years of relocation and building. For much of the populace of the late colonial capital, place of residence was impermanent and contingent on employment or the generosity of kin or strangers. Eating and sleeping were sometimes divided between two different locations. Most of the city's houses and patios, if not also rooms, were shared. In the majority of homes people from different families were lodged under the same roof for days, months, or years at a time. The jumbling and crowding that characterized domestic spaces facilitated sexual liaisons between people who were not married to one another. Lovers may have tried to conceal their activities, but other people—neighbors, relatives, roommates, and co-workers—had ample opportunity to detect illicit affairs.[96] Illicit unions were documented sometimes because of outright denunciations to clerics or alcaldes but other times merely as circumstantial details reported in the processing of other matters.

For unsanctioned couples who did not live together as householders, normative ideologies of marital obligations did not apply. A large economic component of the idealized uxorial role—preparing daily food and drink, washing and maintaining clothes, and cleaning the home for the husband—was irrelevant or impractical outside the setting of a nuclear-family home. Thus, in the urban setting, the economic structure of concubinage did not replicate all of the financial ties created by marriage—neither in the sphere of property and inheritance rights nor in daily economic life.

Nevertheless, some women performed domestic work for their partners in unsanctioned unions, often for wages—notably in relationships between single men and the women they hired to do their domestic chores. The priest don Francisco Carrascal and his housekeeper Paz Palala lived almost as a married couple. As we saw in Chapter 3, they formed a household during twenty-three years until Carrascal's death. Palala traveled with Carrascal to his various parishes, did his domestic chores, and cared for the daughter they had together. He paid her, but when she inherited nothing from him she sued his estate arguing that the wages weren't enough.[97] We also saw in Chapter 3 that the merchant don Blas Bahamonde had a shorter-term, non-cohabitating liaison with María de los Angeles Aragón, an Indian woman he paid to do his cooking and laundry.[98] The illiterate Frenchman don Pedro Ayau appears repeatedly in this sort of thing. As he rose to riches in Guatemala, he made a habit of impregnating young women who were serving him in the houses where he roomed and boarded.[99] A woman named Inés García had a child by the Spaniard don Bartolomé Rigo, who had hired her to make his cigarettes and do his laundry.[100] The twenty-three-year-old don José Matías Molina ran off in a torrid affair with a domestic servant from the home of his mother, doña Martina García. (Doña Martina herself, meanwhile, who owned a sizable *labor* [farm] south of the capital, was reputed to be carrying on with her estate's mayordomo.)[101]

Like tavern keepers Bonita Castro and Rafael Vivas, various illicit couples were partners in business as well as love, but their business partnerships were rarely equal. Unsanctioned couples running enterprises together seem to have shared only limited portions of their resources, and they ultimately faced separate economic fates. Recall Máxima Monroy (we saw her in Chapter 3), who earned her living as a beef retailer in the new capital's central plaza. Her lover, the hacendado don Máximo Coronado, provided her with some of the cattle she sold, and she purchased food for him and hired out his laundry and sewing. Thus, although they did not share a residence, Máxima managed many of don Máximo's domestic chores and marketed some of his hacienda's output. Don Máximo, in turn, contributed a substantial portion of the merchandise for her retail enterprise. When their love affair ended and don Máximo sued Máxima for the cost of some cattle he had advanced her, her attorney argued that the two had shared cash from the beef sales effectively as community property, and that she therefore should not be required to recompense him for his contributions to her operations. Máxima had used their shared resources, the lawyer explained, to pay for food, laundry, and sewing for the both of them. The court's ruling was essentially a compromise between the two; Máxima was ordered to pay don Máximo slightly more than half of what he was demanding. Their partnership, the judge reasoned, had been based on "good faith with payment and trust," and in his estimation Máxima had not been completely honest as "administrator, or retailer of the meat." Though the judge noted that she had spent money for don Máximo's food and laundry, the ruling said nothing further about the intimate nature of the relationship. In effect, the state recognized Máxima as don Máximo's business partner, but not an equal one.[102]

FOR MONEY OR LOVE?

Liaisons between men of European descent and women of Indian, African, or mixed ancestry have long occupied historical imaginations in the Americas.[103] From one perspective, such liaisons could be advantageous for women, offering them gains in social and economic status. From another angle, though, the men in these relationships were exploiting the women and the structural inequities in power.[104] I argued in Chapter 2 that unions between slave women and elite Spanish men were inherently exploitive, based as they were on vast power differentials. In constrast, most illicit unions to appear in the records of late colonial Guatemala were between people of relatively similar social status. Yet gender inequities in salaries gave men access to significantly more money than their female counterparts had through wages. From the 1780s through the first decade of the 1800s, urban men working in construction or as wage laborers in artisan trades could expect to earn between 2½ and 4 reales a day, totaling some 7 to 12 pesos per month.[105] Women working as domestic servants or cooks generally received 2 or 3 pesos each month, although they were often given room and board in addition to their salaries.[106]

Still, the salaries of working men were hardly lavish. On the contrary, for a plebian man supporting a family in the capital, the pay for a day's work was a starvation wage, given that the cost of sustenance in the city for one adult was 1 or 2 reales a day.[107] A man living on this wage could not support a concubine in addition to a wife, much less children. In the Guatemalan capital, as Stern has noted for late colonial Mexico City, "households survived by patching together multiple income streams, and the contributions of plebian patriarchs . . . were often minimal or irregular."[108]

For Guatemala there are remarkably few court records that indicate women were being "kept" outright by their lovers—that is, receiving complete financial support. Among sixty-five cases of concubinage I have identified, only two records clearly depict such scenarios; another two are merely suggestive. In all four cases the man's social status was relatively high—and higher than the woman's status. (We can imagine that the prospect of becoming the kept mistress of a married man may have been a relatively appealing option for single women living as servants in other people's homes.)

One case dates to 1816, when don Francisco Panero offered to provide Mariana Gallegos (not a doña) with money and a place to live if she would consent to a sexual relationship with him. She accepted. Panero arranged for her to live in a "well-reputed" house, hired her a servant, and began giving her 10 pesos a month. The following year they had a daughter, and by 1819 Gallegos was expecting their second child. But Panero's support dwindled. Gallegos petitioned the court, complaining that he had not given her more than a few reales in the past seven months. In addition to caring for her child and being pregnant, she said, she was without good clothing and she had no jewelry, not even "earrings, which are the [appropriate] adornment for a woman." The outcome of her appeal was not documented.[109]

In the second case the relationship may have lasted longer. Domingo José Cisneros, a barber, moved from Santiago to the province of San Salvador (now El Salvador) in the early 1760s. There he established a household with his wife in the town of Zacatecoluca. Some eleven or twelve years later he was denounced for an affair with an Indian woman named María Antonia. Local people said he had brought her with him from Guatemala and maintained her in a separate household in the neighboring pueblo of Analco, where she was called María Antonia Guatemala. Rumors about the illicit relationship and its two participants flourished. Neighbors knew Domingo by a series of aliases and thought his ancestry was racially mixed, though he identified himself as a Spaniard. He was said to have killed a man or two in Guatemala. People in Zacatecoluca claimed that María Antonia had spent the night with Domingo in the same house where he lived with his wife. He had cut María Antonia's braids once in anger, they said (this was a way of publicly humiliating a woman), and he had tried to kill her. Some said he had nearly killed a deputy sent by the alcalde to catch the couple in the act. Witnesses believed Domingo had given some of his legitimate children—they disagreed as to how many—to María Antonia as servants. By the time Domingo was arrested in 1774, his wife had died. He admitted to the amistad with María Antonia, but he contended that it dated back only four years, casting doubt on the neighbors' claims that he had brought her when he settled in the area. Indeed, gossip about this couple seems to have taken on a life of its own, and it is difficult to distinguish between rumor and reality. The content of Domingo and María Antonia's relationship—particularly the extent to which he supported her financially—remains uncertain.[110]

Two additional cases hint at the possibility of women being kept by paramours. In 1800, doña Regina Soto of Nueva Guatemala filed suit contending that don Juan Reyes had proposed to support her in exchange for sex, then failed to fulfill his half of the bargain. Witnesses could not confirm the veracity of Soto's claims, nor even that the couple had been in concubinage. For his part, Reyes denied having had a sexual relationship with Soto beyond a single encounter some nine years earlier.[111]

The other instance, also in the new capital, was recorded in 1810. A mulato tailor in his mid-fifties appealed to law enforcement for help locating his daughter, Manuela Flores, and returning her to his home. Everyone knew that Manuela had been in concubinage for some five years with don Juan Araujo, by whom she had two children. On several occasions the civil authorities had placed Manuela in *depósito* (internment in a neutral private household) at the behest of her father, but she continued in the affair. The alcalde noted that he had tried to get her "to go back to her parents . . . and not to continue in the house where this Araujo has placed her." Perhaps this meant that don Juan was paying for her to live somewhere away from the control of her parents. Neither Manuela nor don Juan testified, and there is no indication as to whether Manuela earned wages. In any case, the couple persisted in the relationship. Manuela's father specified that he had no ill will toward the boyfriend; he and his wife just wanted their daughter to come home, he said. If Manuela was indeed being kept by don Juan, evidently it wasn't for lack of alternative support.[112]

Judicial records suggset that more often than being completely maintained by *amasios*, women may have used unsanctioned sexual relationships as one strategy within a diverse "portfolio" of financial support mechanisms.[113] Juana Aldana, a native of Guastatoya in eastern Guatemala, had come to live in the capital around 1792 at age thirteen. Widowed in her twenties, she worked grinding corn and sewing. In 1805 she was arrested when another woman complained that Aldana was involved with her husband. Aldana admitted to the relationship, which she said had lasted for some sixteen months. She claimed that her poverty had "obligated her to [persist in] the affair," implying that her lover had provided something for her financially. It wasn't housing, though. She did not specify who had employed her in grinding and sewing, but Aldana said she had been living with her brother for some time. It may be that she emphasized her financial need mainly as an excuse when she was placed under arrest.[114]

Indeed, lawyers among Aldana's contemporaries alluded to a notion that men might give women gifts as a standard component of illicit sexual relationships. Paz Palala's litigation against the estate of Padre Francisco Carrascal is an example. As evidence of their liaison, Palala's attorney pointed to gifts that the priest had sent her when the couple were separated during her pregnancy.[115] Another lawyer made the argument that "no woman goes so far as to lend herself to a man's turpitude without having received gifts in proportion to his wealth."[116] To be sure, lawyers' arguments often appear as little more than arguments. In this last case, for one, the court was evidently unconvinced, as it ruled essentially against the lawyer's client.

Speaking about her own life, María Manuela Corpus Chocojay intimated that she had hoped her paramour would provide something for her financially. Chocojay identified herself as an Indian from the pueblo of San Luis del Obispo, on the edge of the capital. In 1803 she and José Gregorio López, an Indian from Ciudad Vieja, were denounced for concubinage in a Guatemala City house where they were both working and living. Testifying in the men's jail, López said he had made up his mind to tie the knot with Chocojay. He asked to be liberated so that he could "work and gather the money to get married." But Chocojay was skeptical. Questioned in the women's jail, she admitted to the affair and concurred with López as to its duration of a week, but she scoffed at the proposal of marriage. "She is not of a mind to marry him," the record reads, "knowing that she is not likely to get ahead at all with such a husband, who until now has not given her one cent." In Chocojay's view, a sexual relationship—licit or illicit—ideally should have offered her some economic mobility. She requested liberty on the grounds that she would "control herself and amend her lifestyle." Both she and López were freed.[117]

A key source of evidence of financial support for *amasias* is litigation by wronged wives, who sometimes complained that their husbands were diverting money to a concubine. Aleja Josefa Sosa, for example, was perfectly aware of her husband's extramarital liaison. She knew who the other woman was, and she knew exactly how long the affair had persisted (fifteen months). Petitioning the court in 1813, Sosa charged that her husband was freeloading at home and spending his wages on his concubine. "He wants me to maintain him and give him clean clothes every week, and [this is without his] maintaining me, nor giving me one cent," she said. "When he does work, it is to take [his wages] to the *amiga*. Indeed she, without working, has better skirts than I, who work and maintain him."[118] While such allegations are suggestive about men's financial or material gifts to their concubines, the petitions should be interpreted cautiously. Womens' charges against their husbands for promiscuity were almost invariably accompanied by accusations of physical mistreatment if not also failure to keep a job, drunkenness, and gambling. The records convey a sense that physical violence was often the main issue but that women needed to elaborate all of their husbands' misdeeds in order to build their cases. Again, Aleja Josefa Sosa illustrates. Her husband's extramarital affair and the money he gave his mistress were secondary complaints in a petition primarily about physical abuse. She contended that in eleven years of marriage, she had miscarried ten pregnancies because of her husband's beatings. The concubine and the misspent money appear almost to have been raised as support for Sosa's larger accusations. (The outcome of her appeal was not documented.)

Nor should we focus solely on financial factors to explain the frequency of concubinage. Tracy Ehlers' ethnographic study of late-twentieth-century San Pedro Sacatepéquez (a Mam and ladino town in Guatemala's western highlands) identifies a complex set of motivations in extramartial sexual relationships. "It is through exploitation of poor or isolated women that men commonly develop a *casita* alliance" (long-term extramarital affair), she noted. "But the exploitation implicit in the male choice of a lower status or economically vulnerable woman is reciprocated in her expectations of him." He would help her create a household, not only by providing "financial support, however minimal," but also by fathering children, who would become the woman's main basis "for economic and social security." Children would provide women with love and companionship, enhanced status in the community, and material support (through their labor) from a relatively young age. In Ehlers's analysis, men are motivated by the sense of status and power they gain from the "parallel marriage" and by the "freedom to act as they please, to debauch and drink with impunity . . . , for the objection of one woman to the arrangement means the man immediately quits her home for the solace of the parallel family."[119] Though based on a much later period, this model resonates with certain patterns we have seen for the capital city in the late colonial years—not just the frequency of concubinage, but also the large number of female-headed households, the huge female majority among the adult population, and the young age at which children could start earning wages to contribute to family income. Ehlers's description also echoes some of the content of late colonial-era wives' complaints about wayward husbands—the men's financial support to mistresses, their capricious comings and goings from the home, their sense of power and impunity in drinking and other vices.

While these explanations suggest a rather bleak portrait of concubinage (not to mention marriage), there were additional factors at play. For one, let us not entirely discount love. Consider the case of Aniceta Portillo. Her lover gave her various gifts, including money, but there was clearly something more to it. Aniceta was a "parda" (woman of dark complexion), married to a man old enough to be her father. She was twenty-three in 1774 when she struck up an extramarital liaison with Francisco Guerra, an acquaintance of both her husband and her parents. Francisco was thirty-five and unmarried, the mestizo son of a family that ran several stores in the city; he and a brother sold supplies to carriage makers and cartwrights. Francisco and Aniceta's story entered the record after Aniceta discovered she was pregnant. Her husband, she later explained, had "not touched her at all in about five months," and she feared he would beat her if he learned she was expecting. Though her parents had expressed their disapproval of her relationship with Francisco, they were by this time aware of the circumstances, and they colluded in an earnest (if unrealistic) attempt to protect their daughter by hiding her from her husband during the pregnancy. But Aniceta's husband reported her missing, and the civil authorities easily discovered her whereabouts. Informed of the situation, the husband eventually dropped all charges and publicly forgave her.

Ironically, the husband's suspicions had not been aroused earlier when Francisco sent several gifts to him and Aniceta at their home (or perhaps the husband had chosen to look the other way). The record does not specify exactly what the gifts were. Francisco later said they were only "trifles" (*menudencias*), though it was precisely the gifts that had alerted Aniceta's mother to the illicit entanglement. Francisco had also given Aniceta a peso to replace a lost pair of shoes. Later, he gave her mother money to pay for her food and lodging during the pregnancy.

Yet the record conveys the impression that Aniceta was following her heart more than her wallet. Admonished by her mother that the affair was wrong, Aniceta had responded in approximate terms that she didn't give a damn (that she was carrying on with Guerra "aunque se la llevara el Diablo").[120] Her mother later told the court that Aniceta had sought escape in the affair with Francisco because she was fed up with her stepchildren. While Aniceta's marriage was apparently troubled or lackluster, one gets a distinct sense that she and the paramour loved each other. Witnesses described how she had often sent secret notes to him by way of a criada, and the depositions show that he had visited her several times while she was in hiding at the homes of various acquaintances.[121]

Other cases too suggest that economic exchange was only one part of a dense web of circumstances that motivated women and men to engage in illicit unions. Factors such as sexual desire, curiosity, and perhaps youthful rebelliousness also played a role. Both men and women explained illicit affairs in terms of their "weakness" (*fragilidad*) and "passion" (*pasión*).[122] Migration patterns put emotional intimacy and affiliation at a premium, perhaps especially in the capital city, as many people there were isolated from their families for extended periods with no direct means of communication. Separations were exacerbated by the earthquakes in 1773 and the gradual relocation of the city (and its populace) over a tortuous road flanked by steep cliffs. Amorous relationships presumably assumed greater emotional importance for people experiencing long absences from family members.

Moreover, the social convention of illicit unions in a certain sense allowed and legitimized them. This convention was not without basis. In a society where matrimony was often ephemeral, infidelity was sometimes relatively insignificant as a betrayal of mutual marital commitment. Many of the records of illicit love reveal that one or both participants' legally married spouse was ausente—absent from the marriage if not also from the community.

Examples include Felipa Guerra, one of the Jocotenango Indian workers on the sugar estate of doña Manuela Dardón (described at length in Chapter 1). The 1765 report on workers there listed Guerra's husband as "ausente," and she was known to be in "mal vivir" with another Indian worker, Martín Chirec. Evidently their relationship was more than a passing dalliance, since she was helping him pay off a debt to Dardón.[123] Also in the 1760s, María Manuela de León, a bakery owner in Quetzaltenango, was engaged in an illicit affair with the traveling flour and sugar wholesaler José Joaquín Santizo. (He was married in the capital to doña Tomasa de Lara, whose baking business was described in Chapter 3.) De León had for several years been separated from her own husband.[124] In the capital in 1798 Lucas García and Marcelina González, both Indians, were jailed for concubinage. Though Lucas was married, his wife was known to be ausente.[125]

Petrona Peralta, a mulata in her twenties, carried on an illicit amistad for some ten years in the 1760s and 1770s, all the while married to someone else. Her husband was a muleteer, away on the highways for months at a time. She contended that they did not get along and that he had essentially abandoned her. She had left their home in Amatitlán and was sharing a house with another woman in the capital when she fell into the company of the other man.[126] Twenty-seven-year-old doña Rafaela Pedroza was arrested in the capital in 1795 for concubinage. Rebuked by the court for her estrangement from her husband, she said that for the past six years she had "not made life with him for just causes."[127] Three years later she entered the record again after the administrator of one of the city's monasteries reported that a certain friar had been sneaking out at night and walking to Pedroza's house. The alcalde and his night patrol then went to her house unannounced and forced their way in. There they found Pedroza "half-covered in a sheet" and the friar "floundering around half-dressed." The judge who heard the ensuing case noted that Pedroza's husband was "absent without it being said where, with what purpose, nor when he will return."[128]

In this context, the lack of distinction in local parlance between adultery and unsanctioned unions of unmarried persons was quite logical. Adulterers, it seems, were often married only in terms of religious law, not in daily practice. This pattern was echoed in Charles Wagley's 1937 ethnographic research in Santiago Chimaltenango, a Mam community in northwestern highland Guatemala. Wagley noted that "there are frequent reshufflings of spouses among the villagers," involving extramarital sex and an apparently normal process of informal divorce and remarriage.[129] Neither the 1930s villagers of Santiago Chimaltenango nor the late colonial-era residents of the capital city consistently observed permanence or monagamy in matrimony.

THE DEMOGRAPHICS OF INFORMAL UNIONS

The skewed gender ratio among adults in both Santiago and Nueva Guatemala presumably shaped patterns of concubinage. Studies of cities with female majorities in colonial Mexico have postulated, in Douglas Cope's words, that "many plebian women sought sexual satisfaction—and some financial security—in concubinage."[130] Given the gender imbalance, it seems logical to think that not all women would find husbands; unmarried women, the reasoning goes, would then resort to concubinage. For men in this picture, the predominantly female cities offered a bountiful multitude of potential mates and opportunities for polygyny. The urban gender ratios would therefore have supported fulfillment of popular ideologies that Stern has described for late colonial Mexico, in which "gender right" gave men exclusive rights to sexual relations with their female lovers but did not give women parallel exclusive rights to sexual relations with their male lovers.

However, these possibilities are not definitively borne out in the initial evidence on concubinage in late colonial Guatemala. In a sample of sixty-five illicit sexual relationships documented in judicial records (chosen at random), the proportions of married men and unmarried women are insufficient to demonstrate widespread polygyny. The cases are summarized in Table 4.2. (Liaisons involving slaves have been excluded in light of the specific circumstances that often surrounded slave women's participation in sexual relationships, as discussed in Chapter 2.)

In the cases where the man's marital status could be determined, twenty-two of the men were married at the time of their affair, and twenty-nine were unmarried. Another three were priests, and three were widowers. Two men are categorized in the table as "other." One of these began his illicit liaison as a bachelor and continued it after being married to someone else; in the other case, accounts disagree as to whether the man continued the affair after getting married. In six of the records, the man's marital status was not documented. Among the female participants, thirteen are known to have been married, twenty-nine went on record as unmarried, and another two were identified as widows. In the remaining twenty-one cases the woman's marital status was not recorded.

There are six "repeat offenders" in the sample. Two were married men, each counted twice in the tabulation (each denounced by his wife for two separate adulterous affairs).[131] Also tabulated twice is the young widower Bonifacio Rogel. He was involved with a widow some twenty years his senior and with a teenage girl whose mother did his cooking.[132] A man named Benito Gueren had an adulterous affair while married, then when widowed he began a relationship with the previous concubine's sister; he is counted once in the table as married and once as a widower.[133] Petrona Peroza, an unmarried Spanish cigarette maker and seamstress who lived with her mother, was documented in affairs with two different men during her late teenage years; she is counted twice among the unmarried women.[134] Among the married women, Agustina Chiboy, a tributary

TABLE 4.2
Marital status of participants in sample concubinage cases, 1770–1832.

	Men	Women
Married	22	13
Unmarried	29	29
Clergy	3	0
Widowed	3	2
Unspecified marital status	6	21
Other	2	0
Total	65	65

Sources: Archivo General de Centro América, Guatemala City (for explanation of document citation numbers, see page 253), A2/150/2831, A2/153/2909, A2/153/2923, A2/153/2914 (two amancebamientos), A2/153/2928, A2/154/2980, A2/154/2954, A2/154/2953, A2/154/2988, A2/154/2997, A2/157/3049, A2/157/3052, A2/157/3064, A1/4068/32049, A2/157/3080, A2/157/3079, A1/5342/45042, A1/4310/34598, A1/4311/34633 (two amancebamientos), A1/4321/34803, A1/4317/34744, A1/2515/20017, A1/4332/34821, A2/185/3704 (two amancebamientos), A2/187/377, fol. 12, A2/186/3731, A2/187/3768, A1/4368/35542, A1/2944/27694, A1/4372/35611, A1/4363/35446, A1/5338/44980, A1/4380/35720, A1/4380/35717, A2/203/4147, A1/le.g 4385/35831, A1/4386/35835, A1/4401/36171, A2/14/318, A1/4398/36121, A1/4400/36153, A2/54/1076, A1/4400/36146, A1/4406/36276, A1/2867/26094, A1/2867/26116, A1/4427/36759, A1/4440/37101, A1/4440/37098, A2/233/4962, A2/247/5364, A2/248/5392, A2/248/5403 "C", A2/250/5440, A1/5909/50454, A1/3006/28794, A2/243/5262, B/1278/31129, A1/6940/57770, B90.1/1252/30589, B85.1/3599/82741; Alejandro Marure Papers, Courtesy Edward E. Ayer Collection, The Newberry Library, Box 1, folders 15 and 29.

Indian who had left her husband in her hometown of San Miguel del Texar, is counted twice. She was living in the capital in 1795 and carrying on with a tributary Indian man whom she had deceived into thinking she would marry him. When he was jailed following a barroom brawl, she ran off with another man.[135] Finally, two separate illicit liaisons were counted involving a doña Regina Soto—likely one and the same person.[136]

The sample itself warrants some critical consideration. Those affairs that entered the written record are not necessarily representative of all illicit liaisons in the society, most of which were presumably never documented.[137] Though many unsanctioned relationships surface as part of the background in litigation about other issues, others entered the court records for reasons arising from the affairs themselves—wives petitioning about philandering husbands; romantic jealousies resulting in criminal violence; parents, landlords, or employers reporting shenanigans taking place under their roofs. Among the sixty-five sample cases, the single most frequent reason for documentation was child support suits. Twelve of these were brought by women who had been jilted after getting pregnant; in a thirteenth case, a woman sued her father for retroactive child support decades after he abandoned her mother (more on these suits in the following pages). Married women did not litigate for child support, since the law assumed that the children were fathered by the husband. The sample therefore probably overrepresents unmarried women, who were more likely than married women to file suits that would document their illicit relationships.

Male participants in illicit sex, on the other hand, were probably more prone to go on record if they were married. Wives frequently knew of their husbands' infidelity and could petition the civil authorities for intervention; such instances account for eleven cases in the sample. Because an unsanctioned union stood a better chance of persisting unrecorded if the man did not have a wife to blow the whistle, the sample likely overrepresents married men as participants in concubinage. (Husbands did sometimes file court proceedings against their wives, but this was less common, with only two instances in the sample.)[138]

Homosexual relationships and acts are not mentioned in any of the court records studied. This absence may be partly an artifact of the reasons behind legal appeals. Heterosexual unions that came before the courts often had been reported by a wronged spouse, or occasionally a disappointed parent. Both wives and husbands among the complainants described their spouses' failures to fulfill prescribed obligations—particularly financial support by husbands and food preparation by wives. Parents who brought charges trying to end their offspring's premarital relationships may have feared the economic repercussions of an out-of-wedlock birth or a marriage to someone of lower status. All these denunciations were essentially protests about the ways that illicit unions threatened prevailing social structures. The state got involved through its judicial apparatus because it sought to protect these structures, particularly marriage and inheritance. Homosexual unions, in contrast, did not present the same threats. In a sense, homosexuality was extraneous to the social institutions that the judicial system sought to preserve. Further, homosexuality may often have been hidden by society's normative homosociality; because it was appropriate for people of the same sex to socialize and work together unchaperoned, neighbors and family members did not necessarily become aware of homosexual liaisons.[139] Finally, people may have been more likely to denounce homosexual acts to religious officials than to secular ones. Studies of other regions of Spanish America have described homosexuality based on documentation in ecclesiastical court records as well as cases brought before the Inquisition.[140]

Despite these gaps in the sample, the data in Table 4.2 suggest several patterns (indeed, adjusting for the gaps would seem to further buttress the patterns). First, men who engaged in illicit sexual unions appear more likely to have been single than married. This probably reflects in part a tendency among men to take concubines while postponing marriage until they were established financially.[141] Single women may have been more frequent participants in illicit unions than were married women, although the sample data are inconclusive since marital status could not be determined for many of the women. Nevertheless, the sample—particularly its substantial number of married women—calls into question the idea of a male populace exploiting the urban gender imbalance for purposes of sexual promiscuity. It also discredits the idea that female concubinage was the exclusive realm of unmarried women seeking sexual satisfaction or material support.

Some of the couples denounced for concubinage were free to get married, and they consented to do so when faced with incarceration upon their arrest.[142] Marriage would immediately legitimize any ongoing sexual relationship and any children that the couple already had. It also might appease parents, employers, or others who shared living space with the couple. In these cases, unsanctioned sex was in effect premarital sex— hardly unusual in the late colonial years despite idealized norms of bridal virginity. As we will see in the following pages, for the majority of people in the capital, courtship was a rather permissive business.

Courtship, honor, and paternity suits

Conventional views have portrayed courtship in colonial Spanish America in terms of ideologically prescribed protocol and restraint. Historians have given particular emphasis to the value that Spanish American societies placed on sexual chastity in girls and women, as scholarship has equated bridal virginity and uxorial fidelity with colonial notions of virtue and family honor.[143]

There were actually two words in colonial Spanish America that are translated in English as "honor," as Lyman Johnson and Sonya Lipsett-Rivera have explained—*honor* and *honra*.[144] The term *honor* referred to high social status, as perceived by contemporaries based on a complex set of factors including a person's ancestry and lineage, race, and wealth (or presumed wealth). This type of honor, which Johnson and Lipsett-Rivera call "honor-status," was accessible mainly to the legitimate children of elite parents; elite children were born with honor-status passed on by the parents. There was potential, albeit slight, for malleability of honor-status over a lifetime, since it was also based on attributes of wealth, dress, and behavior, including sexual chastity or fidelity in women (or the women in one's family).[145] The word *honra* connoted virtue in one's conduct. This type of honor, which Johnson and Lipsett-Rivera call "honor-virtue," was accessible to people of nonelite birth, as it could be attributed based on factors such as integrity, hard work and occupational skill, wealth and generosity, and sexual chastity or fidelity in women (or the women in one's family and household).[146]

I have found that Guatemalan parlance occasionally used *honor* as a synonym for *honra*; that is, *honor* sometimes referred to the honor-virture of plebians. Also, the term *honradez* appears with the sense of honor-virtue. Clearly there were significant connections and interplay among the concepts associated with these various terms. Even as delineated by Johnson and Lipsett-Rivera, the concepts of *honor* and *honra* overlapped somewhat. Both were closely intertwined with public regard; each could amount to something that in English might be called "honorable reputation." Further, elites' access to *honor* overlapped with their access to *honra*, since advantages available to the wealthy—such as luxurious lifestyles and positions of command over laborers—enabled both men and women more easily to behave in ways associated with personal virtue.[147]

In conventional historical understandings of the colonial Spanish colonial honor code, a suitor was supposed to request the bride's hand in marriage from her father, while fathers and other patriarchs were charged with protecting unmarried women's virginity. Research by Ann Twinam shows that among elite Spanish Americans, public knowledge that a girl or woman was not a virgin would lessen her possibilities of marriage or make marriage more difficult.[148] As Ramón Gutiérrez noted for colonial New Mexico, "if a daughter experienced a prenuptial dishonor, such as the loss of her virginity, additional [material] resources would have to be committed to secure her an appropriate mate."[149] Thus a young woman's chastity was essentially a commodity, since it might be exchanged for the fortunes of a desirable marriage. Accordingly, daughters were sheltered within the home and shielded from any interactions that might result in violation of their virginity (and hence their honor). Women and their families orchestrated their activities to ensure their reputations, avoiding any unchaperoned public appearance that could cast doubt on their virtue.[150]

Although some studies of plebian cultures in Spanish America have emphasized the value of bridal virginity, others have found that plebian societies did not necessarily expect virginity in brides.[151] Ann Jefferson's research on early independent-era ladino communities in rural eastern Guatemala is especially revealing. Drawing on church records in which priests recorded their parishioners' stated reasons for pursuing marriages, Jefferson demonstrated that couples were generally formed by

circumstance and by their own initiative—both brides and grooms identified factors such as beauty and productive abilities—rather than parental
matchmaking. Some of the region's wealthier residents mentioned bridal
virginity and honor among reasons for marriage choice, but these hardly
seemed to matter among the poor. On the contrary, it was a rare couple
who were unaware of some past activity in each other's sexual histories.[152]

In native communities in Guatemala, parents and other elders evidently
played a larger role in matchmaking, but with concerns other than Hispanic notions of honor at the foreground. Marriage arrangements in native
Mesoamerican communities did not necessarily focus on bridal chastity.[153]
Hill's depiction of seventeenth-century Cakchiquel culture explains that a
family would consult an *ah q'ih* (native calendrical specialist) about the
advisability of a prospective match before going to the Catholic priest.
If bride and groom were from different parcialidades, then the officers
of each parcialidad would be involved in negotiating the marriage.[154]
Similarly, in the Mam community of Santiago Chimaltenango, parental
arrangements and consultation with a *chimán* (native priest with calendrical knowledge) were the norm into the twentieth century. Wagley described
a process there in which fathers arranged marriages for ther teenage sons
and daughters, though he noted that boys could influence their fathers'
choices; two male informants told of "secret understandings with the girls
whom their fathers chose for them."[155] In the colonial era, Indian parents
in wealthy or tribute-exempt groups (such as nobles or Tlaxcalans) were
concerned with assuring their children's marriages to spouses in the same
category.[156] Studies of native communities in early colonial Mexico have
shown that marriages were arranged by parents and matchmakers, even
for daughters who had been raised as servants in Spanish households.[157]
By the late colonial years in Guatemala, though, Indians who stayed in
the capital as adults generally seem to have been married not by parental
arrangements, but in love matches formed in the relatively unconstrained
social environment of the city.

Overall, concerns about honor seem to have played a limited role in
courtship and marriage in late colonial Guatemala. Among the aristocracy,
honor in the sense of high social status certainly figured as a major factor
in spouse selection, as people sought to marry within their socioeconomic
group. But honor as constituted by female virginity and reclusion was
less consequential, notably among nonelites. In the capital, reclusion was
impractical for the majority of women, who were earning wages; indeed,
many of them had migrated unaccompanied to the city to work. The urban
milieu allowed women and men to fraternize with each other in houses as
well as in the street and other public places. Courtships were carried out

along avenues similar to those we have seen for informal unions, as people went about their daily business and interacted with friends and kin.

An example is that of Cesaria "Tiquiusa" Espinoza and her fiancé José Domingo González, both identified as mulatos.[158] Though they were already planning to be married at the time their activities were recorded in 1803, their case illustrates the atmosphere in which courtships took place. Their story comes to light because they were arrested one night after Tiquiusa got drunk and uttered a string of obscenities to one of the alcaldes de barrio. As part of the prenuptial procedure, Tiquiusa had been placed in depósito in the home of doña Estéfana Ruíz. (Depósito was meant to protect the bride from coercion in expressing her will to marry. Probably Tiquiusa's parents had raised some objection to the marriage, or the priest would not have bothered with the depósito. In theory, a prospective bride put in depósito was meant to be kept interned, secluded from contact with her family or the groom. In practice, though, records show that women carried on their regular activities and associations even during their supposed reclusion.)[159] By Tiquiusa's own account, earlier on the day of her arrest she had left the depósito with doña Estéfana Ruiz's permission "to pick up some *naguas* [skirts or petticoats] from Tomasa who lives in [the barrio of] la Habana." When she arrived at Tomasa's house, the naguas were not yet ready, so she waited in la Habana until nightfall as Tomasa completed her work. Then she went to visit at her own home. From there, her sister accompanied her on the walk back to the depósito.

Although Tiquiusa would acknowledge after her arrest that her mother had admonished her about being out too late at night, she and her sister obviously approached their excursion as an opportunity for relaxation and recreation, and they made no haste. "On the way to the depósito," Tiquiusa explained in her deposition, they walked "by a wine shop, and with her sister she drank a little bit of wine." At some point later in the evening they were joined by her fiancé, José Domingo. It was in José Domingo's company that Tiquiusa crossed paths with the alcalde de barrio. "She spoke very insolently," the alcalde charged, "coming up with as many disgraceful things as can be imagined, to me and to those in my company." Testifying two days after the episode, Tiquiusa contended that she had gotten drunk on the wine with her sister and therefore didn't remember whether she had been disrespectful toward the alcalde, nor what exactly she had said. Both she and José Domingo testified that the ecclesiastical preliminaries for the marriage were complete. The only step left, José Domingo explained, was for him to save enough for the cost of the marriage itself. He was released from the jail after pointing out that he was unable to earn any money there. He was a shoemaker; Tiquiusa's occupation is not known, but she evidently had her own disposable cash (or ready credit) to order the work done by the seamstress and to buy wine.

The testimonies in the case reported Tiquiusa's activities—other than the encounter with the alcalde—in a most nonchalant tone. No one seemed surprised that she had left the depósito and gone to various neighborhoods that evening to get some clothes, visit with family members, and have drinks with her sister if not also with her fiancé. She may have gone to his house to get him to come out with her, or perhaps they joined up elsewhere.

These activities were nothing out of the ordinary. The arrest happened only because Tiquiusa offended the alcalde with her drunken affront. She also had some bad luck; the particular alcalde involved was Manuel Sánchez, notorious for his vigor in pursuing minor offenders.[160] But the fact that Tiquiusa was out drinking with her sister and walking with her fiancé at night did not surprise or scandalize anyone. It was normal for young adults in the capital to use their free hours to do errands and socialize. Gatherings were typically informal and impromptu, as acquaintances met while walking or stopping for a drink and often listened to music or went in search of a musician. There were also acrobatic and comedic street performers in the city (including, in an 1807 record, a female funambulist), and an arena for cockfights attended by both genders. Card playing was popular, though evidence indicates that men predominated among the participants.[161]

To be sure, Tiquiusa and José Domingo were of distinctly middling social status, but young people from more privileged groups engaged in similar activities. Take the three Rivera brothers, all of them dons. Their story begins one evening in 1775 when they went out with some friends. The Riveras, the three of them in their twenties, were decked out in blue and silver *cabriolés* (sleeveless cloaks) trimmed with black velvet and gold galloons. In their company were don Antonio Fernández, a widower merchant in his mid-thirties; a priest, the *bachiller* don José Colomo, wearing a cape and carrying a dagger; an eighteen-year old mestiza named María de la Luz Ubeda, single mother of a small child whom she had left at home that night with a wet nurse; María de la Luz's brother Julián Ubeda; and Julián's wife, a mestiza in her mid-twenties.

The group convened around nine o'clock and headed to the courtyard of the Church of San Sebastián, where batido (a mildly alcoholic beverage) was often sold. They found none of the drink, but hearing firecrackers and musicians in the next block they walked over and sat down in some doorways along with other listeners. While their friends enjoyed the music, two of the Rivera brothers made several runs to buy aguardiente to take back to the group. One witness later testified that the priest don José Colomo and the widower don Antonio Fernández had drunk "with the greatest excess." But everyone in their company, both men and women, consumed some of the liquor. All of this would have constituted a relatively uneventful evening, except that things took an ugly turn after don Antonio Fernández (the widower merchant) called out provocatively to a female passerby. An argument erupted between him and the young woman's male companion, a scuffle ensued, and the Rivera brothers and Father Colomo rushed to defend Fernández. In the end, the priest stabbed the woman's companion in the chest. The victim (Spanish, unmarried, working as a weaver) fortunately recovered from his wound while a judicial inquiry was underway. For some seven months the Riveras and don Antonio Fernández waited in jail until the court ruled that there was insufficient evidence against them. As for Father Colomo, his name is inked out nearly throughout the record because of the ecclesiastic privilege invoked to protect his identity. (The notary charged with the expunging evidently overlooked one spot, leaving us with Colomo's name.) His punishment may have been handled by an ecclesiastical court.[162]

As with Cesaria "Tiquiusa" Espinoza and José Domingo González, the initial evening activities of the Rivera brothers and their friends did not elicit any reproach from the judicial officers who heard their testimony, even though reproaches were a standard element in the interrogations of witnesses and suspects alike. Rather, only the accounts of the melee and its aftermath drew a response and detailed questioning. The witnesses' reports of going out at night to stroll, listen to music, and consume alcohol in mixed company did not raise any eyebrows.

In light of examples like those of Tiquiusa and the Rivera brothers, the possible modes of courtship in the Hispanic city appear relatively licentious. Opportunities for premarital sex were visible in the daily lives of people from various social backgrounds. This unrestrained tenor is harmonious with the frequency of unsanctioned sexual unions and high proportions of illegitimate births that have been identified even among Spaniards.

These findings raise questions about the degree of dishonor for women in premarital sex and pregnancy. Given the permissive patterns of courtship and social mixing between the sexes, one wonders to what extent public knowledge of a woman's premarital relations would have dishonored her or her family. Part of the answer lies in the Spanish concept of *palabra de casamiento* (spoken promise of marriage). Although canon law forbade sexual relations outside marriage, early modern Spaniards tended to view the matrimonial process as underway once a promise was made. In the context of betrothal, attitudes toward sex became more forgiving. Studies of Spain and Spanish America have demonstrated that sexual relations within engagement would not damage even an elite woman's honor provided that the marriage was indeed carried out.[163] Sarah Chambers's study of late colonial and early national-era Arequipa (Peru) has emphasized the importance of betrothal also for Hispanic plebians, among whom a woman who had sex "with a reasonable expectation of marriage . . . could still claim that her conduct was honorable."[164]

But what if a man backed out of an engagement? Historians have shown that women jilted after having premarital sex were wont to bring suits against the men who had abandoned them. Studies have generally viewed such litigation in terms of concerns about honor; men were obligated to fulfill spoken promises of marriage in order to uphold their honor (their reputation for integrity), while women who had gotten pregnant needed to get married to protect their honor (their reputation for chastity). For women who could prove that they had been given palabra de casamiento, both church and civil magistrates would seek to pressure the men with penalties if they insisted in their refusal to marry.[165] Patricia Seed found for Mexico that the punishments were softened toward the beginning of the eighteenth century, as exile and prison sentences gave way to monetary fines paid to the plaintiffs.[166] Such a payment, called a *dote* (dowry), was supposed to better position an abandoned woman to find a husband; improving her financial status would compensate for the damage done to her honor.

However, the suits brought in late colonial Guatemala by women wronged in love centered on concerns other than those about honor and marriage. Primarily, the suits were seeking child support. Issues of *honor, honra,* and promises of marriage played a relatively minor part. The analysis that follows is based on the thirteen records I have found of women's litigation against men who had broken off relationships. (The suits were identified in a random sample, not an exhaustive search, of thousands of judicial records for the period from 1770 to 1824. Presumably the entire corpus of records contains more than thirteen cases.)[167]

The elite quality of *honor* (honor-status) was out of reach for many of the plaintiffs. In only four of the thirteen cases did the plaintiff possess elite status as denoted by the honorific "doña" (and there may be only three doñas in total, since two suits were brought by a doña Regina Soto, probably the same person).[168] The other eight plaintiffs—women and teenage girls sometimes aided by their parents—represent a range of socioeconomic strata. Two were evidently españolas. One of these was María Concepción Arauz (her parents were both identified as españoles), whose case suggests comfortable but not elite status, as we will see in a moment. The other was Francisca Betancur y Moreno. She was able to sign her name, and a court official added "doña" in front of her name on the cover of her case record, but she did not use "doña" in her petition, nor did anyone else involved in the litigation call her "doña."[169] For Francisca Alvarez, who filed her suit in 1824, it is difficult to judge social status since "don" and "doña" (as well as calidad labels other than "Indian") were eliminated from most legal use after 1821.[170] In the remaining records, the woman's calidad is mentioned in only one case (this was María de los Angeles Aragón, an Indian washerwoman who bore a child by don Blas Bahamonde).[171] However, details in the other six cases also connote women of Indian or mixed ancestry in impoverished or middling circumstances. Juana Carrillo, for example, explained that her children's father, don Manuel Najarro y Solórzano, had instructed her to identify them as españoles for the baptismal register, "since that way they would move up, and otherwise they wouldn't" (*pusieron por españoles pues así ascenderían y de otro modo no*). Presumably the children, and hence Carrillo, were not really of purely Spanish ancestry. In another example, Laureana Ríos was relying on the procurator for the poor as her attorney.[172]

Some of the suits do reflect concern with female honor deriving from sexual discretion or modesty. Doña Francisca Izquierdo spoke of her ex-lover's failure "to cover my honor by following through with marriage." The attorney for Laureana Ríos said that the man being sued was planning to marry another woman, thereby "leaving my client with her honor uncovered." Yet only four of the plaintiffs (Izquierdo and Ríos among them) asserted that they had been virginal before their liaisons with the men in question, and this point does not seem to have been central to their demands.

Further, women sued for child support regardless of their sexual histories. Juana Carrillo, for example, was known to have been in a previous consensual union before she got involved with the man she would ultimately take to court.[173] The same was true of doña Regina Soto.[174] Francisca Betancur y Moreno had a child or two from a previous affair before she got involved with don Francisco Molina, whom she then sued for support of their daughters.[175]

Only one of the lawsuits explicitly articulated concerns about damage to the woman's marriageability. This was the case of María Concepción Arauz, the nineteen-year-old who said both her parents were españoles (but not don or doña). Her father owned a brick-making operation (ladrillera) and signed his name in an elegant hand; her mother earned income by doing laundry, sewing, and cooking at their home. Among the mother's clients was don Pedro Ayau, construction tycoon of humble French origins (we have seen him in Chapters 2 and 3). He had been taking his meals in the Arauz household in 1795 when Concepción got pregnant. She fingered don Pedro as the responsible party. Her father helped her bring the suit, demanding a "payment for the horrible harm that he did to her, leaving her pregnant and unable to marry someone else, or at least very unlikely." The father alleged that another suitor, Marcelino González from Zapotitán (in what is now El Salvador), had intended to marry Concepción, and evidence sewn into the judicial case file includes a love note from the young man and a romantic poem obviously penned by a hired scribe. It is not known whether Marcelino and Concepción were ultimately married, though understandably Marcelino would have been rankled to learn of her pregnancy, since according to her testimony she never had sex with him— rather, only with don Pedro Ayau.

At any rate, the remaining content of the Arauz record marks it as a paternity suit, not a case primarily about marriage or honor. The bulk of the litigation consisted of don Pedro making all sorts of arguments to prove he wasn't the baby's father, and Concepción calling numerous witnesses to prove that he was. (Witnesses told how she had twice sent an Indian employee of her father to tell don Pedro to come over when her father wasn't home. Both Concepción and don Pedro admitted that she had sneaked him into her house dressed as a woman to conceal him from her parents and younger sisters.) Notably, Concepción's father Ignacio Arauz expressly stated that he did not want his daughter to marry don Pedro Ayau. Among the father's reasons, don Pedro was a foreigner, and it could not easily be verified "what kind of man he is, or if he is married in his country or somewhere else." Further, Ignacio Arauz charged, don Pedro had two children by another woman and was maintaining them. Finally, Arauz seethed at don Pedro's audacity. "He is so lewd and insolent," Arauz said, "that it is already being said that he is pursuing another woman or that he already has her tricked with a promise of marriage." With the help of her father's dogged efforts in court, Concepción finally extracted from don Pedro an immediate payment of 100 pesos, plus a court order for the impregnator to provide a monthly allowance of 4 pesos to support the child.[176]

As a rule, complainants in paternity suits were not seeking marriage with the men who had wronged them. Some of the plaintiffs initiated their litigation years after the liaisons had ended, and in the meantime they or their ex-lovers had married other people. In at least one case the man was already married at the time of the affair.[177] Felipa Aragón successfully sued her father for back child support decades after he had abandoned her and her mother. (The mother had previously sued him and been awarded a smaller amount.)[178] Four of the thirteen cases suggest that betrothal was discussed at the time of the sexual union. In one of these suits, the plaintiff indicated that marriage would satisfy her claims, but she preferred the alternative of a financial settlement, which was in fact the eventual outcome.[179] In a second case, twelve years had elapsed since the union, and the woman was clearly seeking support for her child, not marriage.[180] A third case was that of Laureana Ríos and Juan Manuel Rodas in the town of Sanarate (along the route from the capital to the Atlantic, in what is now the department of El Progreso). Laureana said she had tried to convince Juan Manuel to marry her, but they could not get the dispensation needed for the marriage. (The record does not specify why it was needed.) When she finally sued him he was already engaged to marry someone else; Laureana was only trying to make him support their child.[181] The other plaintiff who mentioned the possibility of marriage was Felipa Figueroa. She sued Domingo Castro while pregnant with their third child, demanding 40 pesos for the costs of childbirth and additional money to support the baby. She said Castro had spoken of marriage, but it had been impossible to get him to the altar. By the time she began litigation, she no longer wanted to marry him. "If now his behavior has been so strange," she reasoned, "later it will be worse."[182]

In short, women's litigation against their former lovers was not primarily about honor as status, or honor as sexual purity, or marriage. Rather, the suits were mainly about money—specifically, child support. In all thirteen cases found, women were demanding payment for alimentos (literally, food) and other necessities for the children their ex-paramours had sired. The courts typically mandated that the father should pay a sum for the expenses of the birth itself and then a monthly allowance for the child's first three years, which was considered the standard period of lactation.[183] At age three, the child was theoretically supposed to be turned over to the father's care. This premise followed the Siete Partidas, which gave child custody to fathers and charged them with financial responsiblity. In practice, however, mothers in Guatemala generally appear to have retained custody beyond the toddler years—a reality harmonious with the society's understanding of child care as an exclusively female role.

I have found only one instance where a father attempted to assume custody. The child was a girl born in 1796 to don Bartolomé Rigo and Inés García, an Indian woman he had been paying to make his cigarettes and wash his clothes. Their relationship evidently then ended. After their daughter turned three, don Bartolomé sent a representative to take custody. Unwilling to surrender her child, Inés was apprehended by the civil authorities and held in jail while don Bartolomé's agent took the lass into his charge. The mother then appealed to the court several times, accusing the father of "stealing" the child. She contended that don Bartolomé would have to solicit strangers to care for the girl since he had no sisters or female cousins, and that it would be better for the child if he provided support while the mother retained custody. She even offered to place the girl in the Colegio de Niñas or the Beaterio de Indias, but to no avail; the court did not budge. At the end of the case file, however, the notary entered a short addendum reporting that the mother had spirited the child from the father's home and fled on the road toward Petapa. Nothing further was recorded.[184]

It was open to judicial dispute whether fathers would be required to provide support after their children reached age three. Felipa Aragón was twenty-nine when she sued her father, and the judge's ruling obligated him not only to remedy the past but also to improve her present financial situation—to the tune of 600 pesos.[185] In at least one instance, though, a judge viewed a mother's continuing custody as grounds for the father to end his payments. Doña Regina Soto had been receiving 4 pesos per month, deducted by court order from the military salary of don Salvador Buergo, for the support of a daughter they had out of wedlock in 1797 or 1798. After the daughter turned three, don Salvador continued the payments, albeit sporadically. He contended that diminished eyesight and other disabilities had forced him to retire on a limited income, but doña Regina persisted with a stream of appeals to the court between 1802 and 1810. As their daughter entered her teenage years, the mother complained specifically that the father's payments were insufficient to provide proper clothing for the girl to wear to the house of her teacher (maestra), to Mass, and other public places. The judge backed the father, ruling that the mother should turn the daughter over to his custody or accept the cessation of payments.[186]

José Quirino Milán y Oliveros, a barber, was ordered to pay Aurelia Zelado 2 pesos per month indefinitely to support their two illegitimate daughters. By 1801 the girls were teenagers, and Milán asked the Audiencia to relieve him of the responsibility. His attorney claimed that infirmity prevented him from earning wages and that his wife was working to support him and their legitimate children. The Audiencia ruled that the daughters should be placed in reputable homes to earn their living as servants, though no such placement was documented. One imagines that their mother, who had an *estanquilla* (a small shop), kept them with her.[187]

To litigate successfully for alimentos (support or child support), a woman had to prove not only that the union had occurred within the time frame that fit the child's age, but also that the named defendant was the only possible father. Arguments frequently devolved into disputes about paternity, which tended to be denied by men targeted in litigation. Men facing paternity charges often accused the plaintiff of promiscuity, suggesting that another man could have sired the child. In response, mothers called witnesses such as neighbors who had observed trysts and midwives who could testify about a father's presence at a birth.

Most women who sued for child support were awarded some settlement, although it is hard to know how often the judgments were enforced, since only some of the records include information on collection of awards. Rulings were documented in ten of the thirteen cases identified, and in eight of these rulings the court backed the mother.[188] In one case the judge absolved the alleged father, and in one case the court awarded custody to the father.[189] For one of the cases with no recorded outcome, the judge called for a *juicio verbal*—a personal appearance in court by both parties.[190] Probably the result was some sort of payment, since usually at these hearings the magistrates tried to orchestrate a compromise. In a telling comment, one judge noted that in all the suits he had seen demanding *alimentos*, there had never been a ruling against the obligation of the father.[191]

Thus, a man who fathered a child out of wedlock was considered by the courts as financially obligated to the child and the mother, regardless of whether the mother had been virginal at the time of her union with the father.[192] Lawsuits for *alimentos* focused not on claims about women's honor or virtue, but on men's paternity and responsibilities as fathers. By ruling in favor of paternal child-support settlements, judges were in effect recognizing informal unions and legitimizing the mothers' claims.

Indeed, people in various social sectors recognized the concept that men should pay to support children they fathered outside of marriage. In addition to the thirteen cases discussed above, consider the 1793 lawsuit filed by Manuela Ramos (her life was described in Chapter 2). A slave in a Spanish household in Nueva Guatemala, Ramos brought suit against don Pedro Ayau (the same) some seven years after he had been a guest in the house. She alleged that she had consented to have sex with him based on his promise to purchase her liberty, and that she had then become pregnant by him with a daughter who was six years old at the start of the litigation. In her suit she was demanding money for her own freedom, for her daughter's freedom, or for *alimentos* for the child. Though she did not specify an amount, she asserted that Ayau now had his own house and more than a thousand pesos. Her suit was unsuccessful despite an impressive parade of witnesses who testified that Ayau was the girl's father. The judges gave little explanation; they simply absolved Ayau of the charges and sentenced him to pay court costs.[193] Ramos's status as a slave may explain the court's disposition, which was atypical among child support suits.

Nevertheless, her case helps demonstrate that a wide range of people were aware of the possibility of suing for *alimentos*. One might at first imagine that Ramos's attorney—the procurator for slaves who drew up her petition—proposed the tactic of demanding *alimentos* if her request for liberation should fail. But don Pedro Ayau himself said in response to the suit that Ramos had already made the demand orally to him to provide alimentos for the child. Thus, not only the court's procurator but also the enslaved plaintiff knew that she could make such a claim. The alleged father knew it too; even as he denied the child was his, Ayau recognized the nature of the demand, noting that he had heard it already directly from Ramos. (Ramos filed her suit in May of 1793, some two years before Ayau's affair with Concepción Arauz. He therefore understood the scenario of a child support suit long before the Arauz family brought litigation against him.) The nature of such suits was known also to the Indian women, mestizas, mulatas, and españolas who made them, and the suits were implicitly endorsed by the judicial officers who agreed to hear them and then awarded the child support settlements. Women's suits for alimentos and the courts' responses thus foretold national-era legislation that would codify the obligation of fathers to provide child support. This later legislation was not a pure innovation; rather, it was an extension of laws codified in Iberia in the Siete Partidas, and an institutionalization of colonial-era practices.

Paternity suits also served purposes beyond attaining child support. For a woman who had been abandoned with children, the judiciary provided a forum for public declaration and punishment of the man's wrongdoing. Examples suggest that some men named in these suits did feel a degree of shame when their deeds were aired. Don Manuel de Solórzano asked the court to end Juana Carrillo's 1796 suit against him and to make her "stop injuring me with defamatory words."[194] A similar chord was struck by José María Yúdice shortly after independence. Responding to a demand by Francisca Alvarez, Yúdice complained of her insolence and insults. He said he was consenting to provide a pension for her baby only to "cover my honor, and not because I am obligated since I haven't the slightest suspicion that this [pregnancy] was my work."[195] Regardless of his public claims not to be the father, Yúdice clearly wanted to end the litigation, and to do so he was willing to pay.

In 1798 don José Grau y Serra said that doña Francisca Izquierdo y García's litigation against him "has shamed me" and "meant to embarrass me." He retaliated with various epithets, accusing her especially of promiscuity. The litigation was being carried out at long distance; following his affair, don José had left Guatemala to work for a merchant in Comayagua. The court was sending papers back and forth between the two cities. When don José came back to Guatemala on business in 1800, he and doña Francisca were called for a juicio verbal. There the judge had don José taken into custody to prevent his return to Comayagua, pending payment to doña Francisca of 200 pesos for the support of their child. The defendant hailed from humble origins in Catalonia and had styled himself as "don" in America. He was forced to get a loan to regain his liberty.[196] If doña Francisca indeed meant to embarrass him as he charged, she seems to have succeeded.

Although the Guatemalan child-support suits did not foreground women's *honor* or honra in the ways that have been described in terms of a Spanish American "culture of honor," women who challenged their ex-lovers in court seem to have been seeking for themselves a universal kind of dignity. The 1813 case of Eduviges García and don Domingo Herrera is telling. The two had been in consensual union for eleven years, with two children who had died, when Eduviges realized she was pregnant with a third child. Around the same time she also learned also that don Domingo had contracted marriage with another woman. Eduviges went first to their parish priest to oppugn the marriage and then to the home of the fian-cée, a woman named Dolores Lara. Dolores's sister answered the door and later testifed that Eduviges had "explained in friendly terms that she was not going to impede the marriage of [don Domingo] but only to make [Dolores] see that he had been in concubinage for ten or eleven years." As it turned out, Dolores had already received the message (one imagines Eduviges had arranged to get it into the grapevine) and had changed her mind about the engagement. The sister who came to the door told Edu-viges about Dolores's change of heart just moments after Dolores told don Domingo; even as Eduviges was standing in the doorway, don Domingo was still inside the house, enmeshed in confrontation with Dolores. Evi-dently he saw Eduviges or heard her voice carry into the house, and he called to her "Get out of here!" several times. But Eduviges got the last word. "Even if you're married twenty times," she told him as she left, "you'll have to pay for this."[197]

The following night, Eduviges, her best friend, her two brothers, her sister, and another four or five people walked to the house where don Domingo regularly ate supper. They were waiting for him when he fin-ished his meal and emerged onto the street. Eduviges spoke first. "This is what I wanted, you grandiose pig," she told him (*esto era lo qe yo queria grandioso cochino*). Don Domingo began running, but the group caught up and surrounded him. Eduviges's sister grabbed him by the hair, and one of her brothers pulled out a knife; they took his cape, his hat, his machete, and a gold chain he was wearing around his neck before he escaped. The next day, he went to the authorities to report the assault. His head and face were covered with cuts and bruises. He knew the motive for the attack, of course. Presumably it was rather embarrassing for him appear and make the report, but perhaps he was afraid of a follow-up assault. Or perhaps he was driven by sheer anger. In any case, he and Eduviges were ordered to appear in court for a juicio verbal. The notary summed up the outcome by saying that the couple would pardon each other for damages and injuries and that don Domingo would pay Eduviges 25 pesos to cover the cost of the birth, plus another 50 pesos annually in child support during the baby's first three years. She was supposed to turn the child over to him after three years, though the pattern in other cases suggests that she likely retained custody.[198]

Eduviges had thus used a variety of tactics to punish don Domingo. First she sabotaged his marriage plans, and she then marshaled a network of friends and relatives to humiliate him publicly. When the philandering don denounced her vigilante-style justice, the case ended in court and Eduviges gained further retribution—the financial settlement awarded to her for childbirth and child support. Their case is not counted among the thirteen child-support suits previously described, given that she did not initiate the litigation directly.

Yet the story is suggestive about the multiple purposes that such suits could serve. From an economic standpoint, they enabled women to obtain some support from men who had abandoned them with children. In the sphere of interpersonal relationships, the legal system provided a way for women to call publicly for justice against men who had wronged them in love. By ruling in favor of the plaintiffs, the courts gave them institutional validation of their grievances. Eduviges García emerged from her fight with don Domingo Herrera not only with a monetary settlement but also presumably with a renewed sense of dignity. García was outside the elite circles of honor-status, and she was not making claims of honor-virtue. However, anger and the desire for respect are not limited to people of high status or supposed virtue. The way in which don Domingo had jilted Eduviges—contracting another marriage while she was pregnant with his child—would have been degrading to anyone. His abandonment would have economic and emotional impacts for her and the child beyond diminution of their honor. Her counterattack on him in the street and in court had given her a kind of personal and financial redemption that transcended specifically Iberian-rooted notions of honor, resonating with more universal human emotions.

Masculine honor, shame, and desire in affairs of the heart

In contrast to wronged wives and abandoned amasias, spurned husbands and jilted amasios did not often (or did not openly) file suit against their wives or ex-paramours in the courts. It was partly because they did not bear children who would need support, but it was also that masculine honor was at stake. There was something potentially humiliating for a man in being left by a wife or lover for another man. However, a number of stories come to light in other kinds of court records—notably, records generated in response to anonymous denunciations for concubinage and those generated in response to violent disputes between men over romantic jealousies.

Among the affairs represented in Table 4.2, six were documented following anonymous or "private" complaints. The alcaldes and their deputies honored a code of silence in these cases, offering for the notary's report only the fact that an investigation had ensued after the alcalde received "notice" or a "denunciation." One imagines at least some of these were presented by husbands who did not want to detail their cuckolding in a formal petition but who sought help in preserving or reestablishing monogamy with their wives. An example is the 1803 arrest of Gertrudis Guerra (better known to her contemporaries as Gertrudis Carrillo) in the capital's barrio of San Sebastián. On the cover sheet of the case file, the notary wrote that the arrest followed "private complaints" from Gertrudis's husband. Inside the file, the alcalde's report says he received "notice" that Gertrudis was in illicit amistad, and he caught her out on horseback at night with another man. Gertrudis's husband, a mestizo weaver named José María Escalante, eventually testified, revealing that the couple had not been living together for the past year. He also alleged that she had wanted to kill him (though we might suspect he feared her lover would be the one to take action). For her part, Gertrudis contended that José María was abusive and unfaithful. The court ended the case by releasing all parties and instructing the couple to reunite, but the record conveys a sense that the instruction likely had little effect.[199]

Seven of the concubinage cases in Table 4.2 surface in judicial investigations of male-on-male violence between rivals in love. An example is the altercation between don Manuel López, a clockmaker, age thirty-three, and his opponent Joseph Ignacio Corral. Joseph Ignacio was also an español, a fledgling merchant in his mid-twenties. Though don Manuel was married, he was involved with a woman named Josefa Prado, labeled in the record as his "concubina." (Their liaison is immortalized in an ardent love letter from don Manuel that fell into the hands of Joseph Ignacio and ended as evidence sewn into the case record.) Joseph Ignacio also apparently had a share of Josefa's affections, and he and don Manuel had repeatedly confronted each other in verbal sparring. One September night in 1782 Joseph Ignacio cornered don Manuel in the street and began to beat him with the flat of his sword, saying, "Now is the day when the devil will take us if you don't confess to me that you are sleeping with Josefa Prado."[200] Don Manuel escaped with some injuries to one arm. A trial followed, with each man accusing the other of jealousy, but the proceedings essentially came to naught. It is not known what became of either man's relationship with Josefa Prado.[201]

Jousts over sexual jealousies and masculine honor occurred also among more humble people. In 1775 Juan Pimentel, a castizo tailor (single, age nineteen), testified after he was stabbed by a man he named as Joseph the carriagemaker. He didn't know Joseph's last name, he said, but he knew the motive: an affair he was having with a woman named Marcela. Joseph had been threatening him since the previous night.[202] Another example is that of Nasario Domínguez, a mestizo carpenter age eighteen. He was stabbed by a man whose name he didn't know, but he guessed the motive was jealousy of his affair with a woman named María.[203]

Viewed in comparison with women's lawsuits against philandering men (both errant husbands and former paramours), these extrajudicial disputes between men convey particularly masculine concerns about honor. We have seen that women used the court system to seek monetary support, retribution, and renewed personal dignity. In contrast, men likely did not want to be publicly emasculated in legal proceedings that would portray them as unable to stop their wives' affairs or unable to retain the affections of their concubines. A court case would amount to an institutional shaming of the man and his virility. On the other hand, by challenging an interloper, a wronged husband or a two-timed Romeo could emerge with a renewed sense of strength—both by defeating the other man and by reclaiming exclusive access to a wife or girlfriend. His masculine honor would be redeemed.

This was not an exclusively male approach. An occasional fight did break out between women when a betrayed wife or girlfriend took matters into her own hands and tried to end her competitor's pursuits.[204] Usually, though, threats and violence over competing romantic intentions were male strategies. Women were more likely to turn to other people or the courts for help.

Confrontations over jealousies between men were not only about honor; like women's lawsuits against men, male-on-male tilts were also motivated by other emotional elements in the landscape of interpersonal relationships.[205] Among these was desire, particularly desire for exclusive sexual access to specific women. A case from Chiquimulilla (in today's southern department of Santa Rosa, just 20 kilometers from the Pacific coast) illustrates. In the early 1820s, José Manuel López (an Indian) was convicted of having killed his paramour's husband by poisoning. The murder was clearly premeditated; López had gone to request the poison (*leche de habilla*) from an elderly Indian woman, and he recruited another man to slip the toxin into the victim's drink (both accomplices were also convicted). This design to get rid of his lover's husband—without being discovered, López had hoped—would hardly have buffeted his masculine honor. Rather, it appears only as a means to fulfill his desire for an exclusive relationship with his paramour.[206]

Anger, too, must have been a factor in at least some cases. José Francisco "Chico" Valle, for example, a mulato silversmith, at first denied charges that he had challenged don Juan Antonio Milán to a duel over a certain woman (she is unnamed in the record, described only as a "negrita"). Witnesses said the woman had previously been in amistad with Valle but was now involved with Milán; nearly everyone concurred that Valle had gone to Milán's house seeking a duel, but that Milán had declined to fight. (Dueling was outlawed throughout the empire.)[207] Pressed during questioning, Valle finally conceded he didn't remember, having had a "drink of aguardiente" before going to Milán's house and being "blind with rage and ire toward Milán." To be sure, anger was closely linked to honor and jealousy. Valle was angry presumably because Milán had taken something he wanted—and had once had—for himself (the concubine), and because Milán's involvement with her was an affront to his honor. Like women who filed suits against men who had wronged them, Valle sought retribution that would not only redeem him in the matrix of gendered honor but would also assuage his anger.[208]

The case of José Teodoro Arrese depicts an intricate intersection of masculine honor with desire, anger, vengeance, forgiveness, and love. An ex-slave originally from the Sierra de Canales (south of the new capital, in the region of Amatitlán), Arrese achieved a dramatic coup in the righting of his marriage to Eduarda Josefa Rivera. The couple was living in Nueva Guatemala, but they were involuntarily separated in 1778 when Arrese was convicted of a crime and sentenced to three years in the presidio. Rivera, a free mulata, was only about sixteen at the time. She soon took up with a weaver named Severino Agreda, some ten years her senior, and gave birth to a child by him. José Arrese learned of the affair before he had completed his sentence. Allowed to leave the presidio one day accompanied by a soldier, he stopped by the house intending to see Rivera and their children. But Severino Agreda emerged onto the street, Arrese later testified, and threatened him with a knife. His visit foiled, Arrese was then escorted back to the presidio. On his release, now around age twenty-five, he found work as an agricultural laborer and lived in a rented room in the city. For eight months he waited while his wife continued in the affair with Agreda, who was rumored to have beaten her. Arrese's mother urged Eduarda Rivera to end the liaison, and she took Rivera and Arrese's surviving children to their father's home. One child had perished in an epidemic while Arrese was in the presidio.

On a February afternoon in 1781, Arrese finally went to Rivera's house on horseback in the company of his compadre, a muleteer named Calixto Rosales. Rosales stayed in the patio with the mount while Arrese went inside to confront his estranged wife. As Arrese was forgiving her for the "amistad that she had maintained," Rosales alerted him to the arrival of Severino Agreda. "Man, stop talking to your wife," Rosales called. "Here comes the one you're looking for!" (*Hombre deja ablar a tu mujer que hay va el que andas buscando.*) Arrese ran outside. Unarmed, he grabbed Rosales' knife and went after Agreda, stabbing him repeatedly (the authorities later counted ten holes in Agreda's hat). The ministro de vara arrived, and Arrese jumped back on the horse and rode off with Rosales. The two were arrested that night. Meanwhile, Agreda was hospitalized with head wounds, three of which the surgeon judged to be dangerous. Fortunately, he recovered within a matter of weeks. The authorities absolved Arrese of criminal charges given that Agreda had been in concubinage with his wife. As for the concubinage charges against Agreda, Arrese chose to drop them. (Probably it was easier for him to do so knowing that his attack had put Agreda in the hospital.) Evidently, Arrese and his wife had reconciled.[209]

Thus José Teodoro Arrese made a spectacular comeback in the arena of love and marriage. In the months after his release from the presidio he had sunk to a nadir of emasculation, effectively banished from his own household by his wife's lover. Though it took him three years in the presidio and eight months in wait as a free man, in the end Arrese mounted an impressive offense. In uninterrupted sequence, he reentered the house, made up with his wife, and defeated his adversary in a surprise attack. His getaway on horseback with Calixto Rosales must have been sweet indeed.

While Arrese's story portrays themes of masculine honor and shame, it can also be read for other emotions such as desire, anger, and affection. Arrese not only redeemed his honor; he also recovered his wife, his house, and his children—thereby fulfilling several desires and regaining (and returning) affection.

Honor was only one of the multiple cultural and psychological determinants underlying contestations in the sphere of marriage and informal unions. As we have seen, women as well as men engaged in these contestations, though their tactics differed from those of men in accordance with their differing social power and expected roles. The records suggest that women tended to appeal to state authority while men avoided it. Yet both women and men acted to repair their dignity and sense of self, to avenge their anger, and to preserve or correct affective relationships gone awry. And both women and men were, at times, willing to forgive. Their actions and willingness reflect a discernable flexibility in their society's attitudes toward marriage and sexuality.

Women and men making ladino society

The flexibility in marriage and sexuality was part of a broader fissure in late colonial Guatemala between social realities and the patriarchal ideals of Iberian law. The fissure appears concretely in the capital's censuses, where a significant portion of households were headed by women, contrary to the ideal of patriarchal households. The lives of these women contrasted also with ideals of marriage as normative and permanent; the censuses' female household heads included not only widows but also never-married women and wives whose husbands were absent. Contemporary judicial depositions as well as the structure of the census records themselves demonstrate that female-headed households were acknowledged and, to a degree, accepted in both popular and administrative views.

Though the urban populace apparently understood the images of male and female conjugal behavior exalted by civil and ecclesiastical law, people seem only partly to have internalized these ideals. Various behaviors woven into the fabric of quotidian social and business life diverged from prescription. Courtships were typically carried out under the influence of alcohol and without parental supervision or hours of curfew. Within marriages, to be sure, patriarchal authority held significant sway—enough that wife beating apparently was widespread if not also widely expected. Yet wives sometimes rejected the authority of their husbands, fighting back with words, weapons, or litigation. Contrary to church precepts, de facto marital separations were commonplace. Unsanctioned unions reached remarkable numbers, occurring with high visibility in myriad circumstances.

The state through its judiciary provided a means for individuals, particularly women, to contest codified mandates about sexuality and marriage. As in the disputes described in the previous chapters—between Indians and Hispanics, between slaves and slaveholders, between workers and employers—in gendered conflicts between women and men the courts often ruled with considered evenhandedness. At times the judges favored the idealized patriarchal household, ordering separated married couples to reunite. Yet the legal officers seem to have recognized the realities of conjugal life, as they backed married women doing business without their husbands' permission and ruled in favor of single mothers seeking support from men who had fathered their children.

At a fundamental level, the colonial and urban economies tempered the traction of prescribed gender roles. The economic reciprocity of husband and wife was indispensable in small towns and hamlets of the countryside, where most people depended for their survival on male subsistence agriculture and a complimentary set of female productive and reproductive roles. In contrast, most city dwellers worked in a cash-based economy, receiving payments for goods produced or wages for labor performed. Many urban workers slept in rented lodgings and purchased their food and drink with money. As we saw in Chapter 3, women comprised the overwhelming majority of adults in the capital, many of them drawn there as migrants to perform domestic labor for pay. At rural colonial estates as well, a wage economy lessened the need for a spouse; men earned wages for their agricultural work, and they purchased food (or the employer provided food) prepared by women also making money for their labor. Thus, the cash economy expanded the feasibility of living outside a normative marriage.

Economic forces thereby underwrote flexibility in household composition, marriage, and sexuality. Colonial labor demands fueled migration that eroded the permanence of marriage and removed many women and men from the patriarchal vigilance of nuclear-family households and small towns. Migration to the city in particular increased women's access to wages (and hence to livelihood independent of husbands) as well as their access to aid from the colonial state in contesting individual patriarchs. Labor migration increased the rates of interethnic interactions, residential mixing, and hispanization, all of which fostered cross-calidad marriages and informal unions.

The same processes also undergirded the growth of the free ladino labor force. It was partly that migration, social mixing, and hispanization facilitated attrition from coerced labor pools (that is, from native communities and the African slave-identified population). In addition, exogamous unions had the effect of expanding the free labor pool, since children born of these unions (regardless of the parents' calidad) would generally be raised in the ladino world, positioned socially if not legally to be free from labor drafts and enslavement. Labor migration and the resulting reshaping of marriage and sexuality thus accelerated the formation of the free workforce that would supplant tribute labor and slavery. In contestations of gender norms began the dissolution of forced labor.

Conclusion

A Central American assembly convened in 1823, declaring independence from Mexico and establishing a federal system to rule the isthmus. But intraregional conflict and partisan warfare quickly ensued, and by 1839 the confederation would dissolve into the five separate states that would become today's republics of Guatemala, El Salvador, Honduras, Nicaragua, and Costa Rica. Long before these administrative changes, however, a broader set of changes had been underway; the convergence of populations from three continents had unleashed sweeping social transformations starting at the time of the Spanish conquest. These social shifts, perhaps more powerfully than the partisan politics of the Hispanic dominant group, would shape the outlines of society and economy in the new republics.

This book has illustrated these broad processes of social change through an analysis of labor forms on the eve of independence. As in colonial-era Mexico and the Andes, in Guatemala bilingual Indians increasingly began to contract their labor through direct arrangements with their Spanish-speaking employers. This development apparently came later in Guatemala than in areas with larger Spanish populations, and the old repartimiento system endured into the early nineteenth century as one of several ways that Spaniards procured temporary laborers. But it was quickly fading out.

By the end of the eighteenth century, repartimientos of workers from Indian communities in the periphery of Guatemala City persisted in only a few cases. Even in areas more distant from the capital, recruitment systems were already far along in the transition from repartimiento to private arrangement. The workers' experience of draft labor itself contributed to their hispanization, as they toiled in the company of a range of Spanish speakers—typically slaves and free people of mixed ancestry as well as people from other Indian communities. Some draft workers opted to remain on the job beyond their required shifts, working by individual agreement with their employers. A number of native communities negotiated collectively for higher wages or other concessions, thereby partly removing control of labor procurement from the colonial administration. By the start of the nineteenth century, the system of forced indigenous labor had come undone.

A set of cultural and social transitions accompanied the shift in labor procurement. As Indian workers' Spanish language acquisition fostered private labor contracting, work stints grew longer, and women and children increasingly joined men migrating from native communities to Spanish estates. Their departures accelerated the emptying of indigenous towns, a process that had anguished native leaders since the Conquest. High death rates and rising out-migration diminished Indian communities' populations and resources. The same changes that were dismantling the system of forced native labor were also undermining the integrity of native communities.

Both colonial and native states recognized what was happening. Indigenous officers made efforts to intervene, but they could not diminish the social and economic forces driving the transitions. From the Spanish point of view, the changes were not necessarily undesirable. The colonial state's approach was characteristically inconsistent and reactive rather than activist; various edicts called for an end to repartimiento as early as the mid-seventeenth century, but the Audiencia continued granting repartimientos where there was no other way for colonists to recruit native workforces.[1] Procurement practices were dictated more by the availability of workers than by ideologies or state regulatory measures. Several laws decreed in the early decades of independence aimed alternately to ban and reinstate the labor drafts, but they met with little notice.[2] The transition in labor forms was a product of social changes taking place independently of legislation. The supply of hispanized workers contracting their own labor—people of Indian, African, and mixed ancestry—had reached sufficient numbers by independence to meet employers' demands.

These shifts in indigenous communities, identities, languages, and labor forms were part of an even wider scenario of social changes. Not only bilingual Indians but also hispanized people of African descent were increasingly working as free laborers. By the late colonial era, the growing integration of Afro-Guatemalans into Hispanic society had eroded the viability of chattel slavery. Cultural hispanization, and perhaps the racial mixing that often accompanied it, lent some slaves the possibility of passing into free society unnoticed (or at least unarrested). Even among those who remained in slavery, many assumed roles reserved in most slave societies for free people—exercising substantial freedom of movement, earning wages, and providing for themselves and their families. Social networks linked slaves to sources of wage employment and credit, both of which they parlayed into emancipation through self-purchase or purchase of liberty for family members. With each slave who crossed over into free society, the numbers of free people of African descent grew, and the possibilities of further manumissions through social network mechanisms expanded. At the same time, Spanish legal and social ideologies permitted and legitimized the emancipation process.

In 1824 Central America's newly independent Liberal government proclaimed a general emancipation of slaves. This act was hardly reformist. Rather, it essentially ratified an irreversible social process that had already been realized by hundreds, if not thousands, of slaves (and slaveholders) across the colonial centuries. The abolition law served merely to endorse a change that was already largely complete—the result of long-term social and cultural transformations. Like forced Indian labor, African slavery had collapsed under the weight of social change.

This view expands the picture of ethnicity in Central America, where the region's history of African slavery has been nearly obliterated from popular consciousness. The colonial-era process of emancipation was essentially a process of integration into Hispanic society. After independence from Spain, ex-slaves and their descendants would be members of the new republics inasmuch as they had been members of the Hispanic world; their inclusion in the new nations thus rested on the occlusion of their slave past. In contrast to Indian communities, African slaves did not have a separate state within the Spanish colonial system. There was no Afro-Guatemalan body politic, no institution to preserve slave-descendant identity in the postabolition republic.

The story of slavery and emancipation in Guatemala also enlarges historical understanding of Western Hemisphere slavery as a whole. Though Central America was not a major center of the Atlantic slave trade or of slave populations, the Spanish judicial and notarial records there are especially revealing about slavery, partly because they permit longitudinal views of individual slaves and families through enslavement, emancipation, and integration into free society. Studies of slavery elsewhere in Spanish America have used similar types of records to draw the outlines of slaves' hispanization and transition into freedom, depicting emancipation in ways that have not been as clear in studies of Brazil or Anglo America. In at least some parts of Spanish America, the end of slavery appears as a piecemeal social process.[3] We have seen now for Guatemala that the process was part of a larger set of transformations that gave rise to free labor and ladino identity.

These transitions were rooted in mestizaje (racial and ethnic mixing), which in Guatemala was not only an outcome of interethnic unions that produced children of mixed ancestry. It was also a result of indigenous individuals' attrition from the colony's Indian category and of African individuals' attrition from the slave category—that is, the crossing by people from Indian and slave groups into the emerging ladino (hispanized) group. Attrition was fueled by migration in both geographic and cultural senses. Indigenous families and individuals migrated out of Indian communities and out of the tributary population, going to work in the colonial economy as free laborers and joining the Hispanic cultural sphere. People of African descent migrated out of slavery into paid labor, freedom, and Hispanic identities.

The patterns of migration and labor that fueled mestizaje were remarkably gendered. Although most of the migrants arriving to work at colonial agricultural estates were men, the vast majority who came to staff the colonial capital were women. As in other Spanish American colonies, in Guatemala the Hispanic capital city witnessed particularly intense cultural and ethnic mixing (which has continued there into the present). More migrants came to work in domestic service than any other occupation, and their jobs immersed them in Hispanic culture more forcefully than would other types of work. Household service placed workers on a twenty-four-hour schedule in the intimate settings of their employers' homes, usually isolating them from other members of their home communities and requiring them to learn Spanish and adopt other hispanized ways. Thus, the city was a center of hispanization not only because it was a hub for migrants from native and African backgrounds but also because of the particular nature of its jobs and lodging arrangements.

In addition to servant women's position as objects of hispanization, they also played key roles as agents in the formation of free ladino society. Female domestic workers provided a significant portion of the city's child care; servants were on hand daily in elite and middling Hispanic homes, and employers must have relied on their help with the tasks that arise constantly in caring for children. Moreover, while many (if not most) female migrants into the city were Indians, their own children were likely to become members of the free ladino labor force. As mothers, female migrant workers were the primary agents of social and biological reproduction of first-generation urban ladinos. Finally, the labor performed by migrant servant women fulfilled essential daily needs for their employers, relieving much of the urban populace of household chores. Servant women thereby made possible the work of the growing ladino labor force in an array of industries and government functions.

The kaleidoscope of occupations and workers in late colonial Guatemala City was on one hand a product of the disintegration of forced labor systems; it was an outpouring of people and work into a labor market where hiring was now privatized, arranged between individuals. Reflecting these shifts, the trade guilds had become less exclusive along lines of calidad and gender. The guilds' grip on production had also loosened as numerous men and women were practicing without formal guild recognition. Indeed, various female trades were thriving with no guild at all.

On the other hand, though, the labor scene on the eve of independence mirrored its shape from the preceding three centuries. The procurement mechanisms and some of the ethnic identities had changed, but people from the same places (and in some cases the same families) were still doing largely the same kinds of work. Though women had entered a variety of trades, they remained marginalized by inferior wages and exclusion from state and church office holding.

Women's persistent economic and political marginalization is especially paradoxical in Guatemala City, where the 1796 and 1824 censuses suggest that women headed households in numbers roughly equal to men. Given the financial challenges that women faced without spousal support, it is not surprising that some of the census's largest households (that is, those with the most residents) were headed by women evidently renting space to other women and sometimes men; the pooling of rents paid by many tenants afforded the house. Household composition is also suggestive about other social patterns, notably those in marriage and childrearing. The family structures in which urban people actually lived did not generally match the patriarchal units that scholarship has often described as fundamental in Hispanic societies.

The sharing of living space was part of a dense interweaving of public and private life. Most urban households included members of more than one family, with residents linked by credit, patronage, service, or employment—as, for example, with servants and craftsmen who lived in their employers' homes. Further, social relationships tended to overlap with business relationships. In various industries extended kin groups achieved vertical integration as spouses, lovers, relatives, and housemates supplied one another with inputs for their enterprises. Families also exerted horizontal business alliances through groups of siblings, parents and children, or husbands and wives plying a single trade. Even among agricultural laborers, workers were sometimes hired expressly as family groups (recall those from Jocotenango at the sugar estate of doña Manuela Dardón in Chapter 1). At a fundamental level the kinship-network substructure of free labor contracts and businesses was imbricated with the erosion pattern in the old colonial labor systems, since the exodus from coerced labor to free labor was often a collective move by families whose members collaborated in migrating, amassing wages, purchasing liberty, or running small enterprises.

Despite their economic and political marginalization, women were integrated into public economic activities in so many ways that the ideal of female reclusion in a domestic sphere seems to have had little relevance to social reality. The boundary between public and private was nearly invisible for women and men alike. This picture is congruous with recent studies of colonial and nineteenth-century Latin America in which the specific study of women has yielded to a more general consideration of gender as one of various significant features in the overall structure of society. The earlier historiography's emphasis on female reclusion, chastity, and "honor" appears to be partly an outcome of research methods that employed canon law and other codified ideologies as an avenue to studying women. In contrast, sources such as notarial records, court cases, and registers of censuses and business licensing reveal an image of women integrated into the whole of society, rather than a set of idealized behavioral prescriptions.

Late colonial Guatemalans' everyday contestations of idealized gender norms are not really surprising in the contexts we have seen of migration patterns, shared housing, and blurring of public and private arenas. The capital city's permissive style of courtship—which allowed unmarried people to meet, drink, and seek entertainment outside their home—was facilitated by women's participation in the cash economy and was harmonious with their broader participation in a public sphere. The frequency of marital separations and concubinage is partly explained by migratory work that removed laborers from their homes for long periods.

Although colonial officials did not directly question the overarching patriarchal structure of society, the state recognized and in some ways legitimized specific contestations. The courts regularly allowed women who were separated from their husbands to litigate without spousal consent. Further, the judges consistently backed women who sued their former lovers. These women in their litigation expressed little concern with idealized notions of female chastity; few even bothered to assert that their virginity had been violated, nor were they seeking marriage. Rather, they were specifically demanding child support. The courts almost always awarded a monetary settlement to be paid by the presumptive father. By ruling in their favor, the state in effect was recognizing unwed mothers as legitimate parents and guardians. Thus in judicial practice as well as quotidian life, Iberian ideals of female chastity and related honor yielded to more flexible expectations and behaviors.

This legal and lived flexibility toward gender norms in the late colonial period recontextualizes Liberal legislation of the nineteenth century. The early independent-era Liberal administration—chief-of-state Mariano Gálvez and the Legislative Assembly—enacted civil marriage and divorce in 1836 and 1837, but the laws lasted only a matter of months before a Conservative rebellion ousted the Liberals from power and returned exclusive jurisdiction over marriage to the church.[4] The state resumed legislation on gender and the family with the Civil Code of 1877, part of the "Liberal Reform" begun in 1871. Yet, like the nineteenth-century civil codes in other Hispanic American republics, the 1877 legislation in Guatemala largely followed colonial code law rather than case law.[5] It stipulated that wives could not appear in court without their husbands' permission, except to defend themselves in criminal cases or to litigate against their husbands; and it stated that a wife could not buy, sell, receive, or mortgage property—except nonprecious movable property purchased in cash—without written consent from her husband, unless she herself had earned the wages to purchase the property.[6]

To be sure, the 1877 code was reformist in giving the state shared jurisdiction over marriage and divorce; couples could be married by either ecclesiastical or civil magistrates, then had to go to the same institution if they sought divorce.[7] But as in the colonial period, "divorce" as defined in 1877, whether granted by church or state, amounted to a separation that did not dissolve the marriage or allow remarriage.[8] The 1877 laws did offer the innovation of alimony (*una pensión alimenticia*) required of divorced husbands for wives who had not committed "adultery or another crime."[9] However, women with illegitimate children (and the children themselves) fared worse than under colonial law. The 1877 civil code relieved a man of the obligation to support a child fathered out of wedlock, unless he chose to "recognize" the child—a choice the code described explicitly as being voluntary.[10] At least according to the written law, then, men could not be made to pay child support for children born outside marriage. The legislators of the Liberal Reform adhered tightly to ideals of patriarchal nuclear family structure, despite the relative flexibility of their late colonial forebears.

In the sphere of labor structures as well, attention to the late colonial era reframes more recent developments. The Liberal governments of the late nineteenth and early twentieth centuries made legislative efforts to reinstate coerced labor, targeting Indians and "*vagos*" (vagrants) to be drafted.[11] On the surface, the nineteenth- and twentieth-century drafts seem to mirror colonial-era forced tribute labor. Even today's migration patterns appear similar to those of the colonial era, as many indigenous men and family groups leave home seasonally to earn wages in the export plantations of the Pacific coastal lowlands. But modern labor and labor coercion cannot be explained simply as an uninterrupted continuation of colonial ways. Indian tribute labor had gradually but certainly ended by the 1820s, as had African slavery. By the late colonial era indigenous and

Afro-Guatemalan people's labor was, in effect, privatized. Indian office-holders were left on the margins of this new social and economic order, and the Spanish administration—which for much of the colonial period had distributed indigenous labor crews and regulated the institution of slavery—was rendered somewhat unnecessary. Further, the old ethnic categories, once the basis for coerced labor, were made irrelevant for the late colonial economy. Tribute labor and slavery, which had long supported local wealth and privilege, were replaced with newer forms of labor procurement. From the perspective of elite Spanish Americans, these changes undercut the need for colonial rule.

Still, ethnicity would matter in the postindependence era, and it would matter enormously. The "imagined communities" of the Central American nations would be communities of ladinos. Membership in Hispanic society was in effect the basis for membership in the new nations, and the basis for inclusion in the Liberal vision of modernity.[12] As we have seen, people of African descent and many people of indigenous descent had come to be part of the Hispanic sphere. Those who continued to be identified as Indians, though, would be largely excluded from the benefits of Liberal rule in the national era.

This exclusion appears with particular clarity in Guatemala starting in 1871 with the Liberal Reform that followed three decades of conservative rule. The Liberal state took measures to reinstitute coerced labor, specifically at a time when Guatemalan elites were seeking to develop coffee export agriculture.[13] The Liberals also opened the door for foreign investment capitalists, and the result is a well-known story: under the direction of foreign owners and a few elite Central Americans, private companies began to pump coffee from Guatemala and its neighbor countries.[14] Bananas would come next. This growing connection with the international (neocolonial) economy was the major avenue by which Guatemalan Liberals, like their counterparts elsewhere in Latin America, intended to bring their nation into the modern age as they perceived it.[15]

The late nineteenth- and early twentieth-century labor drafts in Guatemala were aimed at people on the margins of the Liberals' nation. By force (or forced labor), Indians and so-called vagrants would be made to work for the wealth and advancement of the ladino leaders' imagined community. Thus, as it was experienced by agricultural workers in Guatemala, the modern age was very like the colonial one. But the seemingly retrograde labor coercion (and labor conditions in general, especially for Indian-identified people) were not simply a legacy of Spanish rule. They were also, in part, a product of modernity as it had taken shape in Guatemala—of the modern (neocolonial) international economy and of the nation itself.

REFERENCE MATTER

Abbreviations Used in the Notes

AGCA   Archivo General de Centro América, Guatemala City. Document call numbers are given as follows: Signatura (subject number)/Legajo (bundle number)/Expediente (document number)

Marure Papers   Alejandro Marure Papers, Courtesy Edward E. Ayer Collection, The Newberry Library, Chicago, Illinois.

Notes

INTRODUCTION

1. Emancipation in the Andes as elsewhere in Spanish America began with slaves purchasing freedom and seizing it through other means; see Aguirre 1993 and Hünefeldt 1994. "Free womb" laws were enacted in various parts of Spanish South America during and shortly after the wars for independence; see Andrews 2004.

2. Examples include Silvio Zavala 1935; Simpson 1950; Chevalier 1963; Taylor 1972; MacLeod 2008 [1973]; Sherman 1979; and Van Young 1981. Studies of African slavery in Mexico and Central America came somewhat later, with those in English perhaps fruits of interest in African American history; see Aguirre Beltrán 1972 [1946]; Palmer 1976; Fiehrer 1979; and Carroll 1991.

3. Recent studies of the Andes have placed indigenous women and marriage within analysis of the colonial structures of tribute, markets, and labor migration, but for Mexico and Central America the new gendered history has generally been more separate from consideration of tribute and labor procurement systems. On the Andes, see, for example, Glave 1989, chap. VII; Wightman 1990, 97 and passim; and Graubart 2007, chap. 1. For an overview on both the Andes and Mesoamerica, see Kellogg 2005, 63–71.

4. On Guatemala, see Contreras R. 1968; Wortman 1982, 182–183; and McCreery 1989. On Mexico, examples include Taylor 1979 and Van Young 2001. On Peru, Walker (1999) shows that nineteenth-century leaders drew support from diverse coalitions including rural and urban, elite and poor, Indian and Hispanic.

5. Arrom 1985b; Guardino 1996; Chambers 1999; Hünefeldt 2000; A. Díaz 2004; Premo 2005; Dym 2006; and Caplan 2010. For an illuminating comparison of the city of Oaxaca with the rural district of Villa Alta, see Guardino 2005.

6. Woodward 1999, 87–90.

7. The classic example is Marure 1960 [1837]. More recent studies include Pinto Soria 1986 (on Central America as a whole) and Taracena Arriola 1997 (on the northwestern region of Los Altos). For an excellent overview of historiography on Guatemala's independence era, see Hawkins 2004, "Introduction." Also on political formation in Central America's independence era, see Dym 2006.

8. On the 1837 revolt, see Solórzano 1987; Woodward 1993; and Jefferson 2000.

9. Instituto Nacional de Estádistica; Plant 1998, 4; and CELADE.

10. McCreery 1994, 187–191, 220–223, 267–268; Grandin 2000, 119; and Reeves 2006, chap. 3. The term *mandamiento*, used in Guatemala to refer to the colonial-era *repartimiento*, continued in the nineteenth century to refer to coerced labor. Even into the 1940s, the state used antivagrancy laws to impress Indian men

into crews sent to work on agricultural estates; see Martínez Peláez 1994, 173 and 176.

11. The Guatemalan state, for example, recognizes African ethnicity in only one ethnic group, the Garífuna, with 5,040 people registered in the 2002 census—less than 0.05 percent of a total population of 11,183,388; see Instituto Nacional de Estádistica.

12. The first of these communities is the Garífuna (plural: Garinagu), estimated to number around 10,000 in Guatemala, concentrated in a few towns on Caribbean coast; this community is descended from slaves deported in 1797 from the British colonies of St. Vincent and Baliceaux in the Lesser Antilles. The refugees were granted freedom by the Spanish Crown when they arrived in what is now Honduras and Guatemala. (On the Garífuna migration and present-day community, see Gonzalez 1988; Kerns 1997; and Euraque 2004. On the size of today's community see Instituto Nacional de Estadística, n11.) Second, a small number of Guatemalans trace their ancestry to people of African descent who arrived from the Caribbean and the United States as free laborers in the late nineteenth and early twentieth centuries; on this migration, see Opie 2009. This later migration is also the background for many black-identified communities elsewhere in Central America.

13. On El Salvador, see Fiehrer 1979; on Costa Rica, examples include Gudmundson 1984 and Cáceres 2010. For a sampling of work on Mexico, see Vinson and Restall 2009.

14. Lutz's analysis of marriage records suggests that blacks and mulatos comprised between about 30 and 40 percent of the city, but Lutz cautions that this figure may be too high, since the numbers of mestizo marriages may have been artificially depressed in the records (Lutz 1994, 102–103). By contrast, he notes, "African ancestry was given undue negative importance," resulting in the use of the mulato identity for those even with very little African ancestry (Lutz 1994, 95).

15. MacLeod 2008, xxvii. The recent volume edited by Gudmundson and Wolfe (2010) takes important strides toward addressing the question.

16. On native cabildos and their officers in Mexico, see Gibson 1964; Farriss 1984, especially 227; Haskett 1991; Lockhart 1992, 48–52; and Restall 1997, chap. 6. Though hereditary female rulers (*cacicas*) have been identified among colonial-era Mixtec communities, women were excluded from the cabildo; see Terraciano 2001, 171–190.

17. Lutz 1994, 43.

18. On the position of Africans in colonial society, see Lockhart and Schwartz 1983, 129–132 For a comparative analysis of Indians' and slaves' positions in the colonial legal system in Peru, see O'Toole 2012, especially 124–125.

19. Santiago was until 1773 sometimes called "Ciudad de Guatemala" (Guatemala City). I avoid using this label for Santiago to avoid confusion with the city now called Guatemala City.

20. The name "Guatemala" was also that of a colonial-era *provincia* (province), comprised by the area of Santiago and Nueva Guatemala and their *comarca* (nearby hinterlands). This region is today sometimes called "the Valley of

Guatemala"; it is significantly larger than the area of today's Departamento de Guatemala. (The area covered by the colonial-era Provincia de Guatemala—approximately the region of Santiago and Nueva Guatemala and their hinterlands—does *not* correspond to the early national-era Provincia de Guatemala, which was much larger, including what is today the area of the Republic of Guatemala.) Confusion caused by the multiple meanings of the name "Guatemala" was apparent even in the colonial era, when petitions and other papers were often redirected after being mistakenly addressed to the wrong government office.

21. The president of the Audiencia was also the captain general and governor of the kingdom (Woodward 1999, 39).

22. On population, see Lutz 1994, 110.

23. Cortés y Larraz 1958 vol. 1, 106, and vol. 2, 155.

24. The decision was made only after much debate; see Zilbermann de Luján 1987, 80; and Sagastume Paiz 2008, 41–46.

25. The plan was to combine some of the outlying pueblos at the new locale, but it is unclear whether this ever happened. See Galicia Díaz 1976, 65; Polo Sifontes 1982, 20–23; and Sagastume Paiz 2008, 60.

26. The move has been treated in Galicia Díaz 1976; Langenberg 1981, chaps. 2–3; Polo Sifontes 1982; Zilbermann de Luján 1987; Sagastume Paiz 2008; and Matthew 2012, 258–267.

27. Antigua and surrounding areas—a jurisdiction called the Partido de Sacatepéquez—retained significant population; in 1820, the members of the ayuntamiento of Antigua argued that they should get a delegate to the Cortes in Spain, noting that the *partido* had 67,000 people whereas the new capital had only 30,000 or 35,000 plus some "villas"; see AGCA A1/3021/29113.

28. Lutz (1976, p. 16) estimated slaves to be about 1.1 percent of the population of Santiago in the 1760s.

29. Galicia Díaz 1976, 40–44.

30. Langenberg 1981.

31. The census report of 1740 made an explicit point about the great female majority among "the common poor." It is not clear that the reported numbers included women and children at all, other than those identified as Spaniards. AGCA A1/210/5002.

32. On other cities see for example Arrom 1985b, 158 and 183–184; Glave 1989, 336–352; Francois 2006, 35; and Pescador 1992, 112–121. On female predominance in rural–urban migration in the United States, see Meyerowitz 1988, 8–9.

33. For an interesting analysis of these gender roles as as perceived by K'iche' elites in Quetzaltenango, see Grandin 2000, 182–185.

34. On increases in the years 1788, 1802, and 1811, see Wortman 1982, 182. On the vaccine, see also Lovell 1985, 161. On the complexities behind apparent Indian population increase, see Grandin 2000, 55–57.

35. On the capitals as a frontier, see MacLeod 1973, 230 and 308; van Oss 1986, 46–48 and 71–72; and Lutz 1994, 162. MacLeod notes that as early as the 1580s, the lower altitudes attracted more Spaniards with agricultural enterprises.

36. The seminal study to use notarial records was Lockhart 1994 [1968] on Peru; more recently on Peru, Graubart (2007) used notarial records, particularly wills, to study indigenous women. On Santiago de Guatemala, Herrera (2003) used notarial records to identify labor and business arrangements among people at all socioeconomic levels. A number of studies have used native-language wills from Mexico; for example Cline 1986; Lockhart 1992; Restall 1997; Terraciano 2001; Melton-Villanueva and Pizzigoni 2008; and Pizzigoni 2012 (which was a few weeks shy of publication at the time the present book went to press).

37. For discussion of the value and problems of court records as sources, see Taylor 1979, 8–9 and 90–92; Stern 1995, 38–40; Ericastilla Samayoa 1997; and Van Young 2001, 111–118. Additional examples of such scholarship include Lozano Armendares 1987; Haslip-Viera 1999; Hünefeldt 2000; and Díaz 2004. In addition to the records of the royal courts, ecclesiastical court records have been fruitful (for example, see Bennett 2003 and 2009). Other scholars have used the records of the Inquisition (also a type of court); for example on Guatemala, see Few 2002.

38. I was not able to locate ecclesiastical judicial records for this study. It is possible that they are stored in the Archivo Arquidiocesano de Guatemala, adjacent to the cathedral in Guatemala City. The archive has been open only sporadically in recent years. As this book went to press, the FamilySearch service of the Church of Jesus Christ of Latter-day Saints began to post on its website images of some of the colonial-era ecclesiastical records from Guatemala; see https://familysearch.org/search/collection/show#uri=http://familysearch.org/searchapi/search/collection/1614809

39. On Mexico's Indian court, see Borah 1983 and Owensby 2008, 43–44.

40. Indian barrio officers also staffed the *rondas*—nighttime policing patrols—throughout the city, under the authority of the Spanish alcaldes (Lutz 1994, 41–43; and Langenberg 1981, 44).

41. Stern 1995, 50–52.

42. Scardaville 1994, 514. Also on Mexico, see Borah 1983; on Ecuador, see Gauderman 2003, 17–21.

43. On notions of calidad, see McCaa 1984; Yannakakis 2008, 14–15; and Martínez 2008, 247. I use the term *race* to refer to notions of biological differences perceived in phenotypes or physical characteristics; I use *ethnicity* to signify a cultural set of identifiers, including but not limited to social association with a particular group (that may be defined along racial lines).

44. These categories are immortalized famously in the "casta paintings" of the seventeenth and eighteenth centuries. I would suggest that the paintings may have been a symptom of elite art-patron anxiety—about social mixing and elision within the racial hierarchy—more than an expression of enduring categories. For a classic critique of the perception that the casta system's stability endured through the colonial period, see Chance 1978, especially 184.

45. On Vela, see AGCA A2/151/2841. On de Jesús, see AGCA A2/157/3058.

46. Lockhart 1984.

47. AGCA A1/4435/36958.

48. AGCA A1/4397/36095.

49. AGCA A2/154/2953.

50. Lutz 1994, 103, 163, 171, and Appendices 1 and 2 (which show increasing numbers of records for people of unidentified race); see also Jefferson 2000, 42–43.

51. Lutz 1994, 171–172.

52. Census records are scattered across various call number areas in the AGCA; many are classified under *signatura* A1.44 and, for the early independent era, B84.3. A partial cataloguing can be found in the AGCA's card catalogue under *Estadística*. The AGCA's records have been microfilmed extensively, and many of the microfilmed censuses can be borrowed from the Genealogical Society of Utah, through the Family History Centers of the Church of Jesus Christ of Latter-Day Saints; see Weathers 1981. As this book went to press, many of the Church's holdings from the AGCA were being made available online at https://familysearch.org/.

53. On etymology of the term *ladino* and the collapsing of various non-Indian categories into the single category of *ladinos*, see Grandin 2000, 84–85, 265–266 n9, and appendix I; and Lokken 2000, 103–111. See also Matthew 2012, chap. 6.

54. On meaning of *mulata* or *mulato*, see Lutz 1994, 46. The records I studied for the later colonial period bear this out also.

55. The term *Maya* is of Yucatec origin; see Restall and Asselbergs 2007, 4.

56. Subsequent studies include McCreery 1994; Taracena Arriola 1997; Grandin 2000; and Reeves 2006.

CHAPTER 1

1. The history of the Quiché (K'iche') is told in the K'iche' book on origins, the *Popol Vuh*. For a translation and study in English, see Tedlock 1996. Cakchiquel history is told in the Annals of the Cakchiquels; see Recinos 1980, and for an English translation see Maxwell and Hill 2006. For an overview of the Spanish-Nahua invasion, see Restall and Asselbergs 2007, 1–20.

2. On the native Mexicans allies, see Matthew 2012.

3. This reputation is rooted partly in his role in the Conquest of Tenochtitlán (Mexico City); left in charge when Hernán Cortés was away from the city, Alvarado ordered a massacre of Mexican nobility in May 1519. Alvarado's version of the events in Guatemala can be found in two surviving letters to Cortés; for an annotated English translation, see Restall and Asselbergs 2007, 23–47.

4. On conquistador procedure and founding of cities, see Restall 2003, 19–20.

5. On Indian slavery in Central America in colonial and precolonial eras, see Sherman 1979; Martínez Peláez 1970, especially chap. 2; MacLeod 2008, part 1, passim; and Herrera 2003, chap. 10.

6. Historians have debated whether the liberation of Indian slaves resulted from the vision of Spanish administrators or from the simple fact that Indian lives and labor under the conditions of enslavement were unsustainable; on the debate, see Lutz 1994, 15–18.

7. On the emancipation and resettlement, see Lutz 1994, 19–32. I suspect that some of the Indian settlements in the Valleys of Panchoy and Almolonga predated the Spanish Conquest; as I describe later in this chapter, for example, the cellular structure of Jocotenango even in the late colonial era reflected a pre-Conquest model. Herrera (2003, 133–134) also argues for pre-Conquest origins.

8. For an overview of the shift in Spanish America, see Lockhart and Schwartz 1983, 128–129 and 134–142, and Lockhart 1969. On the changing structures of labor in central Mexico, see Gibson 1964, chap. 9.

9. On encomienda awards and inheritance in Guatemala, see Kramer 1994.

10. On Mexico, see for example Zavala 1944 and Gibson 1964, 226–228. Subsequent works on Central America have identified similar patterns; see Martínez Peláez 1970 and 1994; MacLeod 2008; and McCreery 1994.

11. MacLeod 2008, 206–207.

12. Martínez Pelaez 1994, 170.

13. Gibson 1964, 249–250; MacLeod 2008, 207–209; and McCreery 1994, 93–94. Employers were also supposed to pay for each man drafted a small tax into the native community *caja* (chest or coffer).

14. On distribution of repartimiento in Guatemala in the 1670s, see Hernández Aparicio 1977.

15. MacLeod 2008, 295–296. On native languages and use of Spanish in various communities in the second half of the eighteenth century, see Cortés y Larraz 1958.

16. Labor drafts were revived in some places in Guatemala with the rise of coffee starting in the 1850s, a point to which I return in the conclusion of this book. Historians have explained the presence (or absence) of the late nineteenth-century drafts as a result of various factors—increased demand for labor, increasing Hispanic state power, integration (or lack thereof) of particular native communities into regional economic structures, and internal class structure in specific native communities. See McCreery 1994, 112; Grandin 2000, 119–122; and Reeves 2006, chap. 3.

17. On conversion to cash in Guatemala, see Wortman 1982, 174–175, and Lovell 1985, 103.

18. Gibson 1964, 235.

19. This point is well illustrated for the Andes in Premo 2000.

20. Zavala 1967, 103-108, and MacLeod 2008, 296. Peru's rotary draft labor system (the *mita*) also lasted until independence; scholars have inferred that its long duration was based partly the Andes' strong pre-Hispanic tradition of rotary draft labor (Lockhart and Schwartz 1983, 140).

21. On central Mexico, see Gibson 1964, chap. 9, and Lockhart 1992, 432.

22. McCreery 1994, 93.

23. McCreery 1994, 94–95. On a similar pattern in the Guadalajara region, see Van Young 1981, 242.

24. AGCA A3/223/3993, 3995, and 4006 (which includes several cases).

25. A suggestive example is a petition from the pueblo of San José, brought to the alcalde mayor of the province of Huehuetenango and Totonicapán, about the abuses by *hacendado* don Rafael de la Torre. The pueblo's Indian officers assumed that the townspeople would continue working in repartimiento at the same hacienda after it changed hands; their request was specifically to be relieved "from sending mandamiento workers for as long as don Rafael de la Torre may be at the hacienda." AGCA A3/227/4192, fol. 2v.

26. For central Mexico, the shifting structure of labor procurement has been linked to concurrent changes in native cultural and political spheres (Lockhart 1992, 429–436).

27. On Guadalajara, see Van Young 1981, 244–245. Comparing Guadajara to Mexico City, Van Young suggests that greater Spanish population density in Mexico City may have intensified Spanish land use in that region, thereby decreasing Indians' access to land and forcing them into wage labor. Their entrance into the free labor market would have lessened the need for draft workers.

28. Taylor 1972, 146–147.

29. Doña Manuela Sunsín described this situation her 1777 repartimiento request, in AGCA A3/225/4060. See also McCreery 1994, 101–102. McCreery notes that wages in both the city and its rural hinterland rose substantially during these decades.

30. Gibson 1964, 232.

31. Fuentes y Guzmán 1882–1883, vol. 2, 138–139. Also see MacLeod 2008, 295 and 449n10. On developments in the sixteenth century, see Sherman 1979, chap. 10. The allowance of 25 percent remained in force until the end of the colonial period, as demonstrated in the repartimiento records (for the late colonial period, see AGCA A3/227, various expedientes).

32. AGCA A3/223–227. On excesses, see McCreery 1994, 108–109.

33. These petitions are contained in AGCA, A3/legajos 223–227.

34. On estimated native populations in various towns in central Mexico, Oaxaca, and Guatemala see Gibson 1964, 142; Taylor 1972, 33; and Sherman 1979, 347–355.

35. For the central Mexican dates, see Lockhart 1992, 428ff; for Guatemala, see MacLeod 2008, 295 and 449n10.

36. On personal service, see Sherman 1979, chap. 10.

37. On the replacement of repartimiento with indigenous *gañán* (nondraft) labor in the Valley of Mexico, see Gibson 1964, chap. 9.

38. On repartimientos in 1814, see McCreery 1994, 111; on 1812, see AGCA A3/227/4194.

39. On the seventeenth century, see Fuentes y Guzmán 1882–1883, vol 2., 138–139. For the eighteenth century, examples can be seen in AGCA A3/224/4024; A3/226/4112; A3/227/4152; and A3/227/4192.

40. AGCA A3/224/4014, A3/224/expedientes 4030, 4035, 4045, and 4049; A3/2561/37586; and A3/226/4114.

41. A collection of indigenous protests from the Valley of Guatemala addressed to the king in the sixteenth century appears in Lutz and Dakin 1996.

42. On the widespread abuses in the draft labor system, see MacLeod 2008, especially chap. 16.

43. AGCA A3/223/3984. Also on the seventeenth century, see Hill 1992, chap. 8.

44. On the first half of the eighteenth century, see AGCA A3/223/expedientes 3986, 3991, and 4001.

45. AGCA A3/224/4014. The towns were Comapa, Conguaco, Azulco, Moyuta, Jutiapa, and Pasaco in today's department of Jutiapa in Guatemala; and Apaneca and Juayúa in today's department of Ahuachapán in El Salvador.

46. AGCA A3/224/4045.

47. AGCA A3/224/4049.

48. AGCA A3/224/4045.

49. AGCA A3/224/4030.

50. AGCA A3/224/4025. See also McCreery 1994, 97.

51. AGCA A3/225/4081 and A3/226/4123.

52. AGCA A3/224/4045 (see entries for 1710 regarding Mixco and San Felipe Nerí); A3/224/4049; A3/226/4094; and A3/227/expedientes 4148 and 4149.

53. On the names Jumay and Jumaytepeque, see Gall 1976–1983 vol. 2, 447–448.

54. AGCA A3/225/4074.

55. AGCA A3/224/4046.

56. On unsatisfactory operation of earlier labor drafts, see MacLeod 2008, 295–296.

57. AGCA A3/224/expedientes 4024, 4025, 4030, and 4046; A3/2561/37586; A3/225/4070; A3/226/4112; and A3/227/4146 and 4193.

58. On this pattern, see also McCreery 1994, 109.

59. AGCA A3/224/4049.

60. AGCA A3/225/4081.

61. There is debate as to whether repartimiento workers were normally paid in advance. For the assertion that the workers were not paid until the end of the week, see Martínez Peláez 1994, 168–169; for description of how advance wages were distributed by the principales of the pueblo as part of the ritual of assigning workers to the weekly shift, see MacLeod 1983, 193–194, and McCreery 1994, 105. In any case, advances were typical if not outright normative for free agricultural laborers in the eighteenth century; for example, see AGCA A3/223/4002 and A3/226/4111.

62. AGCA A3/226/4085.

63. Don Manuel Garrote Bueno's case appears in AGCA A3/227/expedientes 4146 and 4166.

64. For Garrote's petition, see AGCA A3/227/4146. On indigo in colonial Central America, see MacLeod 2008, chap. 10.

65. On the standard wage, see AGCA A3/legajos 224 and 225, various expedientes.

66. One of the repartimientos was issued in 1785, in AGCA A3/226/4118. Another was evidently the object of protest by the Indians of Cuyotenango and Zapotitlán, who complained that repartimiento was too burdensome because they also had responsibilities in cofradías, service for the priest, and civil offices; see AGCA A3/226/4122.

67. AGCA A3/226, 4118, fols. 5–6 and 11–13; and A3/227/4146, fols. 6–7.

68. AGCA A3/227/4146, fols. 6–7.

69. AGCA A3/227/4146, fol. 7.

70. AGCA A3/227/4166. The Audiencia had approved Garrote's 1798 request, issuing orders to the pueblos of Mazatenango and San Gabriel. In 1792 neither Garrote nor the Audiencia had specified the towns from which the workers should be drafted; apparently they were relying on the discretion of the alcalde mayor. Their failure to identify specific towns may reflect a lack of available workers and/ or the lack of conventional repartimientos in the region.

71. AGCA A3/227/4166. On the threat of public disturbance, the Spanish reads "por evitar todo alboroto publico, que parecía muy posible."

72. McCreery 1994, 99.

73. For a history of San Agustín Acasaguastlán, see Gall 1976–1983 vol. 3, 182–186. Gall weighs two explanations for the community's ethnic and linguistic origins in a generally Pocom-speaking area (the Motagua River Valley): either the region was bilingual in the pre-Conquest period, or Nahuatl speakers settled the town after the arrival of the Spaniards. Gall notes that Cortés y Larraz wrote in 1769 that there were 465 Indian families and 2,733 Indian individuals in the pueblo, plus twenty ladino families with 130 individuals. In 1778, don Marcos Victorio Morales requested a repartimiento from San Agustín Acasaguastlán, claiming that there were more than 1,000 eligible draftees (the record does not verify this figure); see AGCA A3/225/4070.

74. On Dardón's estate, see AGCA A2/40/830. On other repartimientos from Acasaguastlán, see AGCA A3/2561/37586 (statement of the fiscal, don Josef Tosta, Aug. 31, 1784); and A3/225/expedientes 4070 (year 1778) and 4081 (year 1776).

75. Dardón's mayordomo (Juan Pascual de Peña, a free mulato) testified that there were eight workers from San Agustín Acasaguastlán presently at the estate. Soon afterwards, Josef Casimiro Estrada (*"al parecer español"*) who evidently worked at the estate, said that of the twelve repartimiento workers from San Agustín Acasaguastlán, six were still at the estate. Another worker (Josef Antonio Rodas, a free mulato) said twelve workers had come from San Agustín Acasaguastlán "de mandamiento" (as a repartimiento) the previous week, and he did not know how many had stayed. He also seemed to indicate that the San Agustín Acasaguastlán workers presently on the estate had arrived at various times, suggesting that Dardón enjoyed a repartimiento for at least several weeks, with crews arriving weekly over some period of time. AGCA A2/40/830.

76. AGCA A3/225/4081; A3/2561/37586; A3/2561/37588; A3/226/4120; A3/225/4070; and A3/225/4081.

77. Lockhart 1969, 426.

78. On the origins of San Cristóbal Cabricán, see Reeves 2006, 23–24.

79. AGCA A3/227/4193.

80. AGCA A3/2540/37302.

81. Ibid.

82. AGCA A1/4400/36140.

83. Taracena Arriola (1997) has found this usage of the word *ladino* even in the northwestern highlands of Guatemala, which in the popular view have been (and are now) the most "indigenous" area of the country.

84. For further discussion, see van Oss 1986, 69–72; Lokken 2000, especially 103–111; and Matthew 2012, chap. 6.

85. Examples of non–Spanish-speaking Indians subject to repartimiento late in the colonial era appear in AGCA A3/227/expedientes 4168 (San Antonio Palopó, year 1799) and 4192 (San José and Santa Lucía Sololá, year 1809). In both cases the native cabildos used an interpreter to communicate with Spanish authorities.

86. For example, AGCA A3/256/37586 (letter from don Thomas Calveros, the priest of Acasaguastlán); A3/224/4046 (statement of *oidor comisionado* don Ramón de Posada); and A3/226/4112. Another example appears in a petition from the Indians of San José and Santa Lucía, in AGCA A3/227/4192. Because their petition was made through the alcalde mayor (a Spaniard), it is unclear whether the Indians themselves used the terms *indios* and *ladinos* or whether this was merely the wording used by the alcalde mayor.

87. On ethnic categories as a reflection of tributary or non-tributary status, see also Lokken 2000, 107–108, and Lokken 2010, 46–47.

88. On the earlier colonial period, see Lutz 1994, 46. The records I have studied from the later colonial period also bear this out.

89. For example, AGCA A3/224/4046 (statement of don Ramón de Posada); and A3/226/4123.

90. Sherman 1979, 225 and 322–326.

91. On private contracting in the sixteenth century, see Herrera 2003, 158–163.

92. This complaint appears repeatedly in AGCA A3/224, various expedientes. On the same problems for draft workers in the sixteenth century, see Sherman 1979, 207.

93. Some native men were employed through tribute labor as cooks in the capital (AGCA A3/224/4045), but I have not found evidence of male labor in preparing food for rural workers. Nor have I found evidence that Indian women worked in the fields on Spanish estates in the colonial period. Starting in the nineteenth century, large numbers of women worked in coffee harvesting; this apparent shift in the gender composition of agricultural labor under the modern trade patterns merits further research.

94. Bauer 1990; and Mallon 1995, 77.

95. Molina 1977a [1571], 23v. and Molina 1977b [1571], 34r.

96. Wagley 1941, 26; Carey 2006, 111–112.

97. Examples are described in the following pages; see also McCreery 1994, 103.

98. AGCA A3/226/4114.

99. AGCA A3/256/37586.

100. AGCA A3/227/4192.

101. Martínez Peláez 1970, 526–531; MacLeod 2008, 316–317; and McCreery 1994, 42. On Mexico, see Kellogg 2005, 67. On the difference between the two senses of "repartimiento," see Martínez Peláez 1994.

102. On the early history of Jocotenango, see Lutz 1994, 19–24. Though historiography on Guatemala typically credits the Spaniards with founding the Indian communities in the Valley of Panchoy (the region of Santiago), Jocotenango's bipartite structure reflects the cellular organization typical of pre-Conquest Mesoamerican communities. On cellular structure in Guatemala, see Hill 1992, 164–165; on central Mexico, see Lockhart 1992, 15–20. In the sixteenth century,

at least, other pueblos and barrios in the Valley of Panchoy also manifested cellular structure (Herrera 2003, 145–146). The petition filed in 1765 (AGCA A2/40/830) was presented by "los Justicias de los Pueblos de Jocotenango y Utateca." It was signed "por los justicias de dhos. Pueblos" (on behalf of the magistrates of said pueblos) by Miguel Bernardo Argaes, who wrote his title simply as "escribano de Cabildo" (Cabildo notary), and by Simón García, who noted his title as "escribano de Utateca" (notary of Utateca). In the investigation sparked by the petition a single Indian *gobernador*, Diego Casanga, represented the entity of "Jocotenango," while another man, Martín Lucas, was identified as "alcalde del Pueblo de Utatleca."

103. Lutz 1994, 19–21.

104. Sansaria was a name for the region of Sanarate and Sansare (Gall 1976–1983 vol. 3, 676). Likely Los Llanos was what is now the *aldea* Llano de Morales (department of El Progreso). At least as late as 1880, Llano de Morales was known as "Los Llanos" (Gall 1976–1983 vol. 2, 547). Strictly speaking, the word *trapiche* signifies the sugar mill, but usage in the late colonial Guatemalan records connoted a more general meaning of the whole plantation—the mill, cane fields, and supporting estate. Though the word *ingenio* might refer to a larger mill and plantation, the two words were often used interchangeably to describe a single operation.

105. Sherman 1979, 249–251.

106. The Dominican order's San Jerónimo sugar estate, with some 600 slaves, also employed free people and repartimiento workers (AGCA A1/2556/20577; deposition of José María Loaisa, Manuel de Guevara, Mariano Espinosa, and Juan Guevara, May 8, 1818). In eastern Guatemala don Josef Jacinto Palomo owned an ingenio with some 100 slaves; beginning in 1794 or 1795 he received a repartimiento of Indian laborers to work the estate's wheat and corn fields (AGCA A3/227/4152).

107. AGCA A2/40/830.

108. Sherman 1979, 289–290 and 297; MacLeod 2008, 141; Martínez Peláez 1970, 544; and Hill 1992, 114. Martínez Peláez (1970, p. 544) described the principales' predicament as that of being stuck "entre la espada y la pared"—literally, between the sword and the wall; they were either "victims of the rigor of the corregidores" or "the hangmen of the macehuales."

109. Martínez Peláez 1970, 536–555; Sherman 1979, 297; Hill 1992, 113; and Carmack 1995, 85 and passim.

110. Grandin 2000, 72–73.

111. AGCA A2/40/830; see the deposition of Lorenza Saquil as well as that of the Indian governor and alcalde, Diego Casanga and Gaspar Sic.

112. Ibid.

113. "Tabardillo" was usually typhus; see Cook and Lovell 1991, 226–227.

114. Malaria, for one, has been endemic in modern times in San Agustín Acasaguastlán; see Gall 1976–1983 vol. 3, 185 (which cites a report from the year 1955).

115. AGCA A2/40/830, testimony of Manuel Silvestre de Peña; see also the testimony of Josef Antonio Rodas.

116. The hours are similar to those described on the San Jerónimo sugar estate in the Verapaz region; see AGCA A1/2556/20577 (the San Jerónimo estate is also discussed in Chapter 2). In the British West Indies, seventeenth-century plantation

owners staggered the planting over several months to lengthen the harvest season, reducing the daily workload during the harvest (Dunn 1973, 191).

117. For explanation of the processing and dangers at sugar mills, see Dunn 1973, 194–196 (quotation, 194).

118. Sherman 1979, 251 and 434n44; see also McCreery 1994, 99.

119. On seventeenth-century wages, see Hill 1992, 112.

120. In 1776 Nueva Guatemala's ayuntamiento stipulated that *peones* in construction projects would earn 2½ reales for a twelve-hour day that included a half-hour rest (Samayoa Guevara 1962, 219). For examples of actual wages for male laborers, see AGCA A1/4311/34626 (petition of don Pedro Ayau dated December 16, 1793, referring to the wage that he had received some eight years earlier); A1/4400/36153 (testimony of Eduardo Quirós, year 1803); and A1/4397/36095 (testimony of Ignacio Quevedo, year 1803).

121. For examples of women's wages, see AGCA A2/185/3704 (year 1797, testimony of Felipa Véliz); A2/205/4191 (year 1803); and A1/2861/25923 (petition dated January 20, 1790, which suggested a salary for the past fourteen years).

122. Data for San Jerónimo are based on AGCA A1/2556/20577. On the amount of the wages, see the May 18, 1818, testimony of José María Loaisa, Manuel de Guevara, Mariano Espinosa, and Juan Guevara. On wages being paid in silver and not in food, see the statement of fray Andrés Pintelos, July 8, 1819.

123. AGCA A2/40/830 (deposition of Diego Casanga and Gaspar Sic, and that of Simón García).

124. MacLeod 1983, 194 and 211n15.

125. On colonial-era Cakchiquel childrearing practices, see Hill 1992, 140–141. I have not found evidence of men who were charged with the responsibilities of child care (other than the financial responsibilities) in either native or colonial society, except in the context of boys being taught chores appropriate to their sex or working as apprentices.

126. I do not know whether Matías and Pascual were related to Miguel and Mateo Lantán, sons of Lorenza Saquil (quoted previously in this chapter).

127. "Que en caso de no querer las precissa diciendo que no les da a sus maridos dinero adelantado, si no ban ellas a moler, que por este motibo se ven obligadas a ir." AGCA A2/40/830.

128. Ibid., statement of Martín Lucas, March 2, 1765.

129. Matías Lucas was among the Jocotenango men interviewed on the road in ibid.

130. Ibid., especially the depositions of Dardón's mayordomo, Juan Pascal de Peña, and Joseph Antonio Rodas. Both men used the term *ladino* in its more modern meaning, referring to people of non-Indian ethnicity. The "ladinos of the Valley of Sansaria" to whom Peña and Rodas referred were probably the same "salaried mulatos and mestizos" that Dardón herself had mentioned—poor and middling people who spoke Spanish and were not identified as Indians or Spaniards (though some of them may well have been of Indian or Spanish ancestry). That Peña and Rodas distinguished between Indians and those they called "ladinos" is clear, given their explanation that it was the ladinos who performed those chores which Indians were legally prohibited from performing. Both Peña and Rodas identified

themselves as free mulatos, not as ladinos. I do not know what, in their view, distinguished mulatos from ladinos. Perhaps they thought of ladinos as people of Indian ancestry who had become so hispanized as to be no longer Indian.

131. Indians who fled Dardón's and other estates may have joined *pajuides*, small settlements hidden from Spanish and Indian authorities (on the Cakchiquel origin of the word *pajuides*, see Hill 1992, 122). However, given the bilingualism of the eighteenth- and nineteenth-century Jocotenango men who fled Dardón's estate, I am inclined to think they likely joined hispanized communities. Some of these communities perhaps originated as maroon communities; on a large band of *cimarrones* in the area, see Gage 1958 [1648], 195–96.

132. For example, Van Young 1981, chap. 11. Much has been written on Latin American "debt peonage," in which debts kept workers—and sometimes their offspring—tied to certain agricultural enterprises. On colonial and nineteenth-century Central America, see for example Lovell 1985, 104–107, and McCreery 1994, 189. However, my findings on indebted Indian workers in late colonial Guatemala suggest a scenario more akin to the finding of MacLeod (2008, 225) about hispanized workers who "accepted advances, and then decamped for other parts of Central America." For debate over interpretations of wage advances, see Bauer 1979a; Loveman 1979; and Bauer 1979b.

133. AGCA A2/40/830, testimony of Tomasa Larios.

134. Ibid., testimony of Simón García.

135. MacLeod 1983, 190.

136. Wortman 1982, 174–175.

137. MacLeod 1983, 191. See also Lovell 1985, 101–105 and 108-113; and Hill 1992, 114–116 and 119–120.

138. For example, AGCA A3/223/3986 and Lutz 1994, 278n108.

139. AGCA A2/40/830, testimony of Diego Casanga and Gaspar Sic. (Though the notary indicated that both men were sworn in to testify, Casanga, the governor, appears to have done most of the talking.)

140. Ibid., testimony of Sebastián Tepep and Martín Lucas, March 2, 1765.

141. Ibid., testimony of Simón García.

142. Lutz 1994, 53–54.

143. Martínez Peláez 1970, 558–564; Hill 1992, 121–123; Lutz 1994, 52–53; and, on the nineteenth century, McCreery 1994, 283–287.

144. For an overview of this literature (which has often involved debate), see Komisaruk 2009, 65n80.

145. AGCA A1/162/4883.

146. On don Pedro de Aycinena (y Larraín), see Brown 1997, 71 and passim. On his uncle, the first Marqués de Aycinena, see Brown 1997; Woodward 1993, 9; and Woodward 1999, 74–75.

147. AGCA A1/154/3063. For studies of the same case, but with different concerns, see Alvarez Aragón 1996 and Webre 2001.

148. For example, see requests from don Josef Antonio de Córdova and don Ventura Nájera in AGCA A1/154/3068, fols. 1–2.

149. AGCA A1/154/3063.

150. Pineda's arguments appear in AGCA A1/154/3063 and A1/162/4883.

151. AGCA A1/162/4883.

152. On early colonial use of Indian wet nurses, see Sherman 1979, 210 and 232.

153. This may have been the son or another younger relative of the Diego Casanga who had served as governor in previous decades. A Diego Casanga had been gobernador of Jocotenango in 1763 (see his testimony in AGCA A2/40/830). In 1805, doña María de Jesús Chicval identified herself as the widow of the late governor of Jocotenango Diego Casanga (AGCA A1/5908/50354); she reported her age as sixty (likely an approximation) in 1809 (AGCA A2/231/4918). If her husband was of similar age, he would have been approximately in his twenties in 1763 and his fifties at the time of the 1797 report. (In Chicval's 1809 testimony she identified herself as the "ex-gobernadora" of the Pueblo of Jocotenango, apparently referring to her position as the late gobernador's wife.) On fathers and sons using the same names among the Nahuas, see Lockhart 1992, 125.

154. AGCA A1/154/3063, fol. 14.

155. Ibid., fol. 62v.

156. Ibid., fol. 28.

157. For Contán's deposition, see ibid., fols. 28–30.

158. "Que ella no queria venir a servir de chichigua a la casa donde está, porque tiene tres hijos. . . . Pero el Governador le mandó, Obligara a servir y ella, por que no le dijera algo el Governador se obligó a servir como está sirviendo de chichigua pero ella por sus hijos, no quería venir." The notary's underlining signals a quotation by the declarant—here, Contán was quoting Casanga.

159. For Aycinena's deposition see ibid., fols. 22–24.

160. Elsewhere Barrutia's first name is identified as Francisca; see Brown 1997, 71.

161. Sherman 1979, 210, 323, and 332; and Lutz 1994, 22–23.

162. The word *chichigua* was being used in Spanish written records by 1578 if not sooner. See Sherman 1979, 323 and 454n100.

163. Lutz 1994, 22–23.

164. For other examples of Indian wet nurses in the capital, see AGCA A1/26/758 and A2/188/3798. For examples of non-Indian wet nurses, see AGCA A2/193/3948; A2/151/2841 (deposition of Antonia Mena, June 20, 1770); and A1/4401/36176 (deposition of Inés Alcayaga, March 18, 1803).

165. Wet nurses in eighteenth- and nineteenth-century Spain were charged with multiple aspects of child care, as described in Sarasúa 1994. On wet nurses in colonial Mexico City, see Pescador 1992, 213–214; on Cuzco, see Wightman 1990, 117.

166. Evidence from seventeenth- and eighteenth-century Guadalajara suggests that most Spanish women did not employ wet nurses; see Calvo 1989, 290–291. On Mexico City, see Pescador 1992, 213–214. On Brazil see Conrad 1994, 112 and 133–140. On Madrid, see Sarasúa 1994.

167. Statement of her husband, don Pedro Aycinena, AGCA A1/154/3063, fol. 22r.

168. "Sus dolores de cabeza, los del hombro, y parte del brazo mutilado quasi continuos, mal estomago, devilidad, y males de Nerbios de qe. padese, la imposi-

bilitan para siempre de poder desempeñar la tierna e importante obligación de criar a sus pechos los hijos qe. pueda tener." Ibid., fol. 27v.

169. Ibid., fols. 26–28.

170. Ibid., fols. 74–75. According to the testimony of don Pedro de Aycinena, María Contán's son was also for a time suckled by a ladina; see ibid. fol. 22v.

171. AGCA A2/153/2951.

172. AGCA A1/154/3063, fols. 72–75.

173. Ibid., fol. 2.

174. The same has been shown for the Andes in Premo 2000.

175. AGCA A3/1603/26416 (the Cruz-Pérez household is number 95). The record is from 1700.

176. This history of Francisca García's life is based on AGCA A1/2958/27971.

177. For a discussion of advantages that Indian women in sixteenth-century Peru could gain through associations with urban Spanish society, albeit often in menial positions such as domestic service and prostitution, see Burkett 1978. On indigenous child domestic service in sixteenth-century Guatemala, see Sherman 1979, 210–211, and Herrera 2003, 159–161.

178. On the ways that Indians used cultural and ethnic mestizaje to lessen their and their children's tribute burdens, see Lutz 1994, 49–62. Some Indians of Ciudad Vieja were exonerated from tribute based on their or their ancestors' role in the Conquest (see Matthew 2012). The record on Fracisca García Victoria does not clarify whether her family was exempt.

179. Her husband was Simeón Vásquez, described in her litigation as "ladino natural de Nueva Guatemala" and "uno de los sacristanes" of the Sagrario parish. The word *ladino* was rarely used alone to describe individuals in Nueva Guatemala (though it was used to describe rural people, particularly groups). In urban usage, *ladino* was normally part of the term *indio ladino*, meaning an Indian who spoke Spanish. Almost anyone named Simeón in late colonial Guatemala was of Indian ancestry, and the fact that Vásquez is identified as "one of the sacristans" suggests that he was one of a group of the sacristan's assistants among whom duties rotated. On rotational duties among the sacristan's Indian assitants (also called *sacristanes*) in eighteenth-century Mexico, see Taylor 1996, 332–333.

180. AGCA A1/2958/27971.

181. Ibid.

182. García noted that she had named the houses where she had worked in a separate *escrito*, which I have not located.

183. AGCA A1/2958/27971.

184. Archbishop don Pedro Cortés y Larraz reported upon his 1768 *visita* to Almolonga (also called Ciudad Vieja) that the residents' "maternal language is Mexican [that is, Nahuatl], and without being ignorant of it they all understand and freely speak Castilian with as much mastery as the maternal language." See Cortés y Larraz 1958 vol. 1, 38 and 41. On dates of the visita to Ciudad Vieja, see p. x of the introduction by Adrián Recinos.

185. I borrow this point from Stern 1995, 258.

186. One son is mentioned in her lawsuit; I have not definitively identifed him or any other children of hers in later records.

187. For examples, see Sherman 1979, 210–211; Herrera 2003, 160; and Lutz 1994, 60. On northern Mexico, see McCaa 1984, 482. On Peru, see Premo 2005, 54, and Graubart 2007, 63.

188. McCreery 1994, 112.

189. Pinto Soria 1986, 120 and 155n80; Grandin 2000, 72–74; and Hawkins 2004, 216.

190. Grandin 2000, 72–74, and McCreery 1989.

191. Various historians have made this point; see, for example, Woodward 1994 and Wortman 1982, 183. On a parallel pattern among the Yucatec Maya communities in Mexico, see Farriss 1984, 377–380.

192. On abolition of the decline of indigenous political autonomy (but increased interdependence between Indian and Hispanic political authority) in nineteenth-century Quetzaltenango, see Grandin 2000, chap. 6.

CHAPTER 2

1. Palomo de Lewin 1992, 56.

2. On the chronology and numbers of slave imports, see Lutz 1994, 162, and Lokken 2004, 45–48. See also Smith 1959, 189–190; MacLeod 2008, 190–191 and 298; and Fiehrer 1979.

3. Lutz 1994, 87–88.

4. This pattern was general for Latin America; see Andrews 2004, 41, Table 1.1.

5. For overviews of these explanations, see Andrews 2004, 37–38, and Schwartz 1977, 70.

6. On small-scale rebellion, see Lokken 2004. A larger rebellion apparently was planned in San Salvador in 1625; see Smith 1959, 189.

7. Studies of slave emancipation elsewhere in Spanish America show similar patterns; see for example Gudmundson 1984; Scott 1985; Aguirre 1993; Hünefeldt 1994; Díaz 2000; Restall 2009; and Lohse 2010.

8. For an overview of Iberian slavery, see Lockhart and Schwartz 1983, 17–19 and 26–28.

9. The idealized model of cultural integration has been modified somewhat by recent scholarship; for discussion see Blumenthal 2009, 3 and 3n6.

10. On the beginnings of racial difference as a basis for enslavement, see Sweet 1997 and Blumenthal 2009, 270–277.

11. Indigo estates may also have employed large slave communities, especially in the province of San Salvador. See Smith 1959, 189.

12. The mother was likely Juliana Rodas, identified in 1775 as a slave of Dardón, as the widow of Juan Pascual Peña, and as mother of the slave Juan Peña who was buying his freedom (AGCA A1/900/9393, fols. 522–523). Juan Pascual Peña was the estate's mayordomo in 1765 (AGCA A2/40/830).

13. AGCA A3/227/4152. Palomo said the ingenio was "four leagues distant from the pueblo of San Pedro Pinula, and that of Jalapa," suggesting a location in today's departamento of Jalapa. Gall identifies a modern-day *aldea* called Ingenio de Ayarza in Jalapa; at this aldea are the ruins of a colonial-era estate known locally to have been a "valuable *finca* [estate]" called the Ingenio de Ayarza (Gall 1976–1983 vol. 2, 318–319). (This is not the town of Ayarza, which is located

in the northeastern part of the departamento of Santa Rosa.) On the number of slaves, Palomo noted that he had bought the ingenio with some 100 slaves (AGCA A1/379/7849). His slaves appear frequently in sale records in the period's notarial books and in the emancipation registries of 1824 (AGCA B/1505/36042 and 36043).

14. AGCA A1/2556/20577 (deposition of the Alcalde Mayor); see also Sherman 1979, 251.

15. Palomo de Lewin 1992, 139. The same had been true in the seventeenth century (Lokken 2010).

16. For lists of the Crown's slaves at Omoa, see AGCA A3/1287/22144 (year 1771); AGCA A3/1772/28371 (year 1773); and AGCA A3/1324/22332 (year 1793). On wages to free workers at Omoa (including the midwife who attended slave births), see AGCA A3/1287/22142 and A3/1939/30117. On the Crown's purchase of these slaves in the 1760s, see Palomo de Lewin 1992, 54; on social organization, see Cáceres 2010.

17. Lutz 1994, 242.

18. Ibid.

19. Slaves also were able to appeal to the Inquisition; for studies of Mexican slaves' Inquisition cases, see for example Bennett 2003 and Owensby 2005.

20. On slaves' knowledge of colonial legal protections in Peru, see O'Toole 2012, chap. 5, especially 156.

21. Alfonso X 1844.

22. Ibid., 3a. Partida, Título II, Leyes VIII and IX; 4a. Partida, Título XXI, Ley VI. For commentary on the impact of the Siete Partidas on slavery in colonial Peru, see Bowser 1974, 273–274.

23. *Recopilación* 1791, 362 (libro VII, título V, ley viii).

24. AGCA A1/900/9393, fols. 522–523; and AGCA A2/40/830.

25. A fourth case is from 1740, in AGCA A1/5357/45277.

26. AGCA A1/5359/45292 (year 1773). The slave was María Rosa Monzón; the owner was Juan de Bacaro.

27. AGCA A1/2870/26226 and A1/1676/10311/fols. 35–36. Medina's petition was filed December 24, 1819; she would have been liberated in the 1824 general emancipation if not sooner.

28. AGCA A1/2296/16824. The record does not indicate the number of family members or their individual prices, except that the total price was increased by 50 pesos because of the birth of the baby.

29. Testimony of José María Loaisa, June 8, 1819 (AGCA A1/2556/20577). Loaisa reckoned it had been five or six years since the earlier appeal; Friar Andrés Pintelos recalled in 1818 that the slaves had petitioned in 1810. I am uncertain whether the two men were recalling the same appeal or two different ones. Regardless, the pattern of repeated appeals and concesssions is clear. The 1810 appeal was presumably the one that resulted in a codified agreement that year, as presented in Gudmundson 2003.

30. On the forced Black Carib (Garífuna) migration to Central America, see Gonzalez 1988 and Kerns 1997.

31. On livestock and pasturage, see the 1810 agreement in Gudmundson 2003.

32. The negotiation bears parallels to those of some slave communities in Cuba and Brazil; see Díaz 2000 and Schwartz 1977.

33. These previous accords about punishment, wages, and workload are referenced by the four slave complainants, the administrator of the hacienda, and Ayuntamiento's síndico in the 1818–1819 litigation (AGCA A1/2556/20577). Some of the same points are specified in the 1810 agreement (Gudmundson 2003).

34. On a parallel scenario on South Carolina rice plantations, where slaves through ongoing conflict with slaveholders helped shaped the task system and volume of work, see Morgan 1998, 179–187. See also Carney 2001, 99-100.

35. Pintelos statement, July 8, 1819, AGCA A1/2556/20577.

36. Loaisa appealed to the Audiencia on June 8, 1819; González petitioned the ayuntamiento on July 7, 1819. Ibid.

37. Miguel González, petition of April, 1820. Ibid.

38. On a similar pattern in Peru, see Hünefeldt, 1994, 121–124, and Premo 2005, 235–240.

39. AGCA A1/2859/25856; A1/5359/45303; A1/5359/45300; A1/177/3633; A1/2791/24470; A1/2760/23915; A1/2862/25957; and AGCA A1/2870/26226.

40. This point has been made also for other regions in the Americas; see for example Berlin and Morgan 1993, 23–32, and Hünefeldt 1994, 68.

41. For a small sample of the enormous historical scholarship on the gendered nature of slavery and emancipation, see Schwalm 1997; Morgan 2004; Robertson and Robinson 2008; and Miller 2008.

42. Petition of Juana Loaisa, February 7, 1820. This is one of the lawsuits contained in AGCA A1/2556/20577.

43. Ibid.

44. See the petition of Miguel González, ibid.

45. The alcalde mayor testified in the case brought by José María Loaisa, ibid.

46. AGCA A1/2859/25856.

47. The hacienda was mentioned by Cortés y Larraz in his 1769 visit to Zacapa (Cortés y Larraz 1958 vol 1., 279). In the early twentieth century, a small *aldea* called Pata Galana existed at or near the former hacienda's location (Gall 1976–1983 vol. 2, 904). Today's community of Pata Galana, presumably the same, is an aldea of the municipio of Río Hondo in the departament of Zacapa.

48. AGCA A1/2859/25856, statement of Marcelo Rivera y Córdova dated Aug. 22, 1783.

49. Palomo de Lewin 1992, 109.

50. AGCA A1/2805/24662 (see also A1/1672/10307, fols. 374–375); A1/2863/25604; B6.17/4125/92802; A2/249/5429"A"; and A1/2791/24470. On reduced price, see AGCA A1/2788/24449 and A1/2867/26095.

51. For example, AGCA A1/2870/26226 and A1/5440/46600.

52. AGCA A1/4069/32109 (year 1774). The nature of Estrada's demands is not specified.

53. AGCA A1/2864/26012.

54. AGCA A1/379/7849.

55. AGCA A1/139/2732.

56. Ibid.; and A1/4303/34471. Olavarrieta served in the same house for decades, and neighbors often referred to the household by her name rather than that of its owner don Pedro Martínez. Martínez apparently delegated extensive responsibilities to Olavarrieta. She represented him in court in a dispute with a neighbor, don Manuel Sánchez, in 1789 (AGCA A1/4005/30417). She was still Martínez's housekeeper when called in 1808 as witness in another case; she was named as Juana Apolonia Olavarrieta y Retana and said she was over age seventy (AGCA A1/4440/37098).

57. AGCA A1/4358/35390.

58. AGCA A1/5359/45294 and A1/379/7849.

59. AGCA A1/2296/16823; A2/157/3047; and A1/939/9432, fols. 77–78.

60. AGCA A1/2861/25906.

61. On Santiago from 1723 to 1773, see Palomo de Lewin 1992, 107–109.

62. For example, see AGCA A1/5359/45292, statement of don Juan de Bacaro.

63. For example, AGCA A1/15/383.

64. On a similar phenomenon in Cuba and discussion of legal theory, see de la Fuente 2007. The papel de venta also appears in various documents in Puerto Rico; see Nistal Moret 1984, 165, 253, 256, and 276. On Peru, Aguirre (1993, 87) notes that a slave who convinced his master to sell him might be sent to "seek a buyer" (*buscar comprador*).

65. AGCA A1/2859/25847 and A1/5358/45280. At least one record connotes a request made in the midst of a conflict that underlay the punishment (AGCA A1/2862/25957).

66. AGCA A1/2863/26000; A1/4358/35390; A1/2799/24580; A1/2859/25847; and A1/2862/25957. On slaves' manipulation of process of their sale in other historical contexts, see Johnson 1999, especially 187, and Blumenthal 2009, 71–72.

67. AGCA A1/2775/24209 and A1/2997/28616.

68. AGCA B1/1505/36042.

69. AGCA A1/1675/10318, fols. 192–193; A1/2800/24593; A1/2556/20577 (papers containing the suit by Juana Loaisa); and A1/2895/25847.

70. On sixteenth-century Guatemala, see Herrera 2003, 126. On the period 1723–1773, see Palomo de Lewin 1992.

71. AGCA A1/2859/25854 (year 1781).

72. AGCA A1/2862/25957 (years 1792–1793).

73. AGCA A1/5284/44380 (year 1803).

74. On coartación in Cuba, see Scott 1985 and de la Fuente 2007.

75. AGCA A1/2870/26226 and A1/2861/25907.

76. On the Marqués de Aycinena, his extended family, and their circle of influence, see Brown 1997 and Woodward 1999, 74–75 and 84–91.

77. AGCA A1/2861/25920.

78. AGCA A1/2800/24593.

79. AGCA A1/4068/32079.

80. AGCA A1/2792/24480.

81. AGCA A1/2861/25907 (year 1796).

82. AGCA A1/2862/25957 (year 1789).

83. AGCA A1/5359/45295.

84. AGCA A1/2772/24146. The initial slaveowner in the case was don Andrés Saavedra, the alcalde mayor of Sacatepéquez.

85. Ibid.

86. AGCA A1/15/383; A1/2769/24051; A1/5359/45303; A1/2788/24449; A1/2869/26175; and A1/4311/34626. On a similar phenomenon in Peru, see Hünefeldt 1994, 131. Although I have found allegations of severe beatings of an eighteen-year-old male slave (AGCA A1/5358/45280), I have not found documentation in Guatemala of sexual abuse of male slaves. Nevertheless, I would argue that men's reproductive role as fathers was exploited by slaveholders as they took ownership of children born into slavery.

87. AGCA A1/4311/34626.

88. See Chapter 4.

89. "Si esta incauta joven no hubiera sido tan facil, nada le sucedería." AGCA A1/2869/26175.

90. On sexual violence against free women, see Komisaruk 2008.

91. "Por desde luego se creyó, que condesendiendo y fecundarse era el camino mas seguro para libertarse."

92. AGCA A1/2869/26175. Her attorney was don Juaquín Eduardo Mariscal, who had also served as procurador for Ramos. The slaveholder, doña Petronila de la Cerda, asked him to take charge of the suit on her behalf when she left town, and he agreed; another attorney was then named for Manuela Ramos.

93. AGCA A1/5359/45303. A daughter of María del Carmen Beteta, Juliana, claimed her liberty in 1824 (AGCA B1/1505/36042); I cannot confirm that Juliana was the same daughter as in the 1821 suit, which does not name the daughter.

94. AGCA A1/2788/24449.

95. "Recabó de ella su prostitución con la promesa de darla el dinero para que se libertase; siendo tan verosimil el que quien desease conocer carnalmente a una esclava la propusiese este estímulo, que sin duda es el mayor" (AGCA A1/4311/34626, statement of Juan Lázaro de Rojas).

96. AGCA A1/2769/24051.

97. For example, see AGCA A1/2775/24209 and A1/5358/45280.

98. On violence against slaves and terror in the United States, see Hartman 1997.

99. The term *rape* had no Spanish-language equivalent in the period studied here. On the absence of a concept equivalent to modern notions of rape, see Komisaruk 2008.

100. On the problems with the notion of "slave agency" and "voluntary" choices see Johnson 2003.

101. AGCA A1/15/383. Her petition was dated May 13, 1791.

102. The history of Ana María Villalonga y Sabater is based on AGCA A1/2561/20642 and A1/15/383.

103. The history of the family of María Apolinaria Castellanos is based on AGCA A1/2487/19695, A1/2859/25850, A1/2869/26175, A1/4311/34626, A1/4560/38993, A1/5359/45299, and B/1505/36043.

104. "Estubo Maria huyendo de mí, tratando y comerciando para sí, como si fuese libre, y dueña de su voluntad sin darme ni medio real." AGCA A1/5359/45299, letter from Barcena dated February 27, 1785.

105. Ibid.

106. Ibid., letter from Barcena dated February 27, 1785.

107. AGCA A1/2487/19695.

108. Although I have not located a document stating Manuela Ramos's age, the fact that she and her brother were sold along with their mother in the mid-1770s suggests that they were probably still dependent on their mother's care. Ramos was presumably a teenager, or perhaps in her early twenties, by 1786 or 1787 when José Estanislao Lara, then around age nineteen, proposed marriage to her. At that time Ramos was pregnant with María de la Asunción. See AGCA A1/4311/34626.

109. AGCA A1/2487/19695.

110. AGCA A1/4311/34626, testimony of doña Francisca Corona.

111. Ibid.

112. Ibid.

113. Ibid.

114. "Pues mirando que se me ha costado la vida y que la criatura quedara pasando trabajos y esclava me he valido por el medio de mi madre para que este sujeto no se quede como hasta la fecha se haya manejando mas de mil pesos y con casa propia la que tiene en la misma calle real" (Ibid., petition of Manuela Ramos, May 11, 1793).

115. Ibid., statement of the *escribano receptor* of the Audiencia, Joseph de Echeverría, April 1, 1794.

116. Ibid., petition of don Pedro Ayau, July 14, 1794.

117. Ibid.

118. At one point in her suit against don Pedro Ayau, Manuela Ramos indicated that she was a slave in the house of doña Josefa Corona and don Ignacio Guerra. It is not clear whether Corona and Guerra lived in the same house or merely shared a patio (a common configuration in the city, especially during the years shortly following the relocation). Or perhaps Guerra was in the process of purchasing Ramos from Corona in installments, making the young woman the slave of both for a time. Clearly Guerra was not married to Corona; each was married to someone else at the time of Ramos's suit. Ayau indicated that, at the time he and Manuela Ramos were living in the same house, it was the house of don Agustín Zavala and his wife doña Josefa Corona (ibid.). A few years earlier Ramos's mother had sought for her to be sold to don Francisco Feijóo, son of doña Juliana López Marchán, who was likely a relative of don Ignacio Guerra Marchán (see AGCA A1/2859/25850). Don Ignacio Guerra Marchán became the executor of don Francisco Feijóo's will (AGCA A1/2760/23915). By 1814, Ramos was a slave of doña Petronila de la Cerda, the widow of don Ignacio Guerra Marchán (see AGCA A1/2869/26175); apparently, Ramos's transfer from Corona to Guerra Marchán had been made complete.

119. Although the exact date of Ramos's transfer is not known, Corona's husband sold Ramos's daughter to Guerra Marchán in 1789 (see AGCA

A1/4560/38993). Since the child was only a toddler at the time, the mother was probably transferred concurrently.

120. AGCA A1/2869/26175.

121. Ibid.

122. AGCA B/1505/36043.

123. The history of the family of Juan Evangelista Castellanos is based on AGCA A1/2760/23915 and B/1505/36043.

124. AGCA A1/2487/19695.

125. AGCA A1/2760/23915.

126. Ibid. Castellanos said it had been twenty-five years; the executor's attorney dated Fejóo's acquisition of Castellanos to the time after the earthquake, which would indicate a period of twenty-two or twenty-three years.

127. Ibid.; statement of don José Ballesteros, June 11, 1801.

128. Ibid.

129. AGCA B/1505/36043.

130. AGCA A1/4396/36055.

131. The history of Salgado and her children is based on AGCA A1/5359/45296; A1/149/2867; and A1/4274/34090.

132. The master silversmith was don Felix Andreu. For his testament and the lengthy litigation over his estate, see AGCA A1/2481/19606.

133. AGCA A1/149/2867.

134. The authenticity of his signature is confirmed by its multiple appearances in the record, in a consistent hand and with spelling ("Albarez") different from that of the notary ("Alvares").

135. AGCA A1/4274/34090.

136. Gómez 2003. On Mexico, see Vinson 2001 and von Germeten 2006.

137. AGCA B1/1505/expedientes 36042 and 36043. I have counted those age fourteen and over as adults.

138. On this construction of *ladino*, see Grandin 2000, 84 and 239, and Lokken 2010, 46–48.

CHAPTER 3

1. Lutz 1994, 110, Table 9, and 141–154.

2. On mestizaje and hispanization of tributaries within the capital city, see Lutz 1994, chap. 3.

3. Lutz 1994, 242.

4. Langenberg 1981, 153 (Table 17) and 157 (Table 19). On the problem of distinguishing landless workers from landholders (both labeled "labradores"), see Langenberg 1981, 149n11. The urban hog dealers may have been raising a few pigs at their homes, but mostly they were bringing animals on the hoof from outside the city. The urban component of their operations seems to have mainly focused on slaughter and sale; for example, see AGCA A1/4435/36958, testimony of Nicolasa de Lara. On hog-raisers at Santiago, see Lutz 1976, 565 and 592–593n41.

5. On early Santiago, see Lutz 1994, chap. 1–2.

6. Ibid., 110. The four communities counted were Jocotenango, San Felipe, Santa Isabel, and San Cristóbal.

7. On gente ordinaria, see Lutz 1994, 171. On naborías, see Sherman 1979, 102–111, and Lutz 1994, 54.

8. Ibid., 110.

9. Ibid., chap. 5 and appendices 1–2.

10. Ibid., 87 (table 6).

11. Ibid., 67, 70.

12. Ibid., 56–61, 95.

13. Ibid., 67 (table 2), 110, 242.

14. Ibid., 242.

15. The first house-by-house census, taken in 1604, lists only vecinos; see Jickling 1982 and Joba 1984, 10 and passim. Earlier estimates also focused on vecinos; see Lutz 1994, 79–80 and 104–106.

16. AGCA A1/210/5002.

17. A1/55/1535.

18. On the significance of categories embedded in censuses and other government statistical inquiries, see Scott 1999, chap. 6.

19. An exception is the Candelaria Parish census of 1820, carried out by the parish priest (Langenberg 1981, 252 and 439). The one 1805 record is for barrio la Habana, taken as part of a vaccination program; to be sure, for this purpose calidad was irrelevant. Single-barrio reports for 1796 include AGCA A1/5263/44221; A1/2752/23, 682; A1/5344/45056; for 1805, A1/4807/41,466; for 1813, AGCA A1/2752/23683; for 1819, B84.3/1130/25982 and A1/5912/50619; for 1820, A1/1811/11960 and A1/1812/11965.

20. AGCA B/1130/25982. Only one record from the capital remains from that year, for the barrio del Perú. The record registers only men, though not surprisingly it indicates that the huge majority—269 of 308—were ladinos, and only thirty-nine were españoles.

21. The intendancy reform divided the city into six *cuarteles* (districts), each with two barrios (Langenberg 1981, 42). For a list of *cuarteles* and their barrios and a map, see Langenberg 1981, 42–44, and Sagastume Paiz 2008, 66–67.

22. The 1824 census reports are archived in the AGCA under Signatura B84 as follows: 1130/25977 (barrio de San Sebastián), 25978 (barrio de Capuchinas), 25979 (barrio de la Habana), 25980 (barrios del Ojo de Agua and Santa Rosa), 25981 (barrios del Tanque and el Marrullero), 25983 (barrio del Perú); 1131/25984 (barrio de San Juan de Dios), 25989 (barrio de San José), 25990 (barrio del Sagrario), and 25991 (barrio Escuela de Cristo).

23. Mörner 1967, 58.

24. Lutz 1994, 128, 137, and 163.

25. On other cities, see Cope 1994; Pescador 1992, 112–121; Calvo 1989; Kuznesof 1986; Matos Rodríguez 1999; and García González 2000, 126–128.

26. AGCA A1/210/5002. It is not clear that the reported numbers included women and children at all, other than those identified as Spaniards.

27. Lutz 1994, 111.

28. The analysis shows 148 females for every 100 males for 1796; 153 females per 100 males in 1805; and 155 females per 100 males for 1824. See Langenberg 1981, 103 and table 1.

29. Ibid., 109, Table 2. On the use of age fourteen as a cutoff, see ibid., 104–105. Also, guild records show that fourteen was typically the age at which boys were apprenticed; see Samayoa Guevara 1962.

30. Zilbermann de Luján 1987, 82–84; Lutz 1994, 49–55.

31. I thank Karen Graubart for this insight, in personal communication.

32. On Túnchez, see AGCA A1/2752/23682, fol. 6r (census of the Barrio del Tanque). The given name and surname, alias, age, marital status, and the location of the house confirm that the woman listed in this census is the same as in the court records cited below.

33. Langenberg 1981, 184, Table 38.

34. AGCA A3/2537/37179; A1/41/1014; and B84.1/1127/25848.

35. AGCA A1/5263/44221.

36. On similar considerations for the census in Mexico, see Francois 2006, 32–33.

37. Langenberg 1981, 180, Table 34. On her use of the term *Dienstmädchen* for "sirviente, etc.," see 152. The term *muchacha*, the most common word for "maid" in today's Guatemalan usage, does not appear in the late colonial records.

38. An interesting example comes from a 1798 criminal trial in AGCA A2/186/3731. An Indian woman in her twenties or early thirties from Jocotenango had been working in a private home in the capital when she was prosecuted for adultery and theft. Her employer, the former alcalde mayor, arranged for the charges to be dropped and turned her over to the custody of the Indian governor of Jocotenango on the condition that she not be allowed to leave the pueblo, "not even under the pretext of serving." Implicit in the order was the notion that domestic service was the normal purpose for which Indian women should come to the city.

39. Langenberg 1981, 173, Table 30.

40. Ibid., 155, Table 18, and 173, Table 30. On the wider variety of male occupations than female ones for both children and adults, see Langenberg 1981, 188n91.

41. There were forty men in 1796 and 218 men in 1824; see Langenberg 1981, Table 19. Langenberg distinguished between those labradores listed as owning land (whom she labeled as *bauer*, or farmer) and those not owning land (*landarbeiter*, or farm worker), with the caveat that lands may not have been reported for the censuses (149n11). In 1796, twenty-nine of the forty labradores owned land; in 1824, 113 of the 218 did (Langenberg 1981, Table 19). The term *labrador* could refer specifically to a wheat farm owner (as in a *labor de pan llevar*), but wheat farm owners in Guatemala were generally a prosperous lot and would have lived closer to the center of the city, whereas the labradores registered in the censuses were mainly living at the edges of town.

42. On mill operators, see Joba 1984, 107–108; the 1604 census (transcribed in Jickling 1982, 171–205), which lists mill owners in entries 28, 94, and 521; Herrera 2003, 123; Langenberg 1981, Table 24. Mills might be operated by a tenant rather than the owner; see A1/4220/33548 (year 1773).

43. On 1777, AGCA A3/2537/37179; on 1793, Samayoa Guevara 1962, 169.

44. Bauer 1990 and Pilcher 1998, 106.

45. An interesting example is the women's jail, where inmates' diet included tortillas, meat, bread, and sometimes plantains "and other things" (AGCA A1/2296/16821). See also Sagastume Paiz 2008, 91. Indian girls in the school at the Beaterio de Nuestra Señora del Rosario ate tortillas at midday with the day's main meal; see Saravia V. 1972, 119.

46. Bauer 1990, 17, and Berman 2007.

47. On public fountains and washing facilities in Santiago, see Luján Muñoz 1982, 159–163; on Nueva Guatemala, see Juarros 1981 [1818], 55, and Langenberg 1981, 58–59. For a late colonial map showing a public washing facility, see Galicia 1976, 129 (item f, "Tanque de Labaderos Públicos"); the same image appears with less clarity in Zilbermann 1987, 247, with source cited on page xi as AGI Mapas y Planos, Guatemala 476. Today's public water system in Guatemala City is spotty, with water running (or trickling) only a few hours a day; water has to be stored for use at other hours. It is not known whether the colonial-era supply was also irregular.

48. For example, conqueror Pedro de Alvarado's 1524 letters describe heavy rains at Yscuintepeque (Escuintla); see Restall and Asselbergs 2007, 38–39. In 1541, heavy rains caused the mudslides that ruined that first city of Santiago (Almolonga); see Lutz 1994, 7 and 258n24.

49. For a description of sewage and drainage problems, see Langenberg 1981, 60–61 and 388–389, and Sagastume Paiz 2008, 82–83.

50. Studying Santiago Chimaltenango (in Guatemala's northwestern highlands) in 1937, anthropologist Charles Wagley (1941, p. 26) commented that many women were at the springs for "two or three hours every day gossiping and visiting as they work."

51. Langenberg 1981, 180, Table 34.

52. Herrera 2003, 92.

53. On beef peddlers, see Lutz 1994, 151 and 305n53; on other trades, see Samayoa 1962, 190–192.

54. Samayoa Guevara 1962, 190–192. On textile and clothing workers, see also Langenberg 1981, 183, Table 37. On bakers, see AGCA A1/2873/26313.

55. Arrom 1985b, 27–28.

56. Samayoa Guevara 1962, 190–192. On bakers, see also AGCA A1/2873/26313. Teachers are chronicled later in this chapter.

57. On Mexico City, see Pérez Toledo 1996, 92–93; on Arequipa, Peru, see Chambers 1999, 54–55.

58. Samayoa Guevara 1962, 43–44 (quotation, 43).

59. On the opening of the guilds to castas, see Samayoa Guevara 1962, 177–181.

60. In contrast, master craftsmen in Mexico City were often called "don" (Kicza 1983, 207–208).

61. AGCA A2/157/3046.

62. AGCA A1/148/2835. Luis de Avila may have been a relative of silversmith Antonio Avila, already mentioned, who was alternately named in the record as Dávila—a contraction from de Avila.

63. AGCA A2/154/2997. The employee was Pedro Nolasco de Avalos, a mestizo, age thirty.

64. AGCA A1/274/5984. Matching signatures confirm that this was the same Luis de Avila. It is possible that the bakery was run by his wife, although he was named as the owner and signed for the bakery.

65. AGCA A1/5359/45296.

66. Exams were administered by one or more masters. If the applicant passed, a license and master status were conferred in an addendum written on the petition itself.

67. AGCA A1/149/2867.

68. On Guatemala's Economic Society and others in the Spanish world, see Shafer 1958 and Luque Alcaide 1962.

69. The plan and addendum appear in Samayoa Guevara 1962, 317–342.

70. As quoted in Sagastume Paiz 2008, 223.

71. Real Consulado 1810, 89.

72. Samayoa Guevara 1962, 81–85, and Pérez Toledo 1996, 88 and 98–101. The repeated passage of legislation in 1820 is likely an indication that people were not complying or that there was significant opposition. Historians of Mexico have debated whether the guilds continued to operate there; see Arrom 1985b, 298n39, and Pérez Toledo 1996, 101–102. Historians of Guatemala have noted that in any case certain structures and customs persisted from the guilds; see Samayoa Guevara 1962, 90–91, and Sagastume Paiz 2008, 237–238.

73. Few 2002, 130.

74. On Mexico, for example, see Arrom 1985b, 200; on the Andes, see Glave 1989, chap. VII.

75. Langenberg (1981, 266) suggested that about one-tenth of 1,478 sample households in the censuses employed domestic servants. However, I believe the proportion is substantially higher but that the censuses did not specify the roles of most servants. Numerous households shown in the censuses included one or more members (often female) with surnames, ages, or other descriptive data suggesting that the individuals were not related to other members of the household. Especially for women, occupations were not always listed (as noted earlier in this chapter and in Langenberg 1981, 205n121).

76. On a similar pattern in late colonial Mexico, see Stern 1995, 259, and Arrom 1985b, 188.

77. Young male household workers of any ethnicity were generally called "*mozos*" if they were teenage or older; the word *indizuelo* seems to suggest that the boy was an adolescent or younger. The term *indizuela*, though, was used to refer to women in their teens and twenties. For example, AGCA A2/153/expediente 2921 (year 1773); A2/157/3058 (year 1781); A1/4321/34803 (year 1795); B/4361/35434 (year 1799). Unfortunately there is relatively little documentation about these girls' lives compared to their large numbers in the city.

78. For comparisons with England and France, see Tilly and Scott 1978. On the United States, see Dudden 1983, 45. On Mexico, see Arrom 1985b, 184.

79. Further, a Spanish cabildo official was entrusted to contract the labor of indigenous orphans; see Herrera 2003, 159–161.

80. AGCA A1/4356/35357.
81. This is the longest labor contract I have seen for late colonial Guatemala.
82. AGCA A1/2958/27971.
83. On ambiguity in treatment of offspring, adopted children, and servants in northwestern Mexico, see Shelton 2007.
84. For example, see AGCA A1/900/9393/fols. 575–579 (will of Francisca Xaviera González).
85. For example, Cayetana Obregón, age nine, was working in the home of doña Ignacia Zalvaljáuregui (AGCA A2/188/3798). On the sixteenth century, see Sherman 1979, 210–211, and Herrera 2003, 160. On the seventeenth century, see Lutz 1994, 60. On similarly young Indian children in domestic service in Parral, Mexico, see McCaa 1984, 482; and on Peru, see Premo 2005, 54; Graubart 2007, 63; and Vergara 2007.
86. On the complex relationships between dress and native identities in colonial Peru, see Graubart 2007, chap. 4. In Guatemala, clothing styles remain a most visible indicator of cultural identity, especially for girls and women. On Maya clothing and identity, see Otzoy 1996 and Nelson 1999, especially chap. 5.
87. Historians studying the Andes as well as Central America have seen both advantages and exploitiveness in Indian girls' and women's positions as domestic servants. For a more positive spin, see Sherman 1979, 210, and Burkett 1978; a more negative view appears in Glave 1989, chap. VII, and Alvarez Aragón 1996. More recently, studies of Peru have suggested that the placement of children from indigenous communities in service in the Spanish cities may have amounted to a strategy for social mobility; see Graubart 2007, 63–70, and Vergara 2007.
88. Langenberg 1981, 203.
89. On the economic lives of migrant domestic servants in Peru, see Graubart 2007, 65–70 and 76.
90. Langenberg 1981, table 45.
91. In Guatemala City today, some lavanderas come to pick up laundry and take it out, or they have their clients drop it off; others come into the client's home to do the wash there if the water supply is plentiful.
92. AGCA A1/2775/24209. It is possible that Cañas lived in the employers' house; nothing was recorded of her husband's whereabouts.
93. AGCA A1/4400/36143. Gálvez was living in Santa Isabel, on the eastern edge of the capital.
94. On tortilleras from Jocotenango selling in Santiago, see AGCA A2/40/830 (note deposition of doña Manuela Dardón); on those from Almolonga (Ciudad Vieja) and nearby towns selling in Santiago, see Cortés y Larraz 1958 vol. 1, 38. On tortilleras from Jocotenango selling in Nueva Guatemala, see AGCA A1/154/3063, fols. 73–75.
95. AGCA A1/4412/36409.
96. I borrow the term *self-management* from Stern 1995, 259.
97. AGCA A2/157/3061.
98. AGCA A1/4435/36958.
99. AGCA A1/4380/35717 (year 1801, Nueva Guatemala).
100. AGCA A2/185/3704 (year 1797, Nueva Guatemala).

101. On migrant working women's "uncontrolled pathways" in urban Mexico, see Stern 1995, chap. 11. On working-class migrant "women adrift" in Chicago, see Meyerowitz 1988, especially xviii.

102. Pratt 2008, 7.

103. AGCA A2/151/2844. Ajau's life comes to light in tragic circumstances—the investigation into her premature death. She was cut in a brachial artery during a scuffle with her husband and bled to death before receiving medical treatment.

104. AGCA A2/186/3731.

105. On Oaxacan Indian migrations to Guatemala (in the Spanish conquest era and again in the late seventeenth and the eighteenth centuries), see Lutz 1994, 28 and 98.

106. AGCA A1/4456/37428.

107. AGCA A1/139/2732.

108. AGCA A2/185/3704. Neither the wife's calidad nor that of the cook was recorded.

109. For a comparative discussion of domestic service as a stage in life in Europe and Latin America, see Kuznesof 1989, 19. On Mexico, see Arrom 1985b, 177–178; on Peru, Graubart 2007, 65.

110. Few 2002, 113–115.

111. The one example I have found is Isidora Morales, a slave discussed in Chapter 2.

112. Few also notes this pattern in colonial Guatemala (Few 2002, 114).

113. Gibson 1964, 255, and McCreery 1994, 109.

114. AGCA A2/250/5443.

115. Menidzábal had ties to Amatitlán (she made a trip there in early 1814), and the majority of people from Amatitlán who migrated to the capital were identified as mulatos. It would not be surprising if she had links to Amatitlán's large cattle industry; such connections could have supplied her business with beef smuggled into the capital to avoid taxes at the city slaughterhouse.

116. Cortés y Larraz (1958 vol. 2, p. 30) subsumed Cubulco's language under the category of Quiché, but today's Achí do not regard themselves as K'iche'.

117. AGCA A2/150/2821.

118. AGCA A2/186/3731. The employer was don Manuel José Pavón.

119. On servants' vulnerability in employers' homes in Brazil, see Graham 1988, 49.

120. AGCA A1/2512/19982.

121. AGCA A1/2527/20118.

122. On similar distinctions made by the Inquisition in Guatemala, see Few 2002, 114–115 and 131.

123. Ascencio's case is in AGCA A2/252/5483 and A1/5908/50410.

124. Taborga had been an alcalde de barrio in the capital in 1804 and 1805; see AGCA A1/4406/36276 and A1/4807/41466.

125. "Sostuvo su palabra añadiendo que si no sabía que le podía pegar y tenía dominio en ella, pero contestandola que quien la había dado dominio para pegarle."

126. Kellogg 2005, 60, and Castañeda 1993. On rape as a tool of the Atlantic World slave system, see Hartman 1997, chap. 3.

127. Barahona (2003, 81–93) has demonstrated for early modern Vizcaya (Spain)—where the history of conquest was in the more distant past and ethnicity presumably less marked—the importance of class and socioeconomic subordination in sexual coercion.

128. On mastery and opportunities for sexual coercion, see Block 2006, 74.

129. On terms and notions, see Komisaruk 2008, 373 and 380.

130. Ibid., 379 and 387.

131. On other regions, see Kellogg 2005, 60; Block 2006, 63–74; and Barahona 2003, 81–92. In today's Guatemala, widespread sexual violence against domestic servants is a public secret. Sexual abuse was named first among the major problems facing domestic workers in 2007 statement by the director of CENTRACAP— the Centro de Apoyo para las Trabajadoras de Casa Particular (Center for Aid to Workers in Private Households), Guatemala City; see http://tejidosypatrones.wordpress.com/2007/12/14/visita-a-centracap/ (accessed on August 5, 2011).

132. In two additional cases, the women successfully fought off their assailants (AGCA A1/4440/37101 and A2/154/2997). Notably, though, these two assaults surface obliquely, in testimony given in trials generated by other charges; see Komisaruk 2008, 389–390. Another two cases each depict seduction by an employer of his servant's teenage daughter (AGCA A1/4321/34803 and A2/185/3704, testimony of Francisca Velis). Since the girls were of marriageable age (indeed, each was considering marriage to her seducer), it does not seem appropriate to apply modern notions for age of consent, which today is eighteen in Guatemala, though lower in some Central American countries; that is, I would not with any certainty classify these two cases as rape.

133. AGCA A2/154/2976; AGCA A2/165/3271; and AGCA A1/4400/36140. Each of the three cases was brought by an immediate relative of the victim.

134. AGCA A2/188/3798.

135. AGCA A1/4435/36958.

136. Block 2006, 64.

137. AGCA A1/4372/35611.

138. AGCA A1/4440/37098; AGCA A1/2543/20362; and AGCA A2/239/5139. The daughter's name was Felipa Aragón.

139. A noblewoman called (Lady) Yoca Xonaxi Palala is named in written text on an early colonial map of Macuilsuchil, now known as San Mateo Macuilxochitl, Oaxaca (Mundy 1996, 231–232).

140. Marure Papers, MS 1131, Box 1, Folder 29.

141. Ibid., Box 2, Folder 26.

142. AGCA A3/2329/34424 and A1/4807/41466; Marure Papers, MS 1131, Box 2, Folder 13.

143. Ibid., Box 1, Folder 29; Box 2, Folder 21; and Box 3, folder 5.

144. Ibid., Box 1, Folder 15.

145. Ibid., Box 1, Folder 29.

146. The executrix, Luisa Sosa, shared a surname with the mayordomo of Carrascal's *labor*, Rafael Sosa. Both apparently had local roots near the *labor* (ibid., Box 2, Folder 21). However, I have been unable to confirm their relationship.

147. Ibid., Box 2, Folder 26.

148. AGCA A1/1763/fol. 233v; AGCA A2/19/454; AGCA A1/6940/57770; AGCA B85.1/3599/82741; and AGCA B90.3/3608/84020. Also, AGCA A1/900/9393, fols. 567–568, is similarly suggestive.

149. Marure Papers, MS 1131, Box 1, Folders 15 and 29.

150. Ibid., Box 2, Folder 26.

151. Ibid., Box 1, Folder 15.

152. Ibid., Box 1, Folder 15 and 29 (quotation is from folder 15).

153. AGCA A1/4267/34006 and A1/5488/47200.

154. AGCA A1/900/9393 fol. 567–568 (year 1775).

155. AGCA A2/239/5139.

156. AGCA A3/224/4045 and A3/226/4114. In 1784, mules were also provided for the mail; chickens, eggs, firewood, and hay were also listed as being given in tribute for the capital.

157. Lutz 1994, 22–23.

158. AGCA A1/154/3063, fols. 13–14.

159. On Mexico, see Kicza 1983, chap. 6. The term was used by Guatemalan clerk don José Grau y Zerra, who was working in the 1790s for a merchant in Comayagua; see AGCA A1/5338/44980.

160. AGCA A1/4440/37098. Coincidentally, this information was provided in the testimony of Apolonia Olavarrieta, who was the servant of don Pedro Martínez for several decades. (We have seen Olavarrieta in Chapter 2, as she housed her syphilitic fugitive slave brother.) Olavarrieta's testimony states that Bahamonde had stayed in Martínez's house as a "criado," and that Martínez had "accommodated him in [the barrio] Belén as a gardener." I have concluded that Martínez's property in Barrio del Belén was separate from his house, based on AGCA A1/4005/30417, which indicates that Martínez and Olavarrieta resided in 1789 in a house next door to that of Manuel Sánchez; and on AGCA A1/5916/50947, which locates the house of a Manuel Sánchez with the same signature on the Calle de la Merced in the barrio Candelaria. However, it is also possible that Martínez lived in Belén at the time that don Blas stayed with him in the 1770s and then moved to Candelaria.

161. AGCA A2/154/2975.

162. Haefkens 1969 [1827], 268.

163. Wortman 1982, 184–194.

164. On weavers and tailors, see Langenberg 1981, 160, table 20; on other crafts, see Langenberg 1981, tables 19–31. I exclude clergy among "trades"; 336 clergymen were indexed in the 1824 census. Langenberg also gives numbers for 1796, but these are less useful since the 1796 records survive for only three barrios, and weavers and tailors were concentrated in particular barrios. Clothing workers had also been especially numerous in early Santiago; see Herrera 2003, 76.

165. On male spinners (*hilanderos*) in Mexico, see Kicza 1983, 209, and Viquiera and Urquiola 1990, passim.

166. The numbers are from Langenberg 1981, 183, Table 37.

167. On spinning, see AGCA A1/2296/16821 (years 1775–1776), AGCA A1/2861/25904 (year 1789), and AGCA B/1131/25991 (year 1824). On food preparation, see AGCA B78.17/676/14585 (which mentions molenderas). On salary paid to the rectora, see A1/5351/45168, A1/2866/26080, and A1/5918/51069.

168. Martínez Peláez 1970, 526–530. See also Martínez Peláez 1994, 172–173; MacLeod 2008 [1973], 316–317; Lovell 1985, 108; and Hill 1992, 118.

169. On tribute requirements, see Lutz 1994, 22, and Kramer 1994, 221–223 and 247. On tailoring as exclusively male work in Mam-speaking northwestern Guatemala in the 1930s, see Wagley 1941, 26.

170. Martínez Peláez 1994, 530 and 757n286.

171. On spinning as "the great bottleneck in textile production" in preindustrial Europe, see Berman 2007, 10. Data from colonial Mexico also show greater numbers of spinners than weavers; see Viquiera and Urquiola 1990, 150–151, Cuadro III; 155; 156, Cuadro IV; 162, Cuadro V; 166–167, Cuadro VI; and 176–177, Cuadro IX.

172. Indians arriving in Guatemala from outside the city to sell thread are mentioned in the declaration of Antonia Mena against her errant husband, the mulato weaver Hipólito Vela. Mena noted that Vela and his partners in crime had the "habit" of stealing thread from these Indians. AGCA A2/151/2841.

173. Fuentes y Guzmán 1882–1883 [1690] vol. 1, 208. See also Haefkens 1969 [1827], 36.

174. AGCA A2/250/5440; A2/151/2841; A2/154/2979; A2/153/2951; A2/157/3053; A2/157/3064; and A1/4398/36121. See also Lutz 1994, 297n32.

175. AGCA A2/240/5170.

176. In theory, the Crown had prohibited the employment of Indians in textile obrajes, though such proscriptive legislation is often more suggestive of violations than efficacy. See MacLeod 2008, 207.

177. Langenberg 1981, 183, Table 37.

178. For example, María Timotea Aguilar's husband mentioned that she had some "sticks for weaving huipiles"; he was probably referring to a backstrap loom. AGCA A1/4274/34090 (deposition of Gregorio Alvarez, May 12, 1790).

179. Langenberg 1981, 184 n85). On women weavers with looms in eighteenth-century Mexico City, see Kicza 1983, 223.

180. Samayoa Guevara 1962, 191.

181. AGCA A1/900/9393, fols. 564–567.

182. AGCA A1/901/9394, fol. 437 (year 1775).

183. On the Mexican obrajes, see Salvucci 1987 and Viquiera and Urquiola 1990.

184. On a 1752 complaint by the weavers' guild about this practice, see Samayoa Guevara 1962, 187. An example is Felipe Toledo, an elderly Spaniard, originally from the San Sebastián barrio in Antigua, who had been a muleteer; see AGCA A2/232/4928 (year 1810).

185. AGCA A2/154/2970.

186. On Santiago, Lutz 1994, 297n32. On Nueva Guatemala, the 1824 census lists numerous weavers, and many as owners of looms, in San Sebastián, in AGCA B/1130/25977. A number of weavers are also listed in the 1824 census for

the barrio del Perú (AGCA B/1130/25983) and barrios del Tanque and del Marullero (AGCA B/1130/ 25981).

187. Lutz 1994, 297n32.

188. Dyers are absent in records from sixteenth and early seventeenth-century Santiago; see for example Herrera 2003, 76, and Samayoa Guevara 1962, 39.

189. MacLeod 2008 [1973], 179–181 and 185–186 on indigo and 170–175 on cochineal. For examples of Indian laborers on a late colonial indigo estate in Guatemala, see AGCA A3/227/4146 and AGCA A3/227/4166.

190. On the twentieth century, see Osborne 1935, 50–55.

191. AGCA A2/153/2939; A1/4332/34821; and A1/4445/37235.

192. AGCA A2/157/3061.

193. AGCA A2/250/5440.

194. Langenberg 1981, Table 72, gives data on tailors' ethnic identities based on an 1820 census of the Candelaria parish, reporting that 12.5 percent of tailors were Spanish, 4.7 percent mestizo, 9.4 percent Indian, 71.9 percent ladino, and 1.6 percent mulatto or black. The "ladino" group probably was constituted by people of mixed or unknown ancestry. The predominance of mixed ancestry among tailors is confirmed in my random sample of court and notarial records from 1765 to 1824, in which calidad is stated for nineteen tailors. Of these nineteen, six are identified as mulato, one alternately as mulato libre and pardo, three as pardo, two as castizo, four as mestizo, and three as Indian, as follows: Domingo Ramírez, mulato, AGCA A1/5499/47343; Simón Flores, mulato, AGCA A2/233/4962; Roberto José Mendia, mulato libre, AGCA A2/154/2975; Mariano Castellanos Santa Cruz, mulato libre, AGCA A1/5499/47343; Ramón Burgos, mulato libre, AGCA A2/157/3081; Teodoro Revolorio, mulato libre, AGCA A2/203/4147; Leandro Carabantes, mulato or pardo libre, AGCA A2/157/3052; Gregorio Alvarez, pardo, AGCA A1/4274/34090; Rafael Vicente Pineda, pardo libre, AGCA A1/4456/37428; Bonifacio Rogel, pardo, AGCA A2/185/3704; Juan Pimientel, castizo, AGCA A2/154/2954; Miguel Gerónimo Lobo, castizo, AGCA A2/204/4166; Luciano Alvarez, mestizo, AGCA A1/4380/35720; Santiago Mendoza, mestizo, AGCA A1/4335/35012; Alejandro Iriarte, mestizo, AGCA A2/157/3050; José Madea, mestizo, AGCA A2/152/2906; José María Juárez, indio de Ciudad Vieja, AGCA A1/4400/36144; Manuel de Zea, "indio cacique del barrio de Mexicanos de Cd. Real, Chiapas, residente en Nueva Guatemala," AGCA A2/204/4166; and José Nicaso Telles, indio de Santa Isabel, AGCA A2/243/5268. Additionally, two tailors whose calidad is not noted in the record likely would have been classified as mulato or pardo; one was the son of a free mulata (Manuel Antonio, AGCA A1/895, fols. 188–189), the other a former slave (Julián Aguilar, AGCA B/1505/36043).

195. The known former slaves were Julián Aguilar and Gregorio Alvarez, both described in Chapter 2.

196. Sources on the prehispanic period recorded in sixteenth-century Mexico include the Florentine Codex and the Tetzcoco Dialogues (see Restall, Sousa, and Terraciano 2005, 219 and 222). For evidence on weaving in a 1583 Kekchí Maya will from Cobán (in Guatemala's Verapaz region), see Restall, Sousa, and Terraciano 2005, 117. On twentieth-century Guatemala, see Ehlers 2000, 46–49 and chap. 5, and Wagely 1941. See also Kellogg 2005, 112–113.

197. Kramer 1994, 221–223 and 247.

198. Samayoa Guevara 1962, 25; and Herrera 2003, 165.

199. Seamstresses using the title *doña* included doña Teresa Toledo, AGCA A2/232/4928, and doña María Josefa García, AGCA A1/4335/35012.

200. For example, AGCA A1/2859/25856 (see the petition from Marcelo Rivera y Córdova dated August 22, 1783, with statements about the slave Gertrudis) and AGCA A1/5359/45296 (see statement dated January 22, 1778, from don Juan Manuel de Zelaya about having purchased a slave as costurera).

201. On state recognition of women's expertise in cigarette making, see AGCA A3/1525/25279 (year 1776).

202. Langenberg 1981, Tables 37 and 38.

203. Samayoa Guevara 1962, 186.

204. Ibid., 190–191.

205. Tanck Estrada 1977, 160–168; Arrom 1985b, 17–18 and 171–172; and Premo 2005, 82.

206. AGCA B/4361/35434, deposition of Bernarda Amaya, September 1798.

207. On convents, see Langenberg 1981, 74 n229.

208. The colegio for elite girls had operated under various names, administrations, and roofs since opening in 1563; often it was simply called the "Colegio de Niñas." See Ciudad Suárez 1996; Saravia V. 1972, 113–116 and 125–127; Lutz 1994, 100. The beaterios were those of Nuestra Señora del Rosario ("Beatas Indias"), Belén, and Santa Rosa; see Saravia V. 1972, 117–132. On the existence of the Beaterio de Santa Rosa as late as 1799, see AGCA B/4361/35434. There was also a school for Indian girls in Santa Catarina Pinula, evidently emphasizing manual crafts; see Salazar 1951, vol. 2, 265; Samayoa Guervara 1962, 67; and Saravia V. 1972, 134–139.

209. Both these factors were mentioned as reasons for the founding of the Colegio de la Visitación in 1795; AGCA A1/16/431, fol. 6.

210. Saravia V. 1972, 107–110; and Langenberg 1981, 74. As early as mid-sixteenth century, three men were working as private teachers in Santiago (Herrera 2003, 98–99). On schools at Santiago, see Langenberg 1981, 317 n218.

211. Samayoa Guevara 1962, 153–154. By contrast, in Mexico City there were efforts to regulate and license female teachers in the late colonial era (Tanck Estrada 1977, 87–130 and 161–165).

212. Except where otherwise noted, the account of Mijangos is based on AGCA B/4361/35434.

213. AGCA A1/5263/44221 (census for barrio de la Habana). The Mijangos household is the fourteenth household listed. María Mijangos identified Mariano Mijangos as her brother in her testimony of October 9, 1798, in AGCA B/4361/35434. A 1777 inventory of bakeries in the new capital (AGCA A3/2537/37179) lists a woman simply as "la Mijangos"—as the maestra María Magdalena Mijangos was later known—among bakery owners in the new capital. This was likely the same woman, who in 1777 would have been in her late twenties. The baking operation was small, not making dough every day.

214. AGCA B/4361/35434.

215. The record leaves unclear whether this witness, doña María Luisa González, was working as a maestra; she may have based her statements on the compensation she gave to the teachers of her own children. Her husband was the doctor don José de Córdoba, chief physician of the Kingdom of Guatemala; theirs was an elite household that presumably did not need her salary, and in this regard she would have been exceptional among maestras.

216. The cost to parents for daughters to enroll in the beaterio is not known. In the Colegio de Niñas for the years 1801 and 1802, the monthly fee was 10 pesos (AGCA A1/296/6354). The Colegio enrolled the daughters of the city's most elite families and may have been somewhat pricier than the beaterios.

217. AGCA A1/2477/19566.

218. AGCA A1/2862/25954.

219. Doña Perfecta's predecessor remained in the office of rectora of the Colegio at least into January of 1797 (AGCA A1/54/1395). Doña Perfecta was in office, facing threat of removal, by 1801 (AGCA A1/113/4783). By March 1803, she was replaced by María Josefa Croquer (AGCA A1/54/1408).

220. AGCA A4/1/36, fols. 1 and 5, and A4/1/37.

221. On Mexico, see Tanck Estrada 1977, 166–168; Arrom 1985b, 197–198; and Lipsett-Rivera 2001, 138–139. On the point that the Enlightenment reconfigured notions ideologies of childrearing, shifting the emphasis from occupational training to literacy and "reason," see Premo 2005, 201-202.

222. The madre rectora of the colegio commented on the growing enrollment in AGCA B80.6/1080/23152. For rosters and overview of curriculum in the 1860s and 1870s, see AGCA B80.6/1085/23500; B80.6/1089/23860; and B80.6/1089/23893. Compare with an account book (with students' names) for 1801 in AGCA A1/296/6354.

223. Zilbermann de Luján 1987, 82–84.

224. On plans for the construction of the new civil and religious buildings, see Zilbermann de Luján 1987; Gellert 1990, 9–11; and Langenberg 1981, chap. 1.

225. Ibid., 154–155.

226. For Ramírez's petition, see Konetzke 1962, 530–535. His life is discussed by Ann Twinam in her forthcoming book on the purchase of whiteness and the history of castas in the Spanish Indies. On his life, see Hernández 1999, 168–172. His life and petition process are also discussed by Ann Twinam in her forthcoming book on the purchase of whiteness in the Spanish Indies. For an overview of work by Jorge Luján Muñoz on architects, builders, and social class in late eighteenth-century Guatemala, see Hernández 1999, 208n4.

227. AGCA A1/4321/34803.

228. On Ayau's contracts and illiteracy, see AGCA A1/2501/19861. On his limited language ability, see AGCA A1/4321/34803. The fact that the French-born Ayau assumed the title "don" despite his humble origins suggests that at least in his case the honorific may have correlated to physical features or coloring that appeared to others as more European than those of many local people.

229. Ibid.

230. AGCA A1/4311/34626 and A1/4321/34803.

231. On this pattern, see Lockhart 1984.

232. This account of Alcayaga and his brick-making enterprise is based on AGCA A1/60/1602. On his age and calidad, see AGCA A1/4442/37150 (his declaration dated June 26, 1808).

233. The Universidad de San Carlos de Guatemala was founded in 1676 in Santiago.

234. Alcayaga identified his nephew as Ignacio Quevedo, in testimony of June 26, 1808, AGCA A1/4442/37150. On Quevedo's work for Alcayaga and salary, and his calidad ("se cree pardo libre"), see his testimony and that of his wife Paula Martínez in AGCA A1/4397/36095.

235. The repartimientos were from San Sebastián and San Miguel el Texar, in the Valley of Chimaltenango. AGCA A3/226/4097. In 1770, a man named Prudencia Tovar, identified as a mulato resident of the barrio of San Marcos in the province of Quetzaltenango, requested and was granted a repartimiento of Indians for his estate; see AGCA A3/226/4086.

236. AGCA A1/60/1602.

237. AGCA A1/4006/30451.

238. On Alcayaga's wife, Cayetana Rogel, see AGCA A2/232/4928; A1/4442/37150; A1/4456/37435; A1/4465/37596; and A2/242/5234.

239. Langenberg (1981, 204 and 245n27) makes the point that the largest single group of artisans, weavers, had suffered from losses when their looms were destroyed in the ruin of the old capital, and that many of these men "temporarily went into other occupations," although she singles out tailoring as the trade that especially attracted these men.

240. AGCA A2/198/4048.

241. AGCA A1/4397/36095.

242. Instability is illustrated for the early 1750s, for example, by the entrance of men trained in other crafts into weaving; see Samayoa Guevara 1962, 187.

243. Viquiera Albán 1999, 97, and Stern 1995, 35.

244. AGCA A1/151/2952.

245. A classic discussion of native drinking and drunkenness and state alcohol policy in colonial Mexico is Taylor 1979, chap. 2. On colonial and early national Guatemala, see McCreery 1994, 87–89; Dunn 1999; and Reeves 2006, 115–135. See also Carey 2012 (which was a few weeks shy of publication as this book went to press).

246. I have found only two mentions of pulque in the area of the late colonial and early national-era capital. One is in a record of Vicenta García, an Indian from Ciudad Vieja identified as a *pulquera*. She and her husband, also an Indian from Ciudad Vieja, were arrested one night in 1803 when she dressed as a man and went out with him to tap their maguey plants. They ran across the alcalde of the barrio del Perú, who evidently was not fooled by the costume and found cross-dressing inappropriate. Further, the husband, José María Juárez, was carrying a knife. Under arrest, he said the knife was necessary for the "exercise of our occupation [of pulque-making]." Both García and Juárez said she had tried to disguise her gender to avoid harassment from a group of "drunken hooligans" who frequented the neighborhood. Juárez identified his occupation as tailor; one imagines he had

some extra men's clothing at home available for his wife's use. Both were released with a warning that García should thereafter dress as a woman. This case, along with the 1679 petition already mentioned, raises the possibility that pulque production may have been a specialization in Ciudad Vieja. Such specialization would mirror a pattern seen in towns near Mexico City (Taylor 1979, 49–50). García and Juárez said they sold their pulque daily to a Spanish woman, doña María de la O Borges; I have not found information about who the end consumers were. See AGCA A1/4400/36144. The other mention was in 1825 by Manuel Aldeco, who brought a maguey plant from Oaxaca to Amatitlán and begun cultivating it. He applied to the state for license to sell pulque in Amatitlán, offering "ten or twelve pesos a month," but his request was denied. See AGCA A3/1847/42378.

247. Lutz 1994, 153.

248. Wortman 1982, 140, 153, 256; Lutz 1994, 152–153, 307n67; McCreery 1994, 87; and Dunn 1999, chap. 1.

249. AGCA A3/2902/43305.

250. AGCA A3/1844/42287 and A3/1844/various expedientes. In 1822, thirty-three of forty-two licensees were women; one woman was named as doña and one of the men as don. The pattern was similar through 1825. In areas outside the capital, particularly the Petén and what is now El Salvador, men's names dominate the lists of licenses to operate chicherías. This may indicate that men were operating most of the chicherías, or it may be that in these less populous areas female chicha dealers charged their husbands or male relatives with going to the government offices to register the license and pay the tax. Study of the nineteenth-century Mam and ladino community of Ostuncalco (in what is now the department of Quetzaltenango) has shown that aguardiente producers were mainly women; see Reeves 2006, 116–123.

251. On costs and distribution of maize in Nueva Guatemala, see AGCA A3/2535/expedientes 37152 and 37156. On Santiago, see Lutz 1994, 147–148.

252. AGCA A1/4312/34658; on Luna's age and ethnicity, AGCA A1/4385/35831.

253. AGCA A1/4445/37235. Téllez was in her mid-thirties.

254. AGCA B84.1/1127/25850.

255. AGCA A2/157/3075 (report by don Lorenzo Montúfar, July 30, 1782).

256. The history of Apolonia Fuentes (alias Túnchez or Tunche) is based on AGCA A1/4068/32049; A2/157/3075; A1/4312/34658; A1/2752/23682/fol. 6; A2/187/3771/fol. 12; A1/4385/35831; A1/4445/37247; and A2/240/5152. On a clan of women named Túnchez who ran liquor stores in the new capital in the late eighteenth and early nineteenth centuries, see Hernández 1999, 81–82.

257. On prostitution in late-nineteenth- and early-twentieth-century Guatemala City, see McCreery 1986.

258. AGCA A2/187/3778. Paz's own account was elided in the record, which gives only the alcalde's statement that she "lied about everything."

259. AGCA A2/202/4125.

260. For additional cases suggestive of prostitution, see AGCA A2/187/3771; A2/200/4096, fol. 114r; and A2/202/4138, fol. 33.

261. AGCA A1/41/1014.

262. For a dispute over the appropriate schedule for drinking chocolate, see AGCA B/4361/35434. The custom of drinking chocolate had taken hold among Spaniards in Santiago as early as 1568; see Herrera 2003, 161.

263. Lutz 1994, 147–148.

264. Herrera 2003, 92, and Lutz 1994, 146. Gender of bakery owners varied across Spanish America. Women predominated in early colonial Peru (Lockhart 1994, 123), late colonial Arequipa, Peru (Chambers 1999, 52), and colonial Quito (Gauderman 2003, 89). In contrast, men predominated in Bourbon Mexico City, where bakery owners were exclusively Spanish (Kicza 1983, 187–188). Both genders appear in colonial Potosí (Mangan 2005, 102).

265. A list of bakers in a tithe account book in 1656–1657 included Spanish women and free mulatas, a free black woman, an Indian woman, and one man (a free mulato); see Lutz 1994, 146 and 302 n24.

266. This contrasts with Lima, where in the nineteenth century slaves were still being deposited in bakeries as punishment (Hünefeldt 1994, 181–182). In Guatemala, presumably women continued in a few very small enterprises making wheaten bread in their homes for sale; the term *pan de mujer* today in Guatemala connotes bread or biscuits made at home by women for informal sale, as opposed to bread made in dedicated commercial bakeries.

267. AGCA A1/4400/36140.

268. On Mexican popular lore that associated bakers with bawdiness, perhaps because of their late-night hours, see Pilcher 1998, 37–38.

269. Samayoa Guevara 1962, 232–233.

270. Ibid., 57.

271. AGCA A1/4400/36163.

272. For example, see the depositions of Tomás Rosales, Francisco Guerra, and Manuel de la Asención Martínez in AGCA A1/4312/34658.

273. AGCA A1/4436/36994.

274. Of the twenty-five bakeries inspected in 1777, three reported normally using four fanegas of flour daily; one reported using three fanegas; ten reported using two fanegas; two used one and a half; five used one; and four reported zero, indicating they did not make dough daily. More flour was used for festival days. AGCA A3/2537/37179. On Mexico City bakeries, see Kicza 1983, 187–196.

275. Samayoa Guevara 1962, 148 and 169.

276. For a discussion of the ways that residents of the Guatemalan capital conceptualized their neighborhood's locations and the ways in which they associated locations with the owners of businesses, see Hernández 1999, 85.

277. I have not been able to identify more than two or three of her family members; some of the ten people she said she was supporting may in fact have been her employees.

278. The history of doña Tomasa de Lara, her family, and her baking enterprise has been reconstructed based on AGCA A2/154/2952, A1/2466/19374, A1/148/2856, and A1/4220/33548.

279. AGCA A1/41/1014.

280. Lutz 1994, 145–146 and 301n14.

281. AGCA A1/41/1014 and Samayoa Guevara 1962, 169–170. On bakers adding maize flour to the dough to cut their costs, see Lutz 1976, 560.

282. The marks were still in use a century later; see Samayoa Guevara 1962, 169–170, and Lutz 1994, 147.

283. Ibid., 145–146.

284. AGCA A3/2540/37302.

285. For example, see AGCA A3/2540/37266 and A1/4015/various expedientes.

286. AGCA A1/2861/25909. A similar petition in 1774 suggested that the Indians of Totonicapán had traditionally sold their wheat freely (see AGCA A3/2535/37156).

287. AGCA A1/2861/25909.

288. For example, AGCA A1/4245/33811 (note the debt of 90 pesos for "harinas"); see also the case of José Santizo, described earlier in this chapter.

289. AGCA A3/2540/37302.

290. On prisoners, see AGCA A1/2296/16821, fol. 10 (year 1775); and AGCA A1/2861/25904 (year 1789).

291. Sherman 1979, 20; Kramer 1994, 220–221, 247; Lutz 1994, 21–22, 148; and Lutz and Dakin 1996, xxviii.

292. Sherman 1979, 92.

293. Lutz 1994, 148–149 and 303n38.

294. AGCA A2/202/4129.

295. AGCA A2/231/4920.

296. Ibid.; see also AGCA A1/4450/37333. Additional information on Vicenta Ozaeta, the mother of Rosalia and Bernardina Arroyo, was gleaned from AGCA A1/4435/36966.

297. The poultry vendors were called "*gallineras*"—literally, hen dealers. The hens may have been chickens or turkeys.

298. AGCA A2/242/5241.

299. AGCA A2/203/4147.

300. Perhaps beef was smaller only in terms of consumption, given that fowls were raised informally in many homes. In the countryside, other than at or near cattle ranches, poultry would have been (as it is today) more readily available than beef.

301. Peláez Almengor 1996, 151.

302. Lutz 1994, 149.

303. On hired cattle drivers, see AGCA A3/2537/37196, 37208, and 37210. On tribute labor in the slaughterhouse, see AGCA A3/2537/37191 and A3/2540/37268.

304. On carnicerías, see Lutz 1994, 149 and 304n42. On the carting concession, see AGCA A3/2537/37178 and A3/2537/37180 and Langenberg 1981, 55–56n162.

305. AGCA A1/155/3081.

306. On the weights, see AGCA A1/155/3081.

307. The set price in 1715 was 6½ pounds of beef for ½ *real* (Lutz 1994, 151). At the new capital in the 1770s and 1780s, prices had nearly doubled; depending on the season, one *real* bought between 4½ and 6½ pounds (Peláez Almengor 1996, 152–153). However, in 1800 the minimum purchase was still ½ *real* (AGCA A1/155/3081, fol. 17v).

308. Lutz 1994, 150–152, 304nn43,45–49, 305nn50–59; Langenberg 1981, 55–56 and 55nn160–162; and Peláez Almengor 1996, 157.

309. The *fiel mayor* (Inspector) of carnicerías described such a shortage around Easter in 1777 that customers were pushing and trampling each other, despite the militia having arrived for crowd control (AGCA A3/2537/37179). Some officials argued that the regatonas themselves were contributing to the shortages in the carnicerías (AGCA A3/2537/37184 and A3/2540/37289 and Peláez Almengor 1996, 157).

310. Lutz 1994, 151 and 305n58; Peláez Almengor 1996, 157.

311. On the system of turns, see AGCA A3/2537/37160 and 37171. On the penalty, see Peláez Almengor 1996, 152n16; AGCA A3/2537/37196 and 37210; A3/2538/37224, and 37236. In one instance, an hacendada (doña Mariana Mencos) was fined (AGCA A3/2537/37179).

312. AGCA A3/2537/37191 and AGCA A3/2540/37268 (which includes a 1799 petition from the Indian officers of Santa Isabel describing the miserable work conditions in the slaughterhouse). On the various locations of the slaughterhouse, see Peláez Almengor 1996, 155–156.

313. AGCA A3/2537/37219 and A3/2365/34876.

314. For regatonas' descriptions of their slaughtering and vending operations circa 1800, see AGCA A1/155/3081, fols. 24r–25r, and AGCA A1/3094/29733. Both documents show for the new capital the persistence of what Lutz (1994, 151) called a "hereditary gremio [guild]" of regatonas.

315. On continued rustling, see AGCA A2/252/5488. On theft in the slaughterhouse, see AGCA A3/2536/37193.

316. AGCA A1/155/3081, fol. 18r.

317. AGCA A3/2538/37235.

318. Peláez Almengor 1996, 158.

319. AGCA A3/2537/ 37160.

320. Langenberg 1981, 56 and 56n166. Complaints followed about supply shortages and carniceras' sales tactics, and the ayuntamiento wavered briefly, trying to reverse parts of the new policy, but reversal efforts failed and were abandoned.

321. It is not clear to me why, even after 1800, some of the cattle were sold only after butchering. Perhaps carniceras were reluctant to buy animals that did not look especially fat or promising, or perhaps some carniceras could not get sufficient credit to buy a whole animal.

322. Reports repeatedly complained of shortages in the cattle deliveries to the slaughterhouse, poor quality of the cattle delivered, and inadequate availability of meat. See also Langenberg 1981, 55n161.

323. The alcabala varied over time but hovered in the late colonial years on the order of 1 or 2 reales per beast; see AGCA A1/155/3081, A3/293/6315 and 6316,

and Peláez Almengor 1996, 153. In addition to the alcabala, fees for butchering and weighing were also charged; see AGCA A3/295/6333 and A1/155/3081.

324. Zilbermann de Luján 1987, 65, and Peláez Almengor 1996, 154.

325. AGCA A1/4397/36089; A2/157/3046; A2/202/4138 (especially fol. 33v); A2/231/4925; A2/239/5130; A2/243/5243; and A2/252/5488.

326. A2/252/5488.

327. An extensive literature has described Spanish American haciendas and their owners. Chevalier's classic study (1963; originally published in French in 1952) posited a largely static pattern of holdings within the hacienda, but subsequent studies have demonstrated fluidity of holdings and wealth of hacendados. See for example Taylor 1972, chap. IV; Mörner 1973; and Van Young 1981, 107–235.

328. AGCA A3/1076/19607 through 19631; A3/1077/19633 through 19658; A3/1356/various expedientes; and A3/1357/various expedientes. Women also appear among the abastecedores (suppliers) for San Salvador (AGCA A3/293/6314), and one appears in the records for Sololá in Guatemala's western highlands (AGCA A3/1077/19658).

329. Don Ventura Nájera is identified as the brother of doña Josefa Nájera in AGCA A3/2539/37246. Doña Lugarda Nájera is identified as don Ventura's sister in AGCA A3/2539/37261. I have not been able to confirm the relationships among don Manuel, doña Manuela, and doña María Josefa and the other Nájeras in the ranching business. A doña María Nájera also appears in a few registries (for example, AGCA A3/293/6310), but I believe she may be the same person as doña María Josefa Nájera. For more on the Nájeras and elite family lineages in Guatemala, see Casaus Arzú 1992.

330. The mayordomo of doña Josefa Nájera's estate was José Gil Guzmán, who was able to write (see AGCA A3/2539/37246). Doña María Josefa Nájera explained her dealings in cattle and her use of other people's lands in AGCA A1/2861/25928.

331. For examples of these marriages, see AGCA A3/2539/37243 and A3/2539/37244.

332. AGCA A3/2539/37244; A3/2539/37252; and A3/293/6317; and A3/294/6323. Additionally, a doña Teresa Rivas was supplying cattle in 1821; see Sagastume Paiz 2006, 64.

333. On use of the term *poquitero* in this context, see AGCA A3/2537/37171 (from the year 1774).

334. On slaves, see Lokken 2010.

335. AGCA A1/4445/37237. The mark of his ranch's cattle brand was known in the area.

336. Ibid.; A3/2686/expedientes 6316 and 6317.

337. On San Salvador, AGCA A3/1357/22771 and A3/293/6314; on León (Nicaragua), A3/293/6315; on Sololá (Guatemala), A3/1077/ 19658; on Patzicía (Guatemala), A3/293/6311; on various pueblos in Sacatepéquez, A3/294/6324; on Santa Ana (El Salvador), A3/295/6328.

338. AGCA A1/5158/43512.

339. Izquierdo's cattle sales are recorded in AGCA A3/1076/expedientes 19619, 19620, 19627, and 19628.

340. Regarding her investments in agriculture, see AGCA A1/895, fols. 213–217. Data on her urban real estate investments appear in AGCA A1/990/9483, fols. 145v–149; A1/5836/49346; A1/895, fols. 130–139, 141–144, and 150–151; and in her will in AGCA A1/2686/22842, which also indicates that she owned a general store (*tienda de pulperías*).

341. Inability to sign her name is mentioned in AGCA A1/990/9483, fol. 149. A *poder* (power of attorney) given in 1764 to her nephew does appear to be signed by her; see AGCA A1/2686/22842. However, notaries and attorneys often signed for illiterate people. Izquierdo's illiteracy is further suggested by the absence of her signature from her testament, its codicils, and the other notarial records of her legal and business transactions.

342. On the militias and social origins, see Gómez 2003, 59–63.

343. Salvador Izquierdo's signature appears in AGCA A1/2460/19216. On his slave trade, see AGCA A1/2460/19216.

344. On Manuela Antonia Ramírez, see AGCA A1/895, fols. 132–139 and 141–144. For more data on property left by Ramírez's mother, see ACCA A1/5836/49346. I have not identified Ramírez's father's name.

345. On García's birth and investments, see AGCA A1/895, fols. 56 and 69–74.

346. He is identified as Capitán and Alférez and as a merchant importing liquor from Peru in AGCA A1/2696/22958. Rafaela Izquierdo's will notes that her brother left some mares on his death—further evidence of his activities as a traveling merchant (AGCA A1/2686/22842).

347. AGCA A1/2733/23436.

348. AGCA A1/895, fols. 69–74. The husband was leasing the hacienda from the Dominican convent, with a nine-year contract that obligated him to pay 1,000 pesos annually and to make some improvements that would become property of the convent.

349. AGCA A1/990/9483, fols. 145–149.

350. AGCA A1/895, fols. 130–132, 132–139, and 141–144.

351. Ibid., fols. 150–151; AGCA A1/5836/49346.

352. AGCA A1/5836/49346.

353. AGCA A1/2686/22842.

354. AGCA A1/2686/22842 and A1/5305/44578.

355. AGCA A1/2686/22842.

356. Her child is mentioned without name in her will, ibid.

357. AGCA A1/895, fol. 213–217; and AGCA A1/2686/22842 (1786 will, clauses 11 and 13).

358. Interestingly, the servant who left, Teodora García, was the only one of the four criadas whose own surname was identified. Perhaps this is not a coincidence; the presence of her surname suggests that her parents were known, and she may have been able to return to their home.

359. Izquierdo's will, codicils, and related materials are contained in AGCA A1/2686/22842.

360. AGCA A1/2959/27977.

361. On the Monroys' beef and tallow trade in the old capital, see AGCA A3/2537/37174.

362. AGCA A1/4313/34675 and A1/5376/45495 (statement of the alcalde mayor).

363. AGCA A1/5376/45495 and A1/4313/34675.

364. AGCA A1/2944/27694.

365. Ibid.

366. For example, Bakewell 1971; Brading 1971; Socolow 1978; Van Young 1981; Kicza 1983; and Hoberman 1991.

CHAPTER 4

1. For a summary of literature on this point, see Kuznesof 2001, 152 and 168n12–14.

2. The Guatemalan Liberal administration promulgated civil marriage and divorce laws in 1837, but the laws were abrogated with the Conservative rebellion later that year. The Liberal civil code of 1877 gave church and state shared jurisdiction over marriage; couples could be married by either church or civil magistrates, then had to go to the same institution if they sought divorce. As in colonial law, however, divorce in the 1877 civil code amounted to a separation but did not dissolve the marriage (República de Guatemala 1877, 19, Libro I, Título IV, Artículo 165). The civil code of 1927 defined divorce as a dissolution of the marriage and allowed divorced men and women to remarry (República de Guatemala 1927, 40, Párrafo VII, Artículo 182, and 47, Párrafo IX, Artículo 215). On the rise of Liberal states and secular divorce elsewhere in Spanish America see Arrom 1985a, Rodríguez Sáenz 2002, and Deere and León 2005.

3. On Guatemala, see Lutz 1994, especially 82–83 and Appendix 3. On other areas, see Lavrin 1989a, 12 and 36n29; Calvo 1989; Dueñas Vargas 1997, 157–160 and 205–243; and Chambers 1999, 131 and 131n23.

4. The literature on honor in Spanish America is extensive. For three overviews, see Stern 1995, 384n13; Johnson and Lipsett-Rivera 1998a; and Chambers 1999, 159–180. Specific studies include Stolcke 1972 and 1974; Gutiérrez 1985; Seed 1988; Socolow 1989; Twinam 1999; Stern 1995; Dueñas Vargas 1997; the various essays in Johnson and Lipsett-Rivera 1998b; Lavallè 1999; Stavig 1999, chap. 2; Lozano Armendares 2005; and various articles in Whitehead, Sigal, and Chuchiak, 2007. Honor has also been a focus in study of sexuality in early modern Spain; see, for example, Barahona 2003.

5. Stern 1995, 20.

6. Arrom 1985b, chap. 2 (quotation, 67).

7. Ibid., 57–58.

8. Premo 2005, 23–25.

9. Díaz 2004, 65–66.

10. On various cities in Costa Rica, see Gudmundson 1986, chap. 3; on São Paulo and Brazil generally, see Kuznesof 1986, 159–163; on Vila Rica, Saõ Paulo, and Guadalajara, see Lavrin 1989a, 43n57; on Antequera (Oaxaca), see Rabell Romero 1996, 93; on Zacatecas (Mexico), see García González 2000, 191; and on Mexico City, see Lozano Armendares 2005, 92–93.

11. Private household heads identified in the censuses as priests—a handful or fewer in each barrio—are indexed in the table and figure as single men. For 1824,

the category of single male heads includes two men with no marital status indicated and no wife present; the category of widowed male heads includes one man with no marital status indicated, but living with his eleven-year-old son; the category of widowed female heads includes one seventy-year-old woman with no marital status indicated and no husband present.

12. This boy is registered in the barrio de San Juan de Dios, *manzana* 14.

13. Jefferson 2000, 59.

14. The 1821 census of the Valley of Santa Rosa (in today's departamento of Santa Rosa, in the eastern countryside) reflected "a strong tendency toward patrilocality" (Jefferson 2000, 59). Stern (1995, 335) describes patrilocal residence patterns in colonial Mexico. (It is not clear to me whether these applied specifically to Indian-identified families; the picture Stern describes for Mexico City is more like Nueva Guatemala.) Also on patrilocal residence patterns in colonial Mexico, see Sousa 1998, 289. On indigenous communities in twentieth-century Guatemala and Nicaragua respectively, see Wagley 1949, 41, and Gould 1998, 162.

15. Hill 1992, 142. A study of 1970s-era San Pedro Sacatepéquez (in the departament of San Marcos), a relatively hispanized Mam community, described a pattern in which upon marriage a woman enters her husbands' parents' home, but that "as soon as they can, [the couple] will build a house of their own and be gone" (Ehlers 2000, 145–146).

16. Jefferson 2000, 135–136.

17. I have not found evidence that such men prepared their own food, although I imagine some may have occasionally reheated tortillas or roasted an animal or ear of corn. The capital city's monasteries had kitchens—staffed in at least one case by an enslaved man (AGCA A1/2556/20577, April 1820 statement of Miguel González).

18. For example, AGCA A1/4400/36144; A2/154/2996; and A2/154/2982.

19. Stern (1995, chap. 11) makes a similar point about late colonial Mexico, noting that, for women in particular, "paths of uncontrolled livelihood" (uncontrolled by fathers or husbands) were more readily available in Mexico City than in the countryside.

20. Arrom 1985b, 208–209. On Brazil, see Nizza da Silva 1989.

21. Arrom 1985b, 224; Rodríguez Sáenz 1995, chap. 4; Gauderman 2003, 51; and Díaz 2004, 84.

22. Arrom 1985b, 208–209.

23. AGCA A1/4274/34090.

24. AGCA A1/901/9394, fol. 441–444.

25. AGCA A2/233/4966.

26. AGCA A2/154/2973.

27. AGCA A2/153/2950.

28. Arrom 1985b, 67.

29. On dowries and arras, see Arrom 1985b, 67–68, and Gauderman 2003, 33. A woman's *bienes parafernales*—properties other than the dowry that she brought to the marriage—legally were to be managed by the wife herself, though there is some evidence that "husbands customarily managed this fund for their wives" (Arrom 1985b, 68); see also Díaz 2004, 75.

30. Arrom 1985b, 67. Single women as well as single men, unless emancipated by the court or their fathers, remained legally subject to the father's authority in legal and financial matters during his lifetime; married and single women were thus more restricted than widows (Arrom 1985b, 57–58).

31. Gauderman 2003, 41–42, and Espejo-Ponce Hunt and Restall 1997, 237.

32. AGCA A1/4213/33476.

33. AGCA A1/990/9483, fol. 145–149.

34. AGCA A1/939/9432, fol. 274–278.

35. Ibid. The witnesses were men, none of them dons.

36. Arrom 1985b, 62–63, and Gauderman 2003, 33–34.

37. For a similar point about Ecuador, see Gauderman 2003, 46.

38. AGCA A2/157/3061.

39. AGCA A2/151/2841.

40. AGCA A1/4283/34191.

41. AGCA A2/150/2831.

42. Arrom 1985b, 209.

43. AGCA A1/4398/36121.

44. For late colonial Mexico, Arrom (1985b, 225) has described evidence of separated couples who stayed separated regardless of court rulings.

45. For example, Stolcke 1974; McCaa 1984; Díaz 2004, 93–94. McCaa found that non-Spanish women in Parral, Mexico, were likely to have to work as servants if they did not marry. In contrast, Arrom (1985b, 226–228) noted for Mexico City that informal separation widened women's options for leaving unhappy marriages, especially among the lower classes, who faced less pressure to keep up appearances.

46. Stern 1995, 275. See also Arrom 1985b, 226–228. A relatively accessible and permissive form of ecclesiastic divorce was instituted in Brazil in the late eighteenth century (Nizza da Silva 1989, 313 and 333–336).

47. On the Bourbon judiciary in Mexico City as a benevolent service along these lines, see Scardaville 1994, 516. On Ecuador, see Gauderman 2003, 57–64.

48. Similar ideals have been described for late colonial Mexico; see Arrom 1985b, 229–247, and Lipsett-Rivera 2001, 125–130.

49. Sixteenth-century Spanish clerics prescribed correction by both spouses but corporal punishment only by husbands; see Lipsett-Rivera 2001, 131–133 and 142n5.

50. Stern 1995, 80.

51. On both acceptance and resistance in Mexico City, see Arrom 1985b, 228–230 and 235–236. Boyer (1989, 260–261) describes Mexican women's internalization of church teachings but also finds that wives refused to tolerate abusive treatment and sought to resist it in various ways. Emphasizing the internalization of popular ideologies, Stern (1995) views wife beating in Mexico as a response by husbands to violations of "gender right"—what men perceived as their rightful authority over their wives. Stern also considers a complex array of women's resistance to the conventions of male gender right. On Mexican notions of men's right to "correct" their wives with corporal punishment, and on a small number of women who used of violence against husbands, see Lipsett-Rivera 2001, 131–133. Rodríguez Sáenz (1994) found wife beating to be commonplace in Costa Rica, but she emphasized women's resistance. On wives' resistance in Quito, see Gauderman 2003, 58.

52. Arrom 1985b, 231–238; Stern 1995, 77; and Lipsett-Rivera 2001, 133.

53. Hünefeldt 2000, 299.

54. See also Hernández 1999, 110–129.

55. AGCA A2/187/3771, fol. 12.

56. The same has been observed for colonial Quito (Gauderman 2003, 128) and Caracas (Díaz 2004, 89–90). See also Arrom 1985b, 218.

57. We can draw parallels with Mexico City, where Bourbon efforts to increase social control resulted in an expansion of judicial and policing activities starting in 1783; see Scardaville 1994, 511–512, and Stern 1995, 267. Stern (1995, 268) has identified for subsequent years in Mexico City "a certain tactical convergence between elite repression and female resistance," as "abused women saw in the new policing systems a potential opening for relief through state intervention." In Guatemala, a parallel jurisdictional reorganization took place in 1791 (see Langenberg 1981, 42–44). Even before that date, however, the capital's concentration of judicial institutions offered women more avenues to the deployment of state intervention than their rural counterparts had. Arrom (1985b, 238) commented that in Mexico City, a battered wife's position was "ambiguous," for despite the recourse of the courts, "the community pressured her to put up with mistreatment in deference to her husband's rightful authority and in order to preserve the marriage."

58. AGCA A2/187/3771, fol. 12. Ramírez's first name is given here as Catarina, but she did not testify; in another document about Miguel García (AGCA A1/4385/35831) a Cayetana Ramírez did testify, and the information in the case is consistent with her having been in concubinage with García. Apolonia Fuentes was known as Apolonia Túnchez throughout her adult life (in addition to the two documents above, see also AGCA A1/4068/32049; AGCA A1/4445/37247; and AGCA A2/157/3075). In the 1796 census she reported her name as Apolonia Fuentes, and Túnchez as an alias (AGCA A1/2752/23682, fol. 6).

59. AGCA A1/4385/35831.

60. Stern 1995, 99–106 and passim.

61. For a range of urban and rural marital disputes in Costa Rica, see Rodríguez Sáenz 1995, chap. 3–4.

62. As Stern notes (1995, 264), the city's cash economy opened a "greater variety and density of uncontrolled female pathways and livelihoods."

63. AGCA, A2/150/2830.

64. AGCA A1/4436/36992 and A1/4442/37150.

65. AGCA A2/157/3078.

66. AGCA A2/157/3061.

67. Hernández 1999, 111–115.

68. Moser and McIlwane 2001, 56–57.

69. República de Guatemala 1996.

70. On Spanish America, see for example Lavrin 1989a, 27; Arrom 1985b, 233; Rodríguez Sáenz 1994; and Stern 1995, passim. On Europe, see Darnton 1985, 29.

71. On the norm of male predominance among assailants, see Taylor 1979, 83–84.

72. AGCA A2/154/2986.

73. AGCA A2/157/3073. Ortiz is identified as mulato libre (see his testimony of October 8, 1782). Sunsín's calidad is not identified. The penal sentence issued August 3, 1782, is sewn out of order in the expediente; it preceded Sunsín's petition of August 23, 1782.

74. For example, AGCA A2/248/5392 and A2/248/5394.

75. AGCA A1/4456/37428.

76. AGCA A1/4311/34633.

77. AGCA A2/154/2997.

78. Fuentes identified her calidad as española and her oficio (occupation) as carnicera (meat seller) in AGCA A1/4445/37247. In this case she was being tried for recurring illegal chicha sales. In the 1796 census she was the head of her household, where apparently she was renting out space to as many as four people (AGCA A1/2752/23682, fol. 6). Her husband is not listed in her house in the census.

79. AGCA A1/4385/35831.

80. AGCA A1/4380/35720.

81. AGCA A1/4427/36759.

82. Stern 1995, 5–6 and passim.

83. For example, see AGCA A1/4283/34191, in which María San Carlos Gaitán refused to resume married life with her husband; and A1/4398/36121, in which Gertrudis Carrillo refused reconciliation even after several court orders. In some trials for concubinage the officials noted that an unfaithful wife or husband had previously been ordered to reunite with her or his spouse but had failed to do so.

84. Lutz 1994, 171–173 and 233–237.

85. On Guadalajara, see Calvo 1989, 295 Table 3; on Mexico City, see Cope 1994, 68; and on Santafé de Bogotá, see Dueñas Vargas 1997, 209–242. For a summary of findings in scholarship on various cities, see Twinam 1999, 11–13.

86. Dueñas Vargas 1997, 214, and Twinam 1999.

87. Arrom 1985b, 71.

88. To compare with São Paulo see Kuznesof 1991, 250–251. Rural rates of illegitimacy may have been much higher if we define legitimate births only as those within church-sanctioned marriages. In small towns in Guatemala in the twentieth century, it was typical for couples forming households together to be married by local custom (costumbre) rather than the Catholic Church or the state (Wagley 1949, 40, and Ehlers 2000, 144). Presumably this pattern dates back indefinitely.

89. AGCA A2/153/2923, petition of Antonio de Nájera; A2/154/2997, note by don Juan Antonio de la Peña, Dec. 14, 1777; A2/157/3052, testimony of Ana Francisca García; A2/157/3061, testimony of María Concepción Galindo; A1/4310/34598, report of don José María Bregante; and A2/248/5403"C," testimony of María Mercedes Paes.

90. This is in contrast to early modern Vizcaya, where *amancebamiento* implied cohabitation (Barahona 2003, 94–97).

91. Arrom 1985b, 112.

92. AGCA A2/154/2953.

93. On marriage and property law, see Arrom 1985b, 63 and 67; Gauderman 2003, chap. 3; and Díaz 2004, 75.

94. Deere and León 2001, 55–57.

95. See, for example, Lockhart 1994; Brading 1971; Stolcke 1974; Socolow 1978; Hoberman 1991; and Gutiérrez 1991. On family and inheritance law in colonial Brazil, see Lewin 2003, vol. 1.

96. Occasional records refer to couples having sex in houses where neither person seems to have lived. These scenarios may have amounted to prostitution rather than sustained amancebamientos. See AGCA A2/187/3771; A2/200/4096, fol. 114r; A2/202/4125; and A2/202/4138, fol. 33.

97. Marure Papers, MS 1131, Box 1, Folders 15 and 29; Box 2, Folder 21 and 26; and Box 3, Folder 5.

98. AGCA A1/4440/37098; A1/2543/20362; and A2/239/5139.

99. In approximately 1786 Ayau fathered a child by Manuela Ramos, a slave in the household where he was staying (A1/4311/34626). In 1795 he fathered a child by María Concepción Arauz. Ayau had been paying Arauz's mother to do his laundry and sewing and to provide his meals, and María Concepción testified that her own job consisted of helping her parents in the house (AGCA A1/4321/34803).

100. AGCA A1/4380/35717.

101. AGCA A2/249/5423.

102. AGCA A1/2944/27694.

103. Famous examples include Cortés and Malintzin in Mexico; in Guatemala, conqueror Pedro de Alvarado and Luisa Xicotencatl; in what is now the United States, Toussaint Charbonneau and Sacajawea, and Thomas Jefferson and Sally Hemings; in Brazil, João Fernandes de Oliveira and Chica da Silva.

104. This view is suggested for example by Octavio Paz's notion of Malintzin as *"la chingada"*—"the one screwed" by the military and sexual force of Cortés and his men.

105. For examples of wages for male laborers, see AGCA A1/4311/34626, petition of don Pedro Ayau dated December 16, 1793 (Ayau was referring here to the wage that he had received as a laborer some eight years earlier); A1/4400/36153 (testimony of Eduardo Quiroz); and A1/4397/36095 (testimony of Ignacio Quevedo). See also Samayoa Guevara 1962, 218–219.

106. For examples of wages for female laborers, see AGCA A2/185/3704 (year 1797, testimony of Felipa Véliz); A2/205/4191 (year 1803); and A1/2861/25923 (year 1790).

107. On food budget, see for example AGCA A1/2861/25904, statement of Angela Montúfar y Berdugo, March 18, 1789, indicating that 2 reales was the daily budget food for prisoners in the jails. It was also "the standard calculation of plebian food costs for one adult" in Mexico City (Stern 1995, 265).

108. Ibid.

109. AGCA A1/5909/50454. Gallegos identified herself in her suit as "criolla," which in the colonial Guatemalan context may have meant "mixed"—that is, of mixed racial ancestry.

110. AGCA A2/153/2928.

111. AGCA A1/4363/35446.

112. AGCA A2/233/4962.

113. For parallels with Mexico, see Cope 1994, 68, and Stern 1995, 261–266.

114. AGCA A1/2867/26116.

115. Marure Papers, Box 1, Folder 29.

116. AGCA A1/4440/37098 (November 15, 1808, statement of don José Ballesteros).

117. AGCA A1/4400/36146.

118. AGCA A2/248/5394.

119. Ehlers 2000, 172–173.

120. The mother's testimony described Aniceta's response, and Aniceta's testimony confirmed it. AGCA A2/154/2980.

121. Ibid.

122. AGCA A1/2475/19556 (opening petition of Francisca Betancurt y Moreno); A1/6940/57770 (opening statement of don José de los Rios y de Guzmán); A1/4380/35717 (opening statement of Inés García); A1/5909/50454 (Mariana Gallegos); A1/4372/35611 (Petrona Alvarez); A1/4321/34803 (María de la Concepción Arauz, December 1795); and A2/154/2953 (Rosalia de Castro, October 5, 1775).

123. AGCA A2/40/830.

124. AGCA A1/2466/19374.

125. AGCA A2/187/3771, fol. 28.

126. AGCA A2/154/2997.

127. AGCA A1/4317/34744.

128. A2/187/3768. In the standard procedure in cases against ecclesiastics, the record concealed the name of the friar and that of his order.

129. Wagley 1949, 41 and 44–47. Wagley also noted that there were in 1937 ten "polygynous households"—none with more than two wives—maintained by "comparatively wealthy" men. (This was among 908 people in the village proper and 400 in its rural sections; see Wagley 1949, 11.) Though these men were not forming two households, Wagley noted that in all cases the man provided the second wife with rooms in which to live and cook separately from the first. However, these polygynous households were generally impermanent, Wagley stated, because the second wife "seldom stay[ed] long," usually leaving to enter another marriage as the only wife.

130. Cope 1994, 68 (on Mexico City). On Guadalajara, see Calvo 1989, 291–292. Stern (1995, chap. 11) seems to make the same assumption in his discussion of Mexico City women who used amasios as sources of income.

131. Severino Vásquez was denounced by his wife Isidora Cárdenas in 1801 for an illicit affair with Eduarda Ibarra or Guzmán (AGCA A1/4380/35720) and in 1807 for an affair with Feliciana Soto (AGCA A1/4427/36759). Miguel García was denounced by his wife Apolonia Fuentes ("Túnchez") in 1798 for concubinage with Cayetana Ramírez (AGCA A2/187/377, fol. 12) and in 1802 for concubinage with Juana Luna (AGCA A1/4385/35831).

132. AGCA A2/185/3704.

133. AGCA A2/153/2914.

134. One of the men was married and the other unmarried. AGCA A1/4386/35835 and A1/4401/36171.

135. AGCA A1/4311/34633.

136. AGCA A1/4363/35446 and A2/14/318.

137. *Diligencias matrimoniales* (church records of marriage proceedings), which may be held in church archives, likely include information on illicit affairs. Study of such records from early independent-era rural eastern Guatemala shows that applicants for marriage freely admitted to past relationships out of concern about ecclesiastically defined "impediments" that required dispensation before a marriage could take place (Jefferson 2000, 137–143). For work with similar records for Costa Rica, see Rodríguez Sáenz 1995, 103–106; for Lima, see Hünefeldt 2000, 93–108.

138. In one of these episodes a man brought suit against his wife, who had been spending nights away from their home (AGCA A1/4397/36095). The other episode was recorded when the husband petitioned the court about his wife's alleged misbehavior, but in the course of litigation it became clear that the husband himself was the one who had been unfaithful (AGCA A1/4398/36121).

139. I am grateful to Pete Sigal for sharing this insight with me.

140. Stern 1995, 426n13; Hünefeldt 2000, 89; Chuchiak 2007; and Lewis 2007. On cases heard by the colonial state, see Spurling 1998 and 2000 (125n2 gives an overview of earlier literature) and Tortorici 2007. Sigal (2005 and 2007) has used linguistic analysis to consider various sexual practices in native cultures. See also Nesvig 2001.

141. On this tendency in Spanish America generally, see Lockhart 1984, 268.

142. See AGCA A1/4400/36153; A1/4310/34598; and A1/4368/35542.

143. For example, Stolcke 1974; Gutiérrez 1985; Seed 1988; Lavrin 1989b; Lipsett-Rivera 1998, 191–192; and Chambers 1999, 169 and 177.

144. Johnson and Lipsett-Rivera 1998a, 3–4.

145. I have found that in records from late colonial Guatemala the term *honor* appears also as a euphemism for female virginity. However, this usage alluded only to the woman's virginity, not to personal or social qualities thought to accompany virginity nor to her public reputation.

146. Johnson and Lipsett-Rivera 1998a, 3–4.

147. Stern 1995, 14–16.

148. Twinam's work on *gracias al sacar* petitions suggests that an illegitimate birth limited the mother's chance of eventually marrying if she did not wed the child's father. In a sample of elite parents of illegitimate children throughout colonial Spanish America, fathers were three times as likely as mothers to have ultimately married someone other than the person with whom they had the illegitimate child. See Twinam 1999, 125, Table 6.

149. Gutiérrez 1991, 230.

150. Concern with virginity was sufficient that if the woman's parents opposed a prospective marriage, the man might abduct her—this was often with her consent—for a few days or weeks, thereby implicitly taking her virginity and thus

her honor. The reluctant parents would then likely support the marriage to salvage their daughter's (and their family's) reputation and to protect her from future unmarriageability. See Stolcke 1972; McCaa 1984, 491–492; and Lavrin 1989b, 65–66.

151. For emphasis on the value of bridal virginity among plebians, see Stern 1995, 270; Boyer 1998, 171–175; and Lipsett-Rivera 1998, 191–192. For the argument that pleblian society did not expect virginity in brides see Waldron 1989, 160; Socolow 1989, 234; and Cope 1994, 69. Stavig (1999, 39) noted that in native Peruvian communities, trial marriage (*sirvincuy*) could be terminated without stigma.

152. Jefferson 2000, chap. 3.

153. Kanter 2008, 83–84; see also Wagley 1949, 41. Gruzinski (1989, 109–110) presents a partly contrasting view, but it is based on clerical-authored prescriptive literature (instructional guides for priests) rather than on actual cases involving native subjects.

154. Hill 1992, 141–142.

155. Wagley 1949, 37–39 (quotation, 39).

156. AGCA A1/192/3921. See also Hill 1992, 142.

157. Anderson 1997, 80; and Sousa 1998, 264–265.

158. AGCA A1/4400/36164.

159. On depósito, see Seed 1988, 78–79; and Kanter 2008, 82–96.

160. On Sánchez's reputation, see AGCA A1/1756, fol. 403.

161. For descriptions of young men and women drinking and listening to music, see AGCA A2/154/2977 and A2/242/5209. On street performers, see AGCA A2/231/4911; on women at the cockfights (*patio de gallos*), AGCA A2/157/3075 (testimony of Irene Polanco, August 3, 1782); on card games, AGCA A2/150/2831 and A1/4400/36143. More generally on recreation in Nueva Guatemala, including theater, bullfighting, billiards, and a botanical garden, see Langenberg 1981, 75–78.

162. AGCA A2/153/2951.

163. Seed 1988, 97–99; Lavrin 1989b, 61; Socolow 1989, 226; and Barahona 2003, 26–27.

164. Chambers 1999, 177.

165. Seed 1988, 99–101; and Lavrin 1989b, 63.

166. Seed 1988, 100–101. In Vizcaya, monetary fines had been the norm at least a century earlier (Barahona 2003, 6, 32–33, 127–132, and 147–156).

167. The thirteen cases are found in AGCA A1/2475/19556, A1/2485/19667, A1/2515/20017, A1/2543/20362, A1/2867/26094, A1/4321/34803, A1/4363/35446, A1/4380/35717, A1/4440/37098, A1/5338/44980, A2/54/1076, A2/5909/1076, and B/1278/31129.

168. AGCA A1/4363/35446 and A2/14/318.

169. AGCA A1/2475/19556. Though she pleaded poverty, this was necessary legal posturing in an appeal for financial support for her children, not necessarily an indicator of her socioeconomic status.

170. AGCA B/1278/31129.

171. AGCA A1/4440/37098 and A1/2543/20362.

172. On Carrillo, see AGCA A1/2515/20017; on Ríos, A1/2867/26094. Other cases are AGCA A2/5909/1076; A1/2485/19667; and A1/4380/35717. A

child-support plantiff named Mariana Gallegos was identified as "criolla," which in the Guatemalan context may have meant "mixed," or it may have meant she was of Spanish ancestry. See AGCA A1/5909/50454.

173. AGCA A1/2515/20017.

174. AGCA A1/4363/35446.

175. AGCA A1/2475/19556.

176. AGCA A1/4321/34803.

177. AGCA A1/2475/19556.

178. AGCA A1/4440/37098 and A1/2543/20362.

179. AGCA A1/5338/44980.

180. AGCA A1/2515/20017.

181. AGCA A1/2867/26094. Ríos's attorney said she had complained repeatedly to the *juez preventivo* in Sanarate, who had been unresponsive.

182. AGCA A2/54/1076.

183. On the lactation period, see for example AGCA A1/4380/35717 (see petition of November 1, 1801); A2/247/5364 (see statement of August 12, 1813); A2/2/14/318 (see petition of November 18, 1802); and A1/4321/34803 (see final ruling of Audiencia). See also Premo 2005, 26.

184. AGCA A1/4380/35717. I deduce García's Indian identity based on her proposal to place her daughter in the Beaterio de Indias.

185. A1/4440/37098.

186. AGCA A2/14/318. A final entry in the case file indicates that the court personnel could not locate the mother to notify her of the decision.

187. AGCA A1/2485/19667.

188. In some of these instances, the documented case is an appeal—such as a request for additional payment—following an earlier ruling awarding a settlement.

189. AGCA A1/4363/35446 and A1/4380/35717.

190. AGCA A2/54/1076.

191. AGCA A1/4440/37098.

192. To compare with Lima, see Premo 2005, 202–207.

193. AGCA A1/4311/34626.

194. A1/2515/20017 (see closing remarks in the first statement of don Manuel de Solórzano).

195. AGCA B/1278/31129 (see José María Yúdice's statement of March 23, 1825).

196. AGCA A1/5338/44980 (see don José Grau y Serra's statement of March 1, 1800). On his origins in Tarragona in Catalonia, see AGCA A1/4800/41459/fols. 75–85.

197. AGCA A2/247/5364. The notary summarized the depositions of two witnesses as: "Reprodujo [don Domingo] por tres o cuatro ocasiones amolarse amolarse; a que le previno la Eduviges que si veinte ocasiones era casado que se la había de pagar."

198. AGCA A2/247/5364.

199. AGCA A1/4398/36121.

200. "Ahora es el día en que el demonio nos lleva si no me confiesa como esta durmiendose con la Josefa Prado." AGCA A2/157/3079.

201. AGCA A2/157/3079. On Joseph Ignacio Corral's fledgling fortunes, see AGCA A1/4295/34368.

202. AGCA A2/154/2954.

203. AGCA A2/157/3080.

204. AGCA A1/4283/34191 and A2/157/3075 (see deposition of Irene Polanco, August 3, 1782).

205. For an excellent analysis linking male-on-male violence to interpersonal relationships and other aspects of social context in colonial Mexico, see Stern 1995, chap. 7.

206. AGCA B/1251/30545 and B/1252/30589.

207. On dueling, see Burkholder 1998, 34, and Johnson 1998, 129.

208. AGCA A2/150/2831.

209. AGCA A2/157/3064.

CONCLUSION

1. MacLeod 2008 [1973], 296, and Wortman 1982, 35–36.

2. McCreery 1994, 111–112.

3. This literature is rapidly growing. Examples on Cuba include Scott 1985, Díaz 2000, and Childs 2006; on Mexico, Aguirre Beltrán 1972 [1946]; Palmer 1976, chap. 7; Carroll 1991; Vinson 2001; Bennett 2003 and 2009; and Restall 2009; on Peru, Bowser 1974, Hünefeldt 1994, and Aguirre 1993.

4. Williford 1963, 69–70, and Estado de Guatemala 1837, 437–452. The 1837 law was remarkably permissive in that it allowed divorce on grounds of mutual consent as well as various other causes, though it was somewhat punitive in that it required the plaintiff spouse to sustain the children (Estado de Guatemala 1837, 448, Capítulo III, and 449, Art. 70).

5. On other republics, see Deere and León 2001, 39–41.

6. República de Guatemala 1877, Libro I, Art. 153, 154, 158, 159. The 1837 legislation made similar restrictions on wives' juridical abilities but explicitly noted that the court could override the restrictions (Estado de Guatemala 1837, 443–444, Capítulo V.)

7. República de Guatemala 1877, Libro I, Art. 142–147; Art. 169.

8. Ibid., Art. 165. In contrast, the 1837 law did allow remarriage after divorce, though it prescribed certain restrictions depending on the cause for the divorce (Estado de Guatemala 1837, 450, Art. 74–78). The civil code of 1927 defined divorce as a dissolution of the marriage and allowed divorced men and women to remarry (República de Guatemala 1927, Art. 182 and 215).

9. República de Guatemala 1877, Libro I, Art. 176–178. The 1837 legislation stipulated that the spouse who petitioned for divorce should pay to support the ex-spouse and children; but that if the plaintiff spouse did not have sufficient resources and the defendant spouse did, then the defendant spouse should maintain the children (Estado de Guatemala 1837, 449, Art. 70–72).

10. República de Guatemala 1877, Libro I, Art. 237, 228–229. The civil code of 1927 upheld recognition by fathers as voluntary (República de Guatemala 1927, Art. 263 ff.). The 1964 civil code stipulates that recognition by the father can be

voluntary or by "judicial sentence that declares paternity" (República de Guatemala 1964, Art. 210).

11. On the laws' construction of vagrancy, see Martínez Peláez 1970, 765n7.

12. On Liberal efforts to westernize the country's Indians, see for example Williford 1969, 35–37. For analysis of K'iche' (Quiché) nationalism and K'iche' efforts to claim a share of modernity, see Grandin 2000.

13. Some labor drafts had been implemented starting in the late 1850s under Conservative rule, primarily for coffee plantations. For comparison of these drafts with those after 1871, see Reeves 2006, chap. 3, especially 75 and 89–91. On the links between coffee agriculture and Liberal-era drafts, see also Martínez Peláez 1970, 579–581 and 765nn6,7, and McCreery 1994, 187–193 and 218–223.

14. For an overview, see McCreery 1994, especially chaps. 6–7.

15. I use the term *modern* advisedly; on problems with perceptions of "modernity," see Cooper 2005, chap. 5.

Works Cited

Aguirre, Carlos. 1993. *Agentes de su propia libertad: Los esclavos de Lima y la disintegración de la esclavitud, 1821–1854*. Lima: Fondo Editorial de la Pontificia Universidad Católica del Perú.

Aguirre Beltrán, Gonzalo. 1972 [1946]. *La población negra de México*. Mexico City: Fondo de la Cultura Económica.

Alfonso X. 1844. *Las Siete Partidas del Muy Noble Rey Don Alfonso el Sabio, glosadas por el Lic. Gregorio López, del Consejo Real de Indias de S.M.*, Tomos I–III. Madrid: Compañía General de Impresiones y Libreros del Reino.

Alvarez Aragón, Rosa María. 1996. "Amas de leche." *Estudios: Revista de Antropología, Arqueología e Historia*, 3a. época, 139–147. Guatemala: Universidad de San Carlos.

Anderson, Arthur J. O. 1997. "Aztec Wives." In Robert Haskett, Susan Schroeder, and Stephanie Wood, eds., *Indian Women of Early Mexico*. Norman: University of Oklahoma Press.

Andrews, George Reid. 2004. *Afro-Latin America, 1800–2000*. New York: Oxford University Press.

Arrom, Silvia M. 1985a. "Changes in Mexican Family Law in the Nineteenth Century: The Civil Codes of 1870 and 1884." *Journal of Family History* 10 (3): 305–317.

———. 1985b. *The Women of Mexico City, 1790–1857*. Stanford, CA: Stanford University Press.

Bakewell, P.J. 1971. *Silver Mining and Society in Colonial Mexico: Zacatecas, 1546–1700*. New York: Cambridge University Press.

Barahona, Renato. 2003. *Sex Crimes, Honour, and the Law in Early Modern Spain: Vizcaya, 1528–1735*. Buffalo, NY: University of Toronto Press.

Bauer, Arnold J. 1979a. "Rural Workers in Spanish America: Problems of Peonage and Oppression." *Hispanic American Historical Review* 59 (1): 34–63.

———. 1979b. "Arnold J. Bauer's Reply [to Loveman's critique]." *Hispanic American Historical Review* 59 (3): 478–485.

———. 1990. "Millers and Grinders: Technology and Household Economy in Meso-America." *Agricultural History* 64 (1): 1–17.

Bennett, Herman L. 2003. *Africans in Colonial Mexico: Absolutism, Christianity, and Afro-Creole Consciousness, 1570–1640*. Bloomington: Indiana University Press.

———. 2009. *Colonial Blackness: A History of Afro-Mexico*. Bloomington: Indiana University Press.

Berlin, Ira, and Philip D. Morgan, eds. 1993. *Cultivation and Culture: Labor and the Shaping of Slave Life in the Americas*. Charlottesville: University Press of Virginia.

Berman, Constance Hoffman. 2007. "Women's Work in Family, Village and Town after 1000 CE: Contributions to Economic Growth?" *Journal of Women's History* 19 (3): 10–32.

Block, Sharon. 2006. *Rape and Sexual Power in Early America*. Chapel Hill: University of North Carolina Press.

Blumenthal, Debra. 2009. *Enemies and Familiars: Slavery and Mastery in Fifteenth-Century Valencia*. Ithaca, NY: Cornell University Press.

Borah, Woodrow. 1983. *Justice by Insurance: The General Indian Court of Colonial Mexico and the Legal Aides of the Half-Real*. Berkeley: University of California Press.

Bowser, Frederick P. 1974. *The African Slave in Colonial Peru, 1524–1650*. Stanford, CA: Stanford University Press.

Boyer, Richard. 1989. "Women, *La Mala Vida*, and the Politics of Marriage." In Asunción Lavrin, ed., *Sexuality and Marriage in Colonial Latin America*. Lincoln: University of Nebraska Press.

———. 1998. "Honor among Plebians: *Mala Sangre* and Social Reputation." In Lyman L. Johnson and Sonya Lipsett-Rivera, eds., *The Faces of Honor: Sex, Shame, and Violence in Colonial Latin America*. Albuquerque: University of New Mexico Press.

Brading, D. A. 1971. *Miners and Merchants in Bourbon Mexico, 1763–1810*. Cambridge, UK: Cambridge University Press.

Brown, Richmond F. 1997. *Juan Fermín de Aycinena: Central American Colonial Entrepreneur, 1729–1796*. Norman: University of Oklahoma Press.

Burkett, Elinor C. 1978. "Indian Women and White Society: The Case of Sixteenth-Century Peru." In Asunción Lavrin, ed., *Latin American Women: Historical Perspectives*. Westport, CT: Greenwood Press.

Burkholder, Mark A. 1998. "Honor and Honors in Colonial Spanish America." In Lyman L. Johnson and Sonya Lipsett-Rivera, eds., *The Faces of Honor: Sex, Shame, and Violence in Colonial Latin America*. Albuquerque: University of New Mexico Press.

Cáceres, Rina. 2010. "Slavery and Social Differentiation: Slave Wages in Omoa." In Lowell Gudmundson and Justin Wolfe, eds., *Blacks and Blackness in Central America: Between Race and Place*. Durham, NC: Duke University Press.

Calvo, Thomas. 1989. "The Warmth of the Hearth: Seventeenth-Century Guadalajara Families." In Asunción Lavrin, ed., *Sexuality and Marriage in Colonial Latin America*. Lincoln: University of Nebraska Press.

Caplan, Karen D. 2010. *Indigenous Citizens: Local Liberalism in Early National Oaxaca and Yucatán*. Stanford, CA: Stanford University Press.

Carey, David Jr. 2006. *Engendering Mayan History: Kaqchikel Women as Agents and Conduits of the Past, 1875–1970*. New York: Routledge.

———, ed. 2012. *Distilling the Influence of Alcohol: Aguardiente in Guatemalan History*. Gainesville: University Press of Florida.

Carmack, Robert M. 1995. *Rebels of Highland Guatemala: The Quiché-Mayas of Momostenango*. Norman: University of Oklahoma Press.

Carney, Judith A. 2001. *Black Rice: The African Origins of Rice Cultivation in the Americas*. Cambridge, MA: Harvard University Press.

Carroll, Patrick J. 1991. *Blacks in Colonial Veracruz: Race, Ethnicity, and Regional Development*. Austin: University of Texas Press.

Casaus Arzú, Marta. 1992. *Guatemala: Linaje y racismo*. San José, Costa Rica: FLASCO.

Castañeda, Antonia. 1993. "Sexual Violence in the Politics and Policies of Conquest: Amerindian Women and the Spanish Conquest of Alta Calfornia." In Adela de la Torre and Beatriz M. Pesquera, eds., *Building with Our Hands: New Directions in Chicana Studies*. Berkeley: University of California Press.

CELADE – División de la Población de la CEPAL (United Nations Economic Commission for Latin America and the Caribbean), Fondo Indígena. "Sistema de Indicadores Sociodemográficos de Poblaciones y Pueblos Indígenas." Retrieved on July 12, 2011, from http://celade.cepal.org/redatam/PRYESP/SISPPI/.

Chambers, Sarah C. 1999. *From Subjects to Citizens: Honor, Gender, and Politics in Arequipa, Peru, 1780–1854*. University Park: Pennsylvania State University Press.

Chance, John K. 1978. *Race and Class in Colonial Oaxaca*. Stanford, CA: Stanford University Press.

Chevalier, Francois. 1963. *Land and Society in Colonial Mexico: The Great Hacienda*. Berkeley: University of California Press. Originally published in French in 1952.

Childs, Matt D. 2006. *The 1812 Aponte Rebellion in Cuba and the Struggle against Atlantic Slavery*. Chapel Hill: University of North Carolina Press.

Chuchiak IV, John F. 2007. "The Sins of the Fathers: Franciscan Friars, Parish Priests, and the Sexual Conquest of the Yucatec Maya, 1545–1808." *Ethnohistory*. 54 (1): 69–127.

Ciudad Suárez, María Milagros. 1996. "El Colegio de Doncellas, una institución femenina para criollas, siglo XVI." *Mesoamérica* 32: 299–314.

Cline, S. L. 1986. *Colonial Culhuacan: A Social History of an Aztec Town*. Albuquerque: University of New Mexico Press.

Conrad, Robert Edgar, ed. 1999. *Children of God's Fire: A Documentary History of Black Slavery in Brazil*. Princeton, NJ: Princeton University Press, 1984; reprint, University Park: Pennsylvania State University Press.

Contreras R., J. Daniel. 1968. *Una rebelión indígena en el Partido de Totonicapán en 1820: El indio y la Independencia*. Guatemala: Imprenta Universitaria de la Universidad de San Carlos.

Cook, Noble David, and W. George Lovell. 1991. "Unraveling the Web of Disease." In Noble David Cook and W. George Lovell, eds., *"Secret Judgments of God": Old World Disease in Colonial Spanish America*. Norman: University of Oklahoma Press.

Cooper, Frederick. 2005. *Colonialism in Question: Theory, Knowledge, History*. Berkeley: University of California Press.

Cope, R. Douglas. 1994. *The Limits of Racial Domination: Plebeian Society in Co-lonial Mexico City, 1660–1720.* Madison: University of Wisconsin Press.

Cortés y Larraz, Pedro. 1958 [1768–1770]. *Descripción geográfico-moral de la diócesis de Goathemala,* 2 vols. Guatemala: Sociedad de Geografía e Historia.

Darnton, Robert. 1985. *The Great Cat Massacre and Other Episodes in French Cultural History.* New York: Vintage.

de la Fuente, Alejandro. 2007. "Slaves and the Creation of Legal Rights in Cuba: *Coartación* and *Papel.*" *Hispanic American Historical Review* 87 (4): 659–692.

Deere, Carmen Diana, and Magdalena León. 2001. *Empowering Women: Land and Property Rights in Latin America.* Pittsburgh: University of Pittsburgh Press.

————. 2005. "Liberalism and Married Women's Property Rights in Nineteenth-Century Latin America." *Hispanic American Historical Review* 85(4): 627–678.

Díaz, Arlene J. 2004. *Female Citizens, Patriarchs, and the Law in Venezuela, 1786–1904.* Lincoln: University of Nebraska Press.

Díaz, María Elena. 2000. *The Virgin, the King, and the Royal Slaves of El Cobre: Negotiating Freedom in Colonial Cuba, 1670–1780.* Stanford, CA: Stanford University Press.

Dudden, Faye E. 1983. *Serving Women: Household Service in Nineteenth-Century America.* Middletown, CT: Wesleyan University Press.

Dueñas Vargas, Guiomar. 1997. *Los hijos del pecado: Ilegitimidad y vida familiar en la Santafé de Bogotá colonial.* Bogotá: Editorial Universidad Nacional.

Dunn, Alvis E. 1999. "Aguardiente and Identity: The Holy Week Riot of 1786 in Quezaltenango, Guatemala." PhD dissertation, University of North Carolina, Chapel Hill.

Dunn, Richard S. 1973. *Sugar and Slaves: The Rise of the Planter Class in the En-glish West Indies, 1624–1713.* Chapel Hill: University of North Carolina Press, 1972; reprint, New York: W. W. Norton.

Dym, Jordana. 2006. *From Sovereign Villages to National States: City, State, and Federation in Central America, 1759–1839.* Albuquerque: University of New Mexico Press.

Ehlers, Tracy Bachrach. 2000. *Silent Looms: Women and Production in a Guate-malan Town,* revised edition. Austin: University of Texas Press.

Ericastilla Samayoa, Anna Carla. 1997. "La imagen de la mujer a través de la crimi-nalidad femenina en la Ciudad de Guatemala (1880–1889)." *Licenciatura* thesis, Universidad de San Carlos de Guatemala.

Espejo-Ponce Hunt, Marta, and Matthew Restall. 1997. "Work, Marriage, and Sta-tus: Maya Women of Colonial Yucatan." In Susan Schroeder, Stephanie Wood, and Robert Haskett, eds., *Indian Women of Early Mexico.* Norman: University of Oklahoma Press.

Euraque, Darío A. 2004. "Negritud Garífuna y Coyunturas Políticas en la Costa Norte de Honduras, 1940–1970." In Charles Hale, Jeffrey Gould, and Darío A. Euraque, eds., *Memorias del Mestizaje: Política y Cultura en Centroamérica, 1920–1990s.* Guatemala: CIRMA.

Farriss, Nancy M. 1984. *Maya Society under Colonial Rule: The Collective Enter-prise of Survival.* Princeton, NJ: Princeton University Press.

Few, Martha. 2002. *Women Who Live Evil Lives: Gender, Religion, and the Politics of Power in Colonial Guatemala.* Austin: University of Texas Press.

Fiehrer, Thomas. 1979. "Slaves and Freedmen in Colonial Central America: Rediscovering a Forgotten Black Past." *The Journal of Negro History* 64 (1): 39–57.

Francois, Marie Eileen. 2006. *A Culture of Everyday Credit: Housekeeping, Pawnbroking, and Governance in Mexico City, 1750–1920.* Lincoln: University of Nebraska Press.

Fuentes y Guzmán, Francisco Antonio de. 1882–1883 [1690]. *Historia de Guatemala ó Recordación florida,* two volumes; Justo Zaragoza, ed. Madrid: Luis Navarro.

Gage, Thomas. 1958 [1648]. *Thomas Gage's Travels in the New World,* edited by J. Eric S. Thompson. Norman: University of Oklahoma Press.

Galicia, Julio. 1976. *Destrucción y traslado de la ciudad de Guatemala.* Guatemala: Universidad de San Carlos de Guatemala.

Gall, Francis, compiler. 1976-1983. *Diccionario geográfico de Guatemala,* 4 vols. Guatemala: Instituto Geográfico Nacional.

García González, Francisco. 2000. *Familia y sociedad en Zacatecas: la vida de un microcosmos minero novohispano, 1750–1830.* Mexico City: El Colegio de México and Zacatecas: Universidad Autónoma de Zacatecas.

Gauderman, Kimberly A. 2003. *Women's Lives in Colonial Quito: Law, Gender, and Society in Spanish America.* Austin: University of Texas Press.

Gellert, Gisela. 1990. "Desarrollo de la estructura espacial en la ciudad de Guatemala desde su fundación hasta la Revolución de 1944." In *Ciudad de Guatemala: Dos estudios sobre su evolución urbana (1524–1950).* Guatemala: Universidad de San Carlos de Guatemala.

Gibson, Charles. 1964. *The Aztecs under Spanish Rule.* Stanford, CA: Stanford University Press.

Glave, Luis Miguel. 1989. *Trajinantes: Caminos indígenas en la sociedad colonial, Siglos XVI/XVII.* Lima: Instituto de Apoyo Agrario.

Gómez, Ana Margarita. 2003. "'Al servico de las armas': The Bourbon Army of Late Colonial Guatemala, 1762-1821," PhD dissertation, University of Minnesota.

Gonzalez, Nancie L. Solien. 1988. *Sojourners of the Caribbean: Ethnogenesis and Ethnohistory of the Garifuna.* Urbana: University of Illinois Press.

Gould, Jeffrey L. 1998. *"To Die in this Way": Nicaraguan Indians and the Myth of Mestizaje, 1880–1965.* Durham, NC: Duke University Press.

Graham, Sandra Lauderdale. 1988. *House and Street: The Domestic World of Servants and Masters in Nineteenth-Century Rio de Janeiro.* Cambridge, UK: Cambridge University Press.

Grandin, Greg. 2000. *The Blood of Guatemala: A History of Race and Nation.* Durham, NC: Duke University Press.

Graubart, Karen. 2007. *With Our Labor and Sweat: Indigenous Women and the Formation of Colonial Society in Peru.* Stanford, CA: Stanford University Press.

Gruzinski, Serge. 1989. "Individualization and Acculturation: Confession among the Nahuas of Mexico from the Sixteenth to the Eighteenth Century." In Asunción Lavrin, ed., *Sexuality and Marriage in Colonial Latin America.* Lincoln: University of Nebraska Press.

Guardino, Peter F. 1996. *Peasants, Politics, and the Formation of Mexico's National State: Guerrero, 1800–1875.* Stanford, CA: Stanford University Press.

———. 2005. *The Time of Liberty: Popular Political Culture in Oaxaca, 1750–1850.* Durham, NC: Duke University Press.

Gudmundson, Lowell. 1984. "'Black' into 'White' in Nineteenth Century Spanish America: Afro-American Assimiliation in Argentina and Costa Rica." *Slavery and Abolition* 5 (1): 35–49.

———. 1986. *Costa Rica before Coffee: Society and Economy on the Eve of the Export Boom.* Baton Rouge: Louisiana State University Press.

———. 2003. "Negotiating Rights under Slavery: The Slaves of San Gerónimo (Baja Verapaz, Guatemala) Confront Their Dominican Masters in 1810." *The Americas* 60 (1): 109–114.

Gudmundson, Lowell, and Justin Wolfe, eds. 2010. *Blacks & Blackness in Central America: Between Race and Place.* Durham, NC: Duke University Press.

Gutiérrez, Ramón A. 1985. "Honor, Ideology, Marriage Negotiation, and Class-Gender Domination in New Mexico, 1690–1846." *Latin American Perspectives* 12 (1): 81–104.

———. 1991. *When Jesus Came, the Corn Mothers Went Away: Marriage, Sexuality, and Power in New Mexico, 1500–1846.* Stanford, CA: Stanford University Press.

Haefkens, Jacobo. 1969 [1827]. *Viaje a Guatemala y Centroamérica.* Trans. Theodora J.M. van Lottum. Guatemala: Editorial Universitaria. Originally published in 1827 in Dutch.

Hartman, Saidiya V. 1997. *Scenes of Subjection: Terror, Slavery, and Self-Making in Nineteeth-Century America.* New York: Oxford University Press.

Haskett, Robert Stephen. 1991. *Indigenous Rulers: An Ethnohistory of Town Government in Colonial Cuernavaca.* Albuquerque: University of New Mexico Press.

Haslip-Viera, Gabriel. 1999. *Crime and Punishment in Late Colonial Mexico City, 1692–1810.* Albuquerque: University of New Mexico Press.

Hawkins, Timothy. 2004. *José de Bustamante and Central American Independence: Colonial Administration in an Age of Imperial Crisis.* Tuscaloosa: University of Alabama Press.

Hernández, Leonardo Fabricio. 1999. "Implicated Spaces, Daily Struggles: Home and Street Life in Late Colonial Guatemala City, 1750–1824." PhD dissertation, Brown University.

Hernández Aparicio, Pilar. 1977. "Problemas socioeconómicos en el Valle de Guatemala (1670–1680)." *Revista de Indias* 37 (149/150): 585–637.

Herrera, Robinson Antonio. 2003. *Natives, Europeans, and Africans in Sixteenth-Century Santiago de Guatemala.* Austin: University of Texas Press.

Hill, Robert M. II. 1992. *Colonial Cakchiquels: Highland Maya Adaptation to Spanish Rule, 1600–1700.* Fort Worth, TX: Harcourt Brace Jovanovich.

Hoberman, Louisa Schell. 1991. *Mexico's Merchant Elite, 1590–1660: Silver, State, and Society.* Durham, NC: Duke University Press.

Hünefeldt, Christine. 1994. *Paying the Price of Freedom: Family and Labor among Lima's Slaves, 1800–1854.* Berkeley: University of California Press.

————. 2000. *Liberalism in the Bedroom: Quarreling Spouses in Nineteeth-Century Lima.* University Park: Pennsylvania State University Press.

Instituto Nacional de Estádistica (Guatemala). "Pueblos por departamento 2002." Retrieved on August 1, 2011, from www.ine.gob.gt/np/poblacion/etnias%20por%20departamento.xls.

Jefferson, Ann F. 2000. "The Rebellion of Mita: Eastern Guatemala in 1837." PhD dissertation, University of Massachusetts at Amherst.

Jickling, David. 1982. "Los vecinos de Santiago de Guatemala en 1604." *Mesoamerica* 3 (3): 145–231.

Joba, Dorothy Jane. 1984. "Santiago de los Caballeros, 1604–1626: Society and Economy in Colonial Guatemala." PhD dissertation, University of Connecticut.

Johnson, Lyman L. 1998. "Dangerous Words, Provocative Gestures, and Violent Acts: The Disputed Hierarchies of Plebian Life in Colonial Buenos Aires." In Lyman L. Johnson and Sonya Lipsett-Rivera, eds., *The Faces of Honor: Sex, Shame, and Violence in Colonial Latin America.* Albuquerque: University of New Mexico Press.

Johnson, Lyman L., and Sonya Lipsett-Rivera. 1998a. "Introduction." In Lyman L. Johnson and Sonya Lipsett-Rivera, eds., *The Faces of Honor: Sex, Shame, and Violence in Colonial Latin America.* Albuquerque: University of New Mexico Press.

Johnson, Lyman L., and Sonya Lipsett-Rivera, eds. 1998b. *Faces of Honor: Sex, Shame, and Violence in Colonial Latin America.* Albuquerque: University of New Mexico Press.

Johnson, Walter. 1999. *Soul by Soul: Life inside the Antebellum Slave Market.* Cambridge, MA: Harvard University Press.

————. 2003. "On Agency." *Journal of Social History* 37 (1): 113–124.

Juarros, Domingo. 1981 [1818]. *Compendio de la historia del Reino de Guatemala, 1500–1800.* Guatemala: Editorial Piedra Santa.

Kanter, Deborah E. 2008. *Hijos del Pueblo: Gender, Family, and Community in Rural Mexico, 1730–1850.* Austin: University of Texas Press.

Kellogg, Susan. 2005. *Weaving the Past: A History of Latin America's Indigenous Women from the Prehispanic Period to the Present.* New York: Oxford University Press.

Kerns, Virginia. 1997. *Women and the Ancestors: Black Carib Kinship and Ritual,* 2nd ed. Urbana and Chicago: University of Illinois Press.

Kicza, John E. 1983. *Colonial Entrepreneurs: Families and Business in Bourbon Mexico City.* Albuquerque: University of New Mexico Press.

Komisaruk, Catherine. 2008. "Rape Narratives, Rape Silences: Sexual Violence and Judicial Testimony in Colonial Guatemala." *Biography* 31 (3): 369–396.

————. 2009. "Indigenous Labor as Family Labor: Tributes, Migration, and Hispanicization in Colonial Guatemala." *Labor: Studies in Working-Class History of the Americas* 6 (4): 41–66.

Konetzke, Richard. 1962. *Colección de documentos para la historia de la formación social de Hispanoamérica 1493–1810,* volumen III, 2° tomo (1780–1807). Madrid: Consejo Superior de Investigaciones Científicas.

Kramer, Wendy J. 1994. *Encomienda Politics in Early Spanish Guatemala, 1524–1544: Dividing the Spoils.* Boulder, CO: Westview Press.

Kuznesof, Elizabeth Anne. 1986. *Household Economy and Urban Development: São Paulo, 1765–1836.* Boulder, CO: Westview Press.

———. 1989. "History of Domestic Service in Spanish America, 1492–1980." In Elsa M. Chaney and Mary Garcia Castro, eds., *Muchachas No More: Household Workers in Latin America and the Caribbean.* Philadelphia: Temple University Press.

———. 1991. "Sexual Politics, Race, and Bastard-Bearing in Nineteenth-Century Brazil: A Question of Culture or Power?" *Journal of Family History* 6 (13): 241–260.

———. 2001. "Gender Ideology, Race, and Female-Headed Households in Urban Mexico, 1750–1850." In Victor M. Uribe-Uran, ed., *State and Society in Spanish American during the Age of Revolution.* Wilmington, DE: Scholarly Resources.

Langenberg, Inge. 1981. *Urbanisation und Bevölkerungsstruktur der Stadt Guatemala in der ausgehenden Kolonialzeit: Eine sozialhistorische Analyse der Stadtverlegung und ihrer Auswirkungen auf die demographische, berufliche, und soziale Gliederung der Bevölkerung (1773–1824).* Cologne: Böhlau Verlag.

Lavallè, Bernard. 1999. *Amor y opresión en los andes coloniales.* Lima: Instituto de Estudios Peruanos.

Lavrin, Asunción. 1989a. "Introduction: The Scenario, the Actors, and the Issues." In Asunción Lavrin, ed., *Sexuality and Marriage in Colonial Latin America.* Lincoln: University of Nebraska Press.

———. 1989b. "Sexuality in Colonial Mexico: A Church Dilemma." In Asunción Lavrin, ed., *Sexuality and Marriage in Colonial Latin America.* Lincoln: University of Nebraska Press.

———, ed. 1989c. *Sexuality and Marriage in Colonial Latin America.* Lincoln: University of Nebraska Press.

Lewin, Linda. 2003. *Surprise Heirs,* vol. 1: *Illegitimacy, Patrimonial Rights, and Legal Nationalism in Luso-Brazilian Inheritance, 1750–1821,* vol. 2: *Illegitimacy, Inheritance Rights, and Public Power in the Formation of Imperial Brazil, 1822–1889.* Stanford, CA: Stanford University Press.

Lewis, Laura A. 2007. "From Sodomy to Superstition: The Active Pathic and Bodily Transgressions in New Spain." *Ethnohistory* 54 (1): 129–157.

Lipsett-Rivera, Sonya. 1998. "A Slap in the Face of Honor: Social Transgression and Women in Late-Colonial Mexico." In Lyman L. Johnson and Sonya Lipsett-Rivera, eds., *The Faces of Honor: Sex, Shame, and Violence in Colonial Latin America.* Albuquerque: University of New Mexico Press.

———. 2001. "Marriage and Family Relations in Mexico during the Transition from Colony to Nation." In Victor Uribe-Urán, ed., *State and Society in Spanish America during the Age of Revolution.* Wilmington, DE: Scholarly Resources.

Lockhart, James. 1969. "Encomienda and Hacienda: The Evolution of the Great Estate in the Spanish Indies." *Hispanic American Historical Review* 49 (3): 411–429.

———. 1984. "Social Organization and Social Change in Colonial Spanish America." In Leslie Bethell, ed., *The Cambridge History of Latin America,* vol. II. Cambridge, UK: Cambridge University Press, 265–319.

———. 1992. *The Nahuas after the Conquest: A Social and Cultural History of the Indians of Central Mexico, Sixteenth through Eighteenth Centuries.* Stanford, CA: Stanford University Press.

———. 1994 [1968]. *Spanish Peru, 1532–1560.* Madison: University of Wisconsin Press.

Lockhart, James, and Stuart B. Schwartz. 1983. *Early Latin America: A History of Colonial Spanish America and Brazil.* New York: Cambridge University Press.

Lokken, Paul Thomas. 2000. "From Black to *Ladino*: People of African Descent, *Mestizaje*, and Racial Hierarchy in Rural Colonial Guatemala, 1600–1730." PhD dissertation, University of Florida.

———. 2004 "A Maroon Moment: Rebel Slaves in Seventeenth-Century Guatemala." *Slavery & Abolition* 25 (3): 44–58.

———. 2010. "Angolans in Amatitlán: Sugar, African Migrants, and *Gente Ladina* in Colonial Guatemala." In Lowell Gudmundson and Justin Wolfe, eds., *Blacks and Blackness in Central America: Between Race and Place.* Durham, NC: Duke University Press.

Lohse, Russell. 2010. "Cacao and Slavery in Matina, Costa Rica, 1650–1750." In Lowell Gudmundson and Justin Wolfe, eds., *Blacks and Blackness in Central America: Between Race and Place.* Durham, NC: Duke University Press.

Lovell, W. George. 1985. *Conquest and Survival in Colonial Guatemala: A Historical Geography of the Cuchumatán Highlands, 1500–1821.* Kingston and Montreal: McGill-Queen's University Press.

Loveman, Brian. 1979. "Critique of Arnold J. Bauer's 'Rural Workers in Spanish America: Problems of Peonage and Oppression.'" *Hispanic American Historical Review* 59 (3): 478–485.

Lozano Armendares, Teresa. 1987. *La criminalidad en la Ciudad de México 1800–1821.* Mexico City: Universidad Nacional Autónoma de México.

———. 2005. *No codiciarás a la mujer ajena: El adulterio el an comunidades domésticas novohispanas, Ciudad de México, Siglo XVIII.* Mexico City: Universidad Nacional Autónoma de México.

Luján Muñoz, Luis. 1982. *El Arquitecto Mayor Diego de Porres 1677–1741.* Guatemala: Editorial Universitaria.

Luque Alcaide, Elisa. 1962. *La Sociedad Económica de Amigos del País de Guatemala.* Seville: Escuela de Estudios Hispano-Americanos.

Lutz, Christopher H. 1976. "Santiago de Guatemala, 1541–1773: The Socio-Demographic History of a Spanish American Colonial City." PhD dissertation, University of Wisconsin-Madison.

———. 1994. *Santiago de Guatemala, 1541–1773: City, Caste, and the Colonial Experience.* Norman: University of Oklahoma Press.

Lutz, Christopher H., and Karen Dakin. 1996. *Nuestro pesar, nuestra aflicción, tunetuliniliz, tucucuca: Memorias en lengua náhuatl enviadas a Felipe II por indígenas del Valle de Guatemala hacia 1572.* Mexico City: Universidad Nacional Autónoma de México, Centro de Investigaciones Regionales de Mesoamérica.

MacLeod, Murdo J., 1983. "Ethnic Relations and Indian Society in the Province of Guatemala, ca. 1620–ca. 1800." In Murdo J. MacLeod and Robert Wasserstrom, eds., *Spaniards and Indians in Southeastern Mesoamerica: Essays on the History of Ethnic Relations*. Lincoln: University of Nebraska Press.

———. 2008 [1973]. *Spanish Central America: A Socioeconomic History, 1520–1720*. Berkeley: University of California Press.

Mallon, Florencia E. 1995. *Peasant and Nation: The Making of Postcolonial Mexico and Peru*. Berkeley: University of California Press.

Mangan, Jane E. 2005. *Trading Roles: Gender, Ethnicity, and the Urban Economy in Colonial Potosí*. Durham, NC: Duke University Press.

Martínez, María Elena. 2008. *Genealogical Fictions: Limpieza de Sangre, Religion, and Gender in Colonial Mexico*. Stanford, CA: Stanford University Press.

Martínez Peláez, Severo. 1970. *La Patria del Criollo: Ensayo de interpretación de la realidad colonial guatemalteca*. Guatemala: Universidad de San Carlos de Guatemala.

———. 1994. "Algo sobre repartimientos." In Edgar Escobar Medrano and, Edna Elizabeth González Camargo, eds., *Antología: Historia de la cultura de Guatemala*, 3d ed. Guatemala: Universidad de San Carlos de Guatemala.

Marure, Alejandro. 1960 [1837]. *Bosquejo histórico de las revoluciones de Centroamérica desde 1811 hasta 1834*. 2 vols. Guatemala: Editorial del Ministerio de Educación Pública.

Matthew, Laura E. 2012. *Memories of Conquest: Becoming Mexicano in Colonial Guatemala*. Chapel Hill: University of North Carolina Press.

Matos Rodríguez, Félix V. 1999. *Women and Urban Change in San Juan, Puerto Rico, 1820–1868*. Gainesville: University Press of Florida.

Maxwell, Judith M., and Robert M. Hill II, trans. 2006. *Kaqchikel Chronicles: The Definitive Edition*. Austin: University of Texas Press.

McCaa, Robert. 1984. "*Calidad, Clase*, and Marriage in Colonial Mexico: The Case of Parral, 1788–90." *Hispanic American Historical Review* 64 (3): 477–501.

McCreery, David. 1986. "'This Life of Misery and Shame': Female Prostitution in Guatemala City, 1880–1920." *Journal of Latin American Studies* 18 (2): 333–353.

———. 1989. "Atanasio Tzul, Lucas Aguilar, and the Indian Kingdom of Totonicapán." In Judith Ewell and William H. Beezley, eds., *The Human Tradition in Latin America: The Nineteenth Century*. Wilmington, DE: Scholarly Resources.

———. 1994. *Rural Guatemala, 1760–1940*. Stanford, CA: Stanford University Press.

Melton-Villanueva, Miriam, and Caterina Pizzigoni. 2008. "Late Nahuatl Testaments from the Toluca Valley: Indigenous-Language Ethnohistory in the Mexican Independence Period." *Ethnohistory* 55 (3): 361–391.

Meyerowitz, Joanne J. 1988. *Women Adrift: Independent Wage Earners in Chicago, 1880–1930*. Chicago: The University of Chicago Press.

Miller, Joseph C. 2008. "Domiciled and Dominated." In Gwyn Campbell, Suzanne Miers, and Joseph C. Miller, eds., *Women and Slavery, Volume Two: The Modern Atlantic*. Athens: Ohio University Press, 284–312.

Mörner, Magnus. 1967. *Race Mixture in the History of Latin America*. Boston: Little, Brown.

———. 1973. "The Spanish American Hacienda: A Survey of Recent Research and Debate." *Hispanic American Historical Review* 53 (2): 183–216.

Molina, fray Alonso de. 1977a [1571]. *Vocabulario en lengua castellana y mexicana*. Mexico City: Porrúa.

———. 1977b [1571]. *Vocabulario en lengua mexicana y castellana*. Mexico City: Porrúa.

Morgan, Jennifer L. 2004. *Laboring Women: Reproduction and Gender in New World Slavery*. Philadelphia: University of Pennsylvania Press.

Morgan, Philip D. 1998. *Slave Counterpoint: Black Culture in the Eighteenth-Century Chesapeake and Lowcountry*. Chapel Hill: University of North Carolina Press.

Moser, Caroline, and Cathy McIlwane. 2001. *Violence in a Post-Conflict Context: Urban Poor Perceptions from Guatemala*. Washington, DC: The World Bank.

Mundy, Barbara E. 1996. *The Mapping of New Spain: Indigenous Cartography and the Maps of the Relaciones Geográficas*. Chicago: University of Chicago Press.

Nelson, Diane M. 1999. *A Finger in the Wound: Body Politics in Quincentennial Guatemala*. Berkeley: University of California Press.

Nesvig, Martin. 2001. "The Complicated Terrain of Latin American Homosexuality." *Hispanic American Historical Review* 81 (3–4): 689–729.

Nistal Moret, Benjamin. 2000 [1984]. *Esclavos, prófugos y cimarrones: Puerto Rico, 1770–1870*. San Juan: Editorial de la Universidad de Puerto Rico.

Nizza da Silva, Maria Beatriz. 1989. "Divorce in Colonial Brazil: The Case of São Paulo." In Asunción Lavrin, ed., *Sexuality and Marriage in Colonial Latin America*. Lincoln: University of Nebraska Press.

Opie, Frederick Douglass. 2009. *Black Labor Migration in Caribbean Guatemala, 1882–1923*. Gainesville: University Press of Florida.

Osborne, Lilly de Jongh. 1935. *Guatemala Textiles*. New Orleans: Tulane University.

O'Toole, Rachel Sarah. 2012. *Bound Lives: Africans, Indians, and the Making of Race in Colonial Peru*. Pittsburgh: University of Pittsburgh Press.

Otzoy, Irma. 1996. "Maya Clothing and Identity." In Edward F. Fischer and R. McKenna Brown, eds., *Maya Cultural Activism in Guatemala*. Austin: University of Texas Press, Institute of Latin American Studies,

Owensby, Brian P. 2005. "How Juan and Leonor Won Their Freedom: Litigation and Liberty in Seventeenth-Century Mexico." *Hispanic American Historical Review* 85 (1): 39–79.

———. 2008. *Empire of Law and Indian Justice in Colonial Mexico*. Stanford, CA: Stanford University Press.

Palmer, Colin A. 1976. *Slaves of the White God: Blacks in Mexico, 1570–1650*. Cambridge, MA: Harvard University Press.

Palomo de Lewin, Beatriz. 1992. "Esclavos negros en Guatemala (1723–1773)." *Licenciatura* thesis, Universidad del Valle de Guatemala, Facultad de Ciencias Sociales.

Peláez Almengor, Oscar Guillermo. 1996. "La Nueva Guatemala y el abasto de carne, 1776–1778." *Estudios: Revista de Antropología, Arqueología e Historia*. Guatemala: Universidad de San Carlos, 3a. época: 149–158.

Pérez Toledo, Silvia. 1996. *Los hijos del trabajo: Los artesanos de la ciudad de México, 1780–1853*. Mexico City: El Colegio de México and Universidad Autónoma Metropolitana Iztapalapa.

Pescador, Juan Javier. 1992. *De bautizados a fieles difuntos: Familia y mentalidades en una parroquia urbana: Santa Catarina de México, 1568–1820*. Mexico City: El Colegio de México.

Pilcher, Jeffrey. 1998. *¡Qué Vivan los Tamales! Food and the Making of Mexican Identity*. Albuquerque: University of New Mexico Press.

Pinto Soria, Julio César. 1986. *Centroamérica, de la colonia al estado nacional (1800–1840)*. Guatemala: Editorial Universitaria.

Pizzigoni, Caterina. 2012. *The Life Within: Local Indigenous Society in Mexico's Toluca Valley, 1650–1800*. Stanford, CA: Stanford University Press.

Plant, Robert. 1998. "Indigenous Peoples and Poverty Reduction: A Case Study of Guatemala." Indigenous Peoples and Community Development Unit, Inter-American Development Bank, Sustainable Development Department; retrieved on July 13, 2011, from http://idbdocs.iadb.org/wsdocs/getdocument .aspx?docnum=363023.

Polo Sifontes, Francis. 1982. *Nuevos pueblos de indios fundados en la periferia de la ciudad de Guatemala 1776–1879*. Guatemala: Editorial José de Pineda Ibarra.

Pratt, Mary Louise. 2008. *Imperial Eyes: Travel Writing and Transculturation*, 2nd ed. New York: Routledge.

Premo, Bianca. 2000. "From the Pockets of Women: The Gendering of the Mita, Migration, and Tribute in Colonial Chucuito, Peru." *The Americas* 57 (1): 63–94.

———. 2005. *Children of the Father King: Youth, Authority, and Legal Minority in Colonial Lima*. Chapel Hill: University of North Carolina Press.

Rabell Romero, Cecilia. 1996. "Trayectoria de vida familiar, raza y género en Oaxaca Colonial." In Pilar Gonzalbo Aizpuru and Cecilia Rabell Romero, coord., *Familia y vida privada en la Historia de Iberoamérica*. Mexico City: El Colegio de México and Universidad Autónoma de México.

Real Consulado de Comercio de Guatemala. 1810. "Apuntamientos sobre agricultura y comercio del Reyno de Guatemala, que el Dr. Antonio Larrazábal, diputado en las Cortes extraordinarias de la nación por la misma ciudad, pidió al Real Consulado en junta de gobierno de 20 de octubre de 1810." *Anales de la Sociedad de Geografía e Historia de Guatemala* 27 (March 1953–Dec. 1954): 87–109.

Recinos, Adrián, ed. 1980. *Memorial de Sololá, Anales de los Cakchiqueles; Título de los Señores de Totonicapán*, trans. Adrián Recinos and Dioniso José Chonay. Guatemala: Editorial Piedra Santa.

Recopilación de las leyes de los reynos de las Indias, mandadas imprimir y publicar por la Magestad Católica el Rey Don Carlos II, tomo segundo, 4a impresión. 1791. Hecha de órden del Real y Supremo Consejo de las Indias. Madrid: Viuda de Ibarra.

Reeves, René. 2006. *Ladinos with Ladinos, Indians with Indians: Land, Labor, and Regional Ethnic Conflict in the Making of Guatemala.* Stanford, CA: Stanford University Press.

República de Guatemala. 1877. *Código Civil de la República de Guatemala.* Guatemala: Imprenta de "El Progreso."

———. 1927. *Código Civil de la República de Guatemala,* Libro Primero. Guatemala: Tipografía Nacional.

———. 1964. *Código Civil.* Publicaciones del Ministerio de Gobernación. Guatemala: Tipografía Nacional.

———. 1996. *Decreto N° 97-96, Ley para prevenir, sancionar y erradicar la violencia intrafamiliar;* retrieved on May 27, 2011, from www.unhcr.org/refworld/docid/3dbe6f367.html.

Restall, Matthew. 1997. *The Maya World: Yucatec Culture and Society, 1550–1850.* Stanford, CA: Stanford University Press.

———. 2003. *Seven Myths of the Spanish Conquest.* New York: Oxford University Press.

———. 2009. *The Black Middle: Africans, Mayas, and Spaniards in Colonial Yucatan.* Stanford, CA: Stanford University Press.

Restall, Matthew, and Florine Asselbergs. 2007. *Invading Guatemala: Spanish, Nahua, and Maya Accounts of the Conquest Wars.* University Park: Pennsylvania State University Press.

Restall, Matthew, Lisa Sousa, and Kevin Terraciano, eds. 2005. *Mesoamerican Voices: Native-Language Writings from Colonial Mexico, Oaxaca, Yucatan, and Guatemala.* Cambridge, UK: Cambridge University Press.

Robertson, Claire, and Marsha Robertson. 2008. "Re-Modeling Slavery as if Women Mattered." In Gwyn Campbell, Suzanne Miers, and Joseph C. Miller, eds., *Women and Slavery, Volume Two: The Modern Atlantic.* Athens: Ohio University Press.

Rodríguez Sáenz, Eugenia. 1994. "'Ya me es insoportable mi matrimonio.' Abuso de las esposas: Insulto y maltrato físico en el valle central de Costa Rica (1750–1850)." *Avances de Investigación* Universidad de Costa Rica, Centro de Investigaciones Históricas, 71: 1–25.

———. 1995. "From Brides to Wives: Changes and Continuities in the Ideals of and Attitudes toward Marriage, Conjugal Relationships, and Gender Roles in the Central Valley of Costa Rica, 1750–1850." PhD dissertation, Indiana University.

———. 2002. "Divorcio y Violencia de Pareja en Costa Rica (1800–1950)." In Eugenia Rodríguez Sáenz, ed., *Mujeres, Género e Historia en América Central durante los siglos XVIII, XIX y XX.* Mexico City: UNIFEM Oficina Regional de México, Centroamérica, Cuba y República Dominicana; and South Woodstock, Vermont: Plumsock Mesoamerican Studies 35–51.

Sagastume Paiz, Tania, coord. 2006. "El abasto de alimentos de la Ciudad de Guatemala, 1821–1871." Guatemala: Universidad de San Carlos de Guatemala, Dirección General de Investigación (DIGI), Instituto de Investigaciones

Históricas, Antropológicas y Arqueológicas (IIHAA); retrieved on July 13, 2011 from http://digi.usac.edu.gt/bvirtual/investigacio_files/INFORMES/PUIHG/INF-2006-010.pdf.

———. 2008. *Trabajo urbano y tiempo libre en la ciudad de Guatemala, 1776–1840.* Guatemala: Universidad de San Carlos, Centro de Estudios Urbanos y Regionales.

Salazar, Ramón A. 1951. *Historia del desenvolvimiento intelectual de Guatemala (época colonial)*, 3 vols. Guatemala: Editorial del Ministerio de Educación Pública.

Salvucci, Richard J. 1987. *Textiles and Capitalism in Mexico: An Economic History of the Obrajes, 1539–1840.* Princeton, NJ: Princeton University Press.

Samayoa Guevara, Héctor Humberto. 1962. *Los gremios de artesanos en la Ciudad de Guatemala (1524–1821).* Guatemala: Editorial Universitaria.

Saravia V., M. Raquel. 1972. *La enseñanza primaria en Guatemala durante la epoca colonial.* Guatemala: Universidad de San Carlos de Guatemala.

Sarasúa, Carmen. 1994. *Criados, nodrizas y amos: El servicio doméstico en la formación del mercado de trabajo madrileño, 1758–1868.* Madrid: Siglo Veintiuno Editores.

Scardaville, Michael C. 1994. "(Hapsburg) Law and (Bourbon) Order: State Authority, Popular Unrest, and the Criminal Justice System in Bourbon Mexico City." *The Americas* 50 (4): 501–525.

Schwalm, Leslie A. 1997. *A Hard Fight for We: Women's Transition from Slavery to Freedom in South Carolina.* Urbana: University of Illinois Press.

Schwartz, Stuart B. 1977. "Resistance and Accommodation in Eighteen Century Brazil: The Slaves' Views of Slavery." *Hispanic American Historical Review* 57 (1): 69–81.

Scott, Joan Wallach. 1999. *Gender and the Politics of History*, revised edition. New York: Columbia University Press.

Scott, Rebecca J. 1985. *Slave Emancipation in Cuba: The Transition to Free Labor, 1860–1899.* Princeton, NJ: Princeton University Press.

Seed, Patricia. 1988. *To Love, Honor, and Obey in Colonial Mexico: Conflicts over Marriage Choice, 1574–1821.* Stanford, CA: Stanford University Press.

Shafer, Robert Jones. 1958. *The Economic Societies in the Spanish World (1763–1821).* Syracuse, NY: Syracuse University Press.

Shelton, Laura M. 2007. "Like a Servant or Like a Son? Circulating Children in Northwestern Mexico (1790–1850)." In Ondina E. González and Bianca Premo, eds., *Raising an Empire: Children in Early Modern Iberia and Colonial Latin America*, 219–237. Albuquerque: University of New Mexico Press.

Sherman, William. 1979. *Forced Native Labor in Sixteenth-Century Central America.* Lincoln: University of Nebraska Press.

Sigal, Pete. 2005. "The Cuiloni, the Patlache, and the Abominable Sin: Sexualities in Early Colonial Nahua Society." *Hispanic American Historical Review* 85 (4): 555–593.

———. 2007. "Queer Nahuatl: Sahagún's Faggots and Sodomites, Lesbians and Hermaphrodites." *Ethnohistory* 54 (1): 9–34.

Simpson, Lesley Byrd. 1950. *The Encomienda in New Spain: The Beginning of Spanish Mexico.* Berkeley: University of California Press.

Smith, Robert S. 1959. "Indigo Production and Trade in Colonial Guatemala." *Hispanic American Historical Review* 39 (2): 181–211.

Socolow, Susan M. 1978. *The Merchants of Buenos Aires, 1778–1810: Family and Commerce.* New York: Cambridge University Press.

———. 1989. "Acceptable Partners: Marriage Choice in Colonial Argentina, 1778–1810." In Asunción Lavrin, ed., *Sexuality and Marriage in Colonial Latin America.* Lincoln: University of Nebraska Press.

Solórzano, Juan Carlos. 1987. "Rafael Carrera, ¿Reacción conservadora o revolución campesina? Guatemala, 1837–73." *Anuario de estudios centroamericanos* 13 (2): 5–35.

Sousa, Lisa Mary. 1998. "Women in Native Societies and Cultures of Colonial Mexico." PhD dissertation, UCLA.

Spurling, Geoffrey. 1998. "Honor, Sexuality, and the Colonial Church." In Lyman L. Johnson and Sonya Lipsett-Rivera, eds., *The Faces of Honor: Sex, Shame, and Violence in Colonial Latin America.* Albuquerque: University of New Mexico Press.

———. 2000. "Under Investigation for the Abominable Sin: Damián de Morales Stands Accused of Attempting to Seduce Antón de Tierra de Congo (Charcas, 1611)." In Richard Boyer and Geoffrey Spurling, eds., *Colonial Lives: Documents on Latin American History, 1550–1850.* New York: Oxford University Press.

Stavig, Ward. 1999. *The World of Túpac Amaru: Conflict, Community, and Identity in Colonial Peru.* Lincoln: University of Nebraska Press.

Stern, Steve J. 1995. *The Secret History of Gender: Women, Men, and Power in Late Colonial Mexico.* Chapel Hill: University of North Carolina Press.

Stolcke, Verena. 1972. "Elopement and Seduction in Nineteenth-Century Cuba." *Past & Present,* 55: 91–129.

———. 1974. *Marriage, Class and Colour in Nineteenth-Century Cuba: A Study of Racial Attitudes and Sexual Values in a Slave Society.* London: Cambridge University Press.

Sweet, James H. 1997. "The Iberian Roots of American Racist Thought." *William and Mary Quarterly* 54 (1): 143–166.

Tanck Estrada, Dorothy. 1977. *La educación ilustrada, 1786–1836: Educación primaria en la ciudad de México.* Mexico City: El Colegio de México.

Taracena Arriola, Arturo. 1997. *Invención criolla, sueño ladino, pesadilla indígena: Los Altos de Guatemala, de región a estado, 1740–1850.* San José, Costa Rica: Editorial Porvenir; and Antigua Guatemala: Centro de Investigaciones Regionales de Mesoamérica.

Taylor, William B. 1972. *Landlord and Peasant in Colonial Oaxaca.* Stanford, CA: Stanford University Press.

———. 1979. *Drinking, Homicide, and Rebellion in Colonial Mexican Villages.* Stanford, CA: Stanford University Press.

———. 1996. *Magistrates of the Sacred: Priests and Parishioners in Eighteenth-Century Mexico.* Stanford, CA: Stanford University Press.

Tedlock, Dennis, trans. and ed. 1996 [1985]. *Popol Vuh: The Definitive Edition of the Mayan Book of the Dawn of Life and the Glories of Gods and Kings.* New York: Simon and Schuster.

Terraciano, Kevin. 2001. *The Mixtecs of Colonial Oaxaca: Ñudzahui History, Sixteenth through Eighteenth Centuries.* Stanford, CA: Stanford University Press.

Tilly, Louise, and Joan W. Scott. 1978. *Women, Work, and Family.* New York: Holt, Rinehart and Winston.

Tortorici, Zeb. 2007. "'Heran Todos Putos': Sodomites, Subcultures, and Disordered Desire in Early Colonial Mexico." *Ethnohistory.* 54:1, 35–67.

Twinam, Ann. 1999. *Public Lives, Private Secrets: Gender, Honor, Sexuality, and Illegitimacy in Colonial Spanish America.* Stanford, CA: Stanford University Press.

van Oss, Adriaan C. 1986. *Catholic Colonialism: A Parish History of Guatemala, 1524–1821.* Cambridge, UK: Cambridge University Press.

Van Young, Eric. 1981. *Hacienda and Market in Eighteenth-Century Mexico: The Rural Economy of the Guadalajara Region, 1675–1820.* Berkeley: University of California Press.

———. 2001. *The Other Rebellion: Popular Violence, Ideology, and the Mexican Struggle for Independence, 1810–1821.* Stanford, CA: Stanford University Press.

Vergara, Teresa C. 2007. "Growing up Indian: Migration, Labor, and Life in Lima (1570–1640)." In Ondina E. González and Bianca Premo, eds., *Raising an Empire: Children in Early Modern Iberia and Colonial Latin America.* Albuquerque: University of New Mexico Press.

Vinson, Ben III. 2001. *Bearing Arms for His Majesty: The Free Colored Militia in Colonial Mexico.* Stanford, CA: Stanford University Press.

Vinson, Ben III, and Matthew Restall, eds. 2009. *Black Mexico: Race and Society from Colonial to Modern Times.* Albuquerque: University of New Mexico Press.

Viquiera, Carmen, and José Ignacio Urquiola. 1990. *Los obrajes en Nueva España, 1530–1630.* Mexico City: Consejo Nacional para la Cultura y las Artes.

Viquiera Albán, Juan Pedro. 1999. *Propriety and Permissiveness in Bourbon Mexico.* Translated by Sonya Lipsett-Rivera and Sergio Rivera Ayala. Wilmington, DE: Scholarly Resources.

von Germeten, Nicole. 2006. *Black Blood Brothers: Confraternities and Social Mobility for Afro-Mexicans.* Gainesville: University Press of Florida.

Wagley, Charles. 1941. *Economics of a Guatemalan Village.* Menasha, WI: American Anthropological Association.

———. 1949. *The Social and Religious Life of a Guatemalan Village.* Menasha, WI: American Anthropological Association.

Waldron, Kathy. 1989. "The Sinners and the Bishop in Colonial Venezuela: The *Visita* of Bishop Mariano Martí, 1771–1784." In Asunción Lavrin, ed., *Sexuality and Marriage in Colonial Latin America.* Lincoln: University of Nebraska Press.

Walker, Charles. 1999. *Smoldering Ashes: Cuzco and the Creation of Republican Peru, 1780–1840.* Durham, NC: Duke University Press.

Weathers, Shirley A. 1981. *Bibliographic Guide to the Guatemalan Collection.* Finding Aids to the Manuscript Collection of the Genealogical Society of Utah 7. Salt Lake City: University of Utah Press.

Webre, Stephen. 2001. "The Wet Nurses of Jocotenango: Gender, Science, and Politics in Late-Colonial Guatemala," *Colonial Latin American Historical Review* 10 (2): 173–197.

Whitehead, Neil L., Pete Sigal, and John F. Chuchiak IV, eds. 2007. *Ethnohistory* 54 (1). Special issue: "Sexual Encounters/Sexual Collisions: Alternative Sexualities in Mesoamerica."

Wightman, Ann M. 1990. *Indigenous Migration and Social Change: The Forasteros of Cuzco, 1570–1720*. Durham, NC: Duke University Press.

Williford, Miriam. 1963. "The Reform Program of Dr. Mariano Gálvez, Chief-of-State of Guatemala, 1831–1838." PhD dissertation, Tulane University.

———. 1969. "Las Luces y la Civilización: The Social Reforms of Mariano Gálvez." New Orleans: Middle American Research Institute, Tulane University.

Woodward, Ralph Lee, Jr. 1993. *Rafael Carrera and the Emergence of the Republic of Guatemala, 1821–1871*. Athens: University of Georgia Press.

———. 1994. "Changes in the Nineteenth-Century Guatemalan State and Its Indian Policies." In Carol A. Smith, ed., *Guatemalan Indians and the State: 1540–1988*. Austin: University of Texas Press.

———. 1999. *Central America: A Nation Divided*, 3rd ed. New York: Oxford University Press.

Wortman, Miles L. 1982. *Government and Society in Central America, 1680–1840*. New York: Columbia University Press.

Yannakakis, Yanna. 2008. *The Art of Being In-Between: Native Intermediaries, Indian Identity, and Local Rule in Colonial Oaxaca*. Durham, NC: Duke University Press.

Zavala, Silvio. 1935. *La encomienda indiana*. Madrid: Imprenta Helénica.

———. 1944. "Orígenes coloniales del peonaje en México," *El Trimestre Económico* 10: 711–748.

———. 1967. *Contribución a la historia de las instituciones coloniales en Guatemala*. Guatemala: Universidad de San Carlos de Guatemala.

Zilbermann de Luján, María Cristina. 1987. *Aspectos socioeconómicos del traslado de la Ciudad de Guatemala (1773–1783)*. Guatemala: Academia de Geografía e Historia de Guatemala.

Index

arship on, 10, 186. *See also* Informal
unions; Love; Marriage
Shame, 234–240
Siete Partidas, 71–72, 231, 234
Silversmiths, 105, 121, 195, 204–205,
208, 239
Sínforo, José Mariano, 88
Single mothers, 55, 128, 172, 207, 241,
248
Sirvientes (servants), 142–45
Slavery: abolition of, 1, 17, 107–8, 245,
259n6; and calidad, 12–13; in capital
city, 113; decline of, 8, 68–69, 71,
107–8, 244–45; emancipation of,
255n1; free labor in relation to, 86–87;
gender and, 106–7; in Guatemala, 4,
68–108; hispanization and, 244–45; for
Indians, 17, 259n6; origins of, 68, 69–70
Slaves: family case examples, 98–107;
flight of, 83–85; food production by,
78; free blacks and mulatos outnum-
bering, 68; fugitive, 73; identity of,
12–13, 107–8; judicial appeals of,
71–76; labor performed by, 70; legal
status of, 12–13; location of, 70–71; as
managers and overseers, 22, 70; means
of attaining freedom for, 83–92; names
of, 69, 103; prices of, 72–73, 88–90;
resistance of, 73–78; sale of, 86–87;
self-manumission of, 72–73, 87–92;
sexual violence against, 92–98, 138;
women as, 78–80. *See also* Blacks
Slave uprisings, 68
Small enterprise, 126–28, 171–73, 183–84
Smallpox vaccine, 10
Social change: domestic service and, 123;
government responses to, 25, 244;
legislative change following, 18, 244;
political change following, 3
Social networks, 80–83, 247. *See also*
Kinship networks
Social reproduction, 9–10, 246
Social status: of bakers, 166, 168; beef
trade and, 177–81; domestic servants
and their employers, 129–30; honor
and, 222–23; maestras and, 150–56.
See also Calidad
Sociedad Económica de Amigos del País
(Economic Society of Friends of the
Country), 122
Society: inequalities in, 15, 92–98,
129–42; judicial records as source of

information on, 12, 13; persistence of
differences in, 14–15
Sololá, 24, 36–37, 52, 264n85,
294nn328,337
Solórzano, Manuel Najarro y, 229,
234
Soriano, Pedro, 89
Sosa, Aleja Josefa, 215
Soto, Regina, 213, 220, 228, 232
Spain, conquest by, 16–17. *See also* Co-
lonial government; Colonial judicial
system
Spanish language, 18, 31, 62, 244
Spinning thread, 145–46
State. *See* Colonial government; Native
governments
Stern, Steve, 12, 186, 196, 197, 199, 212,
219
Streets, 120
Suchitepéquez, 26–29
Sugar mills. *See* Dardón, Manuela; Haci-
enda San Jerómino; Ingenio de Ayarza;
Trapiche
Sugar processing, 43, 39, 74
Sunsín, Lucía de los Dolores, 202–3
Supín, Felipe, 48
Swine, 171–73

Taboara, Manuel de, 89
Taborga, Ignacio, 134–36
Tailors, 149–50
Tavern keepers, 159–64
Teachers, 150–56
Tegucigalpa, 97–98
Téllez, Petrona, 161
Textile and clothing production, 37–38,
145–50
Theft: of cattle, 176; by domestic ser-
vants, 131–32
Tiburcio, José, 147
Toribio Granados, Manuel, 200
Tortilla preparation, 35–36, 118–19,
127–28, 281n94
Tortilleras. *See* Tortilla preparation
Totonicapán, 36, 146, 260n25
Trades. *See* Guilds; Labor
Trapiche: defined, 39, 265n104
Tribute labor system: cash substituted for
labor/commodities in, 18–19, 110 (*see
also* Tribute payments); decline of, 7–8,
18, 22–25, 112–13, 249–50; gender
and, 18–19; persistence of, 249–50,